Curtis
april 2000

Imagining Indonesia:
Cultural Politics and Political Culture

This series of publications on Africa, Latin America, and Southeast Asia is designed to present significant research, translation, and opinion to area specialists and to a wide community of persons interested in world affairs. The editor seeks manuscripts of quality on any subject and can generally make a decision regarding publication within three months of receipt of the original work. Production methods generally permit a work to appear within one year of acceptance. The editor works closely with authors to produce a high quality book. The series appears in a paperback format and is distributed worldwide. For more information, contact the executive editor at Ohio University Press, Scott Quadrangle, University Terrace, Athens, Ohio 45701.

Executive editor: Gillian Berchowitz
AREA CONSULTANTS
Africa: Diane Ciekawy
Latin America: Thomas Walker
Southeast Asia: James L. Cobban

The Monographs in International Studies series is published for the Center for International Studies by the Ohio University Press. The views expressed in individual monographs are those of the authors and should not be considered to represent the policies or beliefs of the Center for International Studies, the Ohio University Press, or Ohio University.

Imagining Indonesia: Cultural Politics and Political Culture

Edited by
Jim Schiller
and
Barbara Martin-Schiller

Ohio University Center for International Studies
Monographs in International Studies
Southeast Asian Series, Number 97
Athens

© 1997 by the Center for International Studies, Ohio University
Printed in the United States of America

03 02 01 00 99   5 4 3 2

Library of Congress Cataloging-in-Publication data available

Typeset by Professional Book Compositors
Cover design by Chiquita Babb
Cover photograph from *Roro Mendut* in *Indonesian Cinema: Framing The New Order* by Krishna Sen gratefully reproduced with permission from Zed Books Ltd.

This book is dedicated to
the memory of
Barbara Martin-Schiller
who died suddenly
on October 9, 1996.

Contents

CONTENTS

Introduction: The Politics of Dramatic Conversations

Jim Schiller and Barbara Martin-Schiller

> Cultures are dramatic conversations about things that matter to their participants.
> —Robert N. Bellah, *Habits of the Heart*

> One of the things that everyone knows but no one can quite think how to demonstrate is that a country's politics reflect the design of its culture. . . . Yet merely to state it is to raise doubts.
> —Clifford Geertz, *"The Politics of Meaning"*

THIS IS A BOOK about Indonesian culture and politics. Its subject matter reflects the effort to advance and reject various notions of what it means to be Indonesian, as well as related perceptions of how Indonesia's citizens and state officials should interact. Because, in recent times, the Indonesian state has been so strong, much of the book is about state-sanctioned and state-supported notions of Indonesian identity and culture and efforts by members of civil society to come to terms with—or sometimes to challenge—official or dominant notions about what constitutes Indonesian culture.

The following chapters grew out of papers presented at a 1991 conference at Flinders University of South Australia entitled "Indonesian Culture: Asking the Right Questions." The contributions presented here represent a wide range of disciplines, points of view, and ideological orientations. The authors are political scientists, historians, anthropologists, artists, and students of Indonesian arts. They are Indonesian, American, and Australian. Some are confident of the resilience and adaptive capacity of Indonesian culture in its response to international influence and local cultural innovation, while others are more anxious. One of the contributors is a creator of Indonesian "popular art" and writes with some anger about restrictions he feels.

The essays share two features. First is the sense that Indonesian culture is complex and dynamic and that the "dramatic conversations" that make up cultural politics in a place as large and complex as Indonesia are likely to be exciting and surprising. Second, they convey the notion that much might be gained by analysts, officials, and activists if they were to abandon the idea that a single understanding of what constitutes Indonesian culture is possible or desirable.[1]

William Liddle begins the collection with a discussion of three prominent innovators who have attempted political cultural change in the New Order period. Goenawan Mohamad is seen by Liddle as a promoter of individual rights and individual liberty against the dominant idea of responsibility to the collective. Sjahrir is portrayed as a supporter of market forces and a challenger of the substantial role played by the state and state officials in the economy. Nurcholish Madjid is described as a champion of Islamic values within a secular state and as an opponent of the idea of an Islamic state.

Liddle weaves the stories of these three innovators into a demonstration of a strategy for studying change in political culture. He suggests that each of the three innovators has been working along a "fault line"—an area of important debate about what sort of society and state Indonesia will be. He notes that there are always defenders of the status quo (or what is taken for it) and that we need to look at the resources possessed by those who would change or maintain culture. Most important, Liddle points out that opportune or poorly considered strategies can change the value of resources and so advance or retard cultural innovation. Unexpected events and unlikely influences can also act as opportunities for cultural change or the promotion of cultural orthodoxy. Against this backdrop of surprise and changing resources and opportunities, cultural innovators and their opponents in or out of government are constantly "improvising" to promote, defend, or reinterpret their values.

William Frederick tells the story of Armijn Pané and the struggle in the 1920s and 1930s over what kind of cultural forms were fitting for the emerging Indonesian nation. He suggests that this story of the 1920s gives us some interesting insights into the 1990s and the current debate about the diversity and integrity of modern Indonesian culture and the nature of the forces at work shaping it. Frederick portrays Pané as an individualist who saw the need for a modern Indonesian culture which would be capacious—able to borrow the best from global and regional cultures—and ever changing. He demonstrates how Pané railed against Balai Pustaka (the government publishing house) for trying to censor what Indonesians read and assuming that Indonesians had poor taste or low intelligence.

Frederick argues that in the 1990s Indonesia has a vibrant culture which the modern Indonesian state still tries to "engineer" but which is too diverse in origins and audience to be managed. The culture is difficult to manage, he argues, because it is driven by the need to cater to a large and diverse class of cultural consumers (wider than the urban middle class). This potential audience has the prosperity and inclination to engage in many forms of cultural tourism. Frederick suggests that we should be particularly interested in popular culture. As an example, he notes the similarity between *dangdut* in the 1990s and *keroncong* in the prewar period. Both are hybrid, "low" culture music forms with substantial commercial appeal but which also have well-placed detractors who perceive them as undignified or unauthentic.

Frederick is enthusiastic about an environment in which authors and performers are innovating by synthesizing regional, international, and newly created art forms in an attempt to attract paying audiences and "to survive physically and intellectually." Like Pané he worries little about cultural borrowing and urges us to look at what culture is appearing and not just what is disappearing. His argument is that cultural creativity may not always please cultural "purists" or those in power, but is responsive to social (market) forces. He suggests that Indonesian culture and Indonesian cultural politics have become more complex and uncertain.

Barbara Hatley discusses gender characterization in modern Indonesian literature in a context which addresses issues both of cultural politics and of political culture. She focuses in particular on the phenomenon of female characters being identified with conservative social values and with Javanese or other regional cultural traditions. She contrasts these conservative representations with other, strikingly different portrayals of women, as symbols of resistance, while suggesting that there is in fact more continuity between these representations than at first appears.

Hatley looks at the historical context of gender characterization. She points out the discontinuity between prewar fiction—which reflected on possibilities for change in customs and attitudes through the depiction of women and gender relations—and that which was written subsequently. Starting with the Japanese Occupation and Revolution, the focus turned to "physical suffering and fighting, [seen, accurately or not,] as male domains of activity." She suggests that one factor "contributing to the association in postwar literature of women characters with nurturance, domesticity, and 'traditional' cultural values" could be the shift from a preponderance of Minangkabau writers in the prewar period to large numbers of Javanese writers subsequently.

She points out the incongruity between the association of women with "esteemed cultural values" and the Javanese tendency "to exclude women from the most prestigious cultural pursuits," suggesting that amid the social change which has occurred since the war, women, "marginalized from [the world of work and politics, seen as the male sphere], can serve as a locus of notions of ongoing cultural values."

Women who are "symbols of resistance" as well as those who are "bearers of traditional values" tend to appear in the works of male authors. Hatley points out the "maleness" of the literary and political discourse which she describes. Female writers of popular romantic fiction, on the other hand, "define women in terms of personal, domestic concerns," focusing on the joys and suffering of middle-class romance and marriage; and the much scarcer "serious" literature by female writers on the whole also depicts personal relations rather than women in the public sphere.

Hatley looks at the social and political context of recent Indonesian literature, both the general climate of social conservatism and political control, and the current gender ideology which stresses "conservative standards of modest, constrained feminine behavior." As in literature, there are alternate traditions of assertive, powerful femaleness, but they are firmly suppressed in the New Order's gender ideology.

The discussion turns finally to the few women writing critically on social and political themes, or "creating female characters who participate . . . , with an assured female identity, in public, national life." Hatley stresses the importance of these voices in the context of the "wider discourse of female constraint and repression," as they present alternate, convincing images with which female readers can identify.

Moelyono writes as an activist with a particular vision of art in service of society. He expresses his concern that Indonesian art under the New Order has become a commodity in which the lives of the poor majority, the *rakyat*, form the backdrop. He wants art to be about the suffering, hopes, and interests of the *rakyat*. He documents some of the efforts by himself and others to make art more accessible, to promote a "people's art" that engages in changing consciousness and advocating the interests of the weak. His story about the process of promoting community art in fishing villages in East Java is an interesting effort to popularize a new perspective. As might be expected, Moelyono has found both allies and opponents in his effort to engage in cultural politics. He notes that nongovernmental organizations (NGOs), social scientists, and student activists have been interested and supportive, as have some foreign donor agencies. He suggests that "mainstream" artists tend to be more commercially oriented. Not surprisingly, some of his efforts at local consciousness raising have been resisted by local government officials and sometimes by villagers who do not seem to understand (or support?) his artistic and activist goals.

Kuntowijoyo writes about Javanese bureaucratic culture in the early twentieth century. His subject is the Abipraya society of Surakarta—an association for members of the Javanese bureaucratic elite. He argues that its power allowed the *priyayi*[2] to promote a rank-conscious, hedonistic culture which justified the position of the elite and prescribed appropriate behavior to accord with status. In his discussion of early-twentieth-century codes of dress, propriety, and submissiveness to authority, he argues that these codes are suggestive of today's Indonesian state culture.

Kuntowijoyo provides us with a historical insight into the resources that are in the hands of the promoters of state culture. The appeal of a corporatist ideology lies in its defense of status. Such an ideology provides state officials and those who would become state officials with a sense of conviction that they are

obliged to rule and that they know how to do so. Finally, the ideology is reconfirmed in the material benefits that the state has
been able to provide its officials and much of the populace, and
in its promise of a better tomorrow.

David Bourchier provides an interesting example of the changing value of resources and opportunities for improvisation in political culture. He writes about the recent debate over what kind
of state Indonesia should be. In the mid-1980s the New Order
government advanced the notion of an integralistic state (sometimes called familial state—*negara kekeluargaan*). It was claimed
that the integralistic state is an authentic Indonesian concept arising out of the village experience in which neighbors supposedly
work together for the common good and decisions are made by
consensus. This line of reasoning suggests that there is no need
for limits on executive power and no need for individual rights
because the state would always defend the interests of society as a
whole.

The idea of an integralistic state, Bourchier argues, was advanced by the armed forces—perhaps concerned about rising
threats (from civil society, organized Islam, and the president) to
its right to play a dominant role (*dwi fungsi*) as defender of the
country and manager of the country's development. Bourchier
suggests the idea was supported by President Suharto and senior
cabinet officials, who stood to gain from acceptance of an ideology which denies a place in politics for opposition and conflict.

Perhaps the most interesting part of the story is the opportunity provided for a spirited defense of democracy, individualism,
and constitutional reform by the government's push for acceptance of integralism. Opponents of integralism—including lawyers, NGO leaders, and other intellectuals—were able to mobilize
resources and concoct arguments that softened the government
line and perhaps made more space for democracy and individual
rights.

Their critique argued that integralism was not the only Indonesian way, that its invention by Supomo in 1945 was not accepted in the constitution, and that the idea should be condemned because of its totalitarian connections. The opponents of integralism pointed out the role of Hatta in moderating the 1945 Constitution and used that as an argument for individual liberty and constitutional reform.

In response, the government pushed a softer, more culturally resonant line, calling for acceptance of the family principle, in which the head of state is like the head of a family. In recent years the government has gone further, paying some attention to notions of individual and press freedoms and universal human rights, while contending that there are unique Indonesian interpretations of those rights which the state should determine.

Fachry Ali writes about the competition between state culture, local culture, and, more recently, an urban, intellectual, cosmopolitan culture. He sees *kebudayaan bernegara* (state culture) as rooted in the revival of Javanese culture and is concerned with the dilemma this cultural situation poses for other nonstate cultures. He uses the Nuaulu (of Molucca province) as an example, admittedly extreme, of nonstate cultures being urged to participate in state-sponsored ceremonies—by putting on dances at state occasions—but not feeling themselves a partner in the state culture.

Fachry stresses the overwhelming dominance of those who would promote state culture. However, he suggests that international and structural changes in Indonesia are providing room for the advocates of cosmopolitan culture and local culture to defend and enhance their positions. The Indonesian state, he suggests, increasingly feels compelled to allow some advocacy of democracy and individual human rights in order to safeguard Indonesia's global economic relationships. Similarly, he argues that the state's need for access to "outer-island" natural resources and the heightened visibility recently given to organized Islam (which is an important part of many of these cultures) provides defenders of local culture with resources which might be used to conserve elements of local culture.

Fachry suggests that the triangular struggle between statist, "enlightened, cosmopolitan" and local culture advocates is a zero-sum situation in which there must be clear winners and losers. Perhaps that is so, but his own evidence that the economic success of the New Order has reduced regionalist and primordialist conflict suggests that further economic growth might provide the lubricant that allows supporters of both Western, liberal, Javanese-cum-statist cultural ideas and non-Javanese local cultural ideas to see themselves as winners or at least to see themselves as having gained something that was worth the loss.

Philip Eldridge examines the political culture of Indonesian NGOs with particular attention to their attitude toward Western-style representative democracy. While most seem to share core values of self-reliance and popular participation, Eldridge suggests that there are important variations in their operational strategies and in their notion of what constitutes "genuine" democracy. He describes three types of NGOs. One group of NGOs sees itself as cooperating with the state in national development and tries to enhance community participation. It is primarily involved in small-scale development programs and negotiates acceptable methods with local officials. A second group of NGOs is more critical of national development policy and more concerned with consciousness raising among the Indonesian middle class. The third group is trying to build an awareness among the politically weak of rights to organize and to manage their own affairs. Eldridge also notes a recent radical challenge questioning the NGOs' lack of a theoretical framework for change and their failure to organize workers, farmers, and squatters.

Eldridge finds that these three groups of NGOs have competing understandings of democracy. The first tends to argue for Western-style representative democracy. The second group is concerned that deliberation and consensus be a part of decision making and fearful of the excesses of individual liberty and market forces, while the third concentrates on local struggles for people's sovereignty and is not likely to be in the forefront of the push for democratization.

Given these differences in accommodation to the state and in understandings of democracy, Eldridge thinks there is little likelihood of a united NGO strategy for challenging the state's corporatist ideology. On the other hand, he predicts that NGOs will continue to be adept at creating space for organizational activity in whatever kind of political system evolves.

Perhaps Eldridge's view of NGO disunity in the push for democracy (or at least the push against corporatist ideology) is too pessimistic. His account of the ways in which NGOs have struggled to find ways to operate under a system which actively discourages nonstate initiatives suggests that NGOs might be more adventurous when there are signs that the system is under challenge from within.

At least the NGOs' use of opportunities to promote their style of activity seems to drive home Liddle's point about culture being constantly redefined by argument and by the use of individual and organizational resources whose value or strength seems to change in unexpected ways. NGOs have pushed the idea that Article 28 of the 1945 Constitution provided them with the right to organize, forged ties with supportive foreign "aid" donors, suggested that political deregulation needs to expand alongside economic deregulation, and, more recently, promulgated a joint declaration on universal human rights that allows NGOs to defend themselves from efforts by Asian states to suggest that human rights were subject to local definition rather than international scrutiny. During most of the New Order period, Indonesian

NGOs have been in a weak political position, but they seem to have found ways to succeed at promoting currents of thought that directly or indirectly challenge corporatist ideology.

Anton Lucas describes the process of compulsory land clearance in Indonesia. He examines the clash between a bureaucracy that cooperates with "developers" to acquire land for commercial purposes and a mainly rural landowning population which is trying to retain its land or obtain reasonable compensation for its loss. Both the state (and its allied "developers") and the landowners have resources, albeit unequal, and opportunities for championing their cause.

The bureaucracy uses development ideology to justify land acquisition for infrastructure, commercial or industrial estates, housing estates, and even recreational purposes (e.g., golf courses). It then uses "compulsory suggestion" (*budaya petunjuk*)—the idea that the populace should do as the state "suggests" because the state must be doing what is in everyone's best interests. When this fails to convince landowners, legal or extralegal intimidation is sometimes used to make them give up the land.

Groups of landowners have resisted land clearances or tried to get better terms for their land by various means, including appeals to the media, visits to the provincial or national legislatures, voting against the government political organization, and occasionally resorting to violence. They have found allies among student groups, NGOs, journalists, and legal aid groups.

The acquisition of farm land for golf—very much an elite sport in Indonesia—provided NGOs and journalists with an opportunity to popularize the cause of those losing their land. The recent period of "openness" has also widened the opportunity for publicizing injustices and inequalities in land clearances. The government, in turn, has often been able to rely on press self-censorship, state control of the legal system, and state connections with gangs and youth groups to help achieve its land acquisition goals.

Lucas notes that where the local bureaucracy obtains fair compensation for landowners and the support of local community leaders, there is little difficulty in land acquisition. He demonstrates that the period of "openness" has allowed landowners to vent their frustration and sometimes gain better compensation. He sees "openness" as a product of intra-elite rivalry but wonders whether it might be hard to turn off the "openness" after the experience of having a somewhat freer press.

Amrih Widodo writes about cultural politics between a strong state and a weak, rural, nonconformist, "religious" community, the Samin of Central Java. He shows how the Samin have "threatened" the established order (as they have since colonial times) by their rejection of Javanese language hierarchy and their attempted rejection of state institutions and policies such as marriage, membership in a recognized religion, and, in the past, taxation.

Amrih notes that the New Order has succeeded in bringing the Samin at least partly into the hegemonic culture through the promotion of high Javanese, *krama*, and through coercing them to accept a recognized religion (Buddhism) and mass marriage within those rites. The Samin, however, have retained some control over the cultural and political struggle, by controlling their own use of language (avoiding terms that express individual interests), and by attaching second meanings to words—for example, *Buda* (Buddhist religion) becomes an acronym for *mlebune uda* ("to enter you must be naked"), symbolic of the Samin's religious belief. (They also exercised some control by defeating the reelection bid of the village head who had been the government's agent in forcing their mass marriage under Buddhist rites.)

Although their numbers are small, the Samin retain considerable interest for the outside world, perhaps because of their ability to use the resources of the weak to stymie efforts by the authorities to make them conform. Amrih suggests that they will continue to negotiate their encounters with outsiders (including state officials) and, in so doing, negotiate their own identity.

Greg Acciaioli writes about the Indonesian state's effort to promote its agricultural development programs in South Sulawesi through the appropriation of local names. The state adds or tries to add value and notions of local participation to its technocratic goals and methods by attaching to them a valued local term (e.g., *Tudang Sipulung*). In turn, the local rice merchants have been able to continue domination of the rice market by adopting a name, KUD (Koperasi Unit Desa, Village Cooperative Unit), that has been sanctified as part of national development ideology. Rice merchants and regional elites have been able to use the guise of "modern" behavior—cooperating in national development efforts by adopting the KUD name for their operations—to continue practices, such as purchase of rice crops before the harvest (*ijon*), that the cooperatives were supposed to end.

The problem that Acciaioli sees is a bureaucratic political culture convinced that it knows what is best for farmers and able to manipulate local culture and language for its own purposes. Farmers may not be in a position to avoid participating on the state's terms, while regional elites may find new opportunities to retain and expand "traditional" patterns and realms of domination.

A Final Word

Whether they are writing about "high politics" or the cosmopolitan culture of Jakarta or the interface between state and societal views of culture in rural and regional Indonesia, the authors are describing an ongoing struggle about how the world is constructed and how, therefore, Indonesians should engage in political or economic or social or religious behavior. Whether they are describing the past or the present, or elucidating notions of what it means to be "modern" or "traditional," the analysts are probing an essentially contested realm in which every point of view will have its defenders and detractors.

Those who would impose designs on cultures or those who struggle to defend cultural orthodoxy or to bring about cultural change will face resistance and may find that the best laid plans of state officials or social activists go astray.

Three recent episodes in Indonesian politics bear this out. In two cases the supposedly weaker party scored some gains. Both the Indonesian state's effort to promote an integralistic ideology in which the state could do no wrong and its more recent endeavor to promote a notion that human rights should be defined locally rather than universally provided an opening for counter-arguments by Indonesian "dissidents" and NGOs. Opponents of the government line vigorously campaigned, in the first instance, for liberal notions of constraints on the behavior of state officials and, in the second instance, for the position that there are universal human rights and that more needs to be done in Indonesia to defend them.

In the third case the Indonesian state strengthened its position against those who would promote political reform. The state managed to convey the interest of the Netherlands, and especially of the Dutch cabinet minister Pronk, in Indonesian and East Timorese human rights issues as "foreign intervention" by the old colonial power. They followed this by cancelling Dutch aid projects and dissolving the Dutch-led aid consortium IGGI with a more compliant one led by the World Bank. In so doing, the controllers of the state managed to reduce the flow of funds to some of the "peskier" NGOs, to coerce those NGOs to show greater loyalty to the state, and to win popular acclaim for defending Indonesian against foreign threat.[3]

That is where events stand now, but in cultural politics no one can be certain of the final word.

Notes

1. Clifford Geertz pointed out this idea in his afterword ("The Politics of Meaning") to *Culture and Politics in Indonesia*, ed. Clare Holt (Ithaca: Cornell University Press, 1972).

2. Heather Sutherland, in *The Making of a Bureaucratic Elite: The Colonial Transformation of the Javanese Priyayi* (Singapore: Heinemann, for the Asian Studies Association of Australia, 1979), defines *priyayi* as an "aristocrat or official, member of the governing elite of Java; characteristics of that class" (p. xix).

3. However, the inconvenience caused by the forced withdrawal of assistance to Indonesian students on aid-funded scholarships in the Netherlands and to Indonesian government agencies receiving Dutch government assistance probably did not improve the government's image in the eyes of those affected.

Chapter One

Improvising Political Cultural Change: Three Indonesian Cases

R. William Liddle

> So long as it is vital, the cultural tradition of a people—its symbols, ideals, and ways of feeling—is always an argument about the meaning of the destiny its members share. Cultures are dramatic conversations about things that matter to their participants.
> —Robert N. Bellah, *Habits of the Heart*

I

IN THE REAL WORLD, cultures are made up of many, often conflicting, patterns of values, beliefs, and customs.[1] These patterns are dynamic, forever changing in response to and in advance of other movements both within and external to society. Nowhere is this truer than in the old-new nation-states of Asia and Africa, where for more than a century indigenous and imported values, beliefs, and customs have been engaging and disengaging, resolving and dissolving like bits of colored glass in a kaleidoscope.

In the world of social science, however, culture is largely treated as a contextual or independent variable useful to explain variations in behavior among societies. The political science locus classicus of this approach is Gabriel Almond and Sidney Verba's *The Civic Culture*, a five-country comparative analysis of the relationship between popular attitudes toward politics and stable democracy.[2] It was applied to the Third World most influentially by Lucian Pye in Pye and Verba's *Political Culture and Political*

Development: "The notion of political culture assumes that the attitudes, sentiments, and cognitions that inform and govern political behavior in any society are not just random congeries but represent coherent patterns which fit together and are mutually reinforcing."[3]

In Indonesian political studies, the most celebrated application of this view of the relationship between culture and politics is Benedict Anderson's "Idea of Power in Javanese Culture."[4] Briefly, Anderson identifies four attributes of what he believes to be the traditional Javanese conception of power—its concreteness, homogeneity, constant amount, and amorality—which contrast sharply with the Western idea of power as he conceives it. He then attempts to demonstrate the merits of the Javanese idea as an analytical tool by employing it to interpret various policy decisions of presidents Sukarno and Suharto.

Anderson's portrayal is lucid, vivid, and original. It focuses our minds wonderfully on a pattern of beliefs associated with the Javanese *kebatinan* (the science of inner being) tradition, and raises intriguingly the question of its contemporary applicability. As a framework for understanding present-day behavior, however (leaving aside the problem of its historical validity),[5] it is partial in two senses. It describes only one among many threads in the fabric of late-twentieth-century Indonesian political culture.[6] And it gives us no tools with which to analyze the historical process by which a set of ideas presumably dominant in precolonial times maintains its influence in postcolonial Indonesian political thought.

On the first point, compare Anderson's single-string approach with Robert Bellah's multi-stranded conception of American political culture:

From its early days, some Americans have seen the purpose and goal of the nation as the effort to realize the ancient biblical hope of a just and compassionate society. Others have struggled to shape the spirit of their lives and the laws of the nation in accord with the ideals of republican citizenship and participation. Yet others have promoted dreams of manifest destiny and national glory. And always there have been the proponents, often passionate, of the notion that liberty means the spirit of enterprise and the right to amass wealth and power for oneself.[7]

Bellah's book goes on to examine how these various subcultures—biblical, republican, nationalist, and individualist—interact today.

On the second point, the absence of analytical tools with which to understand how cultures change or are maintained over time, we need to examine values, beliefs, and customs not just as ideas but as they relate to concrete domestic and international processes and institutions, as well as to the upward and downward movements of powerful social and political forces and currents. Here we must be careful not to succumb to the Scylla and Charybdis of social and cultural determinism.

A good way to begin is to recognize the incompleteness or insuffiency and also malleability of any given cultural inheritance, to be aware that culture is to some extent created anew by every individual in response to the challenges of his or her particular environment. This is not to deny the general stability of cultures, or to exaggerate the effects of the environment, but rather to locate in the individual the mechanism by which cultural change, when it does occur, takes place. Robert Hefner puts the point this way:

> In interpretive social science we sometimes assume that individuals simply "internalize" the values of the group or community of which they are members. . . . . this is for most purposes a much too powerful model of culture. Not all the knowledge we learn in social

life is transmitted in such a prepackaged and comprehensive format. A good portion of the knowledge we need to act in the world is, in fact, reconstructed by each of us as individuals. It depends, then, not on the passive internalization of prefigured symbols and meanings, but on *an ongoing improvisation in the face of environmental demands and opportunities.*[8]

Not all individuals count equally in cultural change, of course. In every large-scale modern society, a relative few are endowed with or accumulate resources—intellectual, persuasive, utilitarian, or coercive—with which they are able to influence, directly or indirectly, the values, beliefs, and customs of many—sometimes very many—others.

Unfortunately, in the theoretical literature of the social sciences there are few helpful guides to analyzing how this business of resource building and resource deploying works in relation to cultural change. My own most basic assumptions tend toward complexity, catholicity, and indeterminacy. With Max Weber and Clifford Geertz, I believe that cultures are "at once a product and a determinant of social interaction."[9] That is, no simple unilinear model can explain why cultures or societies change. Moreover, with Charles Taylor and Albert Hirschman, I believe that outcomes are always subject to, and in fact are often affected by, the intervention of previously unidentified variables.[10] I do not therefore aspire to any kind of closed conceptual framework or lawlike conclusions.

Given these assumptions, Hefner's formulation of cultural change as "ongoing improvisation" is a good description both of my own analytical starting point and of my sense of how it is that individuals in a society actually construct their values, beliefs, and customs. In this essay I will describe the improvisations of three well-known Indonesian intellectuals: Goenawan Mohamad, the editor-in-chief of *Tempo* magazine founded in 1970 and

banned by the Indonesian government in 1994; Sjahrir, a politi-
cal economist who heads his own Sekolah Ilmu Sosial (School of
Social Science) and research and consulting firm, the Institute for
Economic and Financial Research; and Nurcholish Madjid, once
the chair of Himpunan Mahasiswa Islam (Islamic University Stu-
dents' Association), now a lecturer at the Jakarta Institut Agama
Islam Negeri (State Islamic Institute) and chair of the private
Yayasan Paramadina (Paramadina Foundation), a Jakarta-based
Islamic studies organization.

All three of these individuals have engaged in improvisation
because they have not found, in the dominant political cultural
legacy they have inherited, persuasive answers to the challenges
posed by the demands and opportunities of their place and time,
the Indonesian nation-state in the last three decades of the twentieth century. The essayist Goenawan has discarded the state-centered collectivism of his national and ethnic past in favor of a
more individual-centered conception of society; the economist
Sjahrir has rejected his countrymen's belief in the superior morality of the state over the private sector in the economy; and the
religious thinker Nurcholish has disavowed the historical commitment of most Indonesian Muslims to a totalistic view of the
relationship between religion and society, adopting in its place a
render-unto-Caesar secularism toward many questions of social
and political life.

What makes these intellectuals interesting is that they are tack-
ling three of the most central, and in my view harmful, beliefs in
Indonesian political culture—beliefs that have long impeded
progress toward a more participatory polity, prosperous economy,
and integrated society—and that their improvisations have taken
place in public. All three have written and spoken widely for
many years. Their names, ideas, and activities are well known to
the newspaper- and magazine-reading public in Jakarta and
throughout the country. They thus have the potential of shaping

the improvisations of other Indonesians as well. Whether they are in fact having much of an impact is, as I have already suggested, a complex matter that I can only begin to examine here.

II

Goenawan Mohamad was born in 1941 in Batang, a strongly Islamic area on the north coast of central Java. He is undoubtedly the most famous dropout from the University of Indonesia's psychology faculty, which he entered in 1960. During the Guided Democracy period, he was a member of the Manifes Kebudayaan (Cultural Manifesto) group of writers and artists opposed to the communist party-driven politicization of the arts. In 1965 and 1966 he traveled to and studied in Belgium. His journalism career began with the anti-Sukarno, pro-New Order daily newspaper *Harian KAMI*, after which he founded his own newsmagazine, called *Tempo*, from 1970 until it was banned in 1994. He continues to write today for the internet version of *Tempo* called *Tempo Interaktif* and other publications, but has also begun a new career as a political activist. Today he is a very successful journalist–businessperson, and also a highly regarded poet.

Goenawan's ideas are most fully expressed in his weekly *Tempo* columns, now collected in four volumes.[11] At least in the third volume, whose more than 160 essays I read carefully before writing an introduction, it is clear that his central moral and intellectual commitment is to the individual. The institutions and beliefs of society are useful in so far as they create a context in which individual men and women develop the self-knowledge and social resources that enable them to gain mastery over their own lives.

For example, writing about a dam project from which tens of thousands of villagers were forcibly evicted, Goenawan emphasizes that "no matter what, the people cannot have taken away their right—given to them by God—to choose their own way of life." After telling the story of a child prodigy who died young without achievements because of his father's overbearing tutelage, Goenawan writes: "Human beings can be ripened artificially (*dikarbit*), minted (*dicetak*), aimed in a particular direction (*diarahkan*)—who says they can't be? But later on, finally a crisis will hit us as ourselves. Without protection."[12] In a later essay on the 1940s modernist poet Chairil Anwar, he laments that "even now, at a time when we often see individuals beaten up by mobs, tortured by the authorities and slandered by the public, we are still afraid of *I* (*aku*). We feel more secure with *we* (*kita*)."[13]

Accompanying Goenawan's individualism is a cluster of related values and beliefs. He rejects most Indonesian intellectuals' standard dichotomization of cultures into the "spiritual" East versus the "material" West, believing instead that science knows no national or cultural boundaries and that ideas and experiences should be sought from everywhere.

He is hostile to the absolutism of personal rulership ("A country that is governed by one person is not a country at all"),[14] the destructiveness of revolution, the arbitrariness and shackles of bureaucracy, and the fanaticism of ideologues. He favors representative democracy. His columns seek answers to such questions as: What causes democracy? Why are its proponents so often less passionate than its opponents? How can we make choices in a radically uncertain world? How can we reconcile democracy with the selfishness and rapaciousness of human nature?

Goenawan is an autodidact, a born intellectual, and a voracious reader who seems to have formed his essential ideas early.[15] In Batang he read the local press—*Panyebar Semangat* (in Javanese), *Minggu Pagi, Suara Merdeka*—which he valued for its high-quality editing, nonpartisanship, and balanced consideration of issues, unlike the more strident national press of the time. He is an admirer of Albert Camus, and once wrote an introduction to a collection of his essays. If he is heir to any Indonesian intellectual tradition, it is that of the rationalist and Westernizer

Sutan Takdir Alisjahbana. But his small-town Javanese upbring-
ing, or perhaps his temperament, makes him a less one-sided,
more complex, and subtle thinker.

Tempo, modeled after *Time* and *Newsweek,* was designed to appeal to a broad educated audience, to bridge many walks of life,
unlike its more partisan or specialized predecessors. It nonetheless had an explicitly political mission, to defend those who cannot defend themselves. Goenawan links this mission to his
individualism: "in stressing the individual . . . I actually want
to depict the individual as a potential victim, not as a potential
disturber of harmony."[16]

Tempo's linguistic (of course also political, in a broader sense)
mission was from the beginning: to develop a new kind of Indonesian journalistic language, honest and truthful in its re-
portage, stylistically direct, unpretentious and clear, and free of
the clichés and slogans of both ideologues and bureaucrats. It
came very close to achieving those goals, certainly in comparison
both to its predecessors and to its successors.

Sjahrir was born in 1945 in Kudus, Central Java, of West Su-
matran parents. He was educated at the Faculty of Economics,
University of Indonesia, and at Harvard, where he received his
Ph.D. in Political Economy and Government in 1983. During the
political upheavals of the mid-1960s he was a prominent student
activist, becoming chair of the presidium of the national-level
KAMI (Kesatuan Aksi Mahasiswa Indonesia, Indonesian Students
Action Front) in 1969. As a young assistant at the Faculty of Economics in the early 1970s, he was a major intellectual force behind
the student protest movement that culminated in the anti-Japan-
ese and antigovernment riots of January 1974, subsequently labeled *Malari* (*Malapetaka Januari,* the January Disaster).

In Indonesia, Sjahrir studied under the technocrats or so-
called Berkeley Mafia, including Professors Widjojo Nitisastro,
Ali Wardhana, and Mohammad Sadli. He was also associated

with Professor Soemitro Djojohadikusumo, the dean of Indonesian professional economists. At the same time he was strongly influenced by an economist with democratic socialist values, Professor Sarbini Somawinata.[17] Up to 1974, when he was arrested, tried, and convicted for his role in the events leading up to *Malari,* his economics and politics appear to have reflected the ideas of Sarbini more than those of the neoclassical technocrats.

At Harvard, Sjahrir became a convert to the market and a skeptic about the relevance of Western-style democracy for present-day Indonesia. Nonetheless, he remains committed to the goals of broad-based economic growth and distribution. He also believes that the right kind of government intervention—a mix of neoclassical macroeconomic policies, more sectorally targeted policies to increase competition and thereby enhance market efficiency, plus budgetary allocations for distribution—is crucial to achieving both those goals.[18]

Since his return to Indonesia in the mid-1980s, Sjahrir's voluminous journalistic writing has been almost exclusively pro-market, antiregulation, and antimonopoly.[19] Perhaps ironically, this stance aligns him with his former teachers, the reigning technocrats under the leadership of Professor Widjojo, whose policies he once disdained.

To some extent, his current views reflect the temper of the times, as the various nonmarket alternative approaches to which he was once attracted have been discredited. They are also consistent, however, with his earlier anger at the flagrant abuse—through illegal bribes or legal monopolies—by high officials of public position for private gain. But most fundamentally, in my judgment anyway, they reveal Sjahrir's mature convictions about Indonesian economy and society, and in particular about which government policies will solve Indonesia's economic problems at its present stage of development.

Nurcholish Madjid was born in Jombang, eastern Java, in

1939. Jombang is in the heartland of Javanese Islam, and Nur-cholish's father was simultaneously active in the traditional Islamic organization Nahdlatul Ulama (The Awakening of the Religious Teachers: NU) and the Islamic-modernism-influenced political party Masjumi. When NU broke politically with Masjumi in 1952, Nurcholish's father stayed with the latter and transferred his son from a traditional boarding school (*pesantren*) to the famous modernist school at Gontor.

From Gontor Nurcholish entered the State Islamic Institute in Jakarta, graduating with a degree in Arabic literature in 1968. From 1966 to 1971, a time of great ferment in politics and economics, he was national chair of the Islamic University Students' Association. In January 1970 he gave a speech to a meeting of Islamic student groups that electrified and polarized the Muslim community, and whose impact is still palpable today.

The title of the speech sounded bland—"Keharusan Pemba-haruan Pemikiran Islam Dan Masalah Integrasi Ummat" (The necessity for renewal of Islamic thinking and the problem of the integration of the Islamic community)[20]—but it contained a concept—*sekularisasi* (secularization)—that shocked many people. Nurcholish began by asserting that Islam in Indonesia had stagnated. Muslims faced a critical choice: the path of renewal, requiring a thorough rethinking of the meaning of religion in the modern world, at the expense of the solidarity of the community; or the maintenance of that solidarity, at the expense of a freezing of thought and the loss of moral force. Opting for renewal, he proposed a process of *liberalisasi* (liberalization) which in turn had three dimensions: secularization, intellectual freedom, and the Idea of Progress and an Open Attitude.

The concept of secularization Nurcholish borrowed from Robert Bellah, whose paper "Islamic Tradition and the Problems of Modernization" he had read on a trip to the United States and the Middle East in 1968.[21] Bellah's paper focused on early Islam, which he considered more "modern" (in the Western social sci-

ence sense) than the periods that followed it. Here is what Nurcholish read:

> There is no question but that under Muhammad, Arabian society
> made a remarkable leap forward in social complexity and political ca-
> pacity. . . . It is modern in the high degree of commitment, in-
> volvement, and participation expected from the rank-and-file
> members of the community. It is modern in the openness of its lead-
> ership positions to ability judged on universal grounds and symbol-
> ized in the attempt to institutionalize a non-hereditary top
> leadership. [150–51]

Bellah identified four "structural elements" of early Islam that
made it modern in this sense:

> First was a conception of a transcendent monotheistic God. . . .
> Second was the call to selfhood and decision. . . . *Third was the*
> *radical devaluation, one might legitimately say secularization, of all ex-*
> *isting social structures in the face of this central God-man relationship.*
> . . . And finally, there was a new conception of political order based
> on the participation of all those who accepted the divine revelation
> and thus constituted themselves a new community, *umma.* The dom-
> inant ethos of this community was this-worldly, activist, social, and
> political. . . . [151–52; emphasis added]

Nurcholish seized upon Bellah's conceptualization to articulate
his own vision of the proper Islamic society and the shortcomings
of Indonesian Islam:

> By secularization is not meant the implementation of Secularism, be-
> cause "secularism is the name for an ideology, a new closed world
> view which functions very much like a new religion." What is needed
> is every kind of "liberating development." This liberation is espe-
> cially necessary because the Islamic community, due to its own his-

tory, is no longer able to distinguish, among values it considers Islamic, which are transcendental and which are temporal. [4–5]

As a result of this historical process, Islam has lost its "psychological striking force" (1). Muslims have become mere traditionalists and cannot come to grips with the demands of current and future social change. What needs to be done is to "make worldly values that should be worldly, and release the Islamic community from the tendency to make them divine" (5).

These views have implications for politics. Although Nurcholish does not specifically address the issue of an Islamic State, it is clear that he thinks the basic requirement for Muslims is not the form of the state in which they live but the moral character of their political behavior. The loyalty of Muslims is not to institutions but to Islam itself. They are therefore not obliged to form an Islamic party. Nurcholish uses the phrase "Islam yes, Islamic party no" for the first time in this speech (2).[22] An Islamic state is any state in which Muslims can follow the teachings of the Qur'an and *sunnah* (way of life of the prophet). For Nurcholish, these teachings emphasize social justice, egalitarianism, and political participation through democratic institutions.

He also argues for the adoption of useful ideas from outside Islam:

Today, the struggle to improve the fate of the human community is not a monopoly of the Islamic community. The whole human community, staking all of the rationality at its disposal, is involved in efforts to find the best ways to improve the collective life of mankind. Its thoughts in these modern times find expression in such now frequently heard terms as democracy, socialism, populism, communism, and so on. [11]

Nurcholish's views are to some extent a natural continuation of the basic thrusts of nineteenth-century Middle Eastern Islamic modernism, especially that of Muhammad Abduh, which were to return to the Qur'an and *sunnah* as the direct sources of inspiration for belief and practice, and to adopt the tools of modern science in order to catch up with the industrialized West. By the 1940s and 1950s, when Nurcholish was growing up in Jombang, modernist ideas were influential throughout Indonesia, especially in the cities, and were being taught at Gontor.

Nurcholish's concept of secularization, though inspired by a reading of Bellah, seems well within the Islamic modernist principles of his teachers. It nonetheless provoked enormous controversy, almost all of it from within the modernist community itself. One reason was a simple misunderstanding of the word *sekularisasi*, which was taken by many to mean the creation of a nonreligious or wholly secular world, despite Nurcholish's explicit disclaimer. More substantively, many modernists refused to part with the shibboleth that Islam is a holistic religion that knows no separation of the things of God from the things of man. In particular, unlike Christianity (they like to say), there is no separation of church and state in Islam.[23]

At the University of Chicago, from 1978 to 1984, Nurcholish read widely in classical and medieval Islamic literature, under the direction of the neomodernist Pakistani scholar Professor Fazlur Rahman, gaining a new appreciation of nonmodernist thought and practice.[24] Nurcholish had at first intended to specialize in the sociology of religion, but finally wrote his dissertation on the theology and political philosophy of the classical thinker Ibn Taimiya.[25]

Since returning from Chicago in 1984, he has once again become the most prominent intellectual leader of the urban, Western-educated Islamic community. He is a senior researcher at the Indonesian Institute of Sciences (LIPI) and a professor at the Islamic Studies Institute. He is also the founder and head of the private Paramadina Foundation,[26] which conducts religious discussions and in other ways ministers to the spiritual and ethical needs of affluent middle- and upper-class Muslims.

Nurcholish now calls himself a "pluralist" or "inclusivist," by which he means that no single Islamic individual or group can legitimately claim to be in exclusive possession of the truth.[27] Certain knowledge of truth belongs to God, and can only be reached for by man. Intellectual freedom and tolerance for a range of interpretations are therefore basic to a genuinely Islamic society. This approach is of course very compatible, if not identical, with his 1970 views, and he remains a highly controversial figure.

III

So far I have just limned the ideas of three individuals, and elaborated a bit on their origins and characteristics. But the important question is whether something broadly social is going on, whether these individuals are thinking and acting in isolation or are having an impact in changing the values and beliefs of their fellow Indonesians.

This is not an easy question to answer, for both practical and intellectual reasons. The major practical barrier is that Indonesia is not a free society. Fear of government reprisals constrains most people from writing, speaking, or acting authentically in the national political arena. So the observer must sift through the public record for clues as to underlying positions and intentions.

Intellectually, as I stated at the outset, there has been little systematic, cumulative development of conceptual frameworks and hypotheses about the causes of cultural change. There is, however, one fundamental insight on which Karl Marx and Max Weber, together with their respective followers, have been in agreement: that ideas (e.g., Marx's capitalism, Weber's Calvinism) prosper only when they are linked to powerful social forces (e.g., Marx's bourgeoisie, Weber's entrepreneurs).

I accept this insight, and will try to build on it in what follows. At the same time, I am uncomfortable with it, at least when so baldly put, for two reasons. First, it implies that social forces are autonomous of and anterior to ideas, when in fact (or so I believe) ideas often shape both the form and content of social forces in societies under pressure (which is to say all societies in the modern world). Second, it excessively narrows our analytical focus to two variables: ideas and social forces. What we should be looking for, in addition, is the presence or absence of other variables that help new ideas and forces to come together or that keep them apart.

My way of overcoming these problems is to introduce the concept of resources, the means or "factors of production" that give weight to the social and political demands of individuals and groups. My definition of resources is broad, indeed infinite (in the sense that new types are always being created), and my approach to them is empirical, inductive, and formative or emergent.

To be specific, for present purposes: what resources are possessed by the defenders of the dominant culture, what resources do my three cultural innovators hold, and how are these resources being shaped—created, expanded, contracted, destroyed—by the political process—that is, by the working out of conflicts among social and political forces in contemporary Indonesia? In what follows, I will focus primarily on the obstacles thrown up by the defenders and the innovators' current and emerging resources, as I see them, but will also try to give some sense of the possibilities for change that emerge from the political process.

The Defenders

The defenders of the dominant values and beliefs enjoy the luxury of the status quo. They benefit from four important resources: a supporting cast of tens of millions of believers, many of whom are mobilizable against change; the cultural and social inertia that typically accompanies long-held beliefs; a high degree of "recoverability" or capacity to adapt to new situations; and powerful networks of social forces and institutions with an interest in their preservation. In the first case, and to a considerable extent in the second, they command the resources of the most powerful institution in Indonesian society, the state, and of the political force that governs the state, the army.

Without a cumulation of survey research or anthropological case studies, it is difficult to gauge just how pervasive and intensely held, let alone how politically mobilizable, the dominant values of the supporting cast are. My personal impression, derived from long periods of living in both rural and urban Indonesia and a quarter century of reading the daily press, is that they are for sure extremely pervasive.

The intensity with which they are held, and thus their mobilizability and the strength of their inertial force, is another question. To answer it, we need to know something about the extent to which they are a product of each individual's direct experience with the challenges of daily living, which would tend to make them a matter of deeper conviction, rather than a product of the general socialization process, which I suspect results in more easily toppled beliefs.

Without such knowledge, here are a few snippets of direct testimony from Indonesians actively involved in the cultural process. Our Muslim innovator, Nurcholish, believes that Islamic intolerance of non-Muslims is pervasive, intense, and easy to mobilize. In 1991 Arswendo Atmowiloto, editor of *Monitor*, a TV guide and tabloid magazine, and a non-Muslim, was mobbed by angry Muslims and subsequently sentenced to a jail term by a Jakarta court. His crime was insulting Islam by reporting that the Prophet Muhammad was not the public figure most admired by Indonesians, according to a poll of *Monitor* readers.

Commenting on the case, Nurcholish said:

Arswendo did not understand and did not feel how difficult it is to persuade Indonesian Muslims to respect adherents to other religions. I have been involved in polemics, debates, and conflicts for nearly a quarter of a century, and I have felt threats that have made me shudder.[28]

More directly relevant to the issue of the relationship between Islam and the state is a 1990 report from Abdurrahman Wahid, the head of Indonesia's largest Muslim organization, the traditionalist, rural Java-based Nahdlatul Ulama (NU), which claims a membership of 27 million. According to Wahid, Gen. L. B. Moerdani, Minister of Defense and Security, at the time the leader of army opposition to President Suharto's death grip on his office, and a Roman Catholic, asked him if NU would support him as Suharto's successor. Wahid's answer was that, though he himself had no objection, NU's members could not yet accept a non-Muslim president.[29]

On the issue of the general relationship between state and society, the young Muslim poet and essayist Emha Ainun Nadjib, known for his closeness to village people, characterized the attitudes of ordinary Indonesians and officials this way:

All Indonesians I have ever met feel that they are the subordinates (*bawahan*) of the government. Moreover there are very many of our officials in the regions or outlying areas who feel confident that they really are the superiors (*atasan*) of the people. And if you say that popular sovereignty is above the government's sovereignty, you will not only be considered to oppose development, but they will be sure you are really an evil person.[30]

This attitude clearly carries over to the specific relationship between the state and the economy. Perhaps the most worrisome evidence to this effect, worrisome because it shows the extraordinary tenacity of statist views, even among highly educated and well-informed people, is in a recent paper by the economist Bruce Glassburner.[31] In 1989 Glassburner interviewed thirty-six members of the political and governmental elite on questions of economic policy.

All these individuals had been asked the same questions in interviews conducted in the late 1960s by Frank Weinstein.[32] Most elite members, Weinstein found, were hostile to free enterprise and markets and believed in the need for state protection of indigenous capitalists and many other antimarket regulations to prevent monopoly and promote more egalitarian distribution. Twenty years later, and despite the enormous success of the New Order's essentially neoclassical macroeconomic policy during the intervening period, Glassburner found no change in views.[33]

Concerning the relationship between the collectivity and the individual, army officers and civilian government officials are the most vigorous articulators of the pro-collectivity position. At one level, this is because the officers and officials strongly believe that their institutions are the only structures in society that can formulate, articulate, and defend the interests of the whole against the special interests of individuals and groups. That belief is reinforced and sustained by their material and status interests, which have been well served by their control of the government.

In the case of the army, belief in the importance of the collectivity is strengthened by the general corporateness that characterizes all modern military forces. More specifically Indonesian, the ideology of *dwi-fungsi* (the twin functions of defending the country and "playing a positive sociopolitical role") legitimizes the army, in its own eyes at least, as the central organizing and controlling force in Indonesian politics.

The general concept of army intervention in politics, for which *dwi-fungsi* is the current name, goes back to the 1945–1949

Revolution.[34] Senior serving officers appear not to debate either its value as basic doctrine or its current implementation. Retired officers, less bound by military discipline and without a need to please superiors, express a range of views about implementation but do not question the doctrine itself. Younger officers, who were socialized into belief in *dwi-fungsi* in military academy and subsequently have been given training in its practice through assignments outside the Department of Defense and Security, may have other views.

In the case of civilian bureaucrats, belief in the collectivity and in the state's role is strengthened by the government's effective building up of civil service associations, particularly Korpri (Korps Pegawai Republik Indonesia, Officials' Corps of the Republic of Indonesia), and its wives' affiliate, Dharma Wanita (Women's Duty). These organizations are imbued with an ethic of public service and at the same time allow officials to display and enjoy their high social status.

New Order government service is also a world unto itself, superior to and isolated from political parties and other organizations of non–civil servants. Promotions and other career ambitions—especially positioning in jobs that enable one to make money on the side—are satisfied largely through the manipulation of internal patron-client networks. Lower-ranking, younger bureaucrats attach themselves to more senior officials, performing various services that raise the status, power, and income of the seniors in return for boosts up the ladder. This pattern helps to solidify officials' sense of their corporateness and separateness from the rest of society.

For the last several years the head of President Suharto's executive office, Minister for the State Secretariat (and a retired army officer) Moerdiono, has acted as a kind of official philosopher on behalf of collectivism and statism. In speeches and press conferences, he offers a steady stream of often thoughtful commentary and analysis, typically couched in Javanese aphorisms, anchoring government policy to the collective interest. In the New Order's extremely hierarchical bureaucratic system, his style and the substance of his views are emulated by other central officials, governors, district, subdistrict, and village heads. Many non-Javanese officials collect books of Javanese sayings to help them understand and participate in this discourse.

All of this seems to work reasonably well as a cultural system. For example, I recall an evening in 1986 when I was watching the national television news in a small hotel in the remote district town of Takengon, Central Aceh. I was struck by the fact that I was surrounded by a sea of blue Korpri shirts, with their distinctive *beringin* (banyan) tree motif. They were being worn not only by my fellow hotel guests, but by everyone appearing on the screen as well!

To many nonofficials (and even, it must be conceded, to some officials), state television is notorious for its excessive coverage of the doings of officials. But to the people I was with, the images on the screen affirmed an important bond, one that most wearers of the shirt care deeply about. For good reason, since it has made a modern life possible for them and at the same time given them a sense of a larger purpose and social commitment.

Though general support for the idea of the collectivity and for the role of the state is widespread within the state itself, there are nonetheless redoubts of individualism. The state universities, especially the best ones like the University of Indonesia in Jakarta and Gadjah Mada University in Yogyakarta, are perhaps the most important. There, even though the lecturers are all of course state officials, the Korpri shirt and the "safari" daily uniform seen in most government offices are rarer.

The universities provide a kind of protected haven, or atmosphere of relative cultural freedom, where many different ideas are entertained, both in the classroom and in the frequent seminars and conferences that bring in off-campus and foreign speakers. In my experience, mostly at Gadjah Mada, there is a serious attempt at creating an intellectual environment in which faculty and students will not be punished for expressing unorthodox ideas. This intellectual freedom has not gone unchallenged by the government, as the history of repression of student movements and demonstrations attests, but it has never been totally suppressed.[35]

The army's and the bureaucracy's power to defend the ideas of the superiority of the collectivity and the centrality of the state weighs most heavily on the efforts of Goenawan and like-minded intellectuals to raise the dignity and expand the autonomy of the individual. It rests somewhat more lightly on Sjahrir and other pro-deregulation economists, who have at least been able to convince government decision makers to adopt market-oriented policies. The evidence of Glassburner's article, however, argues that the economists have not yet had much impact on the basic pro-state culture of the political elite, even in regard to economic questions.

The belief that an Islamic society requires an Islamic State has a rather different history. It has never been as pervasively held as the pro-collectivity and pro-state ideas. It does nonetheless appear to have intensive support in certain quarters.

To begin with, its greatest popularity has been among the roughly 50 percent of Indonesian Muslims who live outside the Javanese cultural area of east and central Java. Among the Javanese 50 percent, according to the most widely accepted interpretation, it has been a belief only of devout Muslims or *santri*, and not of the probably larger group of Javanese Muslims called *abangan*, whose actual religious beliefs and practices incorporate Hindu and animistic elements.[36]

Secondly, the self-conscious idea of an Islamic State as an obligation, a goal that good Muslims must struggle to achieve, is largely a development of the late nineteenth and early twentieth centuries and of Islamic modernism. It entered Indonesia via students of the Middle Eastern Pan-Islamism of Jamal al-Din al-Afghani and Rasjid Rida, and took its first political form in the debates of the 1930s between the *abangan* nationalist Sukarno and the modernist *santri* Mohammad Natsir.[37] Before 1945, perhaps a majority of Indonesian *santri,* and certainly most rural *santri* in Java, had probably never thought about an Islamic State one way or the other.

Third, no Indonesian government has ever been in favor of an Islamic State. The idea's political heyday was the early to mid-1950s, when virtually all Islamic political party leaders were in principle committed to it, though the intensity of commitment varied from party to party.[38] In the national parliamentary elections of 1955, these parties—led by the hotly pro–Islamic State modernist Masjumi and the more lukewarm traditionalist NU, then a political party as well as an educational and social organization—won nearly half the vote.

Political Islam was defeated in the late 1950s by a coalition of the *abangan* President Sukarno and the *abangan*-led army. Suharto and his army officers are also predominantly *abangan,* and have not allowed it to reemerge. Nurcholish's politics, as I will elaborate below, have paralleled those of Suharto and the army on this issue. His position in relation to the state is thus very different from that of Goenawan, who has few state resources on his side, or even Sjahrir, who enjoys a more narrowly based rapport with the state.

How powerful is the Islamic State idea today, and where does that power come from? Government repression of pro–Islamic State forces makes the first of these questions hard to answer. Most Islamic intellectuals writing and speaking publicly today, including Nurcholish, say that few Indonesian Muslims still believe in the Islamic State. Their testimony is open to question, however, as they themselves oppose the idea. They are also not closely in touch with what we might call the Islamic underground, would-be Islamic political leaders who work with small groups—most visibly on university campuses, but I suspect among lower-middle-class, working-class, and more economically marginal groups as well—and who in the current repressive atmosphere avoid political discussion and, especially, action.

My own view may be biased by a two-year field experience in Aceh, many of whose people take great pride in their Islamic fanaticism. I nonetheless believe that the automatic, unreflective idea that religion can not be detached from any aspect of life is pervasive in the *santri* community. Specifically concerning politics, most local religious leaders, whatever their present relationship with authority, believe that the *ulama* should be the moral overseers of the *umara* (state leadership, an Arabic term used in Indonesian Islamic discourse). The perceived history of Islam, as described above by Bernard Lewis, combined with the interest of the *ulama* in maintaining their elite status, provides much of the explanation for the idea's staying power. Of course, such a view is not in principle incompatible with moderate and pluralist interpretations of *ulama-umara* relations. But it provides a powerful resource to more radical would-be political leaders.

In the last two decades piety has been a growth industry among urban Indonesians of Muslim background, including many *abangan*. The phenomenon is most visible among the middle class and the Western-educated, and is reflected in mushrooming mosque attendance and the now-general use of Islamic symbols and rituals by state officials, including non-Muslims.[39]

In general terms, it appears that religion is filling an identity gap, enabling individuals to become in their own minds complete persons. It is not that modernity (that is, an urban middle-class lifestyle) and nationalism are being rejected, but rather that these ideologies have little to say about either the ultimate or the mundane questions addressed by religion.

The cultural consequences of this new modernity-nationalism-Islam nexus are hard to predict. One possibility, which I describe below, is accommodation with the secular state. Another, however, is a renewed commitment to the idea of the Islamic State, backed by a powerful social force led by intellectuals and middle-class people, but given much of its power by its appeal to working-class, unemployed, and otherwise marginal urbanites, and by its continued positive resonance for rural *santri*. A large number of the latter live in fact in a kind of permanent uprootedness, back and forth between rural and urban employment and lifestyle, and may be becoming increasingly susceptible to all kinds of oppositionist, including Islamic State, ideologies.

Finally, in this discussion of the resources possessed by defenders of the cultural status quo, I mention briefly Maurice Bloch's concept of the "recoverability" of ideology.[40] Citing his own work in Madagascar, Bloch argues that the vagueness and alogicality of ideologies make it possible for them to shift from "one power-holder to another, as an instrument for domination and legitimation" (133).

In Indonesia, all three of the dominant ideas have been around for a long time and, as in Bloch's Madagascar, have survived many political and social upheavals. The strong-state idea in particular, with its deep roots in Javanese political history, seems especially resilient. In another paper, I have attempted to explain how it has been possible for President Suharto to adopt market-oriented macroeconomic policies while at the same time promoting (and undoubtedly himself holding) a pro-state ideology.[41] A third example is the long premodern association between Javanist kings and Islamic legitimation, broken by Dutch colonialism but restored by Sukarno and Suharto.

The Innovators

What resources do the innovators possess? In general terms I see: small but active social forces, or core constituencies; intellectual prowess combined with rhetorical and political skills; additional constituencies that might be brought into a coalition with the core; support from parts of the state; and both specific and diffuse international backing.

Goenawan Mohamad's core constituency is the Jakarta journalistic, literary, and artistic community, together with its small outliers in other major cities and university towns. This group numbers only in the thousands, but it has been very active in the New Order period. General prosperity and the growth of the educational system and of opportunities to study abroad have expanded the group and also given it a larger and more sophisticated audience than ever before.

I do not want to make too great a claim for this community's capacity to promote cultural change, however. Its members still constitute a tiny and beleaguered minority, isolated from the larger society. As a group, they are in their own minds not very talented, and their audience, despite recent progress, remains small in proportion to Indonesian society as a whole. They have not, with very few exceptions—for example, several stories and novels by the former pro-communist Pramoedya Ananta Toer, whose works are banned by the government and who is also a social pariah, and a few stories by the Yogyakarta-based writer Umar Kayam—produced any world-class literature or other great artistic triumphs so far. The fine arts rubric in *Tempo* was the least popular with readers, as the magazine's polls time and again attested.

Goenawan himself has written movingly of this sense of separation. His "Portrait of a Young Poet as Malin Kundang" essay is about a youth who leaves home, becomes rich, denies his mother, is cursed by her, and turns into stone. The implication is of the betrayal by the modern intellectual of his or her cultural heritage, and of the great distance between modern Indonesian and traditional ethnic culture. The essay ends with: "But if for example there is finally no road home, there is still something that is valuable, that is freedom."[42] Unfortunately, while Goenawan and many of his colleagues are willing to make this tradeoff, it doesn't point to any means by which the social gap between individualist intellectuals and the collectivist masses might be narrowed.

In its narrowest construction, Sjahrir's core constituency consists of the tiny group of professional economists and the somewhat larger one of educated Indonesians able to understand his sophisticated commentary on economic events that appears in Jakarta newspapers, newsmagazines, and more specialized business publications. Within this group, Sjahrir is not, of course, the leading figure. That title, for more than twenty years, has gone to Professor Widjojo, President Suharto's long time senior economic advisor and for many years head of Bappenas (National Planning Board). Several other senior economists, including Professors Soemitro, Mohammad Sadli, Ali Wardhana, Sumarlin, and Radius Prawiro, have also had more policy influence than the still youthful Sjahrir. In addition, Soemitro and Sadli are able academic and journalistic writers.

Sjahrir's uniqueness, and the main source of his possible future influence both in the policy process and on cultural change, is that he straddles two constituencies. He is simultaneously taken seriously by economists, whose litmus test of acceptability is knowledge of and respect for the workings of the market, and by the *Malari* and post-*Malari* generations of anti-Suharto political activists, whose basic commitment is to egalitarian redistribution of the benefits of economic growth.

Sjahrir's recent writings, as I have already indicated, are strongly pro-market. Indeed he often takes the economists in power to task for making too many compromises with antimarket forces. In his public appearances, on the other hand, especially at universities, he frequently reminds his audiences of his own leadership role in the *Malari* demonstrations, the years he served in prison as a result, and his continuing commitment to equality and popular welfare. The lecturers at his School of Social Science are recruited disproportionately from the left of the Indonesian political spectrum. His Harvard dissertation, in both its English and Indonesian versions, also contains references to his previous political activism.

Even this double core, however, does not necessarily make Sjahrir's constituency a major force in future policy making or cultural change. Intellectually and politically, Sjahrir inherits the tradition of the democratic socialist Partai Sosialis Indonesia (Indonesian Socialist Party: PSI), banned in 1960. In the 1950s, the PSI already encompassed both market and antimarket egalitarian orientations. It was nonetheless unable to win many votes in the 1955 elections, the one genuine test of popular support in Indonesian political history.

Of the three innovators, it is Nurcholish who enjoys the largest core constituency, large enough perhaps to be considered a genuine social force, consisting of urban, middle-class, Western-educated, reformist- or modernist-minded devout Muslims. Nurcholish is in fact riding the crest of the general Islamization of national Indonesian culture that I have already mentioned but not fully described.

Forty years ago Islam was at the periphery of the modern culture, generally considered "backward" by the best-educated and most culturally sophisticated people. Today, in part as a result of the spread of Western education and of religious instruction in the schools, a new generation simultaneously modern, Indonesian, and Muslim has emerged. Its members are dispersed throughout both the private and the state sectors, and hold many of the most technically and intellectually demanding jobs.

On the available evidence, these people want to be religious but do not want to be led either by the old-fashioned, rural *ulama* or by the newer thinkers within modernist Islam. The *ulama* have long dominated much of Indonesian Islamic life; the new thinkers, inspired since the 1930s by the one-time prime minister and Masjumi leader Mohammad Natsir, have been committed to the idea of an Islamic State.

Instead, they are looking for a new understanding of their religion that gives them a more realistic set of guidelines, really a code of ethics, for private and family life and for dealing with the outside world. They want to know the rights and responsibilities of husbands and wives, how to raise their sons and daughters to be good Muslims and good Indonesians, how to relate to a modern banking system, whether and how to revitalize the concept of *zakat* (religious tax), and even how to deal with such exotica as test-tube babies, organ transplants, and homosexuality.

Many upper- and middle-class businesspeople are especially attracted to Nurcholish because he preaches accommodation with the New Order state. In this he has differed from several other Muslim intellectuals of modernist background, like Dawam Rahardjo of Lembaga Studi Agama dan Filsafat (Institute for the Study of Religion and Philosophy), publisher of the quarterly journal *Ulumul Qur'an,* and Adi Sasono of SEAFDA (Southeast Asian Forum for Development Alternatives), who are to a much greater extent partisans of the poor and critics of the government. In the 1990s, however, this gap has narrowed as many critical modernists, including Dawam and Adi, have been drawn into support of the regime with the creation of a new, state-sponsored association of Islamic intellectuals.

Goenawan, Sjahrir, and Nurcholish are all, in their own ways, skilled communicators to large audiences. Partly this has to do with quality of mind and partly with rhetorical skills. *Tempo* magazine was the creation of Goenawan, more than of any other single individual. Its style and content—Indonesian prose based on sprightly Malay rather than on turgid Dutch, coverage of all sides of issues rather than presentation of a partisan point of view, a high level of journalistic competence—were very different from most of its predecessors and successors.

Goenawan's signature contribution, the 600-word weekly column called *Catatan Pinggir* (Marginal notes), consistently offered the most thoughtful, articulate, and elegant commentary on current events and on Indonesian life in general.[43] *Tempo* sold about 150,000 copies each week. Most of them were bought by Jakarta readers, but enough reached the regions to make *Tempo* (and the daily *Kompas,* with a circulation of about 500,000, whose intellectual and political commitments, if not its prose style, are similar to *Tempo*'s) an important molder of elite opinion throughout the country.[44]

In his field of economics, Sjahrir has established himself through his writings as today's most intellectually formidable commentator on and critic of government policy. With a rhetorical style that combines a grasp of economic science, moral commitment, and a light, humorous delivery (not an easy achievement), he is also a much sought after and persuasive speaker at seminars and conferences.

On first impression, Nurcholish's more straightforward, uncultivated, and unassuming style is not as striking as that of Goenawan the poet or Sjahrir the scientist and raconteur. He is nonetheless very effective, both in print and on the podium. Partly this is due simply to the originality and depth of his ideas and the clarity of his prose, and partly it is due to his articulation of an approach to life that is enormously attractive to his constituency. Behind this approach is the moral authority of a modern man with an American Ph.D., an accomplished theologian and religious historian, and—not least—an able preacher who makes a point of regularly giving Friday sermons at mosques throughout the country.

The style and content of Nurcholish's message also has its weaknesses, however. Perhaps his greater visibility as a cultural and even political leader makes these deficiencies more obvious than in the cases of Goenawan and Sjahrir.

Nurcholish's obsession is to persuade Indonesian Muslims to accept his vision of a rational, tolerant, inclusive, "secular" Islam. He acknowledges, however, that this is a difficult task, because of the deep roots in the community of anti-Westernism, anti-Christianity, indeed intolerance of anything regarded as non-Islamic. In this connection, he often expresses his dislike for certain "romantic-ideological" Muslim intellectuals who reflect and try to capitalize on the intolerant masses for political purposes.

Nurcholish himself is not worried that these leaders will be able to move Indonesian Islam in a militant or fundamentalist direction, even in the more open and democratic political climate that might follow the Suharto era. To an outside observer, however, it is easy to imagine the middle-class appeal of the rational and intellectual Nurcholish being overwhelmed by coarser leaders who know how to inflame the masses.

In terms of reaching out to broader, specifically mass, constituencies, Goenawan and Sjahrir appear to face more daunting obstacles than Nurcholish. Goenawan and his artistic, if not journalistic, colleagues do inhabit a kind of high-culture island that appears foreign and forbidding to many (especially rural and lower-class) people. To adopt a useful phrase from Herbert Gans, the "taste cultures" of upper- and lower-class Indonesians are very different.[45]

How can this gap be overcome? Perhaps one clue can be found in the recent renaissance of *wayang kulit,* the traditional Javanese shadow play, in central Java.[46] In the early 1970s, when I first lived in the Yogyakarta area, the future of *wayang* seemed in doubt. *Dalang* (puppeteers) and their troupes were becoming too expensive for most villagers and even most townspeople to hire. Moreover, young people were said to prefer watching movies, television, and other forms of modern entertainment, and also to be choosing modern occupations over becoming puppeteers.

Everywhere one heard dismay expressed at the negative effects on traditional culture of New Order–style capitalist economic development.

Today *wayang* is still expensive, but it is very much alive. Performances are staged frequently all over the Yogyakarta special region. In 1989 and 1990, at the dozen or so plays I attended, the audiences—full houses, even in the cavernous hall where the monthly Radio Republik Indonesia performances are broadcast —were predominantly young, male, and middle- to lower-class. *Wayang* topics—the relative merits of different puppeteers, the selection of particular plays for performance, even innovations in carving—were popular items of discussion in the local press and among a large and active group of aficionados, many of them university lecturers and other professionals.

What explains this resurgence in interest? Partly, of course, it is the continuing strength of *wayang*'s deep connection with traditional Javanese culture, high and low,[47] a resource not available to the modern artists of Jakarta. Of at least equal importance, however, has been the emergence of a new generation of *dalang* who are strongly motivated to succeed—that is, to make money and enjoy high status in the community—and at the same time happen to be tuned in to recent changes in popular culture.

As a result, today's performances tend to emphasize "action," particularly fight and battle scenes, like so many popular foreign movie and TV programs. The flashback—for example, scenes from a character's earlier life introduced to explain a present situation—is also common. To appeal to the young male audience, there is more "porno" (actually for the most part only mildly risqué dialogue) and less philosophy. One *dalang* has even added trumpets to the gamelan!

There are, to be sure, critics of the new *wayang* in Yogyakarta, especially among representatives of the upper taste culture. Their argument is essentially that low entertainment values are replacing high philosophic ones, and that pure Javaneseness is being subverted by Western theatrical concepts. *Wayang* is not being brought up to date, they claim; rather it has lost its heart and soul.[48] My own sense is that *wayang* is as Javanese as it has ever been (which is to say that it has never been purely Javanese, whatever that may mean) and that its complex appeal endures. Indeed, in another twenty or thirty years, when today's young audience is old, I expect we will all be impressed by the new attention paid to the philosophic side of *wayang*.

To return to my main subject, are such connections possible between high and low taste cultures in Jakarta? One piece of evidence that they are is the popular success, particularly in the 1980s, of Nano Riantiarno's Teater Koma (Comma theater), whose plays regularly enjoyed long runs in Jakarta's larger theaters.[49] Like the Central Javanese *dalang*, Riantiarno wants to be rich and famous. He has also figured out that there is a sizable audience, in this case middle-class but relatively unintellectual young men and women, willing to pay thousands of rupiahs to be entertained by a heady mixture of the Broadway musical and low Surabaya and Jakarta folk comedy.

Riantiarno's productions have come under heavy fire from Jakarta intellectuals for their purported commercialism, low aesthetic quality, and lack of social message. My own view, again, is rather different. Riantiarno is conducting a conversation, if not yet an argument, with his middle-class constituency about issues like social justice (for example in his play *Opera Kecoa,* Cockroach opera) and political leadership (for example in *Suksesi,* Succession). While it may be true that neither party to this dialogue has as yet achieved any great breakthroughs, Riantiarno at least has found an audience and captured its attention, which is more than can be said for many of his peers.

Sjahrir's main hope for a larger constituency is the entrepreneurial or business middle class, which is believed to be growing rapidly as a result of New Order development policies. As the owner of a financial consulting firm and of a seat on the Jakarta stock exchange, Sjahrir himself can claim membership in this group. His firm's clients include some of the largest Sino-Indonesian and indigenous businesses in Jakarta.

Before we can assess the potential of the business class as a social force, however, we need much more information about its size, scope, and internal divisions; its racial makeup; and the extent of its autonomy or dependence on the state. By size, scope, and internal divisions, I mean how many entrepreneurs and business people there now are; whether they are concentrated in Jakarta and a few other large cities like Surabaya and Medan or are dispersed more widely throughout the country, in small towns and even rural as well as urban areas; and whether there are significant differences in interest between big, medium, and small businesses, businesses in different sectors of the economy, and so on.

Racially, the common view—which tends to be disputed by both domestic and foreign economists—is that Sino-Indonesians have been much more successful than indigenous *pribumi* business people in responding to the challenges and opportunities of the deregulation of the late 1980s and early 1990s. This belief creates the potential for conflict between races in addition to or instead of between the business class and statist forces.

On the autonomy question, the common opinion—which few seem to dispute, though I myself take a more optimistic view—is that most prosperous entrepreneurs, of whatever race, at all levels and sectors, owe their success principally to government connections rather than to abilities to meet the challenges of the marketplace. To the extent that this is true, Indonesian business people are not likely to adopt a free-market philosophy.

Of the three leaders, Nurcholish not only enjoys the largest core constituency but has also put together by far the biggest and most influential political alliance, combining elements of modernist and traditional Islam with support from the state bureaucracy (to be discussed below). The traditional part comes from Nahdlatul Ulama (NU), the village- and rural-centered organization of religious teachers, concentrated in East and Central Java but with large followings in several other provinces as well.

Founded in 1926, NU has been led since 1984 by Abdurrahman Wahid, the grandson of one of the organization's founders and son of one of its most respected leaders. To this inheritance, of great importance in NU political culture, he brings resources of his own: a will to lead, a politician's sense of how to cultivate and maintain a network of leaders and followers, intellectual and political creativity and daring, and a neomodernist point of view about the future of Islam and Indonesian society that is very close to that of Nurcholish.

Abdurrahman Wahid's intellectual and political support is a major asset, giving Nurcholish access to the traditional Javanese Islamic community through the leader of its largest organization. If Nurcholish's own constituency is largely urban and middle- to upper-class, Abdurrahman Wahid's is a socioeconomically broad swath of *santri* villagers. This modernist-traditional alliance is reminiscent of the Masyumi political party in the early 1950s, before NU left to become a party on its own. In the 1955 elections, Masyumi and NU combined received nearly 40 percent of the vote.

This is not to argue that, were Indonesia once again to hold democratic elections, a Masyumi-like party led by Nurcholish Madjid and Abdurrahman Wahid would win 40 percent of the vote. On the modernist side, as I have suggested above, there are more radical alternative leaders, now largely operating beneath the surface because of government repression, who might well attract a large and passionate following if controls were lifted.

Among traditionalists, even NU traditionalists, Abdurrahman Wahid is a unique figure who often leads where his people do not want to go. He bubbles over with unconventional ideas, many of which have to do with concern for the substance rather than the form of religion and with tolerance toward non-Muslims. Many of his constituents respond with incomprehension if not hostility.

In politics, Abdurrahman Wahid claims to be against the idea of an Islamic party. Indeed, under his leadership, NU in 1984 removed itself altogether from the partisan arena. He has condemned as sectarian the recently formed ICMI (Ikatan Cendekiawan Muslim Indonesia, Indonesian Muslim Intellectual Association), which Nurcholish and many other self-consciously Muslim intellectuals have joined, and founded in response the Forum Demokrasi (Democratic Forum), whose members include many Catholic and other non-Islamic activists and thinkers.[50]

Were Abdurrahman Wahid to lead a non-Islamic party in a democratic election, many NU members would undoubtedly refuse to follow his lead. He himself has said that this is as it should be, since every citizen has a right to his or her own partisan affiliation. He is nonetheless an important force for cultural change, bringing new ideas to village Muslims and legitimating those ideas through the traditional authority he holds by virtue of his ancestry and his effectiveness as a political leader.

Of the three intellectuals, Goenawan has the least and Nurcholish the most support from the state bureaucracy. Goenawan's individualism runs directly counter to the state's collectivism. Moreover, government bureaucracy was a frequent target of criticism in his columns. Fearing chaos, bureaucrats construct "an order that is upright, cold, compact like the wall of a Dutch house." Bureaucratic rule without accountability leads inevitably to corruption, and "corruption is a cancer that finally crushes hope and belief."[51]

Sjahrir's overall approach to political economy, which combines confidence in markets with a commitment to government intervention both to increase competitiveness and to enhance social welfare, is more hospitable to the New Order state. More concretely, he has formed a kind of de facto alliance with the technocrats. While he is in a sense their major critic, his criticisms come from inside their paradigm, pushing them to adopt and hold to policies that reflect their best selves.

Nurcholish's support within the New Order state goes further than that. Many bureaucrats are attracted to his ideas, which make it possible for them to be openly proud of their religion without being suspected of pro–Islamic State inclinations. At a more structural level, the label Tri-Tunggal (Three-in-One)[52] is sometimes used to describe the similarity in certain ideas and policies among Nurcholish, Abdurrahman Wahid, and Munawir Syadzali, the Minister of Religion from 1987 to 1993, who was educated in Islamic schools but spent most of his government career in the Department of Foreign Affairs before being appointed minister in 1983. Nurcholish was himself widely thought to be a strong candidate to succeed Munawir, a sign of the degree to which he is accepted within the state bureaucracy.

Perhaps the most important factor that makes me optimistic about the ultimate impact of Nurcholish's ideas is that he represents a new kind of Islamic leader, one who can tap a broad potential constituency of support both within and outside the *santri* community. The historian Taufik Abdullah, in a useful essay on patterns of Islamic leadership, identifies two kinds of leaders in precolonial and early colonial Indonesian Islam: the independent *ulama,* usually the head of his own traditional school, and the state Islamic official.[53]

This initial pattern was broken in the early twentieth century with the emergence of a third kind of leader, the Western-style (but Islamic in content and purpose) association activist. The activists did not necessarily know much about Islam—they were educated in Western schools and their skills were organizational and political rather than Islamic-intellectual—but they nonetheless could make a genuine claim to legitimacy as leaders of the *umat.*

These leaders were the first to enjoy geographically dispersed influence, unlike the traditional *ulama,* whose support was concentrated in particular regions. According to Taufik, they were also the first "crossover leaders," simultaneously Muslim and national. They emerged primarily within Islamic organizations, social and educational as well as political, but their membership reach or eligibility was defined in national, Indonesia-wide, terms.

To these three categories Taufik adds a fourth, visible only since the 1970s: new intellectuals like Nurcholish. The new intellectuals have a deeper understanding of religion than most of their predecessors. At the same time they are more thoroughly national, because "more of them have entered the structure of the national community." They work as civil servants, teachers, university lecturers, journalists, and business people. Most of them grew up in devoutly Islamic families and local communities, often outside Java, becoming modern and national through higher education.

Though they do not have their own *pesantren,* the new intellectuals are in other ways reminiscent of the old independent *ulama.* They have acquired status as individuals, respected directly by mass constituencies, not by virtue of holding state office, or even in many cases, positions in Islamic organizations. In an era of rapid mass communications, it is their speaking and writing that makes them known to large audiences.

These are important qualities, because they indicate both high credibility as Islamic leaders and unassailable credentials as full members of the national political community (i.e., as "*Pancasila*ists"[54] who do not threaten the foundations of the Indonesian state. To carry the point a little further than Taufik is willing to, perhaps it can be argued that these intellectuals—Nurcholish foremost among them—have finally bridged the gap between Islam and secular nationalism that has been at the heart of the Islamic State versus *Pancasila* controversy since the 1945 constitutional debates.

Finally, all my cultural figures and their core constituencies extract resources from outside Indonesia. Sjahrir and Nurcholish have advanced degrees from American universities and maintain their connections with former teachers and friends. Goenawan was once a Nieman Fellow at Harvard and has taken sabbaticals to write and teach in Australia. These associations become vehicles through which new ideas, and often money and organization to support their development, enter Indonesia.

The present international intellectual and political climate is favorable to the ideas of all three. This is unambiguously so in the cases of Goenawan and Sjahrir, who enjoy the benefits respectively of the fall of European communism, which has strengthened the confidence of liberal democratizers everywhere, and of the Reagan-Thatcher restoration of economic liberalism as the reigning philosophy of political economy in the West. The influence in Indonesia of world Islam, with its many conflicting strands—including the currently popular radical rejection of the West and call for strict enactment of Islamic law—is more complex and hard to assess. But Nurcholish and his friends have worked hard to introduce and spread a broader range of thinking.

Politics and the Shaping of Resources

Lists of resources possessed by cultural defenders and innovators, such as I have compiled, tend to give a false impression of completeness and permanence. The picture drawn is of a kind of set battle between two armies, each with its social and cultural armor, weapons, and other strengths and weaknesses. But the reality is one of openness and fluidity, the constant decline and disappearance of old resources and creation and deployment of new ones, by multiple participants in a cultural—and ultimately political—process.

The difference is important. The battle metaphor suggests that if we can identify the key resources of the two sides we can predict the winner with some confidence. The process image (which is also a better way to understand battles!) offers no such hope. Rather, it directs us to conceive of culture as history—in the making but not yet made—and to follow closely the development and interplay of social forces and ideas, and the many other variables that may have an impact on the strength and deployability of resources.[55]

Four brief illustrations drawn from high political maneuvering in Jakarta in the early 1990s may give a sense of what I have in mind. The first has to do with how the tides of economic change may affect Sjahrir's store of resources, the second with the way in which the resources of political Islam have been enhanced by President Suharto's struggle to stay in power, the third with how Goenawan's views benefitted from the army's attempt to push Suharto into retirement, and the fourth with the way in which the 1991 Timor crisis for a time ravaged the resources of pro-democracy forces.

Sjahrir's championing of deregulation has a certain tactical appeal for individuals and groups threatened by the business activities of the Suharto family. All six of Suharto's children—but most prominently Tutut, the oldest daughter, Bambang, the middle son, and Tommy, the youngest son—are perceived to be getting the lion's share of government "facilities," in the form of trade monopolies and contracts to build state projects.[56] Sjahrir's public opposition to these projects on market competition grounds makes him a hero to antifamily business people. Put differently, Sjahrir's resources for change are enhanced by the presence in his camp of antifamily business people.

In a few years, when Suharto is no longer president, and many of these same business people are vying for favors from the new government, the climate of opinion may well be less friendly to the pro-market position, and Sjahrir's resources may shrink. My hope, however—and without adequate data, it is admittedly little more than that—is that in the slightly longer run, say in ten to twenty years, presuming continuation of the technocrats' neo-classical influence on policy, a large indigenous, multisectoral, autonomous business community will have emerged.

This group will, of course, be strongest in Jakarta, but it will also be substantial throughout the more urbanized and industrialized parts of the country, and even in small towns across Java. Many of its members should be very receptive to the ideas of pro-market intellectuals. Moreover, through his consulting and writing, Sjahrir may well have succeeded by this time in gaining the confidence of a large portion of the Jakarta business community. Finally, it is, as it was being waged prior to the presidential election of 1993, possible that Sjahrir himself will, under Indonesia's third president, be a key policy maker. I see, therefore, the prospect of a net addition of resources to the pro-change side of the equation.

My second and third illustrations come directly from the struggle for the presidential succession.[57] To counter army opposition to a sixth term in office, Suharto cultivated Islamic support. His actions included: assent to a law strengthening Islamic courts; acceptance of the wearing of the *jilbab* (Islamic headcovering) by female students in state schools; the arrest and sentencing of the *Monitor* editor; approval for ICMI, the new Islamic intellectuals' organization; and consent to the creation of an Islamic (profit-sharing rather than interest-charging) bank.

Most of these are important issues on which there has been controversy for years or decades. Suharto's shift on each gained him the support of many *santri* Muslims, though some others have a different conception of their interests as Muslims (and as Indonesians) and stayed out of the coalition. The latter group includes more radical or militant leaders and intellectuals, who dismissed Suharto's actions as purely self-serving, and also the NU's Abdurrahman Wahid, who has visions both of a more democratic state and of an Islam more autonomous of the state.

The specific cultural consequences of Suharto's opening toward Islam are not clear. One possibility, of course, is the strengthening of Nurcholish's accommodationist position, as more and more urban, educated, middle- and upper-class *santri* become comfortable with a government that responds to their religious as well as nonreligious needs.[58]

No less real, however, is the possibility of a growing gulf between the government and the haves (including upper- and middle-class Muslims) on the one hand, and the much larger number of Muslim have-nots—lower-middle, working-class, and economically marginal people whose interests are less well served by the government and its policies. An important side effect, much feared by Abdurrahman Wahid, may be a slowing down of progress toward democratization, both in culture and in structure. Many of the best cadres who could be working, in organizations such as his Forum Demokrasi, for a more democratic post-Suharto Indonesia have instead been coopted into ICMI.[59]

Interestingly enough, on the other side of the struggle for power, one of the army's principal weapons against Suharto has been support for democratization. The armed forces faction occupies the unelected one-fifth of Parliament's 500 seats. Its leadership—probably under the direction of Minister of Defense Moerdani—used that leverage between 1989 and 1993 to promote a number of popular causes involving defense of the rights of ordinary citizens against specific policies identified with the Suharto government. More broadly, it argued for democratization, defined in part as an enlargement of the role of Parliament and a reduction in the power of the executive.

In early 1992, in the run-up to the parliamentary election to be held later that year, Suharto struck back. Several of the most prominent military MPs, including the chair of the armed forces' faction and the chair of Parliament itself, were notified that they would not be reappointed or renominated.

One of the most outspoken ousted MPs was Police Colonel

Roekmini, who had often been the focus of newspaper and magazine stories about the new pro-democracy stance of the armed forces. Upon hearing the news, she chose to use the only resource available to her at the moment: irony. In a fine parody of an officer's clichéd acceptance of collectivity and hierarchy, she said: "I always say to my superior, the hand of Father [probably implying Suharto] I regard as the hand of God. If he wants to cross my name off, or do whatever else he wants, it's no problem for me. God arranges everything."[60]

The Suharto-army contest for the presidency was of course not over with the 1992 elections. While in retreat for the moment, the army is certain to return to the field, and, as an institution, ultimately to triumph over the mortal president. For my purpose, understanding cultural change, what is important is that this competition has provided and is likely to continue to provide resources and room to maneuver to innovators like Nurcholish and Abdurrahman Wahid. It also creates space for Goenawan and the literary and artistic community, whose freedoms to publish, perform, and promote more individualistic and democratic values have been measurably enhanced, in the short term at least.

My final illustration is the 1992 attack by the government on Non-Governmental Organizations (NGOs), in Indonesia called LSM (Lembaga Swadaya Masyarakat, Community Self-Reliance Agencies).[61] Many observers have seen the growth of LSM in the 1980s as an important resource for political and cultural democratization.[62]

LSM is an umbrella term covering an array of more than a thousand private, voluntary organizations dedicated to providing a public service. Many LSM contribute to development by bringing small amounts of capital, new technology, or organizational skills to bear on local-level projects. Others attempt to modernize traditional institutions, such as the village-level Islamic schools, called *pesantren*. Still others are advocates for consumers, environmental concerns, access to legal assistance, and so on. One of the best known of the latter is the YLBHI (Yayasan Lembaga Bantuan Hukum Indonesia, Indonesian Legal Aid Institute Foundation).

LSM leaders and staff from all over the archipelago form a loose network whose members meet frequently at conferences and seminars. They share a common culture that tends to be suspicious of the New Order government, skeptical of large institutions in general ("small is beautiful"), pro–grass roots, pro–human rights and -democracy, and tolerant of religious and ethnic diversity. Much of their funding comes from foreign foundations and governments.

In the 1980s the LSM began in a coordinated way to press the government to allow them greater freedom to operate in the villages and also to change the general direction of development policy toward more decentralized decision making and more attention to distributive and environmental concerns. A major instrument of this effort was INGI (International Non-Governmental Group on Indonesia), an informal collection of Indonesian and foreign NGOs set up as a deliberate counterbalance to IGGI (Inter-Governmental Group on Indonesia), the consortium of creditor countries that had been giving aid to the Indonesian government since the late 1960s.

Resolutions and aide-mémoires drawn up at INGI meetings, held just before IGGI's annual meetings on the level of aid to be given for the forthcoming year, quickly became a thorn in the side of the government. INGI's relative boldness was made possible by its partially foreign membership, the glare of publicity of an international forum, and the support it received from foreign foundations and governments, in particular from the Dutch government in the person of the Minister for Cooperation and Development, J. P. Pronk.

In March 1992 the Indonesian government struck back at

INGI and the LSM in circumstances created by the international reaction to the Indonesian army's massacre of nationalist Timorese youth in November 1991. The story is complicated, but in essence President Suharto disbanded IGGI, refused any further Dutch aid (including private foundation aid with funds originally from the Dutch government), and told INGI that it should disband also. YLBHI, which received 80 percent of its budget from Dutch sources, was hit particularly hard.

The spur to these actions was an unplanned incident, the November 1991 massacre. Without it, and the foreign reactions it provoked, INGI and the LSM would probably have continued to run up their national and international resources and legitimacy as players in the political and cultural process. With it, they suffered a setback, and the government and other status quo forces scored a victory. As in the other illustrations, however, the contest for Indonesia's future goes on.

IV

Writing at the dawn of independence in Asia and Africa, Edward Shils believed that "the intellectuals will go on playing a large role in the fulfillment of whatever possibilities fortune allots to their societies. . . . as long . . . as they do not disintegrate into tribal and local territorial sovereignties, and as long as they at least aspire to be 'modern.'"[63]

Shils was a close and sensitive observer of Third World intellectuals, particularly in India, and was not generally given to easy optimism or wishful thinking. Nonetheless, reread thirty years later, his view seems too sanguine. Asian and African societies have not disintegrated, and aspirations to be modern are still pervasive. Yet it is hard to argue for the general proposition that intellectuals, of the sort he had in mind and I have been discussing, have played a large role in social and cultural change, large enough at any rate to make a difference.

Why haven't they played a greater role, and how can they be more effective in the future? In search of answers to these questions, this essay has supplied some tools—the concepts of resources and a cultural process driven by intellectuals and other actors acquiring and using resources over time—and applied them to three Indonesian cases. I have argued that cultural defenders ánd cultural innovators alike possess a range of resources, and that both the existence and the value of these resources varies with circumstance and time.

In concrete terms, this approach offers only partial and particular insights—really suggestions for activists in Indonesia and hints to activists elsewhere. It tells them how they might better mobilize and deploy the resources they already have or can create or pick up from their changing social, cultural, political, and economic environment.

This is, to be sure, a limited gain. Nonetheless, it seems to me preferable to the tendency of most social scientists, and certainly of most political scientists, to chase the will-o'-the-wisp of deterministic forces outside the individual human actor. Third World political analysis has accumulated quite a long list of such forces, from the "system of modernity" of Daniel Lerner[64] in the 1950s to the state capabilities of Theda Skocpol[65] in the 1980s and the rational choice models of the 1990s. All these analyses can better be understood as resources than as determinants, and it is now time to put them into a more analytically productive framework.

Notes

1. Values have to do with "how the world should be," beliefs with "how the world is," customs with "how one conducts oneself under the guidance of a particular set of values and beliefs." F. G. Bailey, *Humbuggery and Manipulation: The Art of Leadership* (Ithaca: Cornell University Press, 1988), 36.

2. Gabriel Almond and Sidney Verba, *The Civic Culture: Political At-*

titudes and Democracy in Five Nations (Princeton: Princeton University Press, 1963). For some second thoughts, see Sidney Verba, "On Revisiting the Civic Culture: A Personal Postscript," in Gabriel Almond and Sidney Verba, *The Civic Culture Revisited* (Boston: Little, Brown, 1980). Verba writes that in hindsight "the variations from nation to nation make clear that general sociological processes can easily be modified by political events" (399).

3. Lucian Pye and Sidney Verba, *Political Culture and Political Development* (Princeton: Princeton University Press, 1965), 7. Pye did offer two divisions, between elite and mass culture and between "those more acculturated to modern ways [and those] who are still closer to the traditional patterns of life" (15ff.). He did not see these divisions as elements in a dynamic process, however, but rather as dimensions of culture that would help us understand the relative developmental (read: democratic) prospects of different societies.

4. Benedict R. O'G. Anderson, *Language and Power: Exploring Political Cultures in Indonesia* (Ithaca: Cornell University Press, 1990), 17–77. For examples of similar concepts in other traditional societies, see Elizabeth Colson, "Power at Large: Meditation on 'The Symposium on Power,'" in *The Anthropology of Power*, ed. Raymond D. Fogelson and Richard N. Adams (New York: Academic Press, 1977), 375–86.

5. For a critique, see M. C. Ricklefs, "Unity and Disunity in Javanese Political and Religious Thought of the Eighteenth Century," *Modern Asian Studies* 26, 4 (October 1992): 663–78.

6. As unraveled, for example, in Herbert Feith and Lance Castles, eds., *Indonesian Political Thinking, 1945–1965* (Ithaca: Cornell University Press, 1970).

7. Bellah, *Habits of the Heart*, 28.

8. Robert Hefner, *The Political Economy of Mountain Java: An Interpretive History* (Berkeley: University of California Press, 1990), 239; emphasis added.

9. Clifford Geertz, *The Interpretation of Cultures* (New York: Basic Books, 1973), 250; H. H. Gerth and C. Wright Mills, eds., *From Max Weber* (New York: Oxford University Press, 1946), esp. "The Social Psychology of the World Religions," 267–301.

10. Taylor writes of "the well-known 'open system' predicament, one shared by human life and meteorology, that we cannot shield a certain domain of human events, the psychological, economic, political, from external interference; it is impossible to delineate a closed system." "Interpretation and The Sciences of Man," *Review of Metaphysics* 25 (Fall 1971): 49. Hirschman offers the following "fundamental theorem about the social world . . . : As soon as a social phenomenon has been fully explained by a variety of converging approaches and is therefore understood in its majestic inevitability and perhaps even permanence, it vanishes." *Essays in Trespassing: Economics to Politics and Beyond* (Cambridge: Cambridge University Press, 1981), 134.

11. Goenawan Mohamad, *Catatan Pinggir* (Marginal notes) (Jakarta: P. T. Grafiti, 1982 [vol. 1], 1989 [vol. 2], 1991 [vol. 3], 1994 [vol. 4]. I have also found helpful two collections of essays: *Potret Seorang Penjair Muda Sebagai Si Malin Kundang* (Portrait of a young poet as Malin Kundang) (Jakarta: Pustaka Jaya, 1972); and *Seks, Sastra, Kita* (Sex, literature, us) (Jakarta: Sinar Harapan, 1980).

12. R. William Liddle, "Rumah Seorang Penulis" (The address of a writer), in Goenawan Mohamad, *Catatan Pinggir* (Marginal notes), vol. 3 (Jakarta: P. T. Grafiti, 1991), x–xi.

13. Goenawan Mohamad, "Aku," *Tempo* 22, 29 (19 September 1992), 39.

14. R. William Liddle, "Rumah Seorang Penulis," xii.

15. Much of the information in this and the following paragraph is from an interview with Goenawan in April 1991.

16. "[D]alam mengutamakan individu . . . saya sebenarnya hendak menunjukkan individu sebagai calon korban, bukan sebagai calon pengganggu harmoni." Personal communication, 23 June 1992.

17. The following paragraph is based largely on an interview with Sjahrir in October 1990. I am also indebted to Peter Timmer and Chris Manning for helping me to see both sides of Sjahrir more clearly.

18. For the balance, see his doctoral dissertation, published in Indonesia as Sjahrir, *Ekonomi Politik Kebutuhan Pokok: Sebuah Tinjauan Prospektif* (The political economy of basic needs: A prospective view) (Jakarta: LP3ES, 1986).

19. A collection is Sjahrir, *Kebijaksanaan Negara: Konsistensi dan Implementasi* (State policy: consistency and implementation) (Jakarta: LP3ES, 1987).

20. The speech was subsequently published in Nurcholish Madjid, Abdul Qadir Djaelani, Ismail Hasan Metarieum S. H., and H. E. Saefuddin Anshari, *Pembaharuan Pemikiran Islam* (The renewal of Islamic thought) (Jakarta: Islamic Research Centre, 1970), 1–12.

21. Robert Bellah, *Beyond Belief* (Berkeley: University of California Press, 1970), 146–67. Interview, Nurcholish Madjid, April 1992. I am also indebted to Bahtiar Effendy for helping me to understand Nurcholish and his place in Indonesian Islam.

22. Nurcholish now says that the two figures he most admires among Indonesian Muslims are Mohammad Hatta and Haji Agus Salim, in both cases for their combination of religious and secular knowledge and their nationalism. Interview, April 1992.

23. See especially H. M. Rasjidi, *Koreksi Terhadap Drs. Nurcholish Madjid Tentang Sekularisasi* (Correction of Drs. Nurcholish Madjid concerning secularization), (Jakarta: Bulan Bintang, 1977). This idea is strong among scholars of Islam as well as Muslims. See for example Bernard Lewis, *The Political Language of Islam,* (Chicago: University of Chicago Press, 1988): "When we in the Western world, nurtured in the Western tradition, use the words 'Islam' and 'Islamic,' we tend to make a natural error and assume that the religion means the same for Muslims as it has meant in the Western world, even in medieval times; that is to say, a section or compartment of life reserved for certain matters, and separate, or at least separable, from other compartments of life designed to hold other matters. That is not so in the Islamic world. It was never so in the past, and the attempt in modern times to make it so may perhaps be seen, in the longer perspective of history, as an unnatural aberration which in Iran has ended and in some other Islamic countries may also be nearing its end" (2). On the political implications of this view, Lewis says: "At the present time, the very notion of a secular jurisdiction and authority—of a so-to-speak unsanctified part of life that lies outside the scope of religious law and those who uphold it—is seen as an impiety, indeed as the ultimate betrayal of Islam" (3).

24. For the range of his appreciation, see Nurcholish Madjid, ed., *Khazanah Intelektual Islam* (The intellectual treasure of Islam) (Jakarta: Bulan Bintang, 1984).

25. Nurcholish Madjid, *Ibn Taimiya on Kalam and Falsafah: The Problem of Reason and Revelation in Islam* (Ph.D. diss., University of Chicago, 1984).

26. *Para* means "for" in Spanish, *madina* is "civilization" in Arabic, Nurcholish explained in a speech to the Association for Asian Studies, Washington D.C., 2 April 1992.

27. See the collection of his post-Chicago essays, *Islam: Doktrin dan Peradaban* (Islam: Doctrine and civilization) (Jakarta: Yayasan Wakaf Paramadina, 1992).

28. Personal communication, 15 April 1992. Nurcholish's ideas and person are sometimes harshly criticized in the Islamic press, which now reaches even remote areas like the villages of Aceh in either original or photocopy form. Moreover, it is not just Islamic masses that can be mobilized against innovators. The modern dancer Sardono W. Kusumo was once attacked by protestors in Solo and strongly criticized in Bali for his interpretations of traditional dances. Interview, Sardono W. Kusumo, Jakarta, December 1990. See also Goenawan Mohamad, "Kemerdekaan Kreativitas: Sebuah Pikiran di Sekitar Taman Ismail Marzuki" (Creative freedom: Thoughts on Taman Ismail Marzuki), in *Seks, Sastra, Kita,* 150.

29. Interview, October 1990.

30. "Mereka Menyangka Saya Kiai" (They suppose that I am a kiai), *Matra,* (February 1992), 18.

31. "Economic Openness and Economic Nationalism in Indonesia under the Soeharto Government" (paper presented at a conference on Comparative Analysis of the Development Process in East and Southeast Asia, Honolulu: East-West Center, May 1990).

32. The results were published in Frank Weinstein, *Indonesian Foreign Policy and the Dilemma of Dependence* (Ithaca: Cornell University Press, 1976).

33. Though not one of my concerns in this paper, the racial dimension of these attitudes is also reason for worry. Weinstein's and Glassburner's informants blame Sino-Indonesians for much that is wrong

with the Indonesian economy. On the positive side, the views of younger elites, whose only experience is of the post-1965 period, may be more pro-market. This point was brought to my attention by Don Emmerson.

34. Salim Said, *Genesis of Power: General Sudirman and the Indonesian Military in Politics 1945–1949* (Singapore: Institute of Southeast Asian Studies, 1991).

35. I also have a more humorous example of a redoubt of individualism within the state. In the hotel in Takengon, on the same evening that I saw the sea of Korpri shirts there was a no-shirt, soft-porn program on a closed-circuit TV channel. The hotel was owned by the local public prosecutor, who had presumably been given the film after it was seized by the police.

36. Clifford Geertz, *The Religion of Java* (Glencoe, Ill.: Free Press, 1960).

37. *M. Natsir versus Sukarno* (Padang: Yayasan Pendidikan Islam, 1968).

38. See the speeches of party leaders in the constituent assembly debates of 1957 through 1959, collected in *Tentang Dasar Negara Republik Indonesia Dalam Konstituante* (Concerning the foundation of the state of the Republic of Indonesia in the constituent assembly), 3 vols., n.p., n.d.

39. One sign of this general Islamization is that government officials now routinely begin speeches with the Islamic greeting *Assalamu' alaikum wa rahmatullahi wa barakatuh* (May peace be with you, and the blessing and grace of God). At a conference in 1986 I asked a Christian official of the Department of Education and Culture why he also used the phrase. His answer was that it was not Islamic but national.

40. Maurice Bloch, *Ritual, History and Power: Selected Papers in Anthropology,* (London: Athlone Press, 1989), 131–33.

41. "The Relative Autonomy of the Third World Politician: Suharto and Indonesian Economic Development in Comparative Perspective," *International Studies Quarterly* 3, 4 (December 1991): 403–27.

42. Goenawan Mohamad, *Potret Seorang Penjair,* 20. In personal correspondence (23 June 1992), Goenawan comments further: "Malin Kundang only becomes my tragic hero when he becomes a stone, and is

cursed. Freedom, which for me is a kind of obligation, contains this tragic aspect, because what is confronted is not something that is easy to contradict; on the contrary, it is something that is often true and powerful" (my translation).

43. Goenawan's highly intellectual style does have its detractors, however. The weekly *Barata Minggu,* for example, wrote: "His imagination is high up in the clouds, giving the impression that Goenawan Mohamad is not a real journalist who is oriented to the people" (no. 490 [April 1987]: 7).

44. According to internal marketing surveys, a majority of *Tempo's* readers were university and high school graduates, lived in urban areas, and were employed as civil servants, managers, and other professionals. Interview, Goenawan Mohamad, April 1991.

45. *Popular Culture and High Culture* (New York: Basic Books, 1974).

46. The following paragraphs are based on interviews and observation in the Yogyakarta Special Region from May through October 1971, September through December 1989, and October through November 1990. See also Bakdi Soemanto, *Pergeseran Makna Sakral Dalam Pertunjukan Wayang Kulit* (The shift of sacred meaning in shadow play performance) (Yogyakarta: Pusat Penelitian Kebudayaan Lit-UGM, Universitas Gadjah Mada, 1988).

47. See particularly Benedict Anderson, *Mythology and the Tolerance of the Javanese* (Ithaca: Cornell Modern Indonesia Project, 1965).

48. Interestingly, Anderson, writing in the early 1960s, shares some of the concerns of today's high-culture critics. Specifically, Anderson perceived a secular trend toward a more simplified view of *wayang* as a contest between Good and Evil, a cinema-influenced emphasis on battle and sentimental boudoir scenes, a declining interest in traditional "philosophizing" and its replacement by the values of Westernized bourgeois culture, a muffling of the social and political criticism voiced by the clowns, and a growing attractiveness of characters who represent uncritical loyalty and patriotism. *Mythology and Tolerance,* 27–29.

49. R. William Liddle, "Political Entertainment," (Ohio State University, 1990, manuscript); Barbara Hatley, "Introduction," in *Time Bomb and Cockroach Opera,* ed. John McGlynn and Barbara Hatley (Jakarta: Lontar Press, 1992); Mary Zurbuchen, "The Cockroach Opera:

Image of Culture and National Development in Indonesia," *Tenggara* 23 (1989): 124–50.

50. Nurcholish defends ICMI—led by President Suharto's apostle of hi-tech, Minister of Research and Technology B. J. Habibie—as an organization where previously noncooperating Muslim radicals are now engaging in a debate with other Muslims and with the government. He hopes this debate will give them a better sense of the compromises necessary in politics. Interview with the author, April 1992.

51. Quoted in R. William Liddle, "Rumah Seorang Penulis," xiii.

52. The cultural reference is to the Dwi-Tunggal (Two-in-One) of President Sukarno and Vice President Mohammad Hatta in the early 1950s.

53. "Pola Kepemimpinan Islam di Indonesia," in Taufik Abdullah, *Islam dan Masyarakat: Pantulan Sejarah Indonesia* (Islam and society: Reflection of Indonesian history) (Jakarta: LP3ES, 1987), 54–87.

54. That is, supporters of the state doctrine *Pancasila,* five principles of belief in one God, nationalism, humanitarianism, democracy, and social justice. In New Order political discourse, Islam from the "right" and communism from the left are seen as the chief threats to *Pancasila* as the *asas tunggal* (basic principle) of the state.

55. In a related context, his analysis of the "integrative revolution" in the new states, Clifford Geertz concluded that: "This may seem like a mere wait-and-see policy, inappropriate to the predictive ambitions of science. But such a policy is at least preferable, and more scientific, to waiting and not seeing, which has been largely the case to date." *The Interpretation of Cultures* (New York: Basic Books, 1973), 310.

56. A recent account is Adam Schwarz, "All Is Relative," *Far Eastern Economic Review* (30 April 1992), 54–58.

57. For a fuller treatment, see R. William Liddle, "Indonesia's Threefold Crisis," *Journal of Democracy* 3, 4 (October 1992).

58. Nurcholish says that he tells Minister for the State Secretariat Moerdiono, one of President Suharto's closest advisers, "Do not let us be defeated by our success." He means that the New Order has created, and now must share power with, the Islamic middle class. Interview with the author, April 1992.

59. On the other hand, ICMI supporters like Dawam Rahardjo and Adi Sasono argue that working inside the government for causes like more egalitarian distribution of economic benefits is a better path toward eventual democratization.

60. "Saya selalu bilang sama atasan saya, tangan Bapak itu saya anggap tangan Tuhan. Mau dicoret, mau diapakan, nggak ada masalah bagi saya. Semuanya Tuhanlah yang mengatur." *Tempo* 21, 29 (14 September 1991), 32. For a more direct statement of her view of the New Order, see "Calon legislatif di depan tantangan zaman" (Legislative candidates face the challenges of the times), *Eksekutif* 153 (March 1992), 57–58.

61. See the account in *Tempo* 22, 5 (4 April 1992), 13–26.

62. The best account is Philip Eldridge, *NGOs in Indonesia: Popular Movement or Arm of Government?* (Clayton, Victoria, Australia: Monash University Centre of Southeast Asian Studies, Working Paper 55, 1989). See also Aswab Mahasin, "NGOs and Political Alternatives: Awaiting Surprises," Background Paper Untuk Seminar: Pembangunan Masyarakat Desa Yang Berorientasi Kerakyatan Antara Mitos dan Realita (Background paper for a seminar: Development of village society that is democratically oriented between myth and reality) (Yogyakarta: Fakultas Ilmu Sosial dan Politik, Universitas Gadjah Mada, 1989).

63. "Intellectuals in the New States," *World Politics* 12, 3 (April 1960): 364.

64. *The Passing of Traditional Society* (Glencoe, Ill.: Free Press, 1958).

65. Peter B. Evans, Dietrich Rueschemeyer, and Theda Skocpol, *Bringing the State Back In* (Cambridge: Cambridge University Press, 1985).

Chapter Two

Dreams of Freedom, Moments of Despair: Armijn Pané and the Imagining of Modern Indonesian Culture

William H. Frederick

WHAT IS MODERN Indonesian culture? What does it mean to be a modern Indonesian? The questions may sound new—they are the products of the rapid economic change and heavy exposure to technological civilization that have characterized Indonesia during the past twenty or thirty years—but they have been asked since at least the early years of this century. During the 1920s and 1930s, debate on such issues was particularly intense and did much to shape the character of new cultural forms and the development of the very idea of an independent nation. A rich literature records the many facets of this important intellectual period. In recent years we have seen in Indonesia another, more fractured but not entirely dissimilar, episode of soul searching and reaching for self-definition. An even larger and more wide-ranging body of writings likewise captures the details of this national debate.

The question which rises immediately to mind is what these two eras in Indonesian intellectual history have to do with each other. It is a deceptively simple question, requiring far too large and complicated an answer to take up in its entirety in a short paper; but it is useful to ask nevertheless, because it helps us look at the present in longer perspective than we customarily do, and because it offers some promise of opening up new lines of inquiry into the relationship between culture and society in modern Indonesia. Rather than attempt an overly broad survey, however, what I propose to do here is focus rather narrowly on an individual participant in the 1930s debate, the writer Armijn Pané, with the purpose of suggesting how an examination of his ideas might illuminate an understanding of the "What is modern Indonesian culture?" question in the contemporary setting. My subject, I hasten to admit, has been chosen in anything but a random fashion. I have long regarded Armijn Pané as a neglected and rather misunderstood cultural pioneer, deserving to be better known. But I have singled him out for attention in the present context because he has been so pointedly, though not always entirely approvingly, described (in his own time as well as our own) as the ultimate modern Indonesian, far ahead of his time. If he can't help us on our journey, who can?

I

> Yes, we are modern . . . and yet there still remains, in a corner of our hearts, a little niche where in moments of despair we burn a stick of incense.
>
> —Soewarsih Djojopoespito,
> *Buiten het gareel* (1940)

The great cultural debate of the 1930s, especially as reflected in the literary journal *Poedjangga Baroe* (The New Writer) and the compilation entitled *Polemik Kebudayaan* (Polemic on Culture), has been carefully studied elsewhere,[1] and it will suffice here to make only a few general remarks in order to provide a context for a closer look at Armijn Pané. Despite the vigorous exchange of opinions that took place, it is not very difficult in retrospect to identify several topics on which there was substantial agreement. One of these was that the new, modern Indonesian culture, and the *manusia In-*

donesia baru (new Indonesian) who inhabited it, was to be free. Freedom could not help but be seen in a political, nationalistic light, given the colonial setting of the day. But it was at the same time clearly, and perhaps primarily, seen in a social and intellectual one as well. Freedom was the key to unlocking the dynamism that lay within every society and individual, and dynamism was the essence of modernity. With freedom, all was possible.

Another area in which broad agreement existed was synthesis. Whether to a greater or lesser degree, synthesis was necessary to resolve the contradictions which had to be faced in the process of becoming modern. The dichotomies of East and West, village and city, region and nation, masses and elite, no less than that of tradition and modernity itself, provided the framework for the process, which was not to be haphazard. However much or little of it was to take place, this synthesis was to be selective, marrying the best of the East with the best of the West, the best of tradition with the best of the modern world, and so on. The new culture was to be, well, . . . cultured.

It was also to be national, serving as both embodiment and anchor of a sense of nation, an expression of identity in the broadest sense. The nation was of course still an abstraction, but it played a paramount role in the thinking of the small group of artists and politically oriented figures who argued over the new, modern Indonesian culture. Indeed, one suspects that in their thoughts it took on an ideal and permanent quality that only such an abstraction can have. Did not the creation of a unitary, fixed nation require the building of a unifying, fixed culture? And should not both the nation and its culture be constructed in as ideal a form as possible?

And, finally, modern culture must represent society as a whole. These thinkers were painfully aware of the fact that they were a tiny minority in their own society. Indeed, as writers and artists they were a minority even within the comparatively small group of educated Indonesians, the *kaum terpelajar*. They ardently sought a formula for assuring that their creation would mirror society as a whole. In particular, many insisted, the culture which they fashioned should mirror the *rakyat*, the common folk, for it was they who were intrinsically happy and good, and it was ultimately on them, therefore, that the nation and national culture must rely for its purest values.

Even a brief glimpse at this intellectual program shows that hewing to it and developing it further were not easy propositions. There were still a great many internal contradictions in both the general theories and in their application. As optimistic as individuals might try to be about the possibilities of working these contradictions out, many foundered. How was it possible, for example, to balance the search for individual freedom with the requirements of the *pergerakan* (national movement) for unified thought and action? How could the *rakyat* be happy and good on the one hand, yet ignorant and backward on the other? And how were these qualities to be reconciled? How was faith in the national identity to be weighed against the desire for Westernization? These were troubling conundrums, returned to again and again in print and, doubtless, in interminable nighttime deliberations. More disturbing still, perhaps, were the nagging doubts some were surprised to find deep within themselves—for example, remnants of superstition, the very antithesis of what they had come to understand as "modern."

II

> Armijn [Pané] is identical to the modern age, the technological age, the twentieth century.
> —Karim Halim, review of *Belenggu* (1940)

Many of the participants in the cultural debate of the 1930s have long since been forgotten, but none of the major figures has been so neglected as Armijn Pané (1908–1970). Although his 1940 masterpiece *Belenggu* (Shackles)[2] is nearly universally considered Indonesia's first truly modern novel, and as such seldom fails to receive mention in standard works on Indonesian cultural history, his ideas on the formation of modern Indonesian culture have for the largest part been roundly criticized (in the 1940s and 1950s) and, partly as a result, ignored and forgotten altogether in subsequent years.

The reasons are not far to seek. Invariably identified with the mainstream of *manusia Indonesia baru* opinion in the 1930s, he was in fact sharply critical of some of its central beliefs, particularly those connected with nationalism. His ideas were often subtle and sophisticated, moreover, and therefore easily misconstrued, even by those who might have agreed with him. He was often viewed as being skeptical and fundamentally pessimistic, traits which did not wear well with colleagues and readers who preferred their polemics to be of the sunny, or at least inspirational variety. Certainly not least of all, his uncompromising standards and fondness for many aspects of Western culture led even close friends, accustomed to his natty suits and elegant neckties, to see him as a man who had quite simply abandoned Indonesian culture altogether and opted instead to live a present and fashion a future unrelated to the idea or reality of Indonesia. Armijn was typically referred to as the most Europeanized of a circle already mesmerized by the West and modernism, and that description implies that he was also the most alienated from his own society and its cultural realities. Such judgements, however, are misreadings of the man and his ideas.

Armijn Pané (he seems to have preferred the accented "e" when spelling his name in print) was born on 18 August 1908 in Muara Sipongi, Tapanuli, a small town in the mountains near the northern border of Sumatra Barat.[3] His father, Sutan Pangarubaan Pané, was a man who, unlike many others of aristocratic stock at the dawn of the twentieth century, embraced the prospects of change with enthusiasm. He earned a modest local reputation as a writer and as a journalist and commentator on current affairs, and pushed his children to read and succeed in school. Armijn attended the higher levels of schools available in the Netherlands East Indies, both those designed for Indonesians only and those intended largely for Dutch pupils but occasionally attended by children of the native elite. As was common among youths set on a modern (i.e., Westernized) educational path, he moved frequently as he went from one school to the next. After stints in Tanjung Balai, Sibolga, and Bukittinggi, he moved to Jakarta (then called Batavia). There he attended the famous STOVIA, a school for training native medical personnel commonly known as *dokter Jawa*, a designation which can only have rankled a thoughtful young man from Sumatra. Later he transferred to Surabaya's NIAS, which offered a similar course of study.

Apparently restless and increasingly aware that his interest and talents lay in a different direction, Armijn did not finish his medical schooling. Perhaps following his older brother, Sanusi (1905–1968), in 1927 he abruptly shifted to a government school in Solo that focused on the study of language, literature, and the arts, both indigenous and European. In this new and less rigid atmosphere he began to write in earnest. He also took an interest in politics, acting as a representative to an Indonesia Muda (Young Indonesia, an activist nationalist youth organization) Congress in late 1930. The next year he graduated from school and, the economically and politically depressed times offering nothing better, took a succession of short-term jobs, first as a journalist in Surabaya, then as a teacher in private, Indonesian-run Taman Siswa schools in Kediri, Malang, and Jakarta.

Then, in 1933, Armijn joined Takdir Alisjahbana and the young poet Amir Hamzah to found *Poedjangga Baroe*. He served this literary journal as a contributor and editorial board secretary for the remainder of the prewar period. Virtually all the authors associated with *Poedjangga Baroe* were concerned in one way or another with the building of a new Indonesian culture, largely by arriving at an appropriate synthesis between Western and Eastern influences. None was as original and direct, however, as Armijn Pané, who published a number of articles, and eventually the novel *Belenggu*, to address the issue. While agreeing that synthesis was necessary, he dismissed the proposition that one had to carefully distinguish between East and West in one's borrowings,[4] and he argued that, among indigenous cultural forms, the best source for a modern, national, unifying Indonesian culture was not classical art—traditional Javanese gamelan music, for example—about which some of his colleagues talked so much, but forms of popular culture.[5] He also insisted that the purpose of such a synthesis ought not to be to arrive at a static formulation of a modern Indonesian culture, but to create a living, breathing culture, kaleidoscopic and ever-changing. A truly modern culture, he said, must accept and even seek out change.[6]

One example of popular culture which attracted Armijn's attention was *keroncong*, in the 1930s a hybrid music with a Portuguese and Hawaiian base and considerable influence from regional Indonesian cultures as well, especially those of Ambon and Sumatra.[7] Among intellectuals of the day, *keroncong* players and singers, who often plied their trade in the streets and near open-air restaurants, were viewed as shiftless, low-brow, generally immoral, and definitively lower-class (*kampungan*); the music itself was scorned as mongrel and melodramatic. But it was quite popular: especially in cities like Jakarta and Surabaya, *keroncong* attracted ordinary Indonesians in large numbers. The 1937 box office hit film *Terang boelan* (Moonlight), starring the *keroncong* songstress known as Miss Rukiah, more than made up for what it lacked in the way of story line and cinematographic technique by supplying the audience with a liberal selection of their favorite tunes performed in romantic settings.[8] By the end of the 1930s *keroncong* was so popular that even colonial radio shows and performances in public halls began to feature it, with great success.

Intellectuals were for the most part scandalized, but Armijn defended *keroncong* and went so far as to hail it as a suitable foundation on which to build a modern, unified, and dynamic Indonesian culture.

In a now forgotten but then widely discussed reaction to a live radio broadcast of a public concert in January 1941, Armijn dismissed the criticism of fellow intellectuals by pointing out that *keroncong* was not only not backward, as its detractors claimed, but was in fact markedly progressive.[9] The music was modern and forward-looking because it clearly assimilated many styles, unified them into a seamless whole, and was still capable of accommodating new influences. The people, musicians as well as audience, were also progressive, for they represented a blending of many different groups, and their voice was that of ordinary people, not a handful of aesthetes or aristocrats. This, he said, was much more satisfactory as a potential base for a new Indonesian culture than gamelan, which was after all a court art of the Javanese, rooted in a regional ruling elite and its traditions, and, he thought, unaccustomed to change and synthesis.

In *Belenggu*, Armijn offers us the character of Rohayah, a female *keroncong* singer to whom the unhappily married Dr. Sukartono is deeply attracted, and whose songs seem to offer him a satisfying blend of East and West, of tradition and modernity. It is not too much to see Rohayah as a metaphor for *keroncong* itself: viewed in "polite" society as no better than a prostitute singing cheap tunes, she is gradually revealed to us as in fact a woman of great heart, high morals, and considerable wisdom. So much for class (in several senses of the word). Far more than the petty and confused intellectuals with whom Dr. Sukartono customarily spends his time, Rohayah is not merely a breath of fresh air, she bespeaks humanity itself—and modernity as well— through both her individual confidence and her understanding attitude toward all types of people. *Keroncong*'s universality is Rohayah's, and vice-versa. This was not a thought that many educated Indonesians, including those in the *Poedjangga Baroe* circle, were prepared to accept.

Not content with examining established cultural forms for what they might offer to a future Indonesian society, Armijn was also, perhaps more than any other intellectual figure of his day, committed to new media and the role they might play. In the late 1930s he wrote several articles extolling the virtues of radio as a vehicle for a modern culture of the masses,[10] and beginning at about that time he became a promoter of cinema for the same reasons. In the early 1950s he wrote a long piece, his last major statement of this sort, discussing the past and future of the modern media in helping to create a unifying Indonesian culture.[11]

He was probably fondest of cinema. Like a few other prominent figures—such as the political leader A. K. Gani (1905–1968), who even took up acting in films for a time—he was entranced with cinema because it was so obviously modern, bringing together radio, phonograph, and camera in a fulfillment of technological promise. Like Gani, too, he appreciated the way in which film clearly broke down social barriers and was capable of reaching virtually all people. The visual impact seemed thoroughly direct and nondiscriminatory.

Characteristically, however, Armijn's appreciation of cinema and its role in a modern society went deeper than that of many contemporaries, and had a particular twist. He saw, and was constantly at pains to show, film as an integrative art form in ways that reached far beyond mere technical matters. In order to find an appreciative—and sustaining—audience, for example, a film had to appeal to the tastes and sentiments of significantly more than a single segment of the population. Writers, producers, actors, even cameramen, had always to be aware that the film medium belonged to no single nation or culture: it was truly a part of world culture, always changing and changeable, and therefore requiring a continuing awareness of the possibilities of integration and synthesis. Even cinema as a business enterprise demanded integration (of capital and talent) and ongoing adjustment to trends, tastes, economic conditions, and the like.

The Indonesian film industry, still in its early stages in the years immediately following the struggle for independence, offered numerous illustrations of cultural mixing. Armijn reminded his readers of a very simple one by pointing out that the well-known director Usmar Ismail had training in both indigenous popular stage arts and, at the University of California, the theory and practice of filmmaking; his cameraman for the movie *Dosa tak berampun* (The unforgivable sin, 1951), Max Tera, was the offspring of a Japanese father and an Indonesian mother. Yet who could doubt that the film was Indonesian?[12] With this and other similar examples, Armijn sharpened his point that synthesis rather than efforts to "purify," experimentation rather than conservative classicism, would result in a truly desirable modern Indonesian culture.

With those, even among close colleagues, who persisted in seeing tradition and modernity as opposites, locked in eternal combat, Armijn had little patience. For him, one could no more abandon traditional (or regional) culture than avoid the influence of modern (or national and international) culture; the two were not mutually exclusive, and whatever "modern Indonesian culture" might turn out to be, it must be allowed to develop organically—that is, freely and naturally, not in the context of choosing between one extreme and another. He appreciated jazz as a particularly good example of a cultural form that had risen up from "the people," was the product of many cultural fusions, and could be meaningful to an economically, culturally, and political diverse society, yet was also clearly a national cultural expression.[13]

To those who suggested that somehow such ideas were not properly nationalistic, or perhaps even truly Indonesian, criticisms that had surfaced already before the end of the colonial era, he replied that in his view "national"—and therefore "modern"—Indonesian culture encompassed all regions and classes and cultural forms in Indonesia, on the basis of which acculturation (i.e., synthesis with Western influences in their full diversity) might take place. There was nothing intrinsically exclusive about "national" culture, and indeed exclusivity and stasis were to be guarded against. A modern Indonesian culture must be capacious and ever-changing; it could not help but be always Indonesian.[14]

Not surprisingly, thinking of this kind also brought Armijn into conflict with individuals and institutions seeking to control or manage cultural affairs. In the early 1930s he complained in a number of candid book reviews that the colonial government's publishing house, Balai Pustaka, which he said assumed that the Indonesian reading public had neither intelligence or taste, and attempted through a crude kind of censorship to shape the development of Indonesian culture. (At the end of the decade Balai Pustaka rejected the manuscript of *Belenggu* on what are said to have been "moral" grounds.)[15] Two decades later, Armijn again took up the cause against censorship, this time by the Indonesian government and the intellectual figures advising it on cultural affairs. He noted critically that the 1951 Cultural Congress, though it had called for changing the old colonial rules now that Indonesia was independent, had overwhelmingly approved of film censorship, and of making a distinction in censorship standards between foreign films and indigenous ones.[16] Practices of this sort violated his sense of the healthy development of a modern national culture, and the freedom he believed was crucial to that process.[17]

On the topic of freedom Armijn made his most subtly nuanced and important contribution. Although *Belenggu*, like a number of famous novels preceding it, has widely been understood, by Indonesians as well as foreigners, as primarily an account of the struggle between tradition and modernity, there is a more complex reading which is, I believe, truer to the message its author intended. In this view, the overriding theme of the novel is one of irony. The "shackles" of the title, in postwar editions illustrated on the cover literally as a pair of jailer's cuffs, are not what we might readily believe: the binds of tradition, the oppression of colonialism, or even the strictures of bourgeois "morality." In reality—and Armijn made clear many times his realistic purpose in writing[18]—the principal characters to whom we are introduced are bound up with not external crises but internal contradictions, many of them the result of freedom rather than the lack of it. The characters are limited by the shackles of ambiguity, complexity, and uncertainty.

Rohayah, for example, appears to embody many of the most admired "traditional" values despite having abandoned a proper education and subsequently being "corrupted" by modern urban life; Dr. Sukartono, who prides himself on being the Westernized man of science, nevertheless is particularly sensitive to sentiment and emotion, supposedly the very opposite of science; Sumartini, his unhappy wife, fancies herself thoroughly modernized and yet cannot break through a very rigid notion of what that modernity comprises, and lacks the self-confidence to define her own terms for dealing with the world. Like human beings everywhere, these characters do not and cannot in fact have complete freedom to develop unhindered by contradiction and warring desires. Real people in real life do not have complete independence; freedom always bears with it certain limitations, whatever we might wish to think.

Even the effort to imagine and ensure the development of a modern culture, Armijn seems to suggest, could be seen as a freedom that was in itself naive, contradictory, and limiting. This was a warning against the excessive optimism of intellectuals such as Takdir Alisjahbana, and political figures such as Sukarno, but it was also a shrewd and brave self-criticism. We have no trouble today recognizing it also as a distinctly contemporary skepticism, a "modern" wisdom not easily impressed by ideologies and answers, or by social and cultural absolutes of any kind.

Was this the ultimate, and ultimately unforgivable, form of pessimism in an intensely anticolonial, nationalist age? Many of Armijn's contemporaries seem to have thought so.[19] His own outlook is not altogether clear, and whether his apparent bouts of depression in later life were related to such ideas is a question which remains to be answered. Whatever the case, his writing remained free of cynicism, and merely accepted the realities he had uncovered. Having seen both the necessity for and the limitations of freedom before his nation achieved it politically, Armijn was in a real sense ahead of most of his contemporaries. He considered himself an ardent nationalist, but at the same time he could not revel in the revolution and its outcome, and he never wrote about revolutionary issues or circumstances. During the revolution he worked for the Department of Information, where among other things he attempted to improve the lot of writers, and worked with Usmar Ismail to bring popular theater (and a nationalist message) to Indonesians in both Republican and Dutch-occupied territory. In the 1950s he established a number of bodies devoted to cultural promotion, and wrote and translated a variety of works, including poetry, history, and fiction. But in the postwar era he had, in fact, nothing much new to say, for he had, it seems, seen nothing new. The generation of writers which had risen on the crest of the revolution apparently found him out of date or merely irrelevant, and the cultural struggles of the Guided Democracy period, which can have come as no surprise, only served to sadden and marginalize him further. At the end he emerged from retirement to accept a government award for a lifetime of contribution to the arts, and somewhat later he shared, in a public speech at Taman Ismail Marzuki, some gentle reflections on culture and his life as a writer. He died in early 1970.

III

> [T]he best guarantee against revolutionary ten-
> dencies is an Indonesian society which is as
> [culturally] homogeneous as possible.
> —Ch. O. van der Plas (1927)

Why do Armijn's assessments seem so interesting today, roughly a half century later? I think the main reason is that, in a manner not altogether different from the van der Plas quote which introduces this section, they bring us up short by suggesting very strongly that not much of importance has changed since then. The redoubtable Dutch colonial official's sly recipe for control is highly plausible as a crude statement of New Order cultural policy under the banner of *pancasila*, as relevant a talking point now as then in a discussion of Indonesia's cultural future. Similarly, what Armijn had to say a generation or two ago—a period which, we can hardly forget, was filled with an extraordinary degree of stress, political and otherwise—appears to be not only remarkably fresh but, if anything, more rather than less pertinent. It is not difficult to imagine his criticisms being applied, with very little adjustment, to the ideas and circumstances one finds in many cultural circles today.

The notion that the years between 1940 and 1965 represent little more than a wrinkle in time is hardly new, of course. It underlies the by now common insight that there is a great deal of the colonial pattern in the New Order,[20] as well as the related suggestion that the Indonesian clock has only recently, after a difficult (but in the final analysis historically parenthetical) era, started ticking again, continuing processes begun much earlier.[21] Why else would *Polemik Kebudayaan* (which, when it first appeared in 1948, collected opinions twelve years and the better part of a revolution distant) have received a third printing in 1977, and be revisited yet again in 1986?[22] How else to explain the emergence—perhaps not so coincidentally also in 1977—of the debate launched by Mochtar Lubis on national character and culture, a debate which echoed many of the themes and perspectives of its 1930s predecessor, and in which Armijn could surely have effectively used many of his earlier criticisms?[23]

Evidence with which to construct a view of this sort is not difficult to come by. Perhaps most noticeably, the dichotomies which provided the central dilemmas for prewar writers and cultural commentators persist today. Takdir Alisjahbana's message in a stream of novels and think pieces has varied comparatively little in this regard, and authors as divergent in other respects as Pramoedya Ananta Toer, Mochtar Lubis, and Umar Kayam have either continued with or briefly taken up essentially dichotomous themes or lines of inquiry. Much other writing can arguably be said to have formed around the basic contradictions already in evidence in the 1920s and 1930s—for example, that between national and local languages and cultures. Contemporary exploitation of this theme was taken up by Ajip Rosidi in the early 1970s and has occupied many others since then. Even the editorial columns and letters-to-the-editor sections of the popular press show how dualistically contributors often view contemporary cultural issues. In sentiment, if not their up-to-date details, they are perfectly understandable in the context of the 1930s; the threat posed by Western influence to Oriental culture, the evils of Western commercialism, and the mindless chasing after Western fashion, are all frequent topics of complaint organized along a familiar East-versus-West axis.[24]

In the world of cinema, where enormous change and rapidly changing points of view might reasonably have been expected, one finds instead a depressingly well worn critical landscape. Critics, directors, and thoughtful screen stars dwell rather morosely on the (negative) contrasts between contemporary Indonesian films and those of the West, and argue endlessly about the necessity, and failure, of Indonesian films to reflect the true *wajah Indonesia*, the true "face" or character of Indonesia. Despite the efforts of intellectuals of the industry, like actor-director Eros Djarot, to deemphasize the East-West issue, it inevitably creeps in through consideration of other issues which themselves are handled in the familiar frame of dichotomy.[25] How can tradition determine the nature—the *proper* nature, moreover—of an Indonesian modernity? How can depictions of modern Indonesian culture be at once realistic and idealistic? The critique, like the technology, may have grown more complex over the years, but the focus and frequently even the terms of reference might figure as easily in a contemporaneous discussion of *Terang boelan* as one of, say, *Badai pasti berlalu* (The storm will pass; 1978).[26]

And what is *dangdut* if not today's *keroncong*?[27] All the elements are there: a *kampungan*, crossbred music, scorned by intellectuals and the moneyed elite, and more than a little sensuous. Yet one which, at the same time, intends to speak for common folk and which is indeed enormously popular. Even *keroncong's* association with the movies is replicated in the story of *dangdut*, which was the key to creating mass audiences for a new genre of self-consciously Indonesian films. The circumstances look to be a remarkable case of cultural history repeating itself, and it is difficult to imagine Armijn being able to resist championing *dangdut* just as he had its predecessor, in the same way and for identical reasons.

Finally, we can look to the role of the state in cultural affairs for obvious reflections of the colonial past. Censorship, about which Armijn had been outspoken under both Dutch and Indonesian rule, is still of course very much part of the scene, and one might convincingly argue that despite political changes and nuances, in cultural matters its thrust remains much the same: in the broadest sense, to protect *rust en orde* (roughly, "peace and order"; now *tata tenteram)* and to promote what in the eyes of the government itself constitutes a healthy, civilized society and social outlook. And critics continue to say that censorship prevents artists from reflecting the true condition of society.[28]

Nor should it escape our attention that the New Order—which after all is a direct descendent of *both* the Dutch colonial government and that unified nation-state that existed in the minds of prewar intellectuals—appears to have furthered precisely the kind of cultural unification one might have expected from such a marriage. Most often this has been accomplished under the banner of *pancasila*-ization, which while paying a certain lip service to the value of cultural differences clearly intends to foster something quite different. From Taman Mini to the Festival of Indonesia, critics have tirelessly pointed out, the officially sponsored trend has been toward homogenization of cultures, the creation of pseudotraditions engineered to reflect modern political and social ideals, and toward selecting only "the best" of what both indigenous and foreign influences have to offer: cultural engineering on a scale only dreamed of a generation ago but, for a variety of reasons, now within grasp.

IV

Maybe in the minds of highly educated, "brilliant" folk there is no difference between the Indonesians who lived in colonial times and those of the present day. [That must be why,] without the slightest hesitation, without feeling in the least uncomfortable, they say things about Indonesia and Indonesians which are completely at odds with reality.

—Sayidi Surjohadiprojo,
"Kemampuan menyadari perubahan" (1990)

But there is something awkward, something intuitively amiss, in the whole "déjà vu all over again" analysis. The fault lies largely in the approach, which is built upon the deceptively simple proposition that we can only understand the present in terms of the past. This is a favorite maxim of practitioners of what has come to be called contemporary history, but it is easily taken too far. In short, in our attempt to be historically grounded we often ignore the realities immediately around us, and seldom consider the possibility that they are more the products of change than continuity. There can be little doubt that the cultural polemic of the 1930s still resonates in contemporary Indonesia, or that Armijn, as both proponent and critic in that polemic, makes an uncannily sharp and profitable read today. But at the same time it is equally clear that times—and with them, society—have changed, and have changed sufficiently to render inadequate, if not utterly invalid, even the keenest analysis of a generation or two ago. Earlier terms of reference are less useful, and although new ones may not yet be fully in place, the most cursory riffle through current newspapers and popular magazines suggests that they are rapidly being formed.

To begin with, the context in which Indonesians are coming rather suddenly to see their culture is unmistakably global. Far more than the abstract universalism of earlier days (I would include in this the ideas of Takdir Alisjahbana, the Angkatan '45, and the Lekra artists, usually thought of as being quite disparate) this variety is palpable and its impact direct. Frequently linked in a negative sense with world consumerism, globalization may be seen as a threat to proper values, national identity, and the like.[29] But it is also increasingly treated as an inescapable reality which modern Indonesians, like other peoples of the world, must learn to cope with and, if possible, turn to their advantage. Significantly, there seems to be a growing sense that globalization means not only the world influencing Indonesia, but the other way around as well.[30]

The Indonesian film industry has since its inception possessed a certain degree of international sensitivity, so the recent interest in, for example, competing at Cannes and New York, subtitling films for export, and portraying Indonesian culture in a way that makes sense to (and a good impression on) outsiders, seems new but not entirely surprising. Rather more startling has been the recent internationalization of (and by) *dangdut*, which has perhaps caught proponents as much by surprise as critics, and has altered the way in which both look at this music. Two changes have taken place. First, *dangdut* appears to have escaped at least to some degree the confines of its *kampungan* reputation. It has replaced, for example, the usual musical fare at boutique fashion shows and pricey, ultra-chic, big-city discos.[31] The transition has left even weary journalists on the pop culture beat a little incredulous. At the same time *dangdut* has been a smash hit outside its Indonesian-Malaysian homeland and apparently taken—of all places—Tokyo by storm.[32] Some *dangdut* performers and song writers probably always dreamed quietly of attracting an international audience (as early as 1978 Rhoma Irama produced a demo tape of *dangdut* tunes played by a modified Western-style orchestra, in hopes of cracking the United States market)[33] and they seem undisturbed by this development. But now both friends and foes alike worry aloud about whether all this foreign exposure will change *dangdut* and whether Indonesian popular culture—to say nothing of society—will be corrupted by the big money, perks, and glitz of the international entertainment marketplace. Beginning in this small but not insignificant corner of contemporary Indonesian life, the ways in which Indonesians look at their own culture have begun to shift.

More than self-perception is changing, however. Trite as is may be to say so, today's Indonesian society is remarkably different from that of six, five, or even two decades ago, and cultural issues are thus played out in a setting which in many respects bears little resemblance to those of earlier periods. Perhaps the most obvious change is that Indonesia now possesses a larger population, of which a far greater segment is touched by a plethora of cultural influences. The *Poedjangga Baroe* group consisted of a comparatively small number of artists and political figures talking to each other, and a minuscule readership, about what were still esoteric topics. Now, however, cultural ideas of all kinds are debated by a wide and socially diverse circle of discussants, and followed by a very wide readership. Moreover, that readership has a much higher degree of familiarity with the objects of discussion: the newspaper items, books, magazine articles, radio and television programs, movies, recorded music, and so forth that jostle each other in Indonesian public culture. These media have not only broadened the reach of modern Indonesian culture and involved more people in it, but has at once made it both unifying and more varied. It goes without saying that media technology has played a substantial role in all of this and seems likely to continue to do so as, for example, a rapidly growing number of private television and radio stations take to the air.

One result of this growth is that the contemporary Indonesian public has become accustomed to high levels of both variety and change in its cultural life. Stars and styles come and go at blinding speed; only the flexible and the dynamic survive for long. There is nothing unique or mysterious about this effect, which has been pointed out in other societies, but in Indonesia it has rapidly come to characterize virtually the entire cultural scene; the carryover into other areas is beginning to be clear and may amount to more than a superficial phenomenon. Adaptation to new values, especially the value of competitiveness and the necessity of speaking freely are increasingly common themes on op-ed pages of the press, some authors going so far as to suggest, for example, that "without competition in society . . . we cannot make our way in the world."[34] It is difficult not to conclude that a kind of consensus has begun to arise in Indonesia that competitiveness, openness, criticism, and the like are modern qualities and, more important, that Indonesians can exhibit them without either losing their Indonesianness or going off the deep end.[35] In a sense this has been acknowledged by academic studies defining "modern behavior" from a sociopsychological perspective,[36] and by President Suharto himself, whose comments in the past year or so on the exchange of ideas probably ought to be interpreted as indicating, despite the caution and caveats, that he at least has got the message.[37]

Such thinking has natural connections with the subject of censorship, and it has not gone unexploited, especially in the wake of the celebrated *Suksesi* and *Monitor* affairs of late 1990.[38] What is interesting about the outcry accompanying those two cases is that it focused very heavily on the relationship between government censorship and what it means to be a modern Indonesian. A widespread sentiment seems to have been that the authorities underestimated the intelligence of the public, which, as part of modern society, was discerning and rational enough to take a little outrage, commercialism, suggestive humor, experimentation, and conflicting ideas well in stride. This is no longer a small intellectual elite tugging at the reins, but a large and growing middle class that has changed more rapidly than, and in directions more diverse than, the government has been able to imagine.[39] There is no longer a simple political principle at stake, but a more generalized social one.

What, then, about the question of cultural direction from above? However powerful the official vision of a unitary national culture may be, it seems very unlikely to have been the determining force behind the trends we see today. I would argue that the New Order government has in fact been neither very effective at, nor even (except through its touting of *pancasila* concepts) particularly interested in fashioning a modern culture for Indonesia. Its cultural position is more one of watchdog than initiator or leader, except in the sense that it clearly sees itself as the *modernisator* of society and nation, whatever that may mean with regard to culture. The culture that is now taking shape is, instead, the spontaneous creation of upper and middle classes, shaped by a number of obvious changes such as the passage of time (as the revolution fades into the distance), increasing centralization of the state, growing access to global influences, and improved economic conditions. It is not exclusively an urban phenomenon, nor the sole property of students, well-to-do housewives, or any other group, but is generalized across society and, indeed, across the archipelago.

Some characteristics of this culture are, if not ubiquitous, at least widespread and readily identifiable. It is not, for example, particularly nationalistic. The fact of Indonesia is taken for granted, and little interest is shown in the more syrupy or simplistic representations of patriotism. From time to time an intense interest in national history or heroes manifests itself, but there is little inclination to view these and related subjects reverently. Nor is this new culture particularly self-conscious or introspective. Interest in such topics as national identity, the values of the revolution, and even "the true face of Indonesia" has been fading for some time; one gets the distinct impression that, except where it presents commercial possibilities, and not always then, it is considered out of date.[40] One does see discussion of *jatidiri*, a comparatively new word which of course has the dictionary meaning of "identity" but carries quite unmistakably a more individual focus, and generally a more skeptical, often even humorous, tone.[41] Populism, especially of the treacly, nationalist variety, is a rare indulgence. The *kampungan* style in humor, often invoked to attract (largely middle-class) audiences, is increasingly commercially slick and bittersweet.[42] The *rakyat*, or masses, are also not beyond criticism, and one may occasionally encounter in print suggestions that what some forms of modern Indonesian culture need is not more, but less interest in what the *rakyat* think or want.[43]

But the most important feature of this emerging culture is what seems to be a natural tendency toward homogenization and synthesis. The familiar dichotomies of the culture and cultural dialogue of earlier decades are in the work of many younger authors barely visible, if not altogether absent. Agonizing conflicts between East and West or tradition and modernity are rarely central themes in their writing or performance; in criticism, obsolete. Similarly, the tension between regional and national cultures is at best a minor issue of little permanent interest. Understandably, there are still powerful voices, foreign as well as Indonesian, who cannot help but view contemporary trends in terms and patterns developed earlier. But in my view these observers are missing the point. Yudhistira's *Arjuna* trilogy of a decade ago, for example, has been seen largely in terms of the conflict between Javanese and Indonesian cultures, between tradition and modernity.[44] The analysis makes apparent sense, especially when Yudhistira is placed in the context of a certain kind of literary history, but it ignores the underlying concept, which is that none of those dichotomies are really dichotomies, and in any case are irrelevant in contemporary Indonesia. Yudhistira is not so much intent on maligning Javanese traditions and feudalism—although he manages to accomplish that splendidly, he does so, as it were, on the side—as he is poking fun at the whole establishment that takes such things so seriously it cannot see the complexities and changing realities beneath its very nose. And that, too, is why he can find it both so hilarious and so hopeless that he has been so thoroughly misunderstood by that same establishment.

Breaking convention, or more accurately simply laughing at it and moving beyond it, is in fact very widespread in contemporary Indonesian culture, where the drive to experiment is the result of efforts to attract (paying) audiences quite as much as it may be related to political awareness or artistic sensibilities.[45] This culture may be described as an energetic, often naive, "progressive" eclecticism which creates "new traditions" and cultural fashions from a widely disparate collection of elements. Despite the accusations of anthropologists and commentators with political aims, this eclecticism is not, or certainly not exclusively, the brainchild of government. Especially where regional cultures are involved, it has been made to serve vaguely political purposes, but that is not primarily why it exists and certainly is not why it is popularly accepted.[46]

Increasingly large numbers of Indonesians of all social and economic classes not only have access to world culture, but are cultural tourists in their own nation, even their own region.[47] They neither know nor, truth be told, care very much about the historical niceties of their multifaceted cultural heritage. This is not to say they do not care about having a tradition to be proud of; to the contrary, they want it understandable, polished, and brought up to date. Whether it is a pure or accurate reflection of the past is of no consequence; what matters is how it looks today. In their eyes bastardization of tradition is unimportant and, often, quite unrecognizable; even where it is evident, it may not be considered unacceptable.[48]

This sort of thinking and its physical manifestations drive some foreign Indonesianists and indigenous sophisticates to tears. Macbeth in plumes and a sarong is—for a number of complicated reasons—one thing,[49] but Irianese dancers, dressed in the fashion of the Radio City Music Hall Rockettes of the 1950s with ankle feathers, singing ancient chants to catchy new tunes, is quite another.[50] What are we to make of dance troupes which mix regional styles with abandon yet announce the resulting performance to be, for example, "Balinese" or "Minangkabau"? Or of Guruh's Parisian-Japanese-Javanese confections, at 100,000 rupiahs a seat? What is there to be said about *dalang* who mix *dang-*

dut melodies into their gamelan repertoire or use trumpets and other Western instruments in performances shortened to two or three hours not for foreigners but for Indonesian audiences? Or about *wayang orang* troupes that breakdance or gamelan masters who incorporate *dangdut* themes into their compositions? (*Wayang orang* is a stage show in which human actors play roles taken by puppets in traditional *wayang*.)

One response is to declare it all a confused and confusing travesty to be fought against, another to dismiss it as merely a creation of the alienated (and insensitive) rich, yet another to point out a little condescendingly that such cultural miscegenation has been going on for a long while and that eventually a "real," unified, and refined modern culture will appear. But in all these cases, I think, the important point is again being missed. For better or worse, the examples I have used—and there are many more where they came from, from every region and social level—constitute modern Indonesian culture, or at very least a significant and growing part of it. They show how authors, performers, and others are trying to attract audiences—paying, to be sure, but also approving and interested—and to survive both physically and intellectually. They exist in an Indonesian world that is different not only from Armijn's but, almost certainly, different in many important respects from any he might have imagined. (He certainly underestimated the ability of *wayang* and gamelan to change!)

V

I think the real problem is that the tradition is disappearing, and fast; and I want to know why.

—Robert Brown, "The Performing Arts: Modernity and Tradition" (1979)

Mr. Brown, a musicologist who has done much to preserve Javanese gamelan tradition in the United States, made the above remark at another, earlier conference entitled "What Is Modern Indonesian Culture?" I think the sentiment was wrong for the setting since it in effect ignored the main question, but it does express nicely one of the chief problems facing those who are trying to find ways to define and comprehend modern Indonesian culture. The past weighs very heavily indeed on our consciousness and, whether out of a sense of the importance of history or a sense of the sacredness of tradition, it is difficult to deal with proportionately. I share Mr. Brown's concern about disappearing traditions, and I too am interested in why they are disappearing, but I do not think that on the whole the answers will tell us much, or much that is interesting, about the modern Indonesian culture that is *appearing*, and why it is doing so. These are not merely flip sides of the same coin.

Lest I be misinterpreted here, let me hasten to say that a ready familiarity with the past can be an inspiration and can assist with a contextual understanding; I am simply trying to warn that the connection may not be umbilical. Our brief rendezvous with Armijn, for example, raises the interesting question of what the prewar period has, in fact, to do with the present one, why intellectual patterns established in the 1930s should be at least in some respects so long-lived. It is extraordinary that a figure such as Takdir Alisjahbana should, without having changed his ideas or outlooks in any fundamental ways over the past sixty turbulent years, have been considered relevant by so many for so long. Should we perhaps be discussing the ways in which the revolution and early years of independence (or even, say, the entire two decades between 1945 and 1965) actually *slowed* the pace of intellectual and cultural change, rather than the opposite? Or are we in some kind of intellectual loop?

Essentially the same question can be profitably put somewhat differently. Susan Rodgers's rediscovery of the Batak novel *Sitti Djaoerah: Padan djandji na togoe* (Sitti Djaoerah: The vow; 1927), for example, makes us wonder why its remarkable message of the complementarity of modernity and tradition was not only apparently unusual for its own day, but utterly forgotten in subsequent years.[51] Toward the end of this work there is a stunning chapter in which the experience of riding in an airplane and the enjoyment of a traditional chanted epic are juxtaposed in such a way as to clearly suggest that modernity and tradition are, even in apparently extreme situations, complementary rather than mutually exclusive. In addition, *Sitti Djaoerah* offers an ending of happiness and material success to its chief characters' search for the modern life, a characteristic which sets it entirely apart from the by now "classic" novels of the prewar period as well as many that were published later. Can we help but ask why? And can we help but think that the answer may suggest ways of placing contemporary culture in proper perspective?

For the most part, however, I am inclined to think that asking the right questions about modern Indonesian culture is first and foremost a matter of discovering more about what is happening now. We really know very little about the contemporary cultural scene beyond, perhaps, Taman Ismail Marzuki and the Jakarta Arts Council, not least because we all tend to be a bit snobbish and doubtful about it. (Here I specifically intend to include in that "we" many of my Indonesian colleagues.) We have not taken most of contemporary Indonesian culture very seriously from an intellectual point of view—why shouldn't we take Indonesian pop culture, for example, at least as seriously as we take, say, the American or Italian variety?—and we still are at sixes and sevens regarding its social setting, especially the life and notions of the middle classes.[52]

There is a great deal of basic descriptive work, to say nothing of work with attitudes and ideas, to be done before much helpful analysis can be expected. In that regard, I am inclined to turn Robert Darnton's otherwise very helpful research advice at least temporarily on its head. He suggests searching for what to the researcher appears opaque, and working from that point to construct an understanding.[53] There is a great deal in contemporary Indonesian culture which may seem opaque or odd, however, and in any case what outsiders find opaque and what the majority of Indonesians find opaque may be rather different (depending on a number of variables, they also of course may be quite the same). It seems to me too easy to be misled or confused with this approach. Might it not be helpful to seek first to understand precisely what does *not* seem particularly opaque, what appears, especially in ordinary Indonesian eyes, to be common, everyday, cultural fare (or especially admirable, exciting, or touching . . . in everyday ways), and working from that point to understand why it is so? We know extraordinarily little about how Indonesians outside intellectual circles think about various aspects of their own modern culture, and we know virtually nothing about cultural tastes. Until we are able to improve our knowledge in this area "modern Indonesian culture" seems likely to remain in our minds as either an abstraction or a muddle, or both.

Notes

1. *Poedjangga Baroe* was published between 1933 and 1941. (A postwar series appeared under the title *Pudjangga Baru* between 1948 and 1954.) Achdiat K. Mihardja, ed., *Polemik kebudayaan* (1948; reprint Jakarta: Dunia Pustaka Jaya, 1986) is the key compilation of original essays, but contemporary readers should be aware that many important voices, including that of Armijn Pané, were neglected or omitted altogether. On aspects of the debate, see, for example, Heather Sutherland, "Pudjangga Baru: Aspects of Indonesian Intellectual Life in the 1930s," *Indonesia* 6

(1968): 106–27; Keith Foulcher, *Pudjangga Baru: Literature and Nationalism in Indonesia, 1933–1942* (Bedford Park: Flinders University of South Australia, 1980); H. B. Jassin, *Pudjangga Baru: Prosa dan puisi* (Jakarta: Gunung Agung, 1963); Jakob Sumardjo, "Sastra Pudjangga Baru," *Basis* 32, 7 (July 1983): 242–55; H. T. Faruk and Ryadi Goenawan, "Dimensi-dimensi *Pudjangga Baru*," *Basis* 32, 7 (July 1983): 257–64; and Sue Nichterlein, "An Essay on Transcultural Intellectual Biography: Sutan Takdir Alisjahbana," in *Spectrum*, ed. S. Udin (Jakarta: Dian Rakyat, 1978), 61–91.

2. The novel appeared first in *Poedjangga Baroe* 7, 10–12 (April-June, 1940), and has been reprinted a great many times since. The novel has appeared in English translation as *Shackles*, trans. John H. McGlynn (Athens: Ohio University Monographs in International Studies, 1985), a slightly altered second edition of which was published by the Lontar Foundation (Jakarta: 1988). In addition to the works mentioned in note 2, useful commentary on *Belenggu* may also be found in A. Teeuw, *Modern Indonesian Literature*, 2d ed., 2 vols. (The Hague: M. Nijhoff, 1979); Luigi Santa-Maria, "L'Essor officiel: 1900–1942," in *Sastra: Introduction à la littérature Indonésienne contemporaine*, ed. H. Chambert-Loir (Paris: Cahiers d'Archipel, 1980), 29-55; and Anthony H. Johns, "The Novel as a Guide to Indonesian Social History," *Bijdragen tot de taal-, land- en volkenkunde* 115, part 3 (1959): 232–48.

3. Biographical information on Armijn Pané has been taken principally from Foulcher, *Pudjangga Baru*, 6-7; Jassin, *Pudjangga Baru*, 241; and *Ensiklopedi umum*, (Yogyakarta: Jajasan Kanisius, 1973), 933.

4. The theme runs throughout Armijn's writings, but is often forgotten by his critics and supporters alike. A reminder of the point, and its importance, can be found in Budi Darma, "The origin and development of the novel in Indonesia," *Tenggara* 25 (1990): 9–35, esp. p. 20.

5. Thus he supported not only *keroncong* (see note 7), but popular theater of various kinds, which he considered to reflect truthfully the spirit of the times. See "Dardanella," *Poedjangga Baroe* 1, 12 (1934): 381–83.

6. See esp. "Kesoesastraan baroe," part 1, *Poedjangga Baroe* 1, 1 (1933): 9–15.

7. On *keroncong*, also commonly spelled *kroncong*, see Ernst Heins, "*Kroncong* and *Tanjidor*: Two Cases of Urban Folk Music in Jakarta," *Asian Music* 7, 1 (1975): 20–32; Bronia Kornhauser, "In Defense of *Kroncong*," in *Studies in Indonesian Music*, ed. Margaret J. Kartomi (Clayton, Victoria, Australia: Monash University, Centre for Southeast Asian Studies, 1978), 104–83; and Mona Lohanda, "Majoor Jantje and the Indische Element of Batawi Folkmusic," paper presented to the Third Dutch-Indonesian Historical Congress, Leiden, 23–27 June 1980.

8. The most complete information on *Terang Boelan* is found in Salim Said, *Shadows on the Silver Screen: A Social History of Indonesian Film* (Jakarta: Lontar Foundation, 1991), esp. 24–27, which give a much fuller account than that contained in the same author's earlier *Profil dunia film Indonesia* (Jakarta: Grafitipers, 1982).

9. The original attack on public broadcasting of a *keroncong* concert, in which *keroncong* was flatly declared a "great danger," was launched by Ali Boediardjo, "Volksconcert P.P.R.K. jang pertama," *Poedjangga Baroe* 8, 10 (April 1941): 252–55. Armijn's response appeared in the same issue 256-260, under the title "Kerontjong disamping gamelan" (256–60). G. J. Resink took up the anti-*keroncong* position in his "Indonesische toekomstmuziek," *Kritiek en opbouw* 4, 5 (April 1941): 74–77. Armijn responded directly to Resink and "for obvious reasons" in Dutch, with his long and thoughtful "Gamelan tegenover krontjong, droom tegenover werkelijkheid," *Poedjangga Baroe* 9, 1 (July 1941): 9–30.

10. See, for example, the opinion piece "Radio dan keboedajaan," *Poedjangga Baroe* 5, 9 (1937–1938): 197–98; and the subsequent "Boekoe, pers, radio dan *Poedjangga Baroe*, Nomor Peringatan (1938), 3–16.

11. "Produksi film tjerita di Indonesia, perkembangannja sebagai alat masjarakat," *Indonesia, Madjallah Kebudajaan* 4, 1–2 (January-February 1953): 5–112.

12. "Produksi film," 106–7.

13. These ideas, to which Armijn held with great consistency throughout his career, are discussed in the early "Kesoesastraan baroe," part 1, *Poedjangga Baroe* 1, 1 (July 1933): 9–15, and part 2, *Poedjangga Baroe* 1, 2 (August 1933): 37–43. They appear again in one of his last essays, "Produksi film," particularly forcefully on p. 6.

14. In addition to the items mentioned in the previous note, see also "Lagoe Indonesia Raja," *Poedjangga Baroe* 2 (1934–1945): 27–30.

15. Foulcher, *Pudjangga Baru*, 58.

16. "Produksi film," 103–4.

17. As early as 1933, his penchant for thinking and speaking critically seems to have led some to question Armijn's nationalism. In a piece in which he had less-than-complimentary things to say about the new nationalist anthem, Armijn noted tersely, "Blindly praising a people [nation] is [simply] inappropriate. A nationalism that is brave enough to see and draw attention to its own faults so as to correct them, that is a proper and pure sort of nationalism." "Lagoe Indonesia Raja," 29.

18. He took special pains to distance himself from romanticism, as in the preface to his collection of poems, *Gamelan djiwa* (Jakarta: Bagian Bahasa, DPPK, 1960), also cited in Foulcher, *Pudjangga Baru*, 93.

19. Takdir Alisjahbana, for example, considered *Belenggu* to be defeatist, and therefore not a proper vehicle for a modern, progressive, national culture. *Poedjangga Baroe* 8, 7 (1941): 176–77. See also Foulcher, *Pudjangga Baroe*, 59. Soewarsih Djojopoespito also saw a profound unhappiness in the novel, but viewed it as the "spirit of rebelliousness." *Poedjangga Baroe* 8, 6 (1941): 143.

20. The most forceful statement is Benedict R. O'G. Anderson, "Old State, New Society: Indonesia's New Order in Comparative Historical Perspective," *Journal of Asian Studies* 42 (May 1983): 477–96. For a series of arguments against this point of view, see Robert Cribb, "Heirs to the Late Colonial State? The Indonesian Republic, the Netherlands Indies and the Revolution, 1945–1949," unpublished paper, 1989.

21. See, for example, Thommy Svensson, "The Making of the Late Colonial State in Historical Perspective," paper presented at the conference on The Socio-Economic Foundations of the Late Colonial State in Indonesia, 1880–1930, 1989.

22. In a conference sponsored by the Pertemuan Sastrawan Jakarta, Dewan Kesenian Jakarta, entitled "50 tahun perjalanan *Polemik Kebudayaan*." Many of the presentations at this conference were mimeographed but not, as far as I am aware, subsequently published. It is also interesting that the cultural debate of the 1920s and 1930s is being revived and reexamined by returning to the principal novels of those years

to see, among other things, whether the social conditions and problems they described have changed in the intervening years. See the seminar "*Siti Nurbaya* versus nasib wanita masa kini," sponsored by Televisi Republik Indonesia and *Femina* magazine, held 10 November 1990 in Jakarta and reported in *Femina* 18, 47 (29 November–5 December 1990), 35–37. Some of the papers were later published. See Julia I. Suryakusuma, "Siti Nurbaya pada dekade 1990," and Taufik Abdullah, "Siti Nurbaya: roman, wanita, dan sejarah," *Tempo*, 4 May 1991, 47–61, 43–46, respectively.

23. The debate began with Lubis's three-hour lecture, "Situasi manusia Indonesia kini," presented at Taman Ismail Marzuki, Jakarta, on 6 April 1977, and published by Yayasan Idayu later that year. A great many commentaries, long and short, appeared in the press afterward. For an English translation, see Mochtar Lubis, *The Indonesian Dilemma*, trans. Florence Lamoureux (Singapore: Graham Brash, 1983). For a thoughtful discussion, see David T. Hill, "Interpreting the Indonesian National Character: Mochtar Lubis and *Manusia Indonesia*," unpublished paper, 1989. The link between Mochtar Lubis's ideas and those of Takdir and the *Poedjangga Baroe* is made especially clear when one of the characters in his novel *Maut dan cinta* (Jakarta: Pustaka Jaya, 1977) calls for a *manusia Indonesia baru* (new Indonesian) to arise and both exemplify and lead others to modernity. On this see David T. Hill, "Mochtar Lubis: The Artist as Cultural Broker in New Order Indonesia," *Review of Indonesian and Malaysian Affairs* 21, 1 (1987): 54–87.

24. See, for example, on the subject of automobile stickers: Mochtar Pabottingi, "Bahasa mobil kelas menengah," *Tempo*, 23 March 1991, 104; and on rap music: Letters to the Editor, *Tempo*, 11 and 25 May 1991. Implications of a similar sort, though with perhaps more doubts and certainly more sophistication, can often be found in interviews and short articles by some perhaps unexpected figures. See, for example, pop musician Remy Sylado, "Benarkah menangkat lagu menjadi populer?" *Kompas*, 29 July 1990, and author Y. B. Mangunwijaya, "Renungan Agustus 1990," *Kompas*, 15 August 1990.

25. See his "Membangun sinema Indonesia," *Kompas*, 1 July 1990.

26. It is probably fair to say that even Salim Said's useful and generally discerning *Shadows on the Silver Screen* suffers in this way.

27. On *dangdut* in general, and its relation to the earlier *keroncong*, see my "Rhoma Irama and the *Dangdut* Style: Aspects of Contemporary Indonesian Popular Culture," *Indonesia* 34 (October 1982): 103–31.

28. See the interview with Rosihan Anwar, *Matra* 52 (November 1990): 13–23. Here Rosihan notes, among other things, that the reason film directors cannot accurately depict the true face of Indonesia is that censorship prevents them from doing so, and that things were far freer in Usmar Ismail's day (the late 1940s and 1950s). The same message, but looking forward rather than backward, is contained in the interview with Salim Said, chair of the Jakarta Arts Council, "Pemerintah mengacaukan apresiasi seni," *Tempo*, 29 December 1990, 80–81.

29. Clearly that is the sense, for example, of Eros Djarot's "Membangun sinema Indonesia," *Kompas*, 1 July 1990, and of Mangunwijaya's "Renungan."

30. See, as examples, Sayidi Suryohadiprojo, "Kemampuan menyadari perubahan," *Kompas*, 8 October 1990; the same author's "Jatidiri dan kebudayaan bangsa," *Kompas*, 9 August 1990; and the editorial "Kita harus berantisipasi terhadap terjadinya perubahan paradigma," *Kompas*, 26 September 1990.

31. "*Dangdut* menggoyang diskotek," *Kompas*, 21 January 1990.

32. "Goyang dangdut," *Tempo*, 25 May 1991, 49–66.

33. Untitled cassette tape in my possession.

34. Sayidi Suryohadiprojo, "Jatidiri."

35. See the entire issue of the popular newsmagazine *Editor*, 4 September 1990. The cover depicts a huge open mouth, with the words "Courageous and Free to Speak Out," and several special reports discuss the issue of free speech.

36. For a standard example, see Selo Soemardjan, "Pengembangan sumber daya manusia Indonesia menjelang abad ke 21," *Ilmu dan Budaya* 13, 8 (May 1991), 629–35.

37. See, for example, his comments reported in *Kompas*, 18 August and 21 October 1990.

38. Regarding the October 1990 banning of N. Riantiarno's play *Suksesi*, see especially *Kompas*, 11–13 October 1990; and *Editor*, 20 October 1990. On the *Monitor* affair, in which the magazine was banned and its

editor-in-chief, Arswendo Atmowiloto, jailed, see *Tempo*, 27 October 1990, 27; 3 November 1990, 26–34; and 10 November, 11–13, 35.

39. Concerning the middle class as audience, see literary critic Jakob Sumardjo's commentary in *Kompas*, 15 February 1987. On the middle class in general, see Richard Tanter and Kenneth Young, eds., *The Politics of Middle Class Indonesia* (Clayton, Victoria, Australia: Monash University, Centre of Southeast Asian Studies, 1990).

40. For example, Sartono Kartodirdjo's continued emphasis on the importance of national identity being reflected in history is beginning to sound old-fashioned (and more like a government position). See his "Kesadaran sejarah dan kepribadian nasion," part 1, *Kompas*, 4 October 1990; part 2, *Kompas*, 5 October 1990. Increasingly Indonesia seems to be viewed in a comparative, global fashion, as in Sumarkoco Sudiro, "Kualitas manusia Indonesia," *Kompas*, 11 October 1990. The trappings of nationalism come in for frequent discussion and, often, guardedly critical appraisal in the press. Fairly typical examples by well-known commentators are Subagio Sastrowardoyo, "Upacara bendera," *Tempo*, 13 April 1991, 101; and Daniel Dhakidae, "Pahlawan," *Tempo*, 25 May 1991, 107.

41. See, for instance, Sayidi Suryohadiprojo, "Jatidiri," and the short story by Djoko Quartanto, "Jatidiri," *Kompas*, 16 September 1990.

42. Remy Sylado's activities in this area have an interesting and unusual twist. Recently he has been active in bringing ordinary street hawkers (*pedagang asongan*) to the stage, and in getting them to write short stories and poems. They have natural talent, he says. But he also has used the publicity thus generated to point out that although they were mere hucksters, and were at the bottom of society from the point of view of polite society, they had money and potential clout (and, incidentally, could pay for Remy's tutelage): they earned in the neighborhood of 10,000 rupiahs a day, and they numbered more than 3,000 in Jakarta. This put a rather different face on *rakyatism*. *Kompas*, 14 January, 1990.

43. To take but one example, Misbach Jusa Biran, "Film Indonesia memerlukan kaum terpelajar," *Prisma* 19, 5 (1990): 40–44, notes that the quality of film audiences is too low. The dual yearnings for *kerakyatan*

(populism) or the ability to *merakyat* (be close to the people) on the one hand, and for quality and high-class status on the other, run through much of contemporary discussion of cultural development.

44. The novels in the "*wayang* trilogy" by Yudhistira Ardi Noegraha (who also uses the name Yudhistira ANM Massardi) are: *Arjuna mencari cinta* (Arjuna in search of love) (Jakarta: Cypress, 1977), *Arjuna mencari cinta II* (Arjuna drop-out) (Jakarta: Cypress, 1980), and *Arjuna Wiwa-hahaha . . . !* (Arjuna vs. Arjuna) (Jakarta: Garuda Metropolitan Press, 1984). The analysis I have in mind comes from Savitri Scherer, "Introducing Yudhistira Ardi Noegraha," *Indonesia* 31 (April 1981): 31–52; and, esp., Benedict R. O'G. Anderson, "*Sembah, Sumpah:* The Politics of Language and Javanese Culture," in the same author's collection of essays, *Language and Power: Exploring Political Cultures in Indonesia* (Ithaca: Cornell University Press, 1990), 194–237, esp. 228–35.

45. Certainly one gets the distinct feeling, for example, that individuals such as Riantiarno, Arswendo Atmowiloto, and Guruh Sukarno have a keen eye to business and are molding "art" to the market. But the drive is much more widespread than that, and economics as well as "mass tastes" inevitably push the full spectrum of cultural forms, at all social levels. While widely condemned, in my view this commercialism might well be what has kept the Indonesian cultural scene so lively in the past few decades, especially as compared to that of, for example, Malaysia.

46. We can take two examples at opposite ends of the money-class spectrum. On the "high" side, see the Guruh-directed extravaganza which presented what clearly were terrifically hoked-up renditions of supposedly traditional regional dances, and the like. Producer Abdul Latief noted he was simply offering the (well-off) public what it wanted, that is, what was (and he used the English rendition) marketable. Sri Pudyastuti R., "Gencar semarak Pasaraya," *Tempo*, 30 March 1991, 108. On the "low" side, consider the efforts of the Wayang Orang Bharata, last holdout of *wayang orang* in the capital city, which attempts to be more marketable by shortening performances (and not merely for impatient foreigners!), including break-dance routines in their shows, and

providing both English-language summaries and aphorisms in old-fashioned Javanese for its audiences. *Kompas*, 8 July 1990.

47. One of the promoters of the Abdul Latief production mentioned in the preceding footnote implied that the show was for foreign tourists ("When tourists come to Indonesia, where can they go to see [cultural] things?" he said), but it seems to me rather obvious that these shows are not at all meant for foreigners, but precisely for Indonesians. Some of the sense of Indonesians becoming tourists in their own land, in addition to Indonesian culture reflecting "more and more of ourselves," is conveyed in Gloria Davis, "What Is Modern Indonesian Culture? An Epilogue and Example," in *What is modern Indonesian culture?* ed. Gloria Davis (Athens: Ohio University Papers in International Studies, 1979), 307–18.

48. The trend in performance seems to be to make a distinction not between *modern* and *traditional*, but between *classical* and everything else—that is, between *old-style* and *mode*. For an example see the advertisement for a major—and obviously commercial though serious—production of traditional dances of East Java, in which the designation "traditional" has become "classical" in the same way as Brahms may be considered classical.

49. They appear in an Arifin C. Noer production of Macbeth. For pictures and some commentary, see *Kompas*, 8 September 1990.

50. "Bila tarian rakyat harus dirakyatkan," *Kompas*, 23 August 1990. The title of this article alone is worth an extended analysis.

51. Susan Rodgers, "Imagining Tradition, Imagining Modernity: A Southern Batak Novel from the 1920s," *Bijdragen tot de taal-, land- en volkenkunde* 147, 2–3 (1991): 271–97.

52. Certainly that was the impression left by further examination of the Indonesian middle class in a seminar on the subject sponsored by the University of Indonesia and *Tempo* magazine, held in Jakarta 30 May 1991.

53. Robert Darnton, *The Great Cat Massacre and Other Episodes in French Cultural History* (1984; paper ed., New York: Vintage Books, 1985), 257–63, contains this and some other pertinent suggestions.

Chapter Three

Nation, "Tradition," and Constructions of the Feminine in Modern Indonesian Literature

Barbara Hatley

Introduction: Two Stories of Javanese Women

IN A COLLECTION of short stories by the writer Pramudya Ananta Tur published in 1950, just as Indonesia achieved nationhood, there appears the extended short story "Dia yang menyerah."[1] The tale is set in a Javanese provincial town, Pramudya's home town of Blora, during the preceding years of Japanese occupation, independence struggle, reoccupation by the returning Dutch colonizers, and finally official independence. The central figure is a young girl, Sri, left to care for her family through the terrible deprivation and suffering that these events wreak on ordinary people. Her mother dies and political involvement takes her father and older sister away from home. The title of the story could be translated "She who gives up"—"gives up" both in the sense of giving in, surrendering in defeat, but also of "giving up" *something*, an act of voluntary offering or self-denial. Both these senses are very much present in the author's portrayal of Sri's strategy of survival. To each new calamity and deprivation she surrenders (*menyerah*) without complaint, drawing on the time-honored and meritorious Javanese practices of submission to higher authority and ascetic denial of attachment to the sensual, physical world. While Sri feels pride in thus remaining unaffected by the deprivations which trouble other characters, the author comments that such attitudes of submission and acceptance are always inculcated as virtues by the strong among the weak, making the latter easier to exploit. Sri helps her younger siblings become adept in this practice of acceptance-through-self-denial, and they, like Sri, survive the turmoil, while their more socially active and involved father and older sister do not. But the price is terrible. Along with home, possessions and several of its members, the family has lost all sense of connection or involvement with the surrounding society. When the celebrations of the final peace take place in the town square, Sri and her family, with their numb and shrunken sense of self, have no interest in attending.

In 1975 another Indonesian writer of Javanese ethnic background, Umar Kayam, published a short novel about a Javanese woman named Sri surviving the vicissitudes of social change and political upheaval through a strategy of surrender to circumstance.[2] The title, "Sri Sumarah," would translate much like that of Pramudya's story, except that, as the name of the chief character, it is left untranslated—Sri's attitude of open-hearted acceptance of fate is encoded in her very name. Here the implications are entirely positive. The Javanese term *sumarah,* which the author uses to designate Sri's behavior, in place of the neutral Indonesian *menyerah,* has connotations of religious devotion, submission to a higher power, selfless surrender. It is also the approved attitude of a wife to her husband, that of esteemed female figures from the *wayang* shadow puppet tradition to their husbands. Sri's *sumarah* is learned in submission not to a supernatural being but to her human lord, her husband. By surrendering herself wholeheartedly to the fulfillment of his needs she in turn gains his love and loyalty, and their household runs harmoniously. When her husband dies unexpectedly, Sri uncomplainingly accepts this fate and devotes her energies to raising her daughter. Her daughter, however, moves away from the cultural world of her mother, marries a student activist and becomes involved in the communist movement. When daughter Tun is imprisoned during the anticommunist killings and jailings of 1965 and 1966, Sri Sumarah takes over the care of her young granddaughter. Turning to massage to make a living, Sri on one occasion encounters as a client a young man from the capital, a Javanese who no longer knows his own language, but is passionately attracted to Sri with her traditional Javanese dress and refined ways. Guiltily, Sri surrenders to his caresses, rationalizing her action in images of a mother-child embrace. In this brief incident at the end of the story some commentators have seen considerable symbolic significance.[3] Epitomizing the traditional Javanese cultural world, Sri gives comfort and nurture to the young man from the city, representing brash new Indonesia; Sri/Java is unsettled and disoriented by the encounter but perhaps gains some new sense of self.

Much could be said about the important differences between the two stories. Pramudya's "Dia yang menyerah" was written at a time of political turbulence and intense nationalist feeling, in which the maintenance of political unity and the creation of a national culture were all-important goals; Kayam's story, in a period of political stability that afforded the cultivation of interest in regional cultural traditions, especially that of the numerically and politically dominant Javanese. Pramudya's alienation from many aspects of Javanese cultural tradition, particularly the "feudalism" of the *priyayi* (aristocratic-bureaucratic ruling class), is well documented in his later writings, as is Kayam's identification with Javanese culture and particular interest in the contemporary fortunes of the *priyayi*.[4] Elsewhere I have explored the suggestiveness of language use by the two authors in establishing cultural perspectives:[5] Indonesian allows Pramudya to stand outside the Javanese world and comment critically on it; Kayam, although writing in Indonesian, frequently quotes Javanese terms and sayings in an

BARBARA HATLEY

attempt to capture something of the actual feel of Javanese thought and behavior, and to pass this on to his readers.

What I want to draw attention to here, however, is a different aspect of the two stories—the choice of a *female* figure to embody the archetypal Javanese cultural values of acceptance of fate and submissiveness to higher authority while fulfilling the role of nurturing mother; likewise the silencing of another female figure who turns away from Javanese values and the submissive, supportive mother role, to participate in the more egalitarian world of modern Indonesia. For both Sri's sister Is and Sri Sumarah's daughter Tun this move involves political activity, specifically the joining of communist organizations; eventually both the organizations and the young women themselves are cut down. Is disappears, presumably killed, in the destruction of communist forces involved in the 1948 Madiun affair; Tun is imprisoned after the 1965 coup allegedly inspired by the communists. Inasmuch as any figure in these stories can be seen to legitimately represent "modern Indonesia" it is the young *male* client of Sri Sumarah. Participation by the young women in national affairs is short-lived.

Female Identity and Regional "Tradition" in Contemporary Writing

Those familiar with the writing of Pramudya and Umar Kayam might protest at the less-than-representative nature of this selection from the authors' works. They might cite, for example, Kayam's sensitive and sympathetic portrayal of the woman communist activist Bawuk in the short story of that name, and Pramudya's depiction of various strong female figures, particularly Nyai Ontosoroh, fearless fighter for justice in the *Bumi manusia* novels. Below I will discuss examples of such strong women in fiction, questioning whether their characterizations in fact show more continuity with the above picture than is usually recognized. At this point, though, I admit to choosing these two stories deliberately, for their apt illustration of a widely occurring pattern in modern Indonesian literature—that is, a conjuncture of conservative social values, Javanese cultural tradition, and female identity. Such elements constitute a particular nexus within a more general media stereotyping of women figures, noted by analysts of popular literature and film:[6] the highlighting of women's roles as supportive, subordinate wives and mothers, and their punishment for deviation from this model through excessive ambition, assertiveness, or sexual adventure.

The 1970s and 1980s have seen a particular intensification of this nexus, with the publication of a number of works invoking Javanese folkloric models, explicitly discussing Javanese cultural codes and employing Javanese expressions, while focusing on the experience of a central woman character. One thinks, for example, of Linus Suryadi's extended poem *Pengakuan Pariyem* (The confessions of Pariyem)(1981), adopting the voice of a servant girl in a Yogyakarta household, of Arswendo Atmowiloto's novels *Dua ibu* (Two mothers) and *Canting* (Batik pen), the latter depicting the dual personae of a Solonese batik trader, dynamic market entrepreneur and devotedly compliant wife; also of Ahmad Tohari's *Ronggeng dukuh* (Village dancer) trilogy, tracing the fortunes of a village dancer and prostitute, published between 1982 and 1986. As Anna Clancy points out in an incisive analysis of these works, "one motif of female behaviour which is echoed and re-echoed throughout the texts is a willingness to surrender to fate, to acquiesce to and accept what appears to be inevitable."[7] The author, through the voice of the narrator or another character, explicitly links this behavior with the traditional value of *pasrah* or *sumarah* (surrender, acceptance) and *lega-lilo* (happy acquiescence). While not all women characters in the stories exhibit these traits, it is this model of behavior in terms of which female figures are judged and defined. Those who deviate, often explicitly portrayed like Is in "Dia yang menyerah" as distinctly "unwomanly,"[8] encounter trouble. A key site of womanly surrender and acquiescence is in relationships with men; children are likewise nurtured with loving acceptance and support.

This essay attempts to explore this phenomenon and its ramifications: why it should be women in particular who are chosen as bearers of traditional cultural values and conservative social implication; how this trend in literary representation emerged and how it connects with the sociopolitical context of contemporary Indonesia; what the implications are for conceptions of women's place in society and nation; what alternate female images have been developed, by both male and female writers.

History of Development

That already in 1950 Pramudya depicts the young girl Sri as the embodiment of the Javanese attitude of *menyerah* suggests that the association is not a phenomenon of recent years alone. On the other hand, looking further back into the history of modern Indonesian literature, to prewar fiction, particularly such classics as *Siti Nurbaya*, *Belenggu*, and *Layar terkembang*,[9] one finds much less evidence of a nexus between women figures and traditional, conservative cultural values. Instead women characters and gender relations provide the context for much reflection on *change* in social customs and attitudes—on aspirations to a more individual-oriented rather than group-controlled way of life, on shifting expectations of marriage, on possibilities of expanded social roles for women. Explicit attention is given to women's public activities—as teachers, social workers, organizers, and speech makers.

During this period, one might speculate, greater autonomy for women was an admired, progressive social value for modern-minded Indonesians such as the authors of these novels. Modernizing nationalists in many Third World colonies, as K. Jayawardena points out, have counted the perceived freedom of women in European societies among the progressive aspects of Western civilization that they wished to emulate.[10]

With the coming of the Japanese Occupation and the Revolution, however, a shift seems to take place in the dominant representation of women and gender relations in Indonesian literature. The conception of national struggle becomes that of physical suffering and fighting, as male domains of activity. A focus on the military clashes and political intrigue of the revolutionary period relegates women to background roles as dependents and as victims. The cynical images of women as besotted girlfriends of *pemuda* fighters and destitute, sexually exploited refugees in Idrus's *Surabaya* find more sympathetically drawn parallels in stories such as Pramudya's *Dendam* (Revenge). In Mochtar Lubis's *Jalan tak ada ujung* (Road with no end), the main character is rendered impotent through fear of the dangers of the resistance struggle and the violence of the times. Eventually, however, he loses his fear and regains his virility, in an individual liberation which might be seen to symbolize on a broader level the reinvigoration of the Indonesian nation.[11] Meanwhile, the presence of the hero's wife in the narrative serves not only to highlight her husband's weakness and shame but also as a source of conflict with his close friend and comrade. Pramudya's "Dia yang menyerah"—noteworthy in focusing on the courageous survival strategies of women at home, portrayed both more fully and more sympathetically than the male political domain—nevertheless, like other fictional representations of this period, depicts women as victims. Whatever the historical accuracy of this portrayal—whether or not the fact that huge numbers of women indeed stayed behind and struggled to care for their families while their men were away as forced laborers or guerilla fighters can be seen to outweigh in significance the work of the nurses, female couriers, and others who engaged actively in the war effort—its prevalence in fiction, as well as films and popular recollections of the period, contributes to an understanding of issues of nationhood as *male* territory.

Contributing to the association in postwar literature of women characters with nurturance, domesticity, and "traditional" cultural values may be the emergence in this period of large numbers of ethnic Javanese writers. The Minangkabau authors who predominated in the prewar period, educated and Westernized as they were, would arguably have been influenced also, in writing about gender, by the traditions of their own ethnic group, with its matrilineal family system, emphasis on clan and custom, and reputedly "egalitarian" social relations. Javanese culture, with its history of court cultivation, ongoing emphasis on hierarchy and status display, and dominant ideology of female subordination (viz., the conventional designation of a wife as *kanca wingking*, "background companion") presumably creates different predispositions in representing gender. Though in reality active in many areas of social and economic life, women in Javanese society have nevertheless been associated conceptually with the private sphere of the household, with home management and motherhood.

Such association worked to exclude women from the most prestigious cultural pursuits, from the cultivation of spiritual power through meditation, and from its display through controlled, dignified speech and behavior. Women were said to be simply too bound up with the minutiae of domestic life to be capable of or interested in such endeavor. The depiction of women figures in contemporary fiction as bearers of esteemed traditional values hence seems somewhat at variance with established gender expectations. One factor here may be the perceived appropriateness of female characters as symbols of cultural continuity amid the rapid social changes of postwar, particularly New Order, Indonesia. Men, in their involvement in the world of work and politics, are identified with change and progress: women, marginalized from this public domain, can serve as a locus of notions of ongoing cultural values, of nostalgic celebration of a world that used to be. Mothers, in actuality often key transmitters to their children of traditional cultural lore, in fiction become hallowed symbols of all that is admirable in these regional traditions. The batik-clad feminine figure of Pariyem encapsulates the ongoing richness and almost sensually pleasurable familiarity of Javanese cultural tradition: a young *male* servant in a sarong, by contrast, would be simply an embarrassing anachronism.

The Contemporary Sociopolitical Context

There would seem to be additional forces at work, too, in Indonesia in the 1970s and 1980s, constituting the social context for such literary representations of women. The post-1965 New Order period has seen considerable ideological and practical emphasis on women's "traditional" roles as wives and mothers. The *panca dharma wanita,* the five duties of women, enshrined as the official basis of women's organizations and activities, defines women as companions to their husbands, producers of children, educators of children, contributors to the household, and finally, as citizens. The only two mass organizations for women consist of a government-run program of instruction in family health and welfare and domestic skills (PKK), and a civil servants' wives' movement (*Dharma Wanita,* Women's Duty), ranking in which is determined by the position of one's husband. These developments are part of more general ideological and organizational shifts, away from the popular mobilization through political movements of the 1950s and early '60s toward strong, centralized government control, and the incorporation of citizens into state programs on the basis of their "functional" positions as farmers, laborers, students or, indeed, wives and mothers. Loyal support of state ideology rather than representation of particular interests or ideological views is the mandatory official basis of all organizations.

Such measures are justified as in keeping with traditional Indonesian cultural values, with an understanding of the state as an integrated family system, rather than a site of divisive bargaining between individual interests, as in Western-style democracy. Government policies place considerable emphasis on the preservation and cultivation of traditional, regional cultural forms, as a source of state legitimacy, national cultural identity, and protection against the potentially disruptive effects of rapid modernization.

Central to the ideology of "traditional" stability and order is a discourse directed specifically at women. The notion of an inherently modest and gentle female nature, and a womanly destiny *(kodrat wanita)*, focused on nurturance of husband and family, is constantly invoked as a constraint on women's personal behavior, social relationships, and public activities. It is justified as indigenous, "traditional," "our Indonesian way"—as opposed to alien, excessively Western-influenced conceptions of female equality and independence.

Yet *kodrat wanita* ideology represents, of course, not a "natural" continuation of age-old patterns and expectations of womanly behavior, but a particular construction of these patterns and expectations to accord with contemporary conditions and interests. Above, I mentioned a disjunction between fictional portrayal of women as symbols of ongoing Javanese spirituality, and as social stereotypes of female nature. The fictional characterizations accord with an ideal of refined beauty and wifely devotion once cultivated in royal courts. But they stand at odds with a contrasting stereotype of unrestrained emotions and speech associated particularly with village women, and connecting with a complex of myths and images constituting an alternate understanding of female identity. In the realm of mythology there are figures such as Nyai Loro Kidul, sexually beguiling, magically powerful goddess of the South Seas, and Ken Dedes of the flaming womb, semihistorical queen of the East Javanese kingdom of Singosari, both of whom are manifestations of an ancient female archetype, a chthonic deity of fertility, autonomous, sexually potent, magically dangerous.[12] In contemporary village performances the *ledhek,* solo female dancers at all-male *tayuban* dancing and drinking parties, maintain elements of this tradition of autonomous, powerful female sexuality. Other female performers, such as the star actresses in *kethoprak* popular theater and *pesindhen,* female singers with the gamelan orchestra, share something of this aura.[13] Meanwhile on the plane of everyday domestic interaction, assertive, straight-talking village wives, controlling the purse strings, wield a more practical, mundane form of power. But none of this finds mention in gender ideology as currently promoted in Indonesia; such alternate traditions of the female are firmly suppressed.

That images of female assertiveness should be discouraged in the controlled social climate of an authoritarian, military-connected state is perhaps hardly surprising. The association of military institutions with conservative, repressive constructions of women is well documented.[14] More noteworthy is the vehemence with which the official, approved ideology concerning women is promoted and imposed, through the women's organizations, through the ubiquitous billboards and roadside monuments listing the five duties of women cited above, through the media. Why, one might ask again, are women such a specific focus of attention?

The fact that this gender ideology was developed against the background of alleged cultivation of contrasting aggressive female behavior by the communist movement, defeated enemies of the current regime, is surely crucial. In the aftermath of the 1965 attempted coup, purportedly instigated by the communists, government propaganda contained lurid accounts of sadistic violence and abandoned sexual behavior allegedly carried out by members of the communist-linked women's organization Gerwani. Gerwani had reputedly promoted these licentious practices, along with a general encouragement of female self-expression and promotion of women's issues. One commentator argues that the propaganda "suggested that a powerful evil potency, inherent in female sexuality, was deliberately released by the PKI leaders . . . this force would lead inexorably to mayhem and violence."[15] The main aim of such reports was clearly to stir up outrage against the communists, resulting in public acceptance of and participation in action to eliminate them. At the same time the threat of upheaval arising from such practices justified the assumption of social control by military authorities. The association of control of female behavior with general social control, and conversely, the linkage of female autonomy and assertiveness with political threat, has arguably continued on through the New Order period. With female assertiveness connoting both loose sexual morality and proscribed radical politics,[16] conservative standards of modest, constrained feminine behavior are not difficult to maintain.

Literary images of women such as those described above draw on long-established gender ideology in ways which harmonize with this overall climate of social conservatism and celebration of regional cultural tradition. In an authoritarian "family-based" polity, portrayal of a woman's service to her "lord and master" and devotion to the family group presumably has a broad social resonance. Such characterizations also contribute, along with images in popular media such as film, to a gender discourse associating female with nature, nurture and tradition, the regional vis-à-vis the national, cultural continuity set against a male world of progress and change. The impact on the social experience of women-as-citizens is presumably not encouraging of active participation in national political life.

Alternate Models: Women as Symbols of Resistance

At the same time, alongside these dominant images, contemporary Indonesian fiction displays other, contrasting representations of women. Most strikingly different are the female protagonists of a group of novels produced in the 1980s and 1990s by the prominent male authors Pramudya Ananta Tur and Mangunwijaya. Figures such as Nyai Ontosoroh and Nyai Painah in Pramudya Ananta Tur's *Bumi manusia* (This earth of mankind) quartet and the title character in Mangunwijaya's *Roro Mendut*,[17] assertive and independent minded, display attitudes contrasting to the delight in the traditional female role and serene acceptance of fate of Pariyem, Sri Sumarah, and the rest. Instead, these women fight vigorously for their interests against established authority. In contrast to the connotations of social and cultural conservatism embodied in female characterization in much recent Indonesian writing, these women are paragons of resistance to the status quo.[18]

Pramudya and Mangunwijaya, acknowledged critics of aspects of contemporary Indonesian social reality, appear to be giving expression to such critique through these works. Through the experiences of their female protagonists the authors reflect on the injustice, oppression, and hidebound rigidity of the class and racial hierarchies in which these women are situated. The figure of female servant or concubine, such as Nyai Ontosoroh, mistress of a Dutchman at the turn of the century, or Roro Mendut, a village girl captured in war by a seventeenth-century court official, allows for close, sustained exposure of processes of authoritarian control. Significant, too, is the perceived marginality of women to formal social structures. Mangunwijaya acknowledges that for him women represent forces in Javanese-Indonesian society out-side the structures of hierarchical, authoritarian control. Domi-nant culture imposes on women the duty of serving men, denying recognition of their impressive strength and skills. But at the same time, women's virtual exclusion from status-based male cul-ture allows them to stand as symbols of freedom and potential change. Fictional female characters may be seen to connote the natural strength of the people vis-à-vis the imposed domination of (male) palace or state, or the vigorous and lively cultures of the periphery versus the sophisticated artifice of the court center. Women characters in his works indeed constitute on one level embodiments of his vision of a better Indonesia.[19]

Pramudya, too, has spoken explicitly about his reasons for writing about women in the way he does. His aim, he says, is to give recognition to the strengths and achievements of Indonesian women, so little acknowledged in public discourse, and in par-ticular to the struggle through adversity of his own wife.[20] On the basis of such statements, together with readings of his works, commentators frequently point to the positive nature of Pra-mudya's portrayal of women. His characters are cited as models of autonomous womanhood, free of influence from traditional stereotypes of female subordination.[21]

The female characterization of these two authors thus con-fronts dominant gender ideology. Where women figures in main-stream literary works embody notions of cultural continuity and conservative social values, Pramudya and Mangunwijaya depict female characters of a contrasting type with opposing political suggestion. These women arguably recall age-old images of in-dependent, assertive female power, but here with implications which are positive, even heroic, rather than threatening. Rather than marginalizing them from the national domain, exclusion of such women from traditional structures of political control instead frees them to represent possibilities of a new, transformed Indonesian polity. The stereotypical association of women with nature, nurture, and "tradition" as well as their exclusion from the domain of politics and nation is boldly challenged.

Meanings for Women

In a social climate that strongly discouraged female assertiveness, the celebration of womanly power by respected male authors may be of considerable strategic importance for women, in widening the ideological space for their activities. Alternate, assertive images of women are presumably inspiring to politically critical readers of both sexes. Yet on a personal level one wonders how these fictional characters are read by women readers, what degree of identification and would-be emulation takes place. For the role of resistant female characters within an essentially male discourse on political power, countering the conservative, hierarchical values implied by mainstream representations of women, arguably distances them from womanly experience. As emblems of total resistance, such figures are depicted as unaffected by the inherent expectations of and constraints on female identity in Indonesia, to the extent that they may appear less than convincing as women.

Certain expressions of authorial perspective in these writings tend to reinforce such an impression. The behaviour of the "super nyai," Nyai Ontosoroh, in Pramudya's *Bumi manusia* novels, is explicitly described as unwomanly,[22] and her unwavering, uncompromising attitudes deemed "unnatural" by other characters.[23] Though deeply concerned for her children's welfare she is described as having been unsuccessful as a mother.[24] Motherly nurturance is represented, by contrast, in the person of the mother of the male protagonist, Minke. While Minke's father and brothers display all the negative attributes of Javanese "feudalism," in their oppressive obsession with status, his mother, warm, tolerant, and wise, personifies the humane strands in Javanese culture. Minke's second wife, the Chinese Mai, who plunges into political activity, is not strong enough for the struggle and dies of tuberculosis. Minke's final choice of wife, a beautiful princess from Ambon, while courageous and independent minded, defines herself totally in terms of support of her husband. In the last reported conversation between Minke and his princess, for example, just before his arrest by the Dutch authorities, she kisses his hand and states that for a Moluccan woman like herself "her husband is her star, her moon, her sun. Without him nothing will exist, including herself."[25] Once again occurs the conjunction of female fictional character, regional cultural identity (here Moluccan rather than Javanese), domestic location, and conservative social values. Such aspects of female characterization would seem to echo rather than confront the conservative stereotypes of Javanese male writing cited earlier.

The female characterizations of Mangunwijaya seem to display some of the same contradictions. Strong, resistant female figures are portrayed less than convincingly, or less than completely positively, as women. Larasati, the intelligent, accomplished, and outgoing heroine of the novel *Burung-burung manyar* (The weaver birds)[26] is described as successful in everything *except* her wifely role, in acting too overbearingly toward her pliant, quiet husband. In the case of *Roro Mendut*, the title figure's fiery rebelliousness is eloquently identified with the dynamism of the outward-looking, trade-oriented coastal lands from which she comes (read: dynamic, democratic, entrepreneurial forces in modern Indonesian society) as it relates to the conservative rigidity of the Javanese court world into which she is taken (read: authoritarian, Javanese-dominated contemporary state). But how and why Mendut as an individual woman comes to behave in this way is not explained. A strong commitment to women's interests by the two authors is expressed, nevertheless, within a male literary and political discourse, in ways shaped at times, perhaps unconsciously, by long-standing gender ideology.

Women Figures in Women's Writing

Confirmation of the maleness of the discourse described above might be seen in the fact that women writers depict female experience in completely different ways. The protagonists of short stories and novels by women include no idealized, self-sacrificing Javanese mothers, sexy servant girls, nor tough symbols of resistance. There is no celebration of traditional, regional myths and values. In the popular romantic fiction of the glossy magazines and paperbacks which have flourished in the capitalist boom of the New Order period, and in which women authors predominate, the protagonists are overwhelmingly contemporary middle-class women embroiled in the *suka duka,* the pleasures and pain, of romance and marriage. The wider world, of work and social events, serves as a backdrop for the quest to catch and keep a man. Some commentators lament the narrowness of this canvas:[27] alternately one might posit a connection between this circumscribed subject matter and the ideological pressures on women to indeed concentrate on their roles as wives and homemakers. A most interesting contrast with male writing emerges in regard to portrayal of marriage, which for the female protagonists created by women authors frequently involves neglect, male infidelity, and abandonment, even physical abuse, rather than loving mutual nurturance. The sentimental, melodramatic style of these stories generally causes them to be dismissed as cheap fantasy, but they may perhaps evoke in their (female) readers genuine empathy with what are perceived as quite real social problems.[28] The trials undergone by embattled heroines before the closure of a "happy ending" (such as a marriage newly achieved or restored) might be seen, moreover, to express a muffled protest at the strains and sacrifices for women in maintaining the roles defined for them by currently dominant gender ideology.

Such fiction, inasmuch as it defines women in terms of domestic, personal concerns, continues to marginalize them from the world of public, political life, from the "national" arena as it is usually understood. The much smaller corpus of women's writing accepted as "serious" literature likewise generally focuses on female protagonists and the domain of personal relations, albeit perhaps treated with greater subtlety and individuality. One thinks of N. H. Dini's novels about women characters struggling to define and maintain their own identity vis-à-vis the claims of men and marriage, and Toeti Heraty's sensitive poetic explorations of the joys and strains of male-female interaction. Women's writing that extends beyond these boundaries, to depict women defined independently of men, participating on their own terms in public life, is more rare. To picture women engaged in the public, political realm yet maintaining a distinctive woman's voice, with which readers can identify, and preserving some of that female distance from male structures defined by Mangunwijaya as the basis of potential social transformation—all this presents a daunting task. I have not had the chance to systematically seek out and analyze women's writing of this kind; what follows is in no way a comprehensive review. Rather, some key examples are selected of works by women which do engage these issues, which challenge accepted stereotypes of women's roles in national events, and which present new insights into these events, as viewed and experienced by women.

In 1940 a Dutch edition of Soewarsih Djojopoespito's strongly autobiographical novel *Buiten het gareel* (Out of harness)[29] was published in Holland. The novel deals with the experiences of a woman teacher in a nationalist school during the 1930s. Its protagonist and narrator, Sulastri, works alongside her husband and his colleagues, suffering with them poverty and destitution, persecution by the colonial authorities and betrayal by rivals in the nationalist struggle. Yet she documents with telling irony the condescendingly sexist treatment nevertheless meted out to her, most of all from her supposedly progressive husband. Her story of hard, committed, yet often unacknowledged nationalist struggle presents a fascinating contrast to the portrayal of modern, educated women in two famous male novels of the time—Tini, the bored, idle doctor's wife with no outlet for her skills and aspirations in Armijn Pané's *Belenggu*, and Tuti, the accomplished and much-admired feminist activist experiencing difficulty in finding a husband of her own level in Takdir Alisjahbana's *Layar terkembang*. Soewarsih also provides commentary on famous political figures she knew, often with a frank, critical eye to detail and from an intimate, domestic perspective uncharacteristic of and inaccessible to male authors. Whether her womanly identity contributed to the difficulties she experienced in having the novel published (Balai Pustaka, the Dutch publishing house, rejected her first version, written in Sundanese, ostensibly because of its substandard language, but clearly more for political reasons), whether its account of radical political struggle was judged particularly unseemly in its female provenance, remains unknown.

The short novel *Kejatuhan dan hati* (An affair of the heart) by Rukiah, published in 1950,[30] is set during the 1945–1950 national revolution. Its protagonist, Susi, works as a medical assistant with a group of radical left-wing guerilla fighters, living in their camp and tending those wounded in continuous bloody fighting. Its concerns, however, are strikingly different from male writing of the period dealing with similar events and themes. The story begins with a description of Susi's life as a young girl, in a household dominated by her overbearing, totally materialistic mother, a horrifying manifestation of the stereotypical "financial control" and "domestic dominance" of women. To escape the same female fate, in a marriage forced on her by her mother, Susi joins the revolutionary forces. "I wanted to divest myself of all my feelings as a woman and match my own character with that of the male rebels" (p.43). She works with avid determination, eschewing all feminine softness, but her natural gentleness reemerges when she meets and falls in love with Lukman, a dedicated communist. With Lukman and his friends Susi debates their commitment to violence as a vehicle of social transformation, questioning whether "the people" in whose name they supposedly work share their beliefs or derive any benefit from their actions. She laments the fact that Lukman's beliefs prevent them leading a normal life; rather than taking responsibility for their love in a marriage witnessed by her family, he has to flee to avoid capture by the authorities. The pregnant Susi has no choice but to marry the faithful Par, the suitor who has waited for her during her years away. When Lukman eventually returns, once again on the run, to claim her and the child, she refuses to betray her husband's goodness by going with him. Despite her love for him she cannot live by idealistic dreams but must accept social realities and responsibilities. Male values of total political commitment and dedication to ideals are challenged in the name of a feminine compassion, pragmatism, and concern for others, which at the same time contrasts with negative aspects of the standard "woman's domain" of marriage and household.

Female narratives of involvement in national, political events are rare indeed in the discouraging ideological climate of post-1965 Indonesia, the era of the flourishing "ladies' novel." In 1990, however, at a time of resurgence of the historical narrative in

Indonesian fiction, after a period of dominance by antirealist, absurdist writing,[31] N. H. Dini's novel *Jalan bandungan* appeared.[32] The work embodies an increased female engagement in the shared, public domain—at the level of the narrative, involvement by women in the historical events described, and regarding textual production, in the author's participation in mainstream literary trends. The work begins at the time of the Revolution, when the narrator's family have to flee from the city of Semarang into the mountains to the south. A fascinating picture is given of the life of these refugees. The organization of their bases, the differing roles there of male and female children, the distribution of food through communal kitchens, women's work as nurses at Red Cross posts, the young guerilla fighters who act as guards—all this is described in detail from the straightforward, unsophisticated perspective of the narrator, the young teenage girl Mur. The picture of cooperative endeavor, women alongside men, contrasts with the maleness of the Revolution as portrayed by male writers.

In the next phase of Mur's personal life and of Indonesian national history, however, the domain of political activity is pictured as totally separate from, indeed deeply threatening to, the woman's world of household, children, and nurturance. Mas Wid, the ex-guerilla fighter whom Mur marries largely to please her parents, is a cold, shadowy figure unresponsive to the needs of his wife and children; when he disappears at the time of the 1965 coup and is later found imprisoned for communist activities previously quite unknown to her, Mur's reaction is one of shock and anger at this betrayal of his family. They must suffer the awful stigma, and resulting social isolation and economic hardship, of his communist involvement. The total vilification of Mas Wid, the absence of any development of his character or representation of his views, plus Dini's unproblematic attribution of blame to the communists for the postcoup killings and suffering, is very much in keeping with dominant New Order propaganda on these issues: it surely disappoints any expectations of an alternate, more encompassing and forgiving female perspective. But in another way Dini as a woman writer does contribute distinctively, albeit perhaps disturbingly, to the discourse on Indonesian communism. If in *male* mythology communism is to be feared and condemned in its association with the dangerous, negative potential of *women,* with abandoned, predatory female sexuality, here in a woman's text it connotes the lowest nadir of *male* character, a selfish absorption in ideas and political schemes, to the neglect of personal responsibilities and the endangerment of loved ones. In each case the discourse is strongly gendered, in accordance with long-established stereotypes.

Though Mas Wid's imprisonment indeed brings hardship it also releases Mur from an oppressive marriage, allowing her to regain her own identity and participate once more in the public domain—that is to say, a world constituted by New Order concerns of education, professional work, and international communication, not political activity. In the final section of the novel Mur returns to her job as a teacher, gains a scholarship to study in Europe, and there meets and marries Handoko, the brother of her estranged husband, an engineer long resident in Germany. When this second marriage fails, however, because of Mas Wid's treachery and Handoko's weakness, she faces with quiet equanimity the prospect of life on her own. Dini's narrative engages with national history largely as a context for its own concern with womanly survival and self-actualization: its personal focus and social conservatism contrast strikingly with the conjuncture of female strength and political opposition in the works of male authors.

Most contemporary fiction by women is still more narrowly centered than Dini's works on the private "women's world." There are, however, a few women writers of a generation younger than Dini who do speak with critical female voices on social and political themes. In her collection of short stories *Malam terakhir* (The last night),[33] Leila Chudori depicts the injustice, corruption, and hypocrisy of everyday life as faced by her protagonists. Many of her stories venture into the realm of the surreal, the fantastic (generally an overwhelmingly male literary mode) to highlight the extreme, absurd quality of much accepted social practice and belief. One thinks, for example, of the man whose unbearably foul breath no longer troubles his neighbors once he agrees that the bitter pill given him by the dentist tastes sweet—once he adopts the straitjacket of shared lies in place of disquieting individual truth. The majority of the protagonists in Leila's stories are independent, strong-minded young women like herself. A number of her most memorable stories deal with the contradictions and restrictions of female experience. "Air suci Sita" (The holy water of Sita), for example, exposes the hypocrisy of the sexual double standard as enshrined in the mythology of the *Ramayana* epic, and "Adila," depicts the escape into fantasy and eventual suicide of a young girl hounded by a monstrously dominating mother. But Leila refuses the label of woman or feminist writer, on the grounds that she does not wish to be limited to the territory of "women's themes." Accepting such limits would, in her view, simply confirm dominant stereotypes of women's domestic focus.

One long-standing restriction of women's writing still very much in evidence today relates to the issue of class. In contrast to the servant girls, prostitutes, and concubines of Dutchmen who populate the works of male authors, women writers, as members of the urban middle class, write about people from the world they know. One young poet, Saraswati Sunindyo, does, however, move beyond this standard middle-class terrain. In the poem *Sampah kota Kali Nongo* (The city rubbish of the Nongo River)[34] she writes with fierce anger about the experiences of the women with whom she lived while she was on the south coast of Java carrying out research on prostitution: her descriptions of exploitative police taking their cut and civil servants whiling away the office hours in these poor women's beds make it clear that these women are victims of social and political as well as gender oppression. Saraswati conveys great empathy with the prostitutes Cipluk, Endang, Surti, Marti—an attempted rape in her hotel room by an arrogant local school teacher brings the narrator of the poem to a very vivid understanding of the daily experiences of her subjects and sisters. But Saraswati is acutely conscious, nevertheless, of the huge differences in life chances which distinguish her situation from that of poor, uneducated rural women. She will go back to her books and her middle-class life while Cipluk, Endang, Surti, and Marti must live on by the rubbish-choked river with no such escape. In another poem, *Membayangkan orang lain* (Thinking of another woman), the speaker, sitting in a "modern cafe, Paris-Jakarta style" recalls the image of a young woman she had met in a mountain village with a baby on her hip, telling of a husband who had gone to the city and not returned. Suddenly her favorite black coffee completely loses its taste.

There are other victims, too, of sociopolitical injustice, men as well as women, whose haunting images emerge in Saraswati's poetry. In the remarkable work *Sajak pulau Jawa dan kenangan masih kecil* (The island of Java and childhood memories)[35] the speaker recalls seeing as a small child bloody corpses clogging the meandering rivers of "beautiful Java / with its waving palms and ripening rice." Reference to the massacres of communists which followed the 1965 attempted coup is unstated but unmistakable. The speaker thinks of a beloved teacher who may have been among those bodies, for he disappeared from class at that time and never returned. But who knows for certain, and who can ask, who dares to ask? The image of beautiful Java harbors dark, bloody memories that may not be spoken of.

These examples of women's writing follow no general pattern, develop no general "line," in their different or separate approaches to differing areas of social experience. Degrees of involvement in and ideological perspectives on state politics as such vary sharply. Yet there emerges a sense of female identity quite distinct from the constructs of male authors. Here is no idealization of women figures, either as embodiments of celebrated traditional cultural values or of bold resistance against them. Instead there is clear-sighted depiction of female experience with all its difficulties, and gropings for alternatives. Women's lives are not portrayed as insulated from national events and issues: rather the two intersect in ways which allow critical reflection on the national arena informed by special attention to the dimensions of personal experience and relationships.

Conclusion

It is surely fitting in conclusion to endorse the importance of women writers creating female characters who participate in their own right, with an assured female identity, in public, national life. The phenomenon documented above for much postindependence Indonesian fiction, particularly that of the 1970s and 1980s, the marginalization of female figures from the world of politics and nation, has been shown to reverberate with a wider discourse of female constraint and repression, and a general social conservatism. While "serious" literature in itself might be of limited circulation, its connections with the popular press and entertainment media, their shared participation in common trends, enhance its social relevance. In this context the work of women writers, speaking with their own voices, creating alternate female images with which women readers in particular can identify, takes on considerable importance.

At the same time such writing contributes to a broad field of gender characterization by both male and female authors. To afford legitimacy only to "progressive" female characterization by women writers would be to impose an orthodoxy as narrow and constraining as the repressive mainstream ideology it would confront. As suggested earlier, the strong, resistant female characters of Pramudya Ananta Tur and Mangunwijaya contribute significantly to contemporary gender discourse as well as broader political debate. Other male characterizations of women, too, add depth and richness to an expanding canvas.[36] One striking example is the title figure in Mangunwijaya's recent novel *Durga-Umayi*,[37] named after demonic and benign manifestations of the consort of the god Siva. Mangunwijaya confirms that this woman—who undertakes numerous politically expedient changes of name, identity, and allegiance—on one level, in keeping with her girlhood name, Pertiwi (which might translate as "motherhood") "stands for" twentieth-century Indonesia. Like the past shifts and contemporary contradictions in the identity of this figure, those of Indonesia as a nation are likewise suppressed through a wilfully selective historical memory. Here, amid the multiple layers of the text and the complexities of the social reality to which it refers, there is no suggested resolution, no straightforward celebration of heroic "womanly strength." What does come through is Durga-Umayi-Pertiwi's eventual realization of her situation, her wish to break free of the dualities in which she is enmeshed, to reach out perhaps toward the new "post-Indonesian" reality the author espouses.[38] A female consciousness, with its openness to the existence of multiple perspectives, makes this more possible than the singularity of direction typical of the male. [39]

Durga-Umayi-Pertiwi constitutes, of course, no positive female role model; her depiction in the narrative works on a very different plane. Yet her characterization does add a fascinating di-

mension to constructions of the feminine in Indonesian literature. And this is surely a very positive prospect, a rich plurality of
possibilities of female representation and expression—national-
regional, modern-traditional, assertive-nurturing—bound by no
fixed, imposed image of what a woman must be.

Notes

1. In *Cerita dari Blora* (Stories of Blora) (Jakarta: Balai Pustaka, 1950).

2. "Sri Sumarah" appears with a companion story, "Bawuk," in Umar Kayam, *Sri Sumarah dan Bawuk* (Jakarta: Pustaka Jaya, 1975).

3. See, for example, Tinneke Hellwig, *Kodrat wanita: Vrouwbeelden in Indonesische romans* (Leiden: C. M. S. Hellwig, Drukkerij Sociale Wetenschappen, 1990), 83–84.

4. See his recently published saga of a *priyayi* family, *Para priyayi* (Jakarta: Grafitipers, 1992).

5. In "The New Indonesian Pujanggas," paper presented at a conference on multilingualism in Indonesia held in Pacet, West Java, in 1981.

6. See, for example, Krishna Sen, "The Image of Women in Indonesian Films: Some Observations," *Prisma: The Indonesian Indicator* 24 (March 1982): 17–29.

7. Anna Clancy, "The Cultural Constructions of Javanese Women in Modern Indonesian Literature," honors thesis, University of Sydney (1988), 64.

8. See, for example, "Dia yang menyerah," *Cerita dari Blora*, 296–98.

9. Marah Rusli, *Siti Nurbaya* (Batavia: Balai Pustaka, 1922); Armijn Pané, "Belenggu," *Poedjangga Baroe* 7, 10-12 (April-June 1940); Takdir Alisjahbana *Layar terkembang* (With sails unfurled) (Batavia, Balai Pustaka, 1936).

10. K. Jayawardena, *Feminism and Nationalism in the Third World* (London: Zed Press, 1986).

11. This parallel is inferred by A. H. Johns in the introduction to his translation of Lubis's novel *Road with No End* (London: Hutchison, 1968).

12. Peggy Choy reviews various manifestations of this "chronic female archetype" in discussing the history and cultural meaning of the *ledhek* dancer in her "Texts through Time: The Golek Dance of Java," in *Aesthetic Tradition and Cultural Transition in Java and Bali*, ed. Stephanie Morgan and Laurie Jo Sears (Madison: University of Wisconsin, Center for Southeast Asian Studies, 1984).

Barbara Watson Andaya documents evidence from very early times in Southeast Asian societies of fear of the dangerous power of uncontrolled female sexuality, and of the development of strategies for its containment. See her paper "The Changing Religious Role of Women in Pre-Modern Southeast Asia," presented at the Fourth Women in Asia Conference, University of Melbourne, October 1993.

13. For discussion of connections between the role of the *pesindhen* and this tradition of female performance see R. Anderson Sutton, "Who Is the Pesindhen? Notes on the Female Singing Tradition on Java," *Indonesia* 37 (April 1984).

14. See esp. Cynthia Enloe, *Does Khaki Become You? The Militarization of Women's Lives* (London: Pluto, 1983).

15. Stephen Drakeley, "Torture, Terror and Titillation: The Mysogynous Myth of Lubang Buaya and the Mass Killings in Indonesia," paper presented at the Fourth Women in Asia Conference, University of Melbourne, October 1993. For a very powerful discussion of this phenomenon, relating it to the wider process of the construction of the female in contemporary Indonesia, see Sylvia Tiwon, "Models and Maniacs: Articulating the Female in Indonesia" in *Fantasizing the Feminine in Indonesia*, ed. Laurie J. Sears (Durham: Duke University Press, 1996).

16. An activist friend reports that women arrested by the authorities for participation in political actions such as strikes are often taunted during interrogation about their alleged promiscuity—an association of political and sexual "deviance" is assumed.

17. Pramudya Ananta Tur, *Bumi manusia* (Jakarta: Hasta Mitra, 1980) and subsequent volumes: *Anak semua bangsa, Jejak langkah, Rumah kaca*; Y. B. Mangunwijaya, *Roro Mendut* (Jakarta: Gramedia, 1983).

18. The contrast here with Pramudya's depiction of female character in his 1950 story "Dia yang menyerah," discussed earlier, can perhaps be

seen to parallel a shift in his political orientation over the years. As a generalized concern about injustice and suffering crystallized into socialist critique of class society, so an emphatic depiction of women as victims appears to have shifted to representation of their capacities of resistance. At the same time, though, I would argue that the influence of long-established Javanese stereotypes of the female is still evident in Pramudya's recent writing. His depiction of female characters as "models of autonomous womanhood" is not unproblematic. See the previous section, as well as subsequent discussion.

19. Personal communication. Mangunwijaya stated these views in conversation with a group of friends during the conference on Democracy in Indonesia held at Monash University, 16–20 December 1992.

20. Pramudya is quoted giving this explanation of the background to his characterization of the *nyai* in *Bumi manusia* in an interview with the magazine *Tempo* in 1980.

21. See, for example, Hellwig *Kodrat wanita*, 158–59.

22. Dr. Martinet, her family physician, describes the Nyai as a "tigress," too intimidating to attract the suitors one would expect to gather, given her wealth, beauty, and ailing husband. Pramudya, *Bumi manusia*, 226.

23. See, for example, the comments by Magda Peters, Minke's teacher, in Pramudya, *Bumi manusia*, 210.

24. See the comments by Dr. Martinet in Pramudya, *Bumi manusia*, 225.

25. Pramudya Ananta Tur, *Jejak langkah* (Kuala Lumpur: Wira Karya, 1986), 454.

26. Y. B. Mangunwijaya, *Burung-burung manyar* (Jakarta: Penerbit Jambatan, 1981).

27. See Jakob Sumardjo, "A Peaceful Home: Women in Indonesian Literature," *Prisma: The Indonesian Indicator* 24 (March 1982): 41–52.

28. See Ratih Hardjono, "Wanita tersiksa dalam novel sentimental," *Prisma* 16, 5 (1987).

29. Soewarsih's novel was subsequently published in Indonesian as *Manusia bebas* (A free being). Soewarsih Djojopoespito, *Manusia bebas* (Jakarta: Pustaka Jaya, 1975).

30. The story appears in English translation as "An Affair of the Heart" in *Reflections on Rebellion: Stories of the Indonesian Upheavals of 1948 and 1965*, trans. and ed. William Frederick and John McGlynn (Athens: Ohio University Press, 1983).

31. Keith Foulcher describes these trends in his article "Post-Modernism or the Question of History: Some Trends in Indonesian Fiction since 1965," in *Culture and Society in New Order Indonesia*, ed. V. Matheson-Hooker (Kuala Lumpur: Oxford University Press, 1993).

32. N. H. Dini, *Jalan bandungan* (Jakarta, Penerbit Jambatan, 1989).

33. Leila Chudori, *Malam terakhir* (Jakarta: Grafitipers, 1989).

34. This poem, together with a number of others by Saraswati, was published in the original and in translation by Keith Foulcher in *Inside Indonesia* 31 (June 1992), and is to appear again in introduction to *Fantasizing the Feminine in Indonesia*, ed. Laurie Sears.

35. This poem is remarkable both in its powerful simplicity, and in its direct expression of sympathy with the victims of the anticommunist massacres, together with implied criticism of the expunging of the slaughter from popular memory, the omission of such events from the official record of this period of Indonesian history. Among Indonesian writers not themselves associated with the communist movement, such a stance is very unusual.

36. Umar Kayam's novel *Para priyayi*, for example, reflects on gender roles in *priyayi* Java in greater depth and complexity than do his earlier stories. The novel encompasses inequalities and ambiguities, while also presenting a sympathetic and believable example of traditional marital harmony achieved in old age, in the persons of the grandfather and grandmother of Wanagalih (206–33).

37. Y. B. Mangunwijaya, *Durga-Umayi* (Jakarta: Grafitipers, 1991).

38. See Y. B. Mangunwijaya, "Budaya yang menculik kita," *Tempo* 3 (January 1987), quoted in L. Rae "Liberating and Conciliating: The Work of Y. B. Mangunwijaya," in *Indonesian Political Biography*, ed. Angus McIntyre (Clayton, Victoria: Monash University, Centre for Southeast Asian Studies, 1993).

39. Such consciousness need not be limited, however, to biological women. In Mangunwijaya's *Durga-Umayi* (116–17) it is Pertiwi's Bali-

nese painter boyfriend who speaks of plurality of perspectives, and suggests that women understand such things through their experience of child raising. Pertiwi acknowledges the wisdom of these words, suggesting that they indicate a "more female" (*lebih perempuan*) nature than her own (116–17).

Chapter Four

Seni Rupa Kagunan:
A Process

Moelyono

Poverty of the Ordinary People

ACCORDING TO A World Bank report the number of poor in Indonesia has fallen from 70 million to 30 million. The Netherlands' Minister of Development Cooperation and Chairman of the IGGI, Mr. J. P. Pronk, has also reminded us that any decline in Indonesia's levels of poverty must also be accompanied by an awareness that levels of inequality have not been similarly reduced. In fact the reverse true. For instance, as a result of rapid industrialization, disparities in income and access to land have increased.

Between 1980 and 1990 the issue of land tenure dominated the Indonesian mass media. In Central Java, land cases have taken precedence over other problems. The issue is regarded as serious and complaints to the government on this subject have multiplied.[1]

Still fresh in our minds are the events of November 1988, when dozens of poor people's houses on a coffee estate in the Pulau Panggung district of Southern Lampung were burned to the ground. Thousands of ordinary people were driven off their land because their settlement had encroached on a forest reserve.[2] Other land cases followed in quick succession: Cimacan, Belangguan, and the most celebrated of them all, Kedung Ombo.

Other indicators of poverty can be seen in a decline in public security, safety, and liberty.

Poverty in Modern Art

Several figures in modern Indonesian art have made the issue of poverty a clear subject for their creativity. Several dominant figures have made the people's poverty the subject of their paintings. They include: Soedjojono, Hendra Gunawan, and the late Affandi.

They approach poverty and confront it through their emotions, which in turn gives rise to both their artistic inspiration and aesthetic expression. "Paint with nature! Paint according to your feelings!" said Affandi, who admired both the (Austrian-born) British painter Oskar Kokoschka and the Dutch painter Vincent van Gogh because of "their strong humanism." The poor are, however, seen as a subject of painting, no different from inanimate objects, scenery, flowers, or a woman's body. They are objects that can stimulate inspiration and excite an expressive tension.

In the contemporary world, Affandi's, Soedjojono's, and Hendra's paintings are expensive commodities. Collectors with upper-class aesthetic tastes are thus able to control and possess these commodities. They then display paintings of the poor in their private galleries. The problem of poverty ends up in a collector's gallery. Silenced! Mute! In the aesthetic vision and attitude of modern Indonesian artists, clearly the reality of the poor is reified and alienated.

The Aesthetic Dominance of the "Liberal Arts"

In 1987, the New Arts Movement (Kelompok Seni Rupa Baru) redefined the meaning of art. At the time the recognized definition of contemporary art in Indonesia was restricted to three forms: painting, sculpture, and graphic arts. This definition of *seni rupa* (art) as pure art, in the sense of the English *fine arts*, was a concept that limited art to particular practices that have been called *le Belle Arti del disegno*. These particular practices encompass the equally particular sensibilities of painting, sculpture, and architecture (with the later addition of graphic arts).

This definition is bound to the principles of the liberal arts, where art is the product of free individuals, whose fundamental frame of reference is the High Art of the sixteenth-century European Renaissance, with its belief that there is only one high culture and one type of art that is its legitimate product. The working principles of the liberal arts are related to a particular artistic sensibility, which is not to be found in each and every work, and which must distinguish those works regarded as unrefined (i.e., technique). The New Arts Movement, however, saw art as a plural phenomenon and believed that cultures possess various frames of reference.

The 1987 New Arts Movement wanted to condemn elite domination of Indonesian art by elevating the everyday to the world of art. It was an invitation to democratize art. The intention can be seen in the movement's approach to "everyday art" (*seni rupa keseharian*), where its participants attempted as much as possible to portray a problem without changing its substance. They attempted in one expressive act to unite and harmonize inspiration and expressive rhythm with the problem being explored. The dramatization and reexpression of social problems was not carried out as an individualistic artistic interpretation, but rather as an approach to the problem itself. Where necessary this was accompanied by academic research.[3]

The value of the consciousness afforded by the New Arts Movement is that it smashed the aesthetic hegemony of the "fine arts" over Indonesian art, and liberated a pluralistic concept of art.

"Fine arts" was an exclusive territory, one that could be mastered only by artists from large cities or art academies. The art of the lower classes was regarded as inferior, as mere craft. For the New Arts Movement all artistic phenomena are essentially equal. Differences in their frames of reference give rise to aesthetic differences, notions of value, and artistic function. This means that art should not be classified according to its ranking on some imaginary scale—from A-1 Art to supereconomy-class art. The art of the ordinary people must be given a place and accorded rights.

Nevertheless, in the 1987 New Arts Movement exhibition in Jakarta, *Project I: Fantasy World Supermarket*, popular idioms and icons were displayed, but not the art of the people themselves. The people still stood as objects—mute and passive, while those entitled to speak and appear were only the New Artists. This was a misguided vision of who and what constituted the people.

Art for the Lower Classes

The art critic Dr. Soedjoko rejects this emphasis on fine art. In his "Seni budaya tahun 2000" (Art and culture in the year 2000) he states that for our ancestors art was a skill (*pandai*).[4] The terms *juru, kipu, tukang,* and *utas* all carry implications of "a skilled person." In Javanese the terms *mahir, ahli,* and *pandai* can, among other things, be equated with the term *aguna.* The term *gunawan* means "very skilled, possessed of great knowledge or power." An artist was a *wong guna* (a person of great skill) or a *naraguna.* Art, *seni,* was *guna, kagunan,* or *kapigunan.*

In the *Kamus Jawa Kuno-Indonesia,* (Old Javanese-Indonesian dictionary) the term *guna* is defined as "goodness, good characteristics, character, virtue, ability, skill, expertise, capability, holiness, use, benefit, service, charity, power." It appears that various levels of skill can be called *guna.* The word *guna* also implies moral, religious, authoritative, and ethical dimensions.

The *Bausastra Jawa* (Dictionary of High Javanese) notes the meaning of art as *kagunan* (skill, talent) with the following connotations: 1 *kepinteran* (expertise); 2 *jejasan ingkang adi peni* (a work of great benefit or utility); 3 *wudaring pambudi nganakake kaendahan—gegambaran, kidung, ngukir-ukir* (the outpouring of feeling to produce beauty—in painting, verse, or sculpture and carving). The emphasis on beauty can be sensed in the root word *guna*, which implies character, expertise, creation, and utility.[5]

In defining art in terms of *guna* or *kagunan* (Indonesian: *kegunaan*, skill, utility) both of the above dictionaries define art in Javanese cultural terms. It is obvious from this that a work of art is not something separate from other aspects of life and is not something alienated from the community.

For the Javanese, *kagunan* comes to mean, among other things, painting, poetry/singing, sculpture/carving, musical arts, shadow theater, trance dance, *tayub* dance, *keris* (a Javanese wavy-bladed dagger), mask, dance, and literature.

Based on this understanding of art as *kagunan* [popular craft—*ed.*] it is not difficult to find artists among the ordinary people. We have trance dancers, *tayub* dancers, painters and illustrators, *keris* makers, and many others. The world of art does not know class distinction, only distinctions in the level of quality.

Soedjoko considers ordinary people as art practitioners and art workers. They are subjects. The potential, position, strength, and right to exist of a people's art must be valued. We must guarantee the democratization of art.

The Position of the Ordinary People

The poor are often depicted by some Indonesian artists as objects, with a majority of these depictions centering on the village. At present the poor have to confront an apparatus of power in the form of both formal institutions and a repressive bureaucracy.

Power is an irrefutably instructive power. Faced with such power the poor can only agree and say yes. Powerlessness, the poisoning of norms, the emptiness of meaning, isolation and the self-alienation from new structures engineered by power holders have brought the poor to the level of a "surly but safe" moral subsistence, a condition reflected in a kind of cultural abandon.

The repressive acts of the authorities in land matters, for instance on Pulau Panggung and at Kedung Ombo, provide us with an example of the cultural abandon of the poor. Although people will attempt to endure in the face of powerlessness, the structure and force of the authorities will always give them no other choice than surrender. The roots of this cultural abandon lie in a new form of consciousness, itself rooted in an image of human destiny that is emotional, spiritual, and far removed from the rational.

The institutional mechanisms of the current authorities give the poor very little control over sources of power and their own fate. And this institutional structure does little to accommodate the interests of the poor. This, in addition to the trauma caused by the political events of 1965, has effectively destroyed practical political thought among the poor.

In such repressive conditions, the dynamic of a new lifestyle in the form of various new institutions comes to the fore to overcome this sense of alienation. People lift the gloom from their personal lives by following magical-charismatic leaders or by buying dreams in the form of state lottery tickets every Wednesday.

Apart from this, the poor can find a safety valve for their aspirations and thoughts in artistic expression. Popular art—folklore, for instance—can contain expressions of resistance.

In Surabaya, during the Japanese occupation, there was a popular *ludruk* folk theater figure called Cak Durasim, whose aphoristic songs expressed a particular form of resistance:

> *pagupon omahe doro, melok nipon tambah sengsoro*
> [Keepers of dovecotes, support Japan, increase your misery]

With such lyrics, Cak Durasim directly attacked the Japanese rulers. This resistance is also expressed in the visual arts through glass paintings from Muntilan and Magelang, whose captions included such popular aphorisms as *Melik nggendong lali* (Envy for other's goods; an attitude that easily leads people to forget their basic values), and *Ojo dumeh* (Don't put on airs).

Glass painting is a popular lower-class art form that expresses the aspirations, thoughts, and lore of this class. It is found over a wide area and developed among the ordinary people. It has only been since about 1966 that other vehicles of popular artistic expression have been cut off. Moreover, it is obvious from the "Visit Indonesia Year" program that popular art and culture are being made into commodities to be bought and sold.

The Ordinary People as Subject

Development projects engineered from above by the authorities clearly result in a loss of protection, security, and freedom for the lower classes. Added to this, the lower classes are not always involved in either the planning processes or the realization of these development projects. With regard to land issues, it is quite clear that the lower classes always suffer the consequences of forced resettlement. This is caused by a lack of attention to the idea of social involvement in the development process. The position of the lower classes is one of submission, passive acceptance and that of "object."

Lower-class "cultural resistance" in the face of repressive actions is more often than not based on emotions rather than logic. The lower classes merely adapt, rather than becoming directly involved, because involvement grows out of a critical consciousness. The adaptive human being is a passive human being, an object. The complete human being is a subject, an integrated being. This integration comes from the capacity to adjust to reality, as well as the critical capacity to make choices and change that reality.

Paulo Freire, in his book *Pendidikan sebagai praktek pembebasan* (Education, the practice of freedom) posits the concept of education as a way of transforming people's naive attitudes into critical attitudes, by making people conscious of their role and position not merely as objects, but as subjects.[6] The human being becomes the starting point. Human beings are praxis. We must be aware of our position and role and be actively involved in the course of history. The way to set Freire's concept in train is through being active, through a basic emphasis on dialogue, and by awakening critical attitudes.

Seni Rupa Kagunan

The authorities act in a repressive manner, and the lower classes resort to forms of cultural resistance, which are best seen as a means of temporarily postponing submission and defeat without accentuating the ineffective position of their rights and aspirations. When expressed in art, this cultural resistance has no place of its own nor a place to create. Its place is taken over by the stronger aesthetic norms of modern arts (i.e., the fine arts). While for the lower classes to play a role and become involved in the history, they must become subjects in this process, rather than objects of it.

A people's art attempts to redefine art as both a nonhierarchical practice and a medium controlled completely by the people themselves, as a means of expressing their aspirations for communal autonomy, social justice, and democracy.

The first road we must go down is the one that makes ordinary people aware that they are subjects, who play an active role in propelling the processes of history toward a just and democratic society. As subjects, ordinary people can control media to express their aspirations. The medium of art is one that those aspirations can control.

The fundamental reason for ordinary people to take control of the arts and make artistic activity more a part of their experience is to smash the aesthetic hegemony seen as legitimate by elite arts practitioners in Indonesia.

Indonesian fine artists regard the arena of modern art as something exclusive, to be controlled only by highly talented, sophisticated, and egocentric practitioners, who produce work for a narrow elite band. This frame of reference must be done away with in order to liberate an awareness that art is a skill, a technique, and a practice that can be controlled and practiced by all people. Art is an inalienable aspect of everyday life.

The growth of the awareness that ordinary people should control the medium of the arts needs to be accompanied by arts workers with commitment, care, and partisanship. The function of these assisting arts workers is to give rise to a local arts language and to encourage creative activities for all people. The ordinary people and the arts worker have equal positions as subjects in collectively discussing the social problems they confront.

Art as popular practice is a people's art that expresses the reality, thoughts, reflections, and communal aspirations of ordinary people for autonomy, justice, and democracy.

Y. B. Mangunwijaya's concept of *kagunan* is an appropriate basis for an aesthetic concept of art as a popular practice:

Aesthetic beauty is not some autonomous pleasure, which can be absorbed only by the senses and intellect. Beauty is an aspect of life in its totality. Something is beautiful not because it satisfies a sensory need for harmony or our intellectual desires, but because it is one of life's truths. "Beauty is the splendor of truth" *(pulchrum splendor est veritas)*. Consequently art of quality, whether from near or far, in the final analysis possesses a religious dimension.[7]

Methodology of a People's Art

A people's art is practiced through dialogue, which constitutes a horizontal relationship between individuals. Critical attitudes lie at the core of any dialogue, and dialogue spreads those critical attitudes. Dialogue makes real communication possible. Through trust, dialogue possesses both strength and meaning: trust in people and their abilities, and a conviction that people will become their real selves when others also become genuine.

All people are subjects, and as such they hold equal positions in initiating dialogue. Ordinary people who have problems and an assisting arts worker have an equal position: to engage in a mutual dialogue to discuss and search for solutions through the medium of art.

Ordinary people who have problems represent the central source of information and work according to their knowledge. The assisting arts worker helps put their understanding of their problems into sharper focus. The worker is an arts practitioner who provides his or her creativity as an act of true partisanship. The role of an arts worker is to assist in the regrowth of a popular artistic aesthetic by aiding in the creation of art forms of high quality rooted in traditional culture, the environment, and everyday lifestyles. This also should not be seen merely as "social work." The arts worker can also learn much from his or her involvement that will sharpen his or her own aesthetic dimensions.

This dialogical method is based on the idea that human beings represent praxis. Human beings think, act, work, relate to their environment, have a social existence in the world, and are able to distance themselves from their environment and their actions to alter their environment. While humans live, there will be praxis in the form of action and reflection.

People's Art as Action

In 1986 "people's art" was offered to the inhabitants of the hamlets of Brumbun and Nggerangan in the village of Ngrejo, in the Tanggunggunung district of the Tulungagung Regency. Brumbun and Nggerangan are situated twenty-six kilometers south of Tulungagung, on a bay on the Indian Ocean.

Brumbun is inhabited by approximately a hundred people, including thirty-four heads of household, who occupy twenty-nine simple houses. These people settled here to survive or to improve their lives, after being landless or occupying infertile land in their original villages, or having failed as transmigrants. They originally hailed from the villages of Bangun Mulyo, Tulungrejo, Ngentrong, and Kalidawir, where they farmed small holdings.

In 1963 the Forestry Service Office in Blora and the authorities in the Campurdarat district allowed them to settle on Brumbun Bay on the following conditions: (1) they could occupy land but would have no ownership rights to it; (2) they must cultivate coconuts and pay a rental of two coconuts each month to the local forestry official. Drinking water is taken from a well in the hills to the south of their settlement. Education facilities consist of a small primary school, which uses a modular system of instruction. As of this writing, the school consists of four teachers and twenty-five students.

Nggerangan is situated two kilometers north of Brumbun and is also on the coast. The hamlet consists of fourteen heads of household in a total population of fifty-two persons. Like the people of Brumbun, they are migrants and occupy their land under the same conditions. Their main source of income is farming: approximately four hectares of land are available for wet rice cultivation and there are sufficient groundwater springs for this form of farming. Their socioeconomic conditions are lower than those of the people of Brumbun.

The form of people's art initially offered was drawing, following these stages:

Mastery of Line and Form

Line is a basic element in art. Drawing lines (scribbling) is a fundamental phase in childhood development and is an experience derived from play. This scribbling phase is then followed by making lines into simple shapes (e.g., an egg or a person's head). This in turn is followed by drawing forms from everyday surroundings: fish, boats, people. When people are able to draw objects from their surroundings, they come to the sudden realization: "I can draw!" The arts worker-helper has to convince individuals that they really can draw. Any simple instrument can be used to draw: chalk on a board or the floor, a pencil on paper, or a stick or finger in the sand.

Drawing the Surrounding Reality

This is done by first observing objects and people that are close to the artist. The artist then more sharply focuses on objects or people involved in a particular event (e.g., members of the community quarreling over their allocation of drinking water). The drawing that results is then displayed in a place that is frequently visited by people, and the picture will carry a certain message (e.g., don't quarrel loudly or else a picture will be drawn, displayed, and everyone will know about your quarrel). People then become aware that drawings become a medium for the expression of reality and a form of critical communication to change attitudes.

Drawing as a Medium of Dialogue

When every member of the community is able to draw, then the community is collectively able to enter into a dialogue and critically discuss community problems. Members of the community are subjects at the center of the drawing. The arts worker only assists in sharpening the focus on the particular problem, by eliciting questions from members of the community. It is members of the community themselves who develop their analyses and strategies. Interest in the critical analysis of problems can become intense, and a high level of participation can link the problem to the experiences, interests, and emotions of the participants.

Through the production of collective drawings on a large sheet of paper (or in the sand on the beach) by members of the community, anybody with any thoughts on the problem being discussed becomes involved, immediately and directly, in the process of drawing. This drawing process is a process of collective thought, in the form of a dialogue that maps out and determines attitudes toward that problem.

Art as a Medium for Aspirations

When every member of the community is convinced that they can draw, they are offered instruction in other artistic media, according to their level of ability and their aims, for instance, the production of black-and-white woodcuts. Woodcuts were chosen because not much skill is required and the results can be easily reproduced and distributed. They can also be created from local materials.

If the community faces a particular problem, whose solution requires the involvement of people outside of the community, the community then instigates a program of exhibitions outside the community. Such art exhibitions are useful for information, communication, spreading messages, expressing ideals, inviting dialogue, and searching for advocacy of the problems the community faces.

Reflections of a People's Art

The process of instituting a people's art program in the Brumbun and Nggerangan communities was not as straightforward as suggested above. The first group of artists were primary school students. During the fishing season, parents stop the children from drawing, as the children have to work with their parents, pulling in nets or taking fish from the nets once they are ashore. The parents think that drawing does not produce money and that the children should spend their time pulling in nets, rather than drawing. To convince the people that drawing, too, could produce money, an exhibition of the children's work was organized in the city. Their art works were auctioned off and the proceeds used to buy them school uniforms and to build a cistern and plastic pipes for drinking water for the village.

The second group of artists were local adults. Their task was to discuss the provision of drinking water, community relations, and land matters. This activity was halted by the local district authority, as it was regarded as having political content. Subsequent activities involved only primary school children.

In 1988 the work of the school children and their mentor was exhibited in Jakarta. The results of this exhibition were reported to the regent of Tulungagung, who was clearly interested in the problem of local poverty. The regent then visited the villages and ordered the construction of an asphalt road. The local economy was improved with the availability of transport for the fish catch and transport for local tourists to Brumbun Bay. The positive impact of art as action was felt by the inhabitants of both Brumbun and Nggerangan.

The Indonesian government declared 1991 to be Visit Indonesia Year. The subprovincial government at Tulungagung then declared that Brumbun Bay and Nggerangan were to become tourist attractions. According to a press release, the tourist project proposal of the Tulungagung Local Development Authority and a model of the development mentioned among other things: the building of a parking area at Brumbun, a traditional restaurant, a crocodile farm, and tennis courts. At Nggerangan, a swimming pool was to be built right on the rice fields. Written on the proposal was the note: Local fishing village to be relocated.

This was a crisis. After Brumbun and Nggerangan had become known for their natural beauty, the local pioneering inhabitants were to be moved from their land. It was also a problem because of the impact of art and the reality of the position of the ordinary people as objects of the authorities' engineering plans. We are now preparing an exhibition on the lack of knowledge of the local communities of Brumbun and Nggerangan concerning the Indonesian national priority of tourism.

In Indonesia, people's art has not yet attracted the interest of "professional" artists or led them to become arts assistants to the ordinary people. It has been social scientists, NGOs, and student activists who have been interested. The people's art movement has intensified its efforts as a result of receiving funds for its art assistants from the Ashoka Indonesia Foundation.

A people's arts program has been offered to women workers from the All Indonesia Trade Union (SPSI) in Surabaya, but was stopped by the coordinator at the point of discussing the problem, because they had to get permission from the national leadership of the SPSI in Jakarta.

A wood collector living in a house on the edge of the jungle accepted and applied people's art principles to the medium of glass painting. One of his works, "Ojo dumeh" (Don't put on airs), critically analyzes the control of the economy in Tulungagung by a small group of Indonesian Chinese. He depicted himself as Gareng (one of the clown figures of the *wayang* shadow theater), as a servant. In people's art the process of changing consciousness and promoting a critical autonomy is of greater value than artistic achievement. Artistic supremacy is a way point that must be passed in order to reach a better standard of living. Art is only a medium.

(translated by Paul Tickell)

Notes

1. *Yogya Post,* 24 January 1981.
2. *Tempo,* 16 September 1989.
3. *Katalogus: Seni rupa baru proyek satu "Pasaraya Dunia Fantasi"* (Jakarta: Galeri Baru, Taman Ismail Marzuki, 15–30 June, 1987.
4. Soedjoko, *Seni budaya tahun 2000.*
5. *Katalogus: Seni rupa baru,* 1987.
6. Paulo Freire, *Pendidikan sebagai praktek pembebasan,* (Jakarta: PT Gramedia, 1984).
7. Ariel Heryanto, *Perdebatan sastra kontekstual* (Jakarta: CV Rajawali, 1985).

Chapter Five

Power and Culture: The Abipraya Society of Surakarta in the Early Twentieth Century

Kuntowijoyo

THIS IS A STUDY of the relationship between power and culture: how power defines the production of symbols, and, conversely, how the symbolic world reflects the predominance of power. Michel Foucault once remarked, "We are subjected to the production of truth through power and we cannot exercise power except through the production of truth."[1] Nor can we separate the symbolic from the actual, or culture from political power. In this light, the culture of bureaucracy is certainly related to the exercise of a given political power. Thus, it is regrettable that many studies on the culture of the Javanese *priyayi* (aristocrats or officials) have not taken into account the context of power within which the culture operates: the Javanese political system. Today, we are in need of a critical study of *priyayi* culture. It is only through such a study that a balanced account of the *priyayi* will surface.

The *priyayi* and its culture has attracted many scholars from various disciplines. Clifford Geertz was among the first to be interested in the *priyayi* culture in postcolonial Indonesia. His book *The Religion of Java* (1960) is a study of *priyayi* culture as a religious category within Javanese society.[2] Geertz, however, did not put the *priyayi* in a political perspective—that is, he did not relate the birth of *priyayi* culture to the history of power in Javanese society. Almost at the same time, Leslie Palmier treated the *priyayi* as a distinct social class fully conscious of the relationship between social class and the structure of power. However, his interest was mainly in the study of kinship systems.[3] His study gave much information on social aspects of *priyayi* culture, as did Geertz on the religious aspect; nevertheless it lacked a critical view of the *priyayi*.

Among historians, Akira Nagazumi was probably the first to appreciate the *priyayi* as the early-twentieth-century founder of Budi Utomo, considered the first nationalist movement to arise in Indonesia.[4] He gave much credit to the *priyayi*, but forgot to expose the other side of *priyayi* culture. However, Soemarsaid Moertono was one of the historians who gave too much credit to the *priyayi*. In *State and Statecraft in Old Java: A Study of the Later Mataram Period, Sixteenth to Nineteenth Century* he described the virtuous life of the special social class called *satria* (traditional aristocracy), depicted as being literate and courageous.[5] What he had in mind was certainly the noble characteristics of the *satria* as they were depicted in the literary works of Tripama and Wedatama in the nineteenth century. Savitri Prastiti Scherer's *Keselarasan dan kejanggalan: Pemikiran-pemikiran priyayi nasionalis Jawa awal abad XX* (Harmony and discord: Javanese *priyayi* nationalist thought at the beginning of the twentieth century), also attempts to paint the *priyayi* in a positive light.[6] Mostly a book on the history of ideas, it is also an exposé of the *priyayi* as, to use the contemporary term, *bangsawan pikiran,* or intellectual nobility.[7] It is true that many *priyayi* had contributed to the development of cultural and political activities in the past, but the ignorance of the most critical side of the *priyayi* world is regrettable.

Likewise, *The Making of a Bureaucratic Elite* by Heather Sutherland reveals valuable information on the evolution of the *priyayi*, yet its main focus is the role of the *priyayi* in the administration, as the title suggests.[8] It is a book on the *bupati* (regent) of colonial Java, and the repressive rule of Dutch officials over the native regents. The colonial powers granted only cultural freedoms—for example, it was easy to gain permission to go to the theater and to *tayuban* (Javanese dance) parties, while it was almost impossible for political meetings. This small piece of information tells much of the laxity of the *priyayi* lifestyle. Such cultural activities were the only chance for the *priyayi* to move around. It is precisely the issues of repression and freedom that this paper is trying to elaborate.

Recently, Indonesian scholars have studied the *priyayi* culture. *Kebudayaan Jawa*, (Javanese Culture) by Koentjaraningrat, for example, features one chapter devoted to the *priyayi*, "Kebudayaan Jawa di kota" (Urban Javanese culture).[9] While it is true, Koentjaraningrat says, that *priyayi* are mostly urban, *priyayi*-ness is not a spatial concept. The book discusses the group's kinship system, occupation, leisure time, and artistic activities. Sartono's *Perkembangan peradaban priyayi* (The rise of *priyayi* culture) contains chapters on the symbolic world of the *priyayi*, their lifestyle, and their spiritual life.[10] What Sartono's book lacks is the political context of *priyayi* culture.

The Abipraya Society

Scholars have barely touched one important side of the *priyayi* culture. The Abipraya, a *priyayi* association established in Surakarta at the turn of the century, provides an example of how the life of the *priyayi* was conducted in the early twentieth century.[11] The Abipraya claimed itself to be a *priyayi* organization. A book published by an affiliated association in 1905 mentioned that the publication was intended for the members of the Abipraya and *priyantun sanesipun*, (other *priyayi*).[12] At that time the *priyayi* were the only ones conscious of their role as promoters of progress within Javanese society. The book was thus published to be "jalaraning kamajenganipun bangsa kula tetiyang Jawi," (in the cause of the progress of the Javanese). It is true, for the word *abipraya* was officially taken as a synonym for *olah sengsem*, or an endeavor toward the love of virtue.[13] The official ideology was only practiced in part, when the Abipraya managed to nurse the birth of the Surakarta chapter of Budi Utomo in 1908.[14] Yet, more often than not, as this article is trying to show, the ideology of progress was betrayed by the practice of its members.

The Abipraya was one of the many associations of the *priyayi* which served as avenues for the expression of social and cultural identity. It seems that in the early twentieth century, the *priyayi* had established itself as a distinct social group. The ideology of the Abipraya was shared by other *priyayi* associations; those that appeared in the newspapers were Mardihatmoko of Sukaharjo, a subregency in Surakarta,[15] and Bondolumekso of Surakarta.[16] When Mas Ngabehi Sudiro Husodo, also a *priyayi*, was touring from Yogyakarta to Batavia in 1906 to raise funds for needy students, the *priyayi* newspaper of Surakarta, *Darmo Konda*, published an article entitled "Rukun adamel santosa" (Unity makes us strong), an attempt to unify the members of the *priyayi* class. Although the formal ideology of the Abipraya was progress, Pandrio Hardjo, a *priyayi* association in Banjarnegara, central Java, frankly stated that besides its promotion of the importance of reading books, it was established as an association for leisure activities.[17] It is worth noting that around 1907, in the Mangkunegara part of Surakarta, a *priyayi* association was also founded. It was the Mardi Taya, a cultural association devoted to the advancement of Javanese music and dance.[18] The local newspaper reported that many other associations were established in other cities. In Yogyakarta there were Mardi Harjo and Studie Fonds of Sudiro Husodo; in Surabaya, Rekso Wibowo and Panti Harsoyo; in Madiun, Mardi Harjo; and in Nganjuk, Hamong Projo. The reporter stated that the associations were of the young generation, the *para muda ing jaman sapunika.*[19] A small town like Kudus, in central Java, was reported to have several associations in 1909, some of which were *priyayi* organizations. They were Budi Utomo; Susilo Mardi Prasastra, a recreational (*kamar bolah*) group; Rukun Utama, a business association; Boga Sudarmo, a dinner association; Makhalul Adab, a business and religious learning association; Among Kliyeg, a Monday tour association; Courant Vereeniging, a newspaper-reading association; and, most curiously, mention was made of a Chinese bandit association (Perkumpulan Buaya Barat).[20]

In Surakarta itself there were still more associations. Mention was made in early 1909 of the establishment of Narendro Putra, an association for the nobility,[21] which may have been the forerunner of Narpowandowo. While the Abipraya was a *priyayi* association of the native ruling bureaucracy, those of the colonial *priyayi* established Lenardono, which organized the *priyayi* employees of the Binnenlands Bestuur, their education, and the opium service shops. One of the most important cultural associations was Mardi Basa, an organization founded by Mas Ngabehi Wirapustaka, a great literary figure at the time. Mardi Basa, which was already ten years old in 1912, was intended to be a forum for the advancement of Javanese, especially for the preservation of the refined *krama* level of the language.[22] There may be more unrecorded *priyayi* associations in Surakarta—for example, there is evidence of a certain *priyayi* funeral association established in 1914.[23] Surakarta was already a complex society in the early twentieth century.

While other associations were not reported to have had good management, the Abipraya was not only managed well, but it also had a permanent building for the organization's activities. Every official ceremony of the Abipraya was well organized, with a detailed plan of its proceedings distributed beforehand.[24] The president was elected from among the higher officials (*bupati*) by popular consent. Housekeepers were even appointed through bureaucratic procedure.[25] Such management was possible only because of the involvement of the office of Parentah Ageng Kapatihan (Secretariat of the Royal Government). The Kapatihan released an official order that all *abdi dalam* (court retainers and officials) of the Parentah Ageng (including the positions of *wadana, kliwon, panewu, mantri jawi-lebet sahanon-hanonipun,* and *pulisi pamajegan*), and all the *abdi dalam* of the rank of *lurah* (village head), should join the Abipraya. The maintenance costs of the Abipraya were to be shared by all the associates in accordance with the size of their salary (*lungguh*).[26] The Abipraya included all the *abdi dalam* under the administration of the Kapatihan, but excluded those working for the palace proper or those in the service of the nobility. In so doing, the Abipraya limited itself to the *priyayi* of the bureaucracy.

Who were the *priyayi?* We lack invaluable information of the *priyayi* of Surakarta, because documents that were published annually around 1900 containing lists of the *priyayi* (*Solosche Javaansche almanak*), have not so far been located.[27] We can only use the vague information found in oral statements and writings. Taking account of contemporary sources, the *priyayi* were employees of the colonial government (*abdining kangjeng gubernemen*) and *abdi dalam* of the *susuhunan*. Those who served the king were certainly of the *priyayi*.[28] At the time, *priyayi* seemed to be an ideal position to attain. It was reported that a teacher in a subsidized school, that is, actually a private school, with a monthly salary of f 17.50, was applying for a position in the pawnshop department with a salary of only f 10, in order to become a government official, or *priyayi*.[29]

Priyayi-ness was much honored at the time, when the central powers, the *kraton* (palace), and the colonial bureaucracy monopolized both symbolic and actual properties. It was the time when literature as a symbolic form emphasized the value of an affirmative culture. *Serat mas jenthu inggih mas nganten* by R. M. A. Jayadiningrat I, published in 1907 by his great grandson R. T. Jayadiningrat (an *abdi dalam wadana* in the Surakarta palace), was a *priyayi* document on the importance of hierarchy in society.[30] The book satirized, through stories à la Don Quixote, the impossibility of *wong cilik* (literally, "little people") taking on the symbols of the *priyayi*. The concluding phrase was, "common people must behave as common people, *priyayi* must behave as *priyayi*" (*desa cara desa, priyayi cara priyayi*).

While Jayadiningrat's book was written in the nineteenth century, the works of Padmosusastro on Javanese language (*Serat patibasa*), ceremonies (*Serat tatacara*), and etiquette (*Serat subasita*) were of the early twentieth century. The books illustrate how the concept of *priyayi* was embedded in the heart of everyday life. *Serat subasita*, for example, contains a dictionary of good conduct assigned to the Javanese *priyayi*.[31] In the introduction, the writer tells the readers that existing Javanese etiquette should conform to the dominant culture of the Dutch whenever the two cultures conflicted. The sign of a cultured man was seen as his ability to adopt such etiquette. Padmasusastra lived in a time when progressive culture meant, in the main, Western lifestyle. It was at this time that the Javanese (as well as the Chinese) started cutting their long hair. The first ruler to allow the *priyayi* and members of the military troops to cut their hair was the Kasunanan, which announced its decision only in 1914.[32] It was also the time that the Javanese first used toothbrushes. Padmasusastra told the *priyayi* readers not to keep their teeth black (*sisig*); it was crude behavior (*degsura*). He also advised against wearing baggy trousers like those worn by the Chinese, with flashy blues and greens. This was acceptable for the unlettered, but *degsura* for a *priyayi*. If you wore an eyeglass, you would have removed it when you met a fellow Javanese, but it was acceptable when you met a Dutch person.

Padmasusastra well represented the world of the *priyayi* in the early twentieth century. Not only was the world of the *priyayi* represented in such how-to books, it was also manifested in the fiction of the time. Among the works of Sulardi, the novel *Serat riyanta*, set in the first decade of this century, depicted the love story of a son and daughter of the *priyayi*.[33] Through the novel, we can see closely the lifestyle of the *priyayi*, both of the old nobility and the new bureaucratic families.

Change in the life of the *priyayi* took place in the second decade of the twentieth century. In addition to allowing its members to cut their hair, the Abipraya announced that it would allow them to participate in the activities of the association without uniform dress—including the *kuluk* hat—assigned according to their place in the hierarchy. The proposal for free dress was put forward in 1912, but did not come into effect until 1914.[34] Thereafter, the *jas* and *cripu* became the fashion of the *priyayi* in their leisure time. Despite the progressive culture, however, the *priyayi* themselves could not escape from the old ideology, since the old sources of power were still in place. The most revealing phenomenon of the affirmative culture in Surakarta took place in 1915, when jubilant city dwellers celebrated the official second marriage of Pakubuwana X.[35]

The Priyayi Ideology: Political Mysticism and Hedonism

If we have to summarize the ideology of the *priyayi*, it would be political mysticism on the one hand and hedonism on the other. These two concepts will suffice to describe the world of the most fortunate subjects of the *susuhunan* of Surakarta. The political mysticism was revealed through literary and ceremonial symbolism. *Wedamadya* (Path to higher knowledge) was published in 1898, and republished in 1906.[36] The book was an homage to the king of Surakarta, as symbolized by the inscription (*candrasangkala*) *suka nembah ngesti katong* by a prince of Pakualaman, Yogyakarta, who accompanied the head of the Pakualaman principality in attending a ceremony in the palace of the *susuhunan* of Surakarta. It was known that intermarriage between the two Javanese palaces had resulted in Pakualaman sharing many of the Surakarta cultural patterns. The name of the editor, Padmasusastra of Surakarta, appeared on the front cover, and the author was only secretly alluded to in the text. The book unmistakably depicts the political ideology of the *priyayi*. Pakubuwana X was depicted as Kresna, the King of Dwarawati in the Mahabarata, the reincarnation (*titisan*) of the god Wisnu. It is true that at the time of the celebration, the *susuhunan* of Surakarta could well be described as Kresna, as he had a relatively small figure. The *susuhunan* in his throne was like a god descending to earth (*dewa angeja wantah*). He was also well versed in Western social dances. Skillfully performing the polonaise, he gracefully took the hand of the president's wife and took to the floor. Palace ceremonies, such as the celebration of the coronation day, the birthday of the king, and the *garebeg* (Muslim festivals), were political rituals with a deeper meaning than just celebration. They were political rituals with a more transcendental emphasis. Such ceremony was an exercise of truth, rather than an act of service. Consider how participation in the daily service (*seba*), when the *priyayi/abdi dalam* were on duty in the palace, was described by a literary source. R. M. A. Jayadiningrat's work, published in 1908, claims that *seba* was an act of hermitage. For an *abdi dalam* the best place to meditate was not outside daily life in the kingdom, but in the audience hall (*paseban*) while waiting for the words of the king.[37]

The conduct of *abdi dalam* was standardized. The local newspaper once published advice for proper manners. Good manners included language skill, bodily movement, facial appearance, speaking ability, and moral restraint. Deviant behavior was considered to be a great sin against the king, the *amurbeng bumi*.[38] One may doubt that such literary works have anything to do with the real political world. A newspaper account will certainly eliminate any such doubt. *Darmo Konda*, in 1912, reported on the death of Raden Tumenggung Sastrodiningrat in words that revealed the ideology of political mysticism.[39] Sastrodiningrat was the chairperson of Budi Utomo, Surakarta chapter, when he died. Though he had noble origins, he started his career in the service of the kingdom as a palace apprentice (*punakawan*). His actual appointment did not take place until 1881, and, after some twenty years of service, he was elevated to the position of (royal official (*raden tumenggung*), and appointed as *bupati* to head the secretarial office of the palace (*abdi dalam carik*). His career within the palace and in society made him a popular and much-respected figure in Surakarta. In times of difficulty, when the family of the *susuhunan* faced economic problems due to financial reform, he was reported to have bravely advised the king and his family to be spendthrifts—something nobody else dared to do. Within society, he was known to have lectured the common people in the kampongs with great success. He was known to be friendly to *wong cilik*. Thus, his death deprived the Surakartanese of a living example of a true *priyayi*. When he died, the *susuhunan* awarded him the right of a burial place in the royal tomb of Imogiri. The local newspaper reported that his only obsession, the highest honor he sought, was to die under the feet of the king (*pejah wonten sangandaping sampeyan dalem*).

The Abipraya building was the locus of a specifically *priyayi* culture. In addition to being a meeting place, it was used as an auction place, where people (mainly Dutch) who were moving, or who had died, could sell their property to the public. The building was run by the Abipraya, and a Dutch *vendumeester* would lead the auction.[40] It was also a place where both Western music and Javanese gamelan were performed. On these occasions, the *priyayi* were required to wear proper attire, the *baju sikepan, bebed,* and *kuluk.*

Important events in the building usually related to the palace. In March 1904 a procession was held to replace the old picture of the *susuhunan* in the building with a new one. On that occasion, the picture of the *susuhunan* was placed in a carriage (*kereta*) with two horses, while on the left and the right sides of the *kereta* two men with torches (*obor*) walked slowly.[41] The procession was held in the evening, when the contrast of darkness and light gave an aura of spirituality. The same procession took place in August 1905, this time in honor of the medal presented by the Dutch kingdom to the *susuhunan*, called "Ridder Tweede Klasse van den Rooden Adelaar van Priosen met de Ster." In the evening, the *priyayi* walked from the Abipraya at Coyudan Street to the palace to pick up the medal, which was to be brought to the society building. The medal was placed in a box, wrapped in golden paper, and loaded in a *kereta* that moved in the very front of the line. The medal was removed from the *kereta* and placed in the building, where the attendants could show their respect. Thereafter, they held a toast for the *susuhunan,* listened to the gamelan, and had dinner. The medal was then returned to the palace in the same manner.[42]

Graphic descriptions of such ceremonies usually appeared in the local newspapers. They were announced in the form of *pranatan* (plans) which contained detailed plans of the occasion, sometimes published two weeks before time, and the news of the event appeared about two weeks later. The *pranatan* of the ceremony for the reception of the medal given by the Chinese government in August 1909 to the *susuhunan,* the Siang Liong Po Sing, was to be celebrated at the end of October 1909, yet the detailed plan was published continuously from mid-October. It seems that the standard rule for these ceremonies was, first, the members of the Abipraya collected the medal from the palace; second, the medal was taken to the center of the auditorium; third, the members proceeded to the room to pay homage to the *susuhunan* in groups of eight; and fourth, the *kundisi,* or toast, was held in honor of the *susuhunan.* In the report, the full text of the song was published, sixteen stanzas in all, with a prelude. The song was nothing more than an aggrandizement of the king. It was also reported that when the Patih entered the building, Javanese gamelan, playing "Gending ladrangan," and Western music, "Neerlandsche bloed," were in the air. The Chinese lieutenant and the heads of the five Chinese kampongs attended the ceremony. The ceremony was held from early in the evening until one o'clock in the morning, when the Patih left. Then it continued with an auction and, as usual, was concluded by a *tayuban* dance until morning.[43] We can only guess how much time the *priyayi* spent for their king in a day.

The same celebration took place in April 1910, when the *susuhunan* received a medal from Herzog van Mecklenburg. The proceedings were the same, yet the celebration song was different—this time twelve stanzas—due to the creativity of those *abdi dalam* in charge. Reports in the newspaper describe how the *kundisi* was held. The twelve stanzas were sung while the guests entered the center of the auditorium to pay respect to the medal. After all the members had finished the ritual they sat down, and soon glasses of wine were distributed. The Patih started the toast. Everybody stood up. All the guests responded in a chorus of loud voices, the music played "Neerlandsche bloed," and the gamelan sent a wave of "Pathet barang" in ten stanzas.[44] After the departure of the Patih, the *priyayi* were not willing to miss the *tayuban* party, which lasted until the morning of the next day.

I have mentioned how the *priyayi's* political mysticism is mixed with pleasure. How can we measure this hedonistic ideology? Let us recall the story of the celebration of the replacement of the *susuhunan*'s picture in the Abipraya building in March 1904. I have not mentioned as yet that there was also a kind of *pasar malam,* night market, on that occasion. Those who attended the stalls were deliberately described by local newspaper as being very beautiful (*roggeng*), with very charming faces.[45] The word *roggeng* can also refer to either a dancer or a woman with moral laxity. In either case, the presence of women was emphasized in the report. It is not only the fact itself that reveals something, but also that it was news. It seems that womanizing, in various degrees, was part of the *priyayi* culture. A certain member of the nobility (*mas ngabehi*) was reported to have slept with a village prostitute while serving as an escort to the *susuhunan*'s family in the summer house of Tegalgondo. Unfortunately, said the report, the weather was bad, and the wind blew so hard that the thatched house fell down. The *mas ngabehi* and the woman survived the accident. What makes the story more meaningful is the state of the *bei* and the woman when people came to help: the *mas bei* was lying under the woman. The reporter did not forget to make a cheerful comment, a *pantun,* describing the position they were in while making love.[46] Of course, this is just one newspaper report.

As for alcohol, a report on the party held by a *mas ngabehi* in the Abipraya in 1904 mentioned the use of bright electricity, gamelan music, and champagne. The *priyayi*, the Dutch, and the Chinese toasted three times.[47] Alcohol prepared the *priyayi* for the upcoming *tayuban.* The *Serat Centhini* informs us of how a *tayuban* was held in the nineteenth century. When performing the *tayub,* a man could do many things on the stage. The most usual case was that a man dancing with a *roggeng* should give some money to her. The money would be slipped inside the woman's *kemben* (breast cloth). In the meantime, the man could grab her breast and pinch the nipple with his fingers. What mattered most here was the status of the man and the beauty of the woman. The higher the status of the man, the more be should give to the *roggeng*. The more beautiful the *roggeng*, the more people should give her. Often a man would go bankrupt while dancing with a *roggeng*, because he paid too much money or gave whatever he wore to the woman. It seems that in the early twentieth century, such habits were still common, even among the *priyayi*. The more refined way to give money to the *roggeng* was to put it in a special plate provided for that purpose. However, the influence of alcohol made it unlikely that this rule would be observed.

Almost no reports on activities in the Abipraya failed to mention the *tayub* parties, often with the name of the *roggeng* announced beforehand. The *tayub* parties were even performed for *Wilujengan* in the month of *mulud*, after the *garebag* was over.[48] In the month of *mulud* there was the *sekaten* festival, in commemoration of the birth of the Prophet Muhammad. In the context of strict Islamic *syaria*, such celebrations were unlikely. Not only in the month of *mulud*, but also in celebration of the *lebaran* (fasting month), *tayub* was held. It was reported that the nobilities—the *bupati*, the *wadana*, and the officers of the palace guard—held a *klenengan* (gamelan concert) party and *tayuban* for the celebration of *lebaran*. The *klenengan* took place in the evening, followed by the *tayuban*, which lasted until dawn.[49] The months of *mulud* and *lebaran* were the times for festivities, thus *tayuban* could be considered culturally admissible. The *priyayi* also like to have *tayuban* parties in the month of *sura*, which the Javanese consider to be the sacred month, when no festivities should be performed. Thus, such a celebration was held when the Abipraya elected a new president on the first day of *sura*, the very date which used to be full of mystical meaning. On that occasion, it is reported that they got drunk on gin and lost their self-control.[50]

It was not only in the Abipraya building that the *tayub* was held. A *priyayi* could also have a *tayub* party in his home on his own initiative. In 1909 some fifty-five *priyayi* celebrated the marriage of four daughters of the *susuhunan* with a *tayub* party in one of their homes. It was reported that the people got so drunk that the party was in chaos.[51]

Tayuban was, of course, not the only amusement for the *priyayi*. They also loved music. The Kapatihan orchestra was versed in playing Western classical music. The Abipraya occasionally invited the company to perform such music for its members.[52] In addition, they also loved *wireng*, a choreography consisting of an episode of the *wayang*.[53] As the most fortunate members of Surakartan society, the *priyayi* certainly could afford to consume many things offered by the growing city culture, such as good food, movies, *komidie stambul* (stage shows), circuses, and cigars. Finally, there were also reports on the vices of the *priyayi*, such as cockfighting and gambling, though the government of Surakarta had made such activities illegal for *priyayi*.[54]

Of course, despite the vices, there were also reports on positive things about *priyayi*. They often listened to lectures on education, progress, and the economic condition of the Javanese. They also learned Javanese mysticism and theosophy. Nevertheless, criticism was often directed at the *priyayi*. On *tayub* and women, a writer advised moderately that *priyayi* should not drink too much at a party lest they lose control and humiliate themselves. An honorable man should not make the *tayuban* an opportunity to express his lust for a woman, and if he should do so, he should do it when the party was over, not in the presence of honorable women and nobility.[55] A writer from Ponorogo wrote a serialized article in *Darmo Konda* entitled "Nasehat akan goena mengoerangkan bahaja wang jang ada timboel pada prijaji-prijaji Djawa" (Advice for reducing the danger of spending money that belongs to the Javanese *priyayi*). The writer gave a detailed formula for dancing: a *bupati* should give only f 5 to f 10 while dancing; a *patih,* f 2.50 to f 5; a *jaksa,* with a f 260 salary should only give f 2.50; and lower *priyayi* with only f 15 salaries should give less than f 1, if he did not want to be broke.[56] A book by Swara, *Bab alaki rabi: Wayuh kaliyan boten* (On marriage: Polygamy or monogamy), fiercely attacked the Javanese *priyayi* as being unenlightened, and for becoming the slave of their lust: while their libido was much like that of the Arab, and higher than that of the Chinese, in working and saving they were less diligent than either of those races.[57]

Thus was the picture of an affirmative culture.[58] How affirmative the culture was in early-twentieth-century Surakarta was illustrated by the jubilant celebration of the marriage of the *susuhunan* to the daughter of the Sultan of Yogyakarta in December 1905. Not only did the *priyayi* association Abipraya and the nobility association Narpo Wandowo take part in the occasion, but members of the new *priyayi* association Budi Utomo and the *santri* association Sarekat Islam also rallied in fancy costumes around the city. Certainly, the celebration meant something for one group and something else for other groups. Yet the basic nature was still that of an affirmative culture. In conclusion, what I have in mind is not the Abipraya itself but, through historical parallelism, the KORPRI (Korpus Pegawai Republik Indonesia) in our own time—mutatis mutandis.

Notes

1. Michel Foucault, *Power/Knowledge: Selected Interviews and Other Writings, 1972–1977* (New York: Pantheon Books, 1980), 93.

2. Clifford Geertz, *The Religion of Java* (Glencoe, Ill.: Free Press, 1960).

3. Leslie Palmer, *Social Status and Power in Java* (London: Athlone Press, University of London, 1969).

4. Akira Nagazumi, *The Dawn of Indonesian Nationalism: The Early*

Years of the Budi Utomo, 1908–1918 (Tokyo: Institute of Developing Economies, 1972).

5. Soemarsaid Moertono, *State and Statecraft in Old Java: A Study of the Later Mataram Period, Sixteenth to Nineteenth Century* (Ithaca: Cornell University Modern Indonesia Project, Cornell University Press, 1968).

6. Savitri Prastiti Scherer, *Keselarasan dan kejanggalan: Pemikiran-pemikiran priyayi nasionalis Jawa awal abad XX* (Jakarta: Sinar Harapan, 1985).

7. Si Boeroeng, "Voor Darmo Konda," *Darmo Konda*, 6 January 1908.

8. Heather Sutherland, *The Making of a Bureaucratic Elite: The Colonial Transformation of the Javanese Priyayi* (Singapore: Heinemann, 1979).

9. Koentjaraningrat, *Kebudayaan Jawa* (Jakarta: Balai Pustaka, 1984).

10. Sartono Kartodirdjo et. al., *Perkembangan peradaban priyayi* (The rise of *priyayi* culture) (Yogyakarta: Gadjah Mada University Press, 1987).

11. The birth date of the Abipraya is still to be identified, but it is certain that in 1901 the association already existed; a business advertisement gives its location as next to the Abipraya building, on what is today Coyudan Street. See *De nieuwe vorstenlanden*, 18 March 1901.

12. *Serat pamoring jaler estri* (Surakarta: Vogel van der Heijde for Waradarma Association, 1905). The book was translated from a Dutch text called *De mensch in 't geslachtleven*. The translator was not named, but Ngabehi Wirapustaka or Padmasusastra is mentioned. See the introductory chapter.

13. Ibid.

14. *Darmo Konda*, 15 October 1908. The inaugural meeting of Budi Utomo, Surakarta chapter, was held at the Abipraya building. At the time, Raden Tumenggung Joyonagoro was elected president, and Mas Ngabehi Reksoprojo vice president. Certainly both were members of Abipraya.

15. *Darmo Konda*, 17 October 1904.

16. *Darmo Konda*, 15 March 1906.

17. *Darmo Konda*, 11 May 1908.

18. *Darmo Konda*, 11 March 1907. The Mardi Taya was organized in the house of Raden Ngabehi Citrosantono, an *adbi dalam guru* in Mangkunegara. It had twenty members, each contributing fifty cents a month to pay for music crews (*niyaga*) and snacks. It is reported that the Mardi Taya attempted, among other things, to train its members to be well prepared whenever *tayuban* dances were held, because *priyayi* were *saru* (literally, "indecent") and unlikely to be able to dance properly on such occasions.

19. *Darmo Konda*, 23 May 1907.

20. *Darmo Konda*, 13 June 1909.

21. *Darmo Konda*, 11 February 1909.

22. *Darmo Konda*, 17 July 1912. The elected chairperson at the meeting of 1912 was Mas Ngabehi Reksoprojo.

23. *Darmo Konda*, 18 March 1914. The president of the association was R. M. A. Puspodingrat, and the vice president, R. Ng. Wignyodipuro.

24. See, for example, information published in the local *priyayi* newspaper, the *Darmo Konda*, 31 March 1904, "Pranatan wontenipun parameyan ing Abipraya" (Plan of the ceremony of Abipraya). Such a *pranatan* could be seen in other local newspapers as well.

25. *Darmo Konda*, 18 September 1912, reported that a housekeeper (*nara pramuka*) with the official name Ki Nara Pangsara, was appointed to the rank of *lurah* with a monthly salary of f 15. At the same time, an assistant, Tarunadimejo, was also appointed, with the rank of *jajar* and a salary of f 10 per month. Official dress for the two employees was provided.

26. *Darmo Konda*, 9 July 1906. The monthly share for members living in the city (*negari*), was eight cents for those with one *jung* of wet-rice fields (*sawah*), or f 100 cumulative salary for six months. For those living in the villages, it was five cents for the equivalent level.

27. The Almanak was advertised as containing all the names of the *priyayi*. In 1900 the *Solosche Javaansche almanak* was published by Vogel van der Heijde en Co.

28. *Darmo Konda*, 20 June 1907. This article by Joko Setyarjo, in the column of "Gagasan," was intended as a criticism of the mentality of the young generation, who would rather be *priyayi* than have other jobs.

29. *Darmo Konda*, 24 September 1908.

30. R. M. A. Jayadiningrat I, *Serat man jenthu inggih mas nganten* (Surakarta: Albert Rusche, 1907).

31. Padmasusastra, *Serat subasita* (Surakarta: Budi Utama, 1914).

32. Hair cutting as a cultural movement had already begun in the second half of the first decade. The Mangkunegara principality was ahead of its time, by letting the nobility, as well as the subjects, cut their hair. The Chinese began popularizing the movement after the Russo-Japanese War, but adopted it most aggressively after the Chinese Revolution. The Kasunanan government was behind; it announced the right to cut hair for the *adbi dalam* and its military troops only in 1914. See *Darmo Konda*, 9 February 1914.

33. Raden Bagus Suluardi, *Serat riyanta* (Weltevreden: Papyrus, 1920).

34. *Darmo Konda*, 4 February 1912; 7 December 1914.

35. For a detailed description of the marriage see *De Indische gids*, vol. 2, 1915.

36. Pangeran Aria Sasraningrat, *Wedamadya*, edited by Padmasusastra (Surakarta: 1898).

37. See Soemarsaid Moertono, *Negara and Usaha Bina-Negara di Jawa Masa Lampau: Studi Tentang Masa Mataram II Abad XVI Sampai XIX* (Jakarta: Yayasan Obor Indonesia, 1985), 113.

38. "Tetedhaken serat piwulang tumrap kangge nyuwita," *Darmo Konda*, 4 July1904.

39. *Darmo Konda*, 13 March 1912.

40. *Darmo Konda*, 25 May 1905.

41. *Darmo Konda*, 28 March 1904.

42. *Darmo Konda*, 25 August 1905.

43. *Darmo Konda*, 18, 21 October 1909; 4, 8, 11, 15, 16 November 1909.

44. *Darmo Konda*, 28, 30 April 1910; 2 May 1910.

45. *Darmo Konda*, 21 March 1904.

46. *Darmo Konda*, 16 July 1906. I will quote the *pantun* in order to give some idea of the style of Malay used by the local newspaper at that time: "Botjah klentang toemboeh di atas, Ikan blenak di rawa-rawa, Masbehi di bawah prampoean di atas, Ampir mati bersama-sama".

47. *Darmo Konda*, 29 August 1904.

48. *Darmo Konda*, 16 April 1908.

49. *Darmo Konda*, 4 October 1910.

50. *Darmo Konda*, 25 December 1911.

51. *Darmo Konda*, 15 February 1909.

52. See, for example, *Darmo Konda*, 23 September 1905.

53. See, for example, *Darmo Konda*, 18 February 1909, a report on the *wireng* in the house of Joyonagoro, a son-in-law of the *sunan*.

54. *Darmo Konda*, December 1908. Mention was made of the *priyayi* members of the Abipraya, but the fact that the government specifically took measures to prevent *priyayi* taking part in cockfighting and gambling is evidence that such habits existed.

55. *Darmo Konda*, 25 February 1909.

56. *Darmo Konda*, 12 June 1905; 21 August 1905.

57. Swara, *Bab alaki rabi: Wayuh kaliyan boten* (Semarang: H. A. Benyamins, 1913).

58. I owe much of the concept of affirmative culture to a book on the critical theory of culture by John Brenkman, *Culture and Domination* (Ithaca: Cornell University Press, 1987).

Chapter Six

Totalitarianism and the "National Personality": Recent Controversy about the Philosophical Basis of the Indonesian State

David Bourchier

IN FEW COUNTRIES has state ideology been so closely linked to notions of "indigenous" cultural identity as in Indonesia. When Sukarno stood before the Constituent Assembly in 1959 and implored delegates to vote to put an end to parliamentarism and return to the 1945 Constitution, he did so in the name of the "national personality" (*kepribadian bangsa*). Indonesia's economic decline, political conflict and military unruliness, Sukarno argued, all stemmed from a fundamental lack of fit between "Western" liberal philosophies embodied in the parliamentary constitution of 1950 and the authentic personality of the people. Ever since that time a central theme of government rhetoric has been that the country's political structures and procedures reflect a uniquely "Indonesian" approach to authority and decision making.

The harnessing of the "national personality" in the service of politics has seen politicians devote a lot of energy to molding and systematizing the notion of indigenous culture. John Bowen for example, shows how, from a wide variety of labor exchange practices in rural Indonesia, the tradition of *gotong royong* (usually represented as a pattern of "mutual assistance" common to village communities throughout the archipelago) was first constructed and then used by Sukarno and later Suharto to justify a range of political measures—from the restriction of party freedoms to the mobilization of village labor to do unpaid work for the state.[1] The ubiquitous political mantras *musyawarah* (deliberation) and *mufakat* (consensus) are also the product of diverse traditions of customary law (*adat*) having been distilled into simple formulas and then used as "cultural-ideological instruments" by both the Guided Democracy and New Order governments. *Pancasila* too doubles as a political ideology and as the authentic embodiment of a deep-seated indigenous Indonesian philosophy of life. The central image in this carefully cultivated ideology of Indonesian-ness is the traditional village, where social harmony reigns, neighbors pitch in for the common good, and decisions are reached by consensus under the guidance of a wise leader. *Pancasila, musyawarah, mufakat,* and *gotong royong* have come to define, in official discourse, essential traits of both the political system and of the national personality.

The controversy I wish to explore in this paper arose from an attempt by the New Order government to take the process of meshing constructions of traditional culture with political ideology one step further and link the Indonesian Weltanschauung with a totalitarian theory of the state. In fact, the government did more than just make the linkage; it attempted to formalize it by enshrining this theory in the corpus of state ideology and thereby affect the legal foundations of the Indonesian state. I am referring to the move in the mid-1980s to embrace what has come to be known in Indonesia as the theory of the integralist state (*negara integralistik*).

I will begin by examining the background to the theory of integralism in Indonesia and then describe its resurrection by the New Order and the debates which followed. I will go on to analyze possible reasons behind integralism's reemergence and assess the significance of the issue as a whole. I argue that integralism is essentially an ideological device deployed by Indonesia's rulers in an attempt to preserve and extend their grip on society in the face of demands by new social forces for greater political rights and effective limits on executive authority. While the New Order's adoption of an explicitly totalitarian theory of politics provides a worrying insight into the thinking of some of the regime's most powerful figures, I suggest that one of its most important consequences has been to provoke the government's critics to formulate a coherent response and thereby improve the quality of political debate in Indonesia.

The central point of reference for all discussion about integralist ideology in Indonesia is a speech made in 1945 by the customary law expert Raden Supomo.[2] Supomo studied law in Leiden in the 1920s and returned to become Indonesia's foremost *adat* scholar and a judge in the colonial administration. During the Japanese military occupation he was appointed chief Indonesian advisor to the Justice Department and headed the Japanese Law Research Association (Nippon Hoo Kenkyu Kai). It was by virtue of his legal expertise and high standing in the Japanese administration that he was called upon in April 1945, several months before the Japanese surrender, to take part in a committee to prepare for independence called the Badan Untuk Menyelidiki Usaha-usaha Persiapan Kemerdekaan (Dokuritsu Zyunbi Tyoosakai; Investigating Committee for Independence Preparations). The committee consisted of sixty-two of the most prominent "collaborating" nationalists, including Sukarno, Mohammad Hatta, Radjiman Wediodiningrat (chairman), Wachid Hasjim, and Mohammad Yamin.

The main task of the Investigating Committee was to draft a constitution and to propose what basic form the independent nation should take (i.e., whether it should be a monarchy or a republic, a federation or a unitary state, and so on). On 31 May 1945, during a debate about the appropriate philosophical foundation of the Indonesian state, Supomo outlined his vision of an integralist state.

In essence, Supomo's argument was that the fundamental political institutions of every state must reflect the unique cultural and legal heritage of its people. Drawing on a large body of *adat* scholarship as well as his own standing as an authority on customary law, Supomo held that village communities all over the archipelago were characterized by their attachment to values of communal harmony, social solidarity, and their feeling of oneness with their leaders. For this reason the only appropriate philosophical basis (*staatsidee*)[3] for the Indonesian state was one which put the highest value on social harmony and the preservation of time-honored bonds between rulers and ruled.

Supomo classified political philosophy into three broad streams: individualism, class theory, and integralism. The first, he explained, was propounded by Hobbes, Locke, Spencer, and Rousseau, and was aligned with the idea of a social contract among all individuals. This philosophy, in which the state acted to uphold individual legal rights, had been worked out most fully in Western Europe and the United States. According to the second stream, taught by Marx, Engels, and Lenin, the state was the instrument by which one class exerted its domination over others. Supomo explicitly rejected both of these approaches to social organization—the first because it led to alienation, greed, and ultimately to imperialism, and the second because it promoted a fractured and antagonistic conception of society. Neither, he argued, were appropriate to the basic traditions and ways of thinking of the Indonesian people.

The third major tradition of political philosophy, however, for which Supomo chose the name *integralism*,[4] was very much attuned to Indonesia's national character, and, he argued, already implicit in indigenous structures of authority and modes of social organization. Supomo characterized integralism as a theory in which the state was committed not to individual rights or particular classes but to society conceived of as an organic whole. As the Dutch legal scholar J. H. A. Logemann[5] has pointed out, the integralist state Supomo spoke about corresponds to the concept of the organic state in continental legal philosophy, the notion that the state is synonymous with "organized society" and an embodiment of the national spirit (*Volksgeist*). Supomo indeed named Hegel, along with Spinoza and the early-nineteenth-century German Romantic Adam Müller, as the leading theorists of integralism.

The two contemporary examples Supomo chose to illustrate the qualities of integralism were the Japanese imperial regime and the recently defeated Third Reich. Both, he maintained, attached tremendous importance to the spiritual unity of the national community and emphasized the "family" bonds between rulers and ruled.[6] Supomo, who had been introduced to National Socialist ideology while studying in Holland,[7] referred approvingly to the notion of *das Ganze der politischen Einheit des Volkes* (the totality of the political unity of the people) as well as the idea of the *totaler Führerstaat* and the *Blut und Boden Theorie*.[8] He was also explicit about the totalitarian character of integralism, using the term *totaliter* interchangeably with *integralistik* throughout his speech.

To some extent Supomo was paying lip service to the ideological orthodoxy of the time. The outright rejection of "materialistic" liberalism and communism in favor of the more "spiritual" Japanese and German philosophies of rule was a prominent theme in the propaganda of the occupying forces,[9] which, after all, were still very much in control in May 1945 when Supomo made his speech to the Investigating Committee. But Supomo went much further in his defense of these totalitarian concepts than the other members of the committee, arguing that they were very much in accord (*sangat sesuai*) with Indonesia's traditional political and cultural order and therefore helped illustrate the kind of philosophical basis on which he maintained the future Indonesian state should be built. This is not to say, however, that Supomo was a fascist or that he dreamt of replicating the militaristic Japanese regime or the Third Reich in Indonesia. His vision was of a state which mirrored the institutions and ethos of a (highly idealized) traditional village community in which there was no sense of separation between rulers and ruled. Supomo stressed the centrality of the notion, beloved in Javanese mythology, that the people and their lord (*kawulo dan gusti*) were as inseparable as the body and the spirit: . . . even today in villages, not only in Java but also in Sumatra and in the other Indonesian islands, state officials remain *spiritually united* with their people and are committed to forever preserving unity and balance within their communities."[10] Individuals living in traditional communities, Supomo said, do not live apart from one another or from the outside world; everybody cooperates in a spirit of community mindedness (*gotong royong*) and familyness (*kekeluargaan*).

In practical terms, Supomo wanted a constitution premised on total faith by the people in their ruler. He argued against the inclusion of any guarantees to protect the fundamental rights and liberties (*Grund- und Freiheitsrechte*) of individuals or groups against the state and against checks on executive authority. If such measures were adopted, the fundamental principle of oneness between the people and their rulers, between state and society, would be violated.[11]

Supomo's opinions carried a great deal of weight in the Investigating Committee and most of the 1945 Constitution is his work. The constitution as a whole, however, cannot be seen as a complete fulfillment of Supomo's totalitarian vision. While it does give enormous power to the president, it also contains an article dealing with political rights, which in itself implies a separation between state and society. Supomo, who was keenly aware that the incorporation of political rights in the constitution would go against the logic of integralism, argued strongly for their exclusion. In the end, however, he was forced to compromise with Mohammad Hatta and his supporters, who argued that without provisions for citizens' rights Indonesia could develop into a *negara kekuasaan*, an all-powerful state which relied on coercion rather than law.[12] For Hatta, Germany's experience illustrated precisely such dangers. It was thanks to Hatta's persistence, and his ability to transcend the hazy optimism which colored the thinking of many of the leading nationalist figures at the time, that Article 28, guaranteeing freedom of association and expression, was included in the 1945 Constitution.[13]

Perhaps because of this compromise, perhaps because totalitarianism became taboo worldwide, the theory of integralism was rarely raised in public for the next forty years. The first (and apparently the only) person to make a serious attempt to have it adopted as part of the national ideology in this period was the constitutional lawyer, Colonel (now Brigadier General, retired) Abdulkadir Besar.[14] As secretary general of the Interim Peoples Consultative Assembly (MPRS) Abdulkadir wrote a long "academic appraisal" advocating that Supomo's integralism (which he most often referred to as the *staatsidee kekeluargaan*, the familial state concept) be adopted as the philosophical basis of the Indonesian political system.[15] Although his ideas were not then explicitly embraced by the New Order government, they do appear to have been influential in military doctrine and reportedly were incorporated in the curriculums of armed forces staff colleges, including Seskoad (the Army Staff and Command College in Bandung), where Abdulkadir was responsible for courses on ideology and the state constitution in the late 1970s.[16]

In retrospect, an interesting prelude to the revival of integralism was the 1981 publication of a controversial booklet on the origins of the *pancasila* by Nugroho Notosusanto, one of the army's principal ideologists, who was to be Indonesia's Minister for Education and Culture in 1983 through 1985. Nugroho attempted to cast doubt on Sukarno's authorship of the *pancasila* by arguing that the former president had simply articulated concepts already formulated by Mohammad Yamin and Supomo in the Investigating Committee. In a table, Nugroho lists first Yamin's five principles (outlined on 29 May 1945) then Supomo's five (31 May) and, last of all, Sukarno's five (1 June).[17] What is most curious, for present purposes, is that unlike Yamin and Sukarno, Supomo's five principles, listed by Nugroho as *persatuan* (unity), *kekeluargaan*, *keimbangan lahir dan batin* (equilibrium between body and soul), *musyawarah*, and *keadilan rakyat* (popular justice) were never itemized by their author. In other words, Nugroho himself had sifted through his 1945 speech and assembled an inventory of "principles" in a deliberate attempt to credit Supomo with a greater role than Sukarno in the formulation of the state ideology.[18]

The term *integralism* gained widespread currency only in the mid-1980s, when high-ranking members of the BP-7,[19] the government's supreme ideological control council, began referring to Indonesia's *staatsidee integralistik*. According to Marsillam Simanjuntak,[20] who has traced the history of integralism in Indonesia, the term first resurfaced in an ideological training manual written in 1984 by BP-7 member Suntjojo.[21] Senior State Secretariat officials, including its powerful minister Lieutenant General (Ret.) Sudharmono, were also at work promoting integralism as the driving spirit behind the constitution and relating it to all aspects of national life.[22] By 1987 it had been incorporated into the curriculum of P4[23]—the ideological education sessions attended by many million Indonesians every year—as well as school and university courses.[24] Supomo's 1945 argument, minus the references to Germany, Japan, and totalitarianism (but, oddly enough, including the mention of Hegel, Spinoza, and Müller) has been adopted almost as a canon. Students are examined on it and senior officials regularly refer to it as an established truth: Indonesia is a *negara integralistik* and therefore does not recognize opposition, does not recognize individualistic or liberalistic attitudes, does not recognize notions such as minorities and majorities, core and periphery, workers and bosses, military and civilian.[25] These concepts are all said to belong to an alien, dichotomistic way of thinking which is both un-Indonesian and against the spirit of the constitution. As a journalist for the magazine *Forum keadilan* (Justice forum) put it: "The *negara integralistik* has become a sort of phenomenon. It is a kind of new idiom, which needs to be inserted into speeches, welcoming addresses, seminars, gatherings, and even informal occasions."[26] Supomo's integralism, in short, was gradually retrieved from history and adopted as a central tenet of *pancasila* orthodoxy.

The key ideologues behind the resurrection of integralism were two senior members of the BP-7—Abdulkadir Besar and Professor Padmo Wahyono, dean of the prestigious law faculty at the University of Indonesia. In 1984, while working as an assistant to the Coordinating Minister for Politics and Security, Abdulkadir wrote a fascinating and rather bizarre article in which he held that Supomo's integralism should be employed as a sort of master concept for organizing all aspects of public life in Indonesia; he spoke of an integralist system of justice, integralist culture, integralist historical method, an integralist way of thinking, and, of course, the integralist state. He maintained that the integralist state was the apex not only of historical progress but also of a natural evolutionary process. Just as microorganisms evolve into more complex beings, he argued, so do human societies become more complex, differentiated, and hierarchical. Supomo's integralist *staatsidee* implied, he argued, a "neogenetic hierarchy" in which all people are organically linked to one another and find their ultimate expression in a benevolent and all-encompassing state.[27]

It was Padmo Wahyono, though, who adopted the mantle of chief protagonist of Supomo's integralist theory of the state. A constitutional lawyer by training, Padmo spent most of his career lecturing at the University of Indonesia and at various military and police academies. From 1983 until his death in 1991 he was deputy chairman of the BP-7. Padmo wrote several articles after 1989 that quote Supomo at length and maintain that his vision provides the authentic philosophical underpinning of the Indonesian legal order. In a long and convoluted 1990 article entitled *Integralistik Indonesia* Padmo argued that the Indonesian state had come into being not as the result of a "dualistic" social contract between rulers and ruled but of a "collective act" (*Gesamtakt*) and was therefore a manifestation of the public interest (*respublica*). The public interest, he maintained, was thus synonymous with the objectives of the state embodied in the GBHN (Garis Besar Haluan Negara; Broad Outlines of State Policy). Because the GBHN were formulated not by victorious political parties but through a process of deliberation, they were, he reasoned, "clearly the product of integralist state policies."[28]

Continuing in this vein, Padmo asserted that the "simplification" of political parties in the 1970s, the existence of Golkar, *dwifungsi* (the "dual-function" doctrine which requires the military to play a permanent political role) and the (highly restrictive) 1985 Law on Social Organizations are all in accordance with the "Indonesian integralist outlook."[29] Padmo expressed some reservations about developments in the economic sphere, which he regarded as reflecting an individualistic approach, but suggested that these problems could be resolved if the integralist philosophy were sufficiently worked into the culture (*dibudayakan*),[30] presumably through the agency of P4 courses. It is ironic that whereas Supomo took indigenous cultural values as his starting point, Padmo was saying in effect that Indonesians were insufficiently attuned to their authentic cultural heritage and therefore needed to be "Indonesianized."

Resistance

Given that the revival of integralist ideology was so clearly a policy initiative originating from the top levels of government, it met a surprising amount of opposition. It is also surprising, given the level of agreement that now exists among the critics of integralism, that it took as long as it did to have the issue discussed publicly. The Legal Aid Foundation in Jakarta appears to have been the first group to target integralism as a potential threat to the struggle for human rights in Indonesia.[31] The real controversy, though, did not begin until July the following year, when a series of high-level seminars were held to mark the thirtieth anniversary of Sukarno's decree returning Indonesia to the 1945 constitution.

These seminars, held at the law faculties of the University of Indonesia in Jakarta and Padjadjaran University in Bandung, provided a rare national forum for intellectuals, lawyers, NGO activists, and bureaucrats to debate constitutional questions. One of the issues most hotly contested at the University of Indonesia seminar was the constitutional validity of the law reserving a permanent quota of 100 seats in parliament for armed forces appointees. Abdulkadir Besar insisted that the law was constitutional while veteran legal scholar Dr. Ismail Suny, supported by the human-rights lawyer Mulya Lubis and Marsillam Simanjuntak, maintained that it was not. The essential difference in the two positions turned not on legalities but on interpretations of the constitution, that is, whether it was integralist in inspiration. Abdulkadir claimed that it was, and that the participation of the armed forces in Parliament simply reflected this, while his challengers argued that to regard Supomo's integralism as the authentic spirit of the 1945 Constitution was both anti-democratic and a misrepresentation of Indonesian national history.[32]

In subsequent months there were a number of polemics published in the pages of Indonesia's newspapers, magazines, and journals. Critics of the integralist *staatsidee*—which, apart from lawyers included historians, political scientists, sociologists, and journalists—made three kinds of arguments.

One was that Supomo's theory of integralism was based on mistaken assumptions about indigenous Indonesian culture. The political scientist Arbi Sanit, for instance, argued that village communities in different parts of Indonesia were neither as similar to one another nor as democratic as Supomo wanted to believe. Arbi Sanit highlighted differences between the highly centralized power structures of traditional Javanese villages and the relatively egalitarian character of Minangkabau communities in West Sumatra. According to the Javanese conception of power in the village, Sanit said, everyone had a right to speak, but only landowners had a right to contribute to decision making.[33]

The second argument, made most forcefully and comprehensively by Marsillam Simanjuntak in his 1989 thesis *Hegelian Elements in the Integralist View of the State*, was that it is historically fraudulent to regard the constitution as a realization of Supomo's integralist vision. Marsillam argued that the incorporation of political rights into the constitution in 1945 completely demolished the coherence of Supomo's concept and consigned it to the scrapheap of history. He went on to explore the political philosophies of the three European thinkers to whom Supomo paid homage: Spinoza, Müller, and especially Hegel, highlighting the antidemocratic and absolutist aspects of their thought. Supomo, he held, following Hegel and German National Socialist ideology, was arguing in favor of state sovereignty and stood, therefore, in direct opposition to the ideal of popular sovereignty (*kedaulatan rakyat*) enshrined as a fundamental principle in the final form of the 1945 Constitution.

The historical defeat of the integralist *staatsidee*, Marsillam argued, was further confirmed by the fact that the idea was never taken seriously again, either by governments or by Supomo himself. Marsillam argued that even those responsible for the resurrection of integralism were aware of the unacceptability of Supomo's proposal. At a seminar held by *Kompas* in December 1989 there was an interesting exchange in which Marsillam accused Padmo Wahyono—who was at the time dean of his own law faculty—of attempting to disguise the totalitarian basis of Supomo's thought by quoting Supomo on several occasions as having advocated not totalitarianism but the idea of totality, (i.e., replacing Supomo's *"totaliter"* with *"totalitas,"* even in direct quotations). Padmo's response was to admit that he had indeed changed Supomo's original text, but he defended his action on the grounds that he felt that Supomo had not actually meant to advocate totalitarianism.[34]

The third argument basically held that no matter how much influence Supomo's ideas may have had in 1945, they had no place in present-day Indonesia. Legal Aid Foundation Chairman Abdul Hakim G. Nusantara (1988), for example, labeled integralism a patrimonial concept that was hostile to the notion of individual rights and incompatible with the government of modern societies. It should be recognized, he argued, that the behavior of any state reflects the interests of the social groups which control it. Priority, therefore, should be given not to peddling a philosophy which claims that the interests of the state and society are identical but to establishing reliable mechanisms which prevent abuses of authority, facilitate the expression of popular political aspirations, and provide impartial arbitration of conflict between individuals, groups, and the state.

The eminent historian Sartono Kartodirdjo sounded a similar note of concern, if not alarm, when he warned that if Indonesia wanted to regard itself as a modern country it would have to rid itself of feudalistic attitudes and irrelevant old values, such as *musyawarah*, and concentrate on introducing legal certainty and controls on power. Sartono feared that the revival of integralism was taking the country in the opposite direction. "Supomo's integralist state [concept] legitimates the absence of *trias politica* (the separation of powers)" he remarked. "So where is the integralist state concept taking this country? Are there any guarantees that law can be upheld in an integralist state? . . . Moreover, how is development supposed to be supervised in an integralist state?"[35] A. E. Priyono, editor of the journal *Prisma*, expressed the same sentiments, highlighting what he saw as the incompatibility between a pluralistic economy and a totalitarian political philosophy: "In building a complex economy which has to deal with the interaction between the state and various private or social groups it is not appropriate to set up a constitutional apparatus which guarantees hegemonic power."[36]

One of the most interesting aspects of the debate was how the notion of indigenousness was used by both sides. Some opponents of integralism, such as Ismail Suny and Arbi Sanit, used the New Order's indigenist rhetoric against itself by accusing the government of trying to smuggle dangerous foreign concepts into the country by pretending that they were Indonesian.[37] It was probably in response to such criticisms that the more culturally resonant term *negara kekeluargaan* (familial state) began to appear alongside, or in place of, *negara integralistik*. Regime spokesmen, including Padmo Wahyono and Brigadier General (Ret.) Harisoegiman, the Director General of Social and Political Affairs in the Department of the Interior, also went to great lengths to stress that the integralism they were talking about was not the prewar European variety but *Indonesian* integralism, "adapted

from traditional culture in Indonesia, especially from the villages."[38] Against this, Bambang Sulasmono, a lecturer at Satya
Wacana University in Central Java, argued that the younger generation, growing up in a predominantly "liberal and capitalist"
reality, found it increasingly difficult to relate to integralism. Far
from reflecting a traditional agrarian sensibility, he ventured that
the integralist outlook "existed only among the elite in the capital city."[39]

Looking for Reasons

It is clear that the government had trouble convincing the
opinion makers in the intelligentsia both of the authenticity of
the integralist *staatsidee* and the need for it. Indeed, as has been
suggested, some of the writing of the regime ideologists, especially after late 1989, took on an uncharacteristically defensive
tone. Clearly the government did not expect the level of criticism
that its revival of integralism attracted.

This begs the question: What was at stake? Why, at a time of
apparent political calm at home and a trend in the outside world
toward a greater tolerance of political pluralism, did the Indonesian government decide to introduce a theory, derived at least
partly from totalitarian models, that prescribes virtually un-
bounded executive authority and denies the validity of political
life independent of the state?

Douglas Ramage, who interviewed several military figures in
Jakarta, has argued that the promotion of integralism was essentially a military initiative to remold *pancasila* discourse in such a
way as to make the doctrine of *dwifungsi* an inseparable part of
the state ideology and thereby preserve the military's privileged
position in the political system.[40] He found that the military
leadership's anxiety about their power base, and about the future

of the New Order's nonsectarian political formula more generally, was fueled in particular by Suharto's courtship of political Islam.

There is no question that the military leadership was strongly in favor of integralism taking its place as Indonesia's *staatsidee*. After all, military ideologists maintain that integralism has long been established in Indonesian military ideology and that the concepts of integralism and *dwifungsi* are closely entwined. *Dwifungsi* doctrine indeed rests on notions inherent in integralist ideology, such as paternalism, the legitimacy of nonelected rulers, and the idea that it is possible for an elite to represent the whole society's interests rather than simply its own. Both Abdulkadir Besar and Lieutenant General (Ret.) Sarwo Edhie Wibowo, who headed the BP-7 in the mid 1980s, were passionate defenders of *dwifungsi*. Moreover, the military had reason to be concerned about the changing constellation of power in the New Order and their future place within it. The absence of any genuine threats to national security coupled with the consolidation of a substantial civilian technocratic elite have seen the arguments for maintaining a high level of military participation in political life come under increasing challenge. It is well documented also that the relationship between the president and the military leadership deteriorated in the second part of the 1980s and that Suharto's sponsorship of Islamic groups was as much a result of this breakdown of trust as a cause of it.[41]

These factors explain the military's backing of integralism, but they do not adequately account for the broad institutional support the campaign received. The BP-7, for instance, which is responsible directly to the president, could not have embarked on a crusade to redefine the basis of the Indonesian state without Suharto's explicit support. His blessing would also have been necessary for integralism to be introduced to school and university curriculums nationwide. More importantly, if the promotion of integralism was primarily a military initiative, we would have to explain why Sudharmono's State Secretariat—the legal-administrative core of the New Order—took an active role in its propagation from at least 1986. Although Sudharmono and some of his aides were military, neither he nor his office were on good terms with the armed forces leadership during the 1980s. The military were especially resentful of Sudharmono's efforts to minimize their influence within Golkar, the organization he chaired between 1983 and 1988, and later actively opposed his nomination as vice president.[42] This does not mean that Sudharmono was against *dwifungsi*, but it does make it difficult to accept that when he and other members of the State Secretariat advocated integralism they were doing the military's bidding.

So while the armed forces had their own good reasons for supporting the integralist agenda, the revival of Supomo's integralist *staatsidee* should be seen as having enjoyed the backing of a wider section of the regime leadership, including the presidency.

In general terms, the adoption of the integralist *staatsidee* is probably best seen as a defensive maneuver on the part of the New Order leadership to preserve its authority in the face of challenges from a number of directions. One perceived challenge came as a result of the recession and the sharp decline of the price of oil in the early to mid-1980s, when the government was forced to privatize and deregulate large sectors of the economy. The loosening of central control over economic decision making that this involved appears to have been compensated for with a marked tightening of political controls. Most spectacular was the 1985 package of five political laws which, among other things, increased the proportion of armed forces representatives in parliament, strengthened the powers of the government to control the activities of political parties and social organizations, and introduced procedures which made it virtually impossible to alter the constitution. The integralist *staatsidee* can be interpreted as their ideological complement.

Deregulation and economic liberalization, as well as the extension of personal taxation, have been major factors in generating demands for political deregulation—a code word for greater power sharing and political liberalization. This argument has gathered momentum in recent years and has put pressure on the government to formulate a response. If the government's *keterbukaan* (glasnost) initiative was calculated to give the appearance of greater freedom, integralist ideology defined its limits. Brigadier General Moerdiono, Sudharmono's successor as State Secretary and one of the government's strongest proponents of integralism said in 1990: "We are indeed moving toward greater freedom. But the rhythm must be arranged (*diatur*). It is like in an orchestra, where each of the instruments has its own particular function to perform in accordance with the melody."[43] The analogy with an orchestra (and in earlier manifestations, the gamelan)[44] illustrates splendidly the image of society as an organic, harmonious, and hierarchically ordered whole nurtured by the champions of integralism.

The 1980s also saw a marked growth of pressures on the Suharto government on human rights issues, particularly by the rapidly expanding population of nongovernment organizations. Domestic criticism was reinforced by international pressure as a result of several developments, including: (a) the linking up of domestic and foreign NGOs in the International NGO Group on Indonesia (INGI) in 1985; (b) the rapid growth in exports of Indonesian manufactured goods onto the world market in the mid-1980s, leading to increased scrutiny of oppressive labor practices by international organizations such as the ICFTU and the AFL-CIO; (c) the trend toward greater democracy in other parts of the Third World; and (d) the collapse of communism, which provided a huge boost for the prestige of liberal democratic ideology and the liberal conception of human rights worldwide. The espousal of the integralist *staatsidee* can be seen as an attempt to formulate a coherent counterargument to this growing wave of "human rights" criticism. The government's response to both domestic and international human rights criticism in recent years has been to say that Indonesia must not be judged according to "Western" standards that stem from an individualistic intellectual and political tradition but by its own value system based, once again, on the primacy of the well-being of the collectivity.[45]

Apart from general human-rights-based criticism and demands for more openness, the government also found itself having to respond to growing criticism framed in terms of constitutionalism. One of the constant themes in the critiques made by the Petition of 50, as well as a variety of NGOs and intellectuals throughout the 1980s was that the political ground rules laid down by the New Order concerning such matters as elections, political parties and the composition of parliament contravened basic constitutional rights and freedoms. As Priyono has argued, the enshrinement of integralism as Indonesia's *staatsidee* suggests an attempt to cut the ground from under the feet of the New Order's constitutionalist critics.[46] The logic here is that according to the dominant school of constitutional thought in Indonesia, a *staatsidee* occupies the supreme position in the hierarchy of legal norms and therefore determines how all subordinate legal products, including the constitution, should be interpreted. If the government's jurists and ideologists declare the "source of all sources of law" to be integralist, then it is all the more difficult for critics of the government to use constitutionalist arguments to press for democratic reform. The rights and freedoms the constitution guarantees melt into air.[47]

Intentionally or not, the government's depiction of Supomo's integralism as the legitimate basis of the state has redefined not only the spirit of the constitution but the entire character of the independence movement that brought Indonesia into being. By privileging Supomo's neofeudal vision as historically and culturally authentic, the government is in effect writing off mainstream nationalism, which took the notion of popular sovereignty (*kedaulatan rakyat*) as its starting point.[48] The idea that the rulers had to be answerable to the people was a central concept in the writings of Hatta from the 1920s, and was accepted in all but the most conservative sections of the independence movement. The assertion that conflict and opposition within the national family is culturally unacceptable makes it politically awkward for present-day reformers to draw on Indonesia's own rich traditions of confrontationalist political activity and democratic thought. "The dominance of integralism," writes Ramadhani Aksyah, "is an obstacle to people even talking about opposition."

Unintended Consequences

I have characterized the government's adoption of integralism primarily as a defensive tactic, an attempt to erect an ideological bulwark to preserve the status quo against rising demands for an extension of democratic rights and freedoms. But in another sense it simply articulated a logic of rule that the New Order had been following more or less since its rise to power in the mid-1960s. The political history of the New Order can be construed as a long, albeit uneven, effort to realize one of the key tenets of the integralist *staatsidee*—the elimination of the separation of state and civil society, or in Supomo's words, "*dualisme 'Staat und staatsfreie Gesellschaft.'*"[49] The dismantling of the party system; the corporatization of youth, women, farmers, workers and professionals' organizations; the requirement that all social organizations submit to government supervision; and the proliferation of restrictions on the freedom to organize are all consistent with the idea of a progressive incorporation of civil society into the state. Although the Suharto regime cannot be categorized as totalitarian, its adoption of integralist ideology lends weight to what Richard Tanter, in his excellent study of surveillance and militarization in Indonesia, describes as the New Order's "totalitarian ambition."[50]

Having said that, I want to finish by suggesting that, politically speaking, the revival of integralism may have done the government more harm than good. Although it is fair to say that appeals to exceptionalism—the argument that Indonesia is unique and that state institutions and procedures should express that uniqueness—have tended to enjoy a good degree of support among the political public, the *negara integralistik* debates suggest that the government overplayed its hand in this instance. The revelation of Supomo's open affinity with totalitarianism provided Indonesia's democratic opposition with a clear target to focus on and to define itself against.

Challenged to formulate a coherent response, critics of the New Order have directed much of their energy toward unearthing and reclaiming Indonesia's democratic past. Marsillam Simanjuntak's historical study triggered great interest among the critical intelligentsia in the constitutional debates of 1945 and in particular the antitotalitarian stream of Indonesian political thought associated most closely with Sutan Sjahrir and Mohammad Hatta. Hatta, in fact, has emerged as a hero figure among opponents of integralism, while the historically resonant idea of popular sovereignty has crystallized as a key counterconcept.

Others have looked to the country's more recent political history. One of the central points which Buyung Nasution highlights in his major study of the debates in the Constituent Assembly from 1956 to 1959 is the depth of commitment to political rights and freedoms among the elected delegates to the assembly.[51] He argues that this shows that arguments which claim that notions of human rights and democratic checks on executive authority do not have a legitimate basis in Indonesian history are misleading. Another prominent human rights lawyer, Mulya Lubis, makes a similar point in his doctoral thesis, arguing that the concept of universal human rights was widely accepted in the mid to late 1960s.[52] He maintains that it was the New Order's preoccupation with order and stability, rather than any fundamental incompatibility between human rights and indigenous culture which saw popular rights come under sustained attack at both the ideological and political levels during the tenure of the Suharto government.

A further unintended consequence of the government's attempt to revive the integralist *staatsidee* has been the reopening of the agenda of constitutional reform, which since about 1968 has been considered taboo. While most opponents of integralism have concentrated on arguing for a more democratic interpretation of the constitution in its current form,[53] there are now a number of intellectuals and lawyers, the most high profile being Buyung Nasution, who argue that the 1945 Constitution is intrinsically undemocratic and ought to be revised.[54] The constitution's weak provisions for civil and human rights, the need to circumscribe the powers and term of the president, the dubious legality of the constitution's adoption in 1959, and Sukarno's 1945 remark that the constitution was "temporary" and "would of course be rewritten in more peaceful times"[55] are the grounds most frequently mentioned by advocates of reform. Although the government rejects all suggestions that the constitution be altered in any way, its attempt to marry it to a theory that denies the legitimacy of popular political rights and genuine accountability may simply ensure that such calls increase in the future.

A final and more general point about the controversy over integralism is that it highlights the problematic nature of the concept of political culture, at least as it has been used by many Western writers about Indonesia and other non-European countries. Political culture is not an entity, the logic or essence of which can be discovered, but rather a realm full of competing and often contradictory impulses. To equate Indonesian political culture with the hierarchical and paternalistic ethic promoted by the current rulers is to ignore countercurrents which are not only very much alive today but, as the opponents of integralism also stressed, a vital part of Indonesia's political history.

Notes

1. John Bowen, "On the Political Construction of Tradition: *Gotong Royong* in Indonesia," *Journal of Asian Studies* 45, 3 (May 1986), 545–61.

2. Raden Supomo (1903–1958) was a Javanese aristocrat who studied law in Leiden from 1921 to 1927. He was part of a circle of young men in Holland, including Mohammad Hatta, who formed the nationalist group Perhimpunan Indonesia. After returning to the Indies in 1929 he worked in the colonial bureaucracy as a judge and later joined Parindra, a traditionalist Javanese party at the conservative end of the political spectrum. In September 1945 he was appointed Justice Minister in Indonesia's first republican government and became the first Indonesian ambassador to Britian.

3. Mainstream Indonesian constitutional philosophy derives from prewar Dutch traditions, which in turn borrowed heavily from Germany. The concept that every constitution must base itself on an irreducible master concept, or *staatsidee*, owes much to the thought of Georg Jellinek and Hans Kelsen, who used the term *Grundnorm* (basic norm). I explore German influences on constitutional thought in Indonesia in "Reflections on the Integralist Tradition of Political Thought in Indonesia" (paper presented to the Asian Studies Association of Australia 9th Biennial Conference, Armidale, New South Wales, 5–9 July 1992).

4. It is unclear how Supomo arrived at this term, as it was uncommon in legal or political philosophy. Several right-wing Catholic groups in Latin America used it, however, including the Brazilian Integralist

movement (Ação Integralista Brasileira), which was active in the 1930s. See M. T. Williams, "Integralism and the Brazilian Catholic Church," *Hispanic American Historical Review* 53, 4 (August 1974).

5. J. H. A. Logemann, *Keterangan-keterangan baru tentang terjadinya UUD 1945,* (New accounts of the origins of the 1945 Constitution; a translation of the 1962 essay "Niewe gegevens over het ontstaan van de Indonesische grondwet van 1945" by Darji Darmodihardjo) (Jakarta: Aries Lima, 1982), 29.

6. Mohammad Yamin, *Naskah persiapan undang-undang dasar 1945* (Documents relating to the preparation of the 1945 Constitution), vol. 1 (Jakarta: Jajasan Prapantja, 1959), 112.

7. Ahmad Subardjo Djoyoadisuryo, *Kesadaran nasional: Otobiografi* (Jakarta: Gunung Agung, 1978), 201, reveals that he and his fellow members of the nationalist organization Perhimpunan Indonesia studying in Leiden in the early 1920s were flooded with Nazi propaganda and visited by several Nazis who tried (unsuccessfully) to win them over. Two of Subardjo's closest associates at the time were Supomo and A. A. Maramis. All three were to play important roles in the Investigating Committee.

8. Mohammad Yamin, *Naskah persiapan undang-undang,* 112.

9. See for instance the widely disseminated 1937 tract *Kokutai no hongi* published by the Japanese Department of Education, quoted in Ivan Morris, ed., *Japan 1931–1945: Militarism, Fascism, Japanism?* (Boston, Heath, 1963), 44ff. and Prof. Chikao Fujisawa's 1942 pamphlet *The Great Shinto Purification Ritual and the Purification of Nippon* (1942), referred to in Peter de Mendelssohn, *Japan's Political Warfare* (London: George Allen and Unwin, 1944), 165ff.

10. Mohammad Yamin, *Naskah persiapan undang-undang,* 113; italics in original.

11. Ibid., 114.

12. Ibid., 299–300.

13. Article 28, like many other parts of the 1945 Constitution, is extremely brief and imprecisely worded: "The liberty to associate and organize, and to express opinions either orally, in writing or by other means will be regulated by law."

14. Abdulkadir Besar is one of the foremost ideologists in the armed forces. He studied law at the Military Law Academy in the early 1960s while serving in various intelligence and security positions under Nasution. After six years as secretary general of the MPRS (1967–1972) he fell from grace (with MPRS Chairman Nasution) and joined the teaching staff at Seskoad, where he was very influential. According to Nasution (in David Jenkins, *Suharto and his Generals: Indonesian Military Politics, 1975–1983* [Ithaca: Modern Indonesia Project, Cornell University, 1984], 124) he was the "key personality" at the third army seminar in Bandung in 1972. From 1976 to 1979 he was the deputy commander of Seskoad.

15. Abdulkadir Besar, "Academic appraisal tentang tata tertib MPR" (Academic appraisal of procedural aspects of the MPR), in *Laporan Pimpinan MPRS tahun 1966–1972* (Jakarta: Penerbitan MPRS, 1972), 493–548 (the appraisal is dated 18 April 1968). Marsillam Simanjuntak, *Unsur Hegelian dalam Pandangan Negara Integralistik* (Hegelian Elements in the Integralist View of the State) (Master of Laws thesis, Faculty of Law, University of Indonesia, Depok, 1989), 49, first pointed this out. I would like to acknowledge here that Marsillam's work triggered my interest in the subject of this essay.

16. Abdulkadir in interviews with Douglas Ramage in Jakarta in August and October 1992. Ramage, "Pancasila Discourse in Soeharto's Late New Order" (paper prepared for the conference on Indonesian Democracy: 1950s and 1990s, Monash University 17–20 December 1992), 9. I have not been able to check Seskoad materials to confirm this, although the phrase *faham integralistik* (integralist approach) is used in an internal document issued in 1982 by Kopkamtib (*Komando Operasi Pemulihan Keamanan dan Ketertiban* (The operations command to restore order and security)). See Sudomo, *Kebijaksanaan Kopkamtib dalam penanggulangan ekstremitas kiri* (Kopkamtib's Policy to Tackle the Extreme Left), Terbatas [restricted] (Jakarta: Sekretariat Komando Operasi Pemulihan Keamanan dan Ketertiban, 1982) 10, 14. Curiously, another of the army's leading intellectuals, Lieutenant General (Ret.) Sayidiman Suryohadiprojo, claimed in 1989 that he had never heard of integralism before its current revival. See Kompas, *Menuju masyarakat*

Baru Indonesia: Antisipasi terhadap tantangan abad XXI (Toward a New Indonesian society: Anticipating the challenges of the 21st century) (Jakarta: Kompas and Gramedia, 1990), 199.

17. Nugroho Notosusanto, *Proses perumusan pancasila dasar negara* (The process of formulating the *pancasila* state philosophy) (Jakarta: Balai Pustaka, 1981), 54–55.

18. Prof. Darji Darmodihardjo, another prominent military lawyer-ideologist who served on the BP-7 in the late 1980s, did the same thing in his 1981 lectures at Seskoad but came up with five quite different principles. Darji Darmodiharjo, *Pancasila dalam beberapa perspektif* (Several perspectives on *pancasila*) (Jakarta: Aries Lima, 1982), 32.

19. Badan Pembinaan Program Penataran Pedoman Penghayatan dan Pengamalan Pancasila (Body for the Teaching of the Guidelines, Inculcation, and Practice of *Pancasila*).

20. Marsillam Simanjuntak, *Unsur Hegelian*, 58.

21. There is in fact an earlier discussion of integralism in Subardjo's autobiography (396–98) which, although supportive, was in a historical framework and not part of the "new wave." Subardjo quotes Supomo at length and without acknowledgement. Given that Subardjo had studied the philosophy of Hegel and Savigny (117, 135) and that he was an intimate friend of Supomo (236) it is quite possible that Subardjo felt entitled to take some credit for formulating the theory of integralism as espoused in 1945.

22. See, for example, Sudharmono "Wawasan masa depan kita dan peranan ilmu-ilmu sosial" (Our conception of the future and the role of the social sciences), *Pelita*, 16 December 1986. *Pelita*, the newspaper controlled from 1985 by Golkar while under Sudharmono's leadership, played an important part in pushing the integralist agenda.

23. P4 stands for Pedoman Penghayatan dan Pengalaman Pancasila (Upgrading Course on the Directives for the Realization and Implementation of Pancasila).

24. See, for example, Widiada Gunakaya and Surayin *Penuntun pelajaran tata negara* (Constitutional studies manual; based on the 1984 curriculum and revised in accordance with the 1987 teaching guidelines) (Bandung: Ganeca Exact Bandung, 1987).

25. Vice president and former armed forces Commander General Try

Sutrisno is the most dependable, but certainly not the sole, source of such statements. See his comments reported in *Kompas*, 20 September 1990 and *Suara Pembaruan*, 15 February 1991 and 13 March 1991.

26. Suhunan Situmorang et al., "Revivalisasi negara integralistik: Polemik yang belum selesai" (The revival of the integralist state: An unfinished polemic), *Forum Keadilan*, no. 22 (1990): 36.

27. Abdulkadir Besar, "'Negara Persatuan': Citanegara integralistik anutan UUD 1945" ("The unitary state": The integralist state-philosophy as the basis of the 1945 Constitution), in Guru Pinandita, *Sumbangsih untuk Prof Djokosoetono SH* (Jakarta: Lembaga Penerbit Fakultas Ekonomi Universitas Indonesia, 1984).

28. Padmo Wahyono, "Integralistik Indonesia" (Indonesian integralism), *Majalah Persahi*, no. 3 (January 1990): 43

29. Ibid., 43–45.

30. Ibid., 48.

31. YLBHI, *Hukum, politik dan pembangunan* (Law, politics, and development; a submission to the DPR concerning the Social Organizations Bill) (Jakarta: Yayasan Lembaga Bantuan Hukum Indonesia, 1985); Abdul Hakim G. Nusantara, *Politik Hukum Indonesia* (The politics of law in Indonesia) (Jakarta: YLBHI, 1988).

32. See *Suara Pembaruan*, 3, 4, 5, and 7 July 1989; *Pelita*, 4 July 1989

33. Situmorang, "Revivalisasi negara integralistik," 39.

34. For a bowdlerized version of this exchange see *Kompas, Menuju masyarakat Baru Indonesia,* 188ff.

35. Sartono Kartodirdjo, "Rakyat jangan dianggap bodoh" (Don't treat the people as if they are stupid), *Prisma* 6 (1989).

36. *Bernas*, 1 and 2 July 1991.

37. Situmorang, "Revivalisasi negara integralistik," 37; *Suara karya*, 22 March 1990; *Kompas*, 20 April 1990.

38. *Suara karya*, 22 March 1990. See also, for example, Padmo Wahyono, "Integralistik Indonesia" ; *Suara karya*, 24 March 1990; *Suara pembaruan*, 26 March 1990.

39. Bambang S. Sulasmono, "Kristalisasi pemikiran kenegaraan" (A crystallization of constitutional thinking), *Kompas*, 14 May 1991.

40. Ramage, "Pancasila Discourse in Soeharto's Late New Order. "

41. See, for example, Max Lane, *"Openness," Political Discontent and*

Succession in Indonesia: Political Developments in Indonesia, 1989-91, (Nathan, Queensland, Australia: Centre for the Study of Australia-Asia Relations, Griffith University, 1991), 3–16.

42. Vatikiotis describes this antipathy. He writes "If Abri agrees on anything it is on a fervent dislike of Sudharmono. " Michael Vatikiotis, *Indonesian Politics under Suharto: Order, Development and Pressure for Change* (London: Routledge, 1993), 84–88.

43. *Kompas*, 18 October 1990.

44. The gamelan as a metaphor for a smoothly functioning social-political order goes back at least as far as the early days of Indonesian nationalism. It was a favorite image of Raden Soetomo (1888–1938), one of the founders of the pioneering "cultural nationalist" organization Budi Utomo.

45. This argument is now used by several Southeast Asian countries in response to human rights criticism. (See, for instance, James Walsh, "Asia's Different Drum," *China News Digest Book and Journal Review*, 14 June 1993). The reemergence of the notion of *ketimuran* (Eastern-ness) in Indonesia, popularized during the Japanese occupation, may indicate that Indonesia is interested in spearheading a campaign to define a broader Asian conception of human rights. Singapore and Malaysia have used similar 'cultural relativist' arguments to rebut criticisms framed in terms of human rights in recent years.

46. *Bernas*, 1 and 2 July 1991.

47. Examples can be found in the recent doctral thesis of Indonesia's highest-placed constitutional lawyer, Deputy Cabinet Secretary Dr. A. Hamid S. Attamimi, who uses Supomo's 1945 speech as an authoritative guide to the interpretation of the constitution. Analyzing the place of *trias politica* within the constitution, Attamimi argues that while the constitution differentiates between legislative, executive, and regulatory powers, this should not be regarded as endorsing *trias politica* because according to Supomo in 1945 this concept is not in accordance with Indonesia's *staatsidee*. See A. Hamid S. Attamimi, "Peranan keputusan presiden Republik Indonesia dalam penyelenggaraan pemerintahan ne-gara" (The role of presidential decisions in the governance of the Indonesian Republic) (Doctor of Laws dissertation, University of Indonesia, Jakarta, 1990), 143–46.

48. Ramadhani Aksyah, "Paham integralistik dan oposisi" (Integralism and opposition), *Kompas*, 28 October 1989.

49. Mohammad Yamin, *Naskah persiapan undang-undang*, 114.

50. Richard Tanter, "Intelligence Agencies and Third World Militarisation: A Case Study of Indonesia, 1966–1989" (Ph. D. thesis, Dept. of Politics, Monash University, 1991).

51. Adnan Buyung Nasution, "The Aspiration for Constitutional Government in Indonesia; A Socio-legal Study of the Indonesian Konstituante 1956–1959" (Ph. D. dissertation, Rijksuniversiteit, Utrecht, 1992).

52. T. Mulya Lubis, "In Search of Human Rights: Legal Political Dilemmas of Indonesia's New Order, 1966–1990" (Doctor of Laws dissertation, School of Law, University of California, Berkeley, 1990).

53. See, for instance, Marsillam Simanjuntak, "Konstitutionalisme dan demokrasi di Indonesia" (Constitutionalism and democracy in Indonesia), *Detik*, no. 565 (30 November 1992).

54. See, for example, *Kompas*, 4 July 1989; *Suara Pembaruan*, 28 May 1990; Bambang S. Sulasmono, "Kristalisasi pemikiran kenegaraan"; Adnan Buyung Nasution, "Adakah hak asasi manusia di Dalam UUD 1945?" (Does the 1945 Constitution contain human rights?), *Forum Keadilan*, no. 20 (21 January 1993).

55. Mohammad Yamin, *Naskah persiapan undang-undang*, 410.

Chapter Seven

Sharing a Room with Other Nonstate Cultures: The Problem of Indonesia's Kebudayaan Bernegara

Fachry Ali

PERHAPS IT IS irrelevant to question whether the emergence of a state is the product of cultural processes. The degree of people's acceptance of the existence of the state and the depth of their consciousness of their civil rights requires deep socialization of a particular frame of values—what can be termed here *kebudayaan bernegara*, or a state culture. The gap between ethnic groups that have a state culture and those that do not has become the source of endless problems for many new states. As the problems extend to the national level, issues that were originally rooted simply in a cultural context might be extending to economic and political fields as well.

Before proceeding with the argument, I would like to define what I mean by culture. Culture, in this instance, is a fabric of meanings through which people can interpret their experience and which thereby become a blueprint for action.[1] Such a cultural concept is very loose. I tend to employ it purposively, however, in order to accommodate the dynamic of problems relevant to *kebudayaan bernegara*.

Kebudayaan bernegara fits within this conceptual framework.: It is *a set or a fabric of meanings through which the state elite take control of the development of people's ideas, and particularly of their notion of how the state should be organized.* The *kebudayaan bernegara*, therefore, contains elements of beliefs, expressive symbols, and a set of particular values. It thus constitutes a vehicle whereby the people it encompasses find their world, reflecting both their feelings and ideas, and, to some extent, express their political assessments of state affairs.

It was through this conceptual framework that Clifford Geertz explained the Indonesian political struggles in the 1950s and 1960s, with what he called *the struggle for the real* or the politics of meaning;[2] that is, a kind of struggle among political groups to fight for a strategic position in providing an ideal interpretation of Indonesian realities. The stakes of these struggles were not positions of real power, but they were symbolic.[3]

To make this complicated framework easier to understand, it seems worth approaching the Indonesian *kebudayaan bernegara* —its state-oriented political culture—by setting forward some extreme examples of how that political culture has been accepted by Indonesian ethnic groups. Hopefully, these examples will provide an opportunity to elucidate the development of the "state culture" in the Indonesian New Order.

State Culture: Nuaulu and Java

Nuaulu is a traditional village, part of the *desa* of Sepa, in the Amahai administrative district (*kecamatan*) of Seram Island (in the province of Maluku), whose people still strongly adhere to their ancient beliefs. The population of the village of Sepa is about 2,000. In the entire *kecamatan* 18,538 people live in twenty villages. Roughly 49 percent are Muslims, and as many are Christians, mostly Protestants. Less than 3 percent adhere exclusively to traditional religious practices. The Nuaulu are therefore a very small population, surrounded by much larger settlements which differ in terms of religious orientation, degree of integration into the state, and general lifestyle.[4]

The Nuaulu have had some kind of corporate identity for over 300 years, and have been recognized by outsiders as a distinct group for at least that long. Their traditional belief system, which is still profoundly rooted within the Nuaulu, has served as a tool and as a cultural model in structuring the "outside world." The outside world is conceived as Sepa village and other villages surrounding Amahai district whose residents now have converted to different religions: Islam and Protestant Christianity. Above all, however, from the Nuaulu cultural perspective, the Republic of Indonesia (which in the Amahai district is represented by Javanese as well as Ambonese officials) is seen as part of the outside world as well. For historical, geographical, and socioeconomic reasons, the Nuaulu people find themselves distinct from their neighbors. Thus, they are separated from the "outside world."

When linked with the concept of *kebudayaan bernegara*, this separation means that the Nuaulu people do not see themselves as hemmed in by new sociocultural, economic, and political developments. They see, instead, the incompatibility of their fabric of ideas (culture) and the "modern" one produced by the state.

Their first introduction to the state took place through their indirect involvement in the rapid development of the surrounding societies. They then became aware of how heterogeneous the Indonesian people were. The outbreak of the traumatic South Moluccan Republic (RMS) affair made them aware that they had a larger identity (as Moluccan people) than their tradition suggested. However, they were again shocked as the Indonesian Army shattered the RMS force. Consequently, this brought about a new consciousness: behind the regional boundaries which they had just found, there was a realm of power, far stronger and more powerful than that ever possessed by Moluccan groups: the Indonesian state.

However, incorporation of the Nuaulu into this latter realm was conducted through unique means, for example, through participation in modern state ceremonies. Theoretically, the state ceremonies have become modern rituals through which the state tries to cultivate a single and new loyalty beyond ethnic lines, and to sanctify the state itself. The *Tujuhbelas Agustus* (Independence Day) and Veterans Day ceremonies, which are held annually in Amahai district, are conceived, from the Nuaulu's cultural point of view, as a form of new ritual which has been incorporated into their lives.

Nevertheless, their participation in those state ceremonies is not completely sincere. The aim of making the ceremonies more lively, and inserting a recreational element into them, has prompted the local government officials of Amahai to invite the Nuaulu to perform their ritual dance, *cakalele*. Consequently, the dance they perform became rigorously unifocal, demystified, and wholly reduced in semantic content. It is at this point that the problem of cultural and national integration comes to the fore, and the *kebudayaan bernegara* collides with local culture.

For the Nuaulu it is difficult, because of the restricted nature of their participation in the state rituals, to experience Indonesian state ceremonies as anything more than an encounter with some ethnic other, let alone attain any sense of belonging. It is extremely difficult for them to think of themselves as Indonesians in the fullest sense, unless they cease to practice their own rituals —that is, to cease to be Nuaulu. As stated by Roy F. Ellen, the Nuaulu people are ready to compromise on the role they are expected to perform. The role, however, is performed *by Nuaulu people, not Indonesians*. The modern Indonesian culture expressed through these state rituals, from the Nuaulu point of view, is simply another culture to be tolerated, but it is interpreted wholly from the view of their own traditional culture, not as an inclusive culture of which they feel an integral part.

The Javanese experience is the exact opposite of that of the Nuaulu.[5] For the Javanese villager, the distinction between Indonesia and Java is far from clear, because in the creation of the national state, the villager sees the reconstruction of Javanese society and the reinvigoration of Javanese values. Such a consciousness is firmly rooted in the Javanese historical experience under colonialization. Consequently, the Javanese experienced a kind of permanent disintegration and division of power.[6] They experienced a general formlessness of life, an essential vagueness of social structure, and a looseness of ties between individuals, especially when compared to places such as Bali, where traditional institutions continue to shape social behavior precisely and explicitly.

The causes of this general social malaise and loss of structural solidity can mainly be traced to Dutch economic and administrative policy in Java from the beginning of the nineteenth century. That policy aimed at extracting large agricultural surpluses from the island, using the native population to provide those surpluses, and yet accomplishing this without seriously disturbing native life. The intent was to keep the natives native, and yet to make them produce exports saleable on world markets, a self-contradictory aspiration on the face of it. Especially under the Culture System, Java's crops were to come into the modern world, but Java's people were not.

The intention of all the welfare measures undertaken by the colonial government was to shield the Javanese village from the presumptively destructive forces of the rationalized, modern West, rather than to help it adjust to those forces. It meant that the Javanese were indeed prevented from reacting freely to the changed conditions they found themselves in, and that they were unable to develop new institutions through which they might cope more effectively with modern life. They were forced, therefore, to rely on a series of ad hoc, desperate, and almost entirely defensive adjustments to the series of social crises that the hundred and fifty years of intensive Dutch rule brought.

Geertz imaginatively describes postcolonial Javanese society:

Pulled this way and that, hammered by forces over which it had no control, and denied the means for actively reconstructing itself, village social structure lost its traditional resiliency and grew flaccid, pliant, and generally indeterminate. The so called "advance towards vagueness" which has sometimes been remarked of Javanese rural social organization is in fact a result of this peculiarly passive kind of social change experience which it has been obliged to endure; such vagueness is functional to a society which is allowed to evade, adjust, absorb and adapt but is not really allowed to change.[7]

It is within this uncertain and vague situation that the Javanese conceived the emergence of the Republic of Indonesia, which, through a series of social and political revolutions, would act as a vehicle for their own reintegration and, above all, as a tool for their cultural revival. The nation-state, therefore, reconstructed their old fabric of meanings and ideas that had been shattered by Dutch and Japanese colonial regimes.

The Dynamics of State Culture: The New Order Era

It is, of course, incomplete to raise only these two extreme examples of the Nuaulu and the Javanese in the context of this discussion. Because of their extreme nature, however, such cases provide striking examples of the intricacies of the processes involved in the encounter between the emerging modern state and the various ethnic groups in Indonesian society. The Nuaulu people, on the one hand, do not conceive the modern state as a continuation of their ancient system of ideas. They perceive the presence of the state as merely a complement to their own culture. In the eyes of the Nuaulu, the state culture and the Nuaulu culture stand independent and equal. *For the Nuaulu, the state culture and local culture are not substantially integrated.*

The Javanese people, on the other hand, perceive the state as an integral part of their system of ideas. The unconscious, ancient appeal of cultural solidarity, after having been thrown into almost complete disarray by the colonial regimes, came to be focused on the Indonesian state. Here, in the main, the desire to be united under a strong leadership was almost entirely associated with the newly emerging Indonesian state. *For the Javanese, the state culture and the old cultural desires were thus complementary.*

However, the real problem still remains. The Nuaulu's case seems to foreshadow the situation elsewhere in the "outer islands," whose people remain firmly in the grasp of their own system of ideas. The problem may be getting more serious as the state attempts to impose its standardized system of values on the surface of local cultures. Several ethnic and regional outbreaks in the 1950s and 1960s can be partly understood as resulting from the supralocal party's system of ideas being superimposed on realms whose people had not yet abandoned their own system of culture. The previous regional movements derived partly from this incompatibility between the state and local systems of ideas. In other words, in the context of the fifties and sixties, the *struggle for the real* was not only valid in the arena of central political power, but was also reflected in the relationship between the center and peripheries: a clash between the central government and the local parties themselves over the right to determine, and to interpret, local realities.

From this vantage point, the Indonesian political dynamic under the New Order can be seen. The central elite believed in the state's fabric of ideas and meanings, partly because of structural problems which are becoming increasingly self-evident (and to some extent because of pragmatic considerations). The state, in order to be effectively dominant in society, increasingly emphasizes its own system of ideas. The emphasis on political stability and security and the choices of a particular direction for the future of societal development, reflected, for instance, in the "imperative" to comply with a single model of development, are striking examples of the implementation of that articulation of state culture.

The state culture's claims to acceptance lie almost entirely in the development of the Indonesian economy. Because economic development has transformed society, the state culture is thought to have its structural roots in that development and transformation. *At this stage of development the standardization of the state culture's claims fits its economic calculation.* Conversely, the implementation of economic development fits its cultural calculations.

The economy-based nature of the societal transformation has, to a large extent, produced the expected results. Indonesian society under the New Order is almost completely free from the context of its previous systems of ideas—most notably among the urbanized populace. One of the most impressive results of the transformation is the radical decrease of regionalist motives and primordialist sentiments, which previously had been the basis of political conflicts. With various exceptions, Indonesian society today has been transformed into a new, or more accurately, a different form. This form has not yet become permanent, but it is clear that it is almost totally removed from the old forms.

It is precisely because of such a transformation that some parts of society have gained wider opportunities, much wider than before, to absorb various universal ideas. The growth of democratic movements and the desire of some educated Indonesians to be free of state control—features of society that are clearly seen today—owe much to the transformation under the New Order. But these developments are not in accordance with the expectations of the state culture.

It is here that the struggle for the right way to define Indonesian realities is being played out. The "enlightened" parties, who have absorbed universal ideas which are not structurally tied to the New Order economic sphere, have employed those systems of ideas to interpret Indonesian realities in a way that is different from the interpretation of state officials. The emergence of various society-based movements (student, intellectual, and environmental, among others), whose members covet a more democratic Indonesia, can be understood as a part of the articulation of the struggle for the right to influence Indonesian realities today.

However, it would be misleading to take for granted the conviction that these new developments have, in themselves, entirely erased the old realities: the persistence of the local cultural systems. Those systems still exist. The *kebudayaan bernegara* now involves layers of cultural struggle—the cosmopolitan, the localist, and the statist itself. It is at this point that interesting questions could be raised: in what ways will such a struggle materialize? And, above all, who will emerge as the sole winner?

No party in this triangular struggle, however, could definitively shape its own destiny. The unofficial members of the cosmopolitan cultural network of the Indonesian enlightened party, on the one hand, lean heavily on the support of international opinion in putting forward their interpretation. To some extent, this kind of power has demonstrated its effectiveness. Often the state is able to launch only moderate measures against them, and they have been able, in part, to push the state into a defensive position.[8] But it is quite certain that the force of this movement is confined artificially, and is not deeply internalized within the consciousness of contemporary Indonesian society. Thus, it is doubtful that they will have enough power to achieve significant influence. The most important shortcoming of this new group is their lack of any wealth that could be transferred into a cultural weapon, or, at least, could allow them to endure.

The state, on the other hand, still has strong control over several strategic factors that maintain the effectiveness of its cultural system. The state's control over productive and strategic capital sectors, on which almost all the new economic middle and upper classes depend, provides the avenues through which the state can perpetuate its own ideas and legitimize itself. Above all, the power of the armed forces, who have physically integrated the whole nation, is officially on the side of the state.

However, the ground on which the state articulates its culture has changed. At the international level, the role of nonstate actors has not only received more attention,[9] but has also been fostered by the changing processes of world politics, wherein the role of the state in resolving the world's problems has been challenged by nonstate actors (in terms of both individuals and institutions).[10] This situation has reduced the dignity of the state before its cosmopolitanized society. The process of articulating the state culture, therefore, must be shared with other cultures.

Moreover, though it is still only vaguely accepted, partly because of internal political considerations, the previously uncompromising stand of the Indonesian military has changed slightly. The military's attitude toward the intellectuals' concept of freedom is no longer as tough as it was. As a result of this changing attitude, the military, a core force within the state culture, has demonstrated its readiness to compromise with other cultures—something it almost completely rejected in previous decades.

Finally, there is the issue of the local cultures in the outer islands. Constrained by their diverse nature, they are overcoming some fundamental shortcomings. Though those cultures are, in the main, supported by Islamic values, they nevertheless are unable to develop strategic responses to the modernizing process. However, the abundant natural resources in these regions can be used as weapons in the struggle of local cultures to maintain and promulgate their own ideas, at least in their own territory.[11] Ultimately, however, given the isolated nature of these regions, they will not be able to compete with the state culture.

As a result, the Indonesian cultural struggle, is facing a zero-sum situation. The victory or the loss of one of the participants will cause an imbalance of power, and lead to further political conflict. The Indonesian struggle for the real still goes on.

Notes

1. C. Geertz, *The Interpretation of Cultures* (New York: Basic Books, 1973), 154. Geertz's cultural conception has been expounded by Diane Austin-Broos. See her article "Clifford Geertz: Culture, Sociology and Historicism", in *Creating Culture*, ed. D. Austin-Broos (Sydney: Allen and Unwin, 1987), 141–62.

2. See Clifford Geertz, afterword ("The Politics of Meaning") to *Culture and Politics in Indonesia*, ed. C. Holt (Ithaca: Cornell University Press, 1972), 319–36.

3. Geertz, afterword.

4. All the information on the Nuaulu is derived from Roy F. Ellen, "Ritual, Identity and Management of Interethnic Relations on Seram," in *Time Past, Time Present, Time Future*, ed. David Moyerd and Hendri Claessen (Dordrecht: Foris Publications, 1988), 117–35.

5. This description of Javanese culture is taken from Clifford Geertz, "Javanese Village," in *Local, Ethnic and National Loyalties in Village Indonesia: A Symposium*, ed. W. Skinner (Cultural Report Series, Southeast Asian Studies, Yale University, 1959).

6. The permanent division of Javanese power in the eighteenth century has been expounded by M. C. Ricklefs in his Cornell doctoral dissertation, "Yogyakarta under Mangkubumi, 1749–1792: A History of the Division of Java," 1973.

7. Geertz, "Javanese Village," 36.

8. The frequent presence of J. P. Pronk, Dutch Minister of Foreign Aid and the Chairperson of IGGI before its disbanding in 1992, is an example of how the state may seem powerless before the Indonesian supporters of "universal ideas". Pronk not only rejected many official programs put forward by the Indonesian government, but also chose to visit many dissident groups in Indonesia. Influential efforts of the gov-

ernment were not able to prevent this colonial style of inspection without dismantling the entire group. This example clearly demonstrates the strength of the cosmopolitan culture network that has been formed.

9. The emergence of INGI (International Non-governmental Group on Indonesia) is an interesting example. These nonstate actors (mostly from NGOs), produce very provocative statements about the Indonesian government at every annual meeting. One annual statement, for example, addressed *Kedung Ombo*—a controversial dam project funded by the World Bank. Through a series of appeals to the World Bank, the statement caused a commotion within Indonesia. The Indonesian INGI members were accused of embarrassing their own government. The Minister of Domestic Affairs did not conceal his dissatisfaction; he stated: "Right or wrong, it is my country." But the state took no action against INGI.

10. See B. Hocking and M. Smith, *World Politics* (London: Harvester, 1990), 8-9.

11. Aceh may be a good example of this. Even up to recent times, limited outbreaks have been occurring in this region. The collision between the state culture and the local culture can be seen clearly here. The central power, however, seems to be recognizing the Acehnese system of ideas as a distinct one. The richness of their region in natural resources has helped the Acehnese to maintain their cultural identity.

Chapter Eight

Non-government Organizations, the State, and Democratization in Indonesia

Philip Eldridge

Momentum for democratic change in Indonesia has been building since the late 1980s. Demands for reform appear to enjoy more broadly based support than during the previous major upsurge of political activity (during the 1970s). While urban-based professionals and intellectuals still form the core of this movement, its links with rural people and industrial workers are now a good deal more diverse and extensive. In that context, demands for electoral and constitutional reform reflect broader struggles for democratization of Indonesia's legal and institutional structures.

While significant differences exist between these groups with respect to both strategy and ideology, a lack of legal autonomy or security for their own organizations or those established by groups at the grassroots level with whom they work has increasingly provided a common focus of interest and action, with elements that seek change coalescing around demands for freedom to organize. Pressure on this issue has been concentrated particularly on struggles relating to land tenure, labor rights, the urban informal sector, and the environment. These activists believe that freedom of association is guaranteed by Article 28 of Indonesia's 1945 Constitution.[1] In practice, such rights are abridged by heavy government intervention and monopolization of major fields of mass organization by official networks of "functional groups" (Golongan Karya—GOLKAR). The Social Organizations (ORMAS) Law of

1985 also has the potential to seriously constrain the operation of a wide range of groups outside the formal arena of politics, although I have argued elsewhere that the impact of that legislation has been blunted a good deal by a variety of informal strategies.[2]

Non-government organizations (NGOs) —commonly referred to in Indonesia as self-reliant community (development) institutions (LSM, Lembaga Swadaya Masyarakat, or LPSM, Lembaga Pengembangan Swadaya Masyarakat)[3]—represent one important element within this loose coalition for "democratization." NGO/LSM/LPSMs are defined, in the context of this discussion, as nonparty and nonprofit organizations, although cooperative enterprises that share profits among their members are included. Most claim to focus on promoting the interests of the poor and disadvantaged, though many pursue more general public-interest objectives.[4] Organizations oriented purely toward charity or welfare are not covered in this paper, although they can reasonably be seen as having a stake in greater freedom for nonstate associations to manage their own affairs. To some extent, cultural and recreational associations of those who are not poor also have such a stake. Educational institutions feature in this discussion only insofar as they support developmental or advocacy activities similar to those of NGOs—although some have contributed significantly to the developing of the understanding of democratic values in Indonesia.

Most discussion of prospects for a greater measure of democracy and openness (*keterbukaan*) in Indonesia has tended to assume that NGOs give unqualified support to such demands. This is understandable in view of their sustained rhetoric, which emphasizes self-reliance, popular participation, bottom-up, small-scale, and decentralized styles of development. NGOs themselves have sought to extend application of the "deregulation" policies pursued in the economic sphere since the mid-1980s to social and community organization more generally. The World Bank and several Western governments have supported them in this endeavor, urging a greater measure of community participation in official programs as a condition of aid. NGOs' capacity to mobilize support from their counterparts overseas to assist the government of Indonesia (GOI) in meeting these demands has enhanced their leverage still further. To the extent that pressures for political democratization are perceived as coming from the same sources, Indonesian NGOs are assumed to hold similar views.

Such a view is too simplistic—notions of democracy embrace several levels of meaning in the Indonesian context, and the heterogeneous nature of LSM/LPSMs results in different understandings of that notion. It cannot therefore be assumed that demands for "democratization" or "rights to organize" necessarily translate into support for Western-style "liberal" democracy. This is true in the case of many younger radical groups also. Care must also be taken in projecting goals and strategies derived essentially from local experience into the macropolitical sphere. Despite the obvious antithesis between many LSM/LPSM values and those of the New Order "corporatist" state, close examination of their normative framework reveals some divergence from values of Western-style liberal democracy as well as considerable convergence with many aspects of Indonesia's official ideology of *pancasila*. Also, while NGOs' insistence that they are "nonpolitical" is partly tactical and prudential, it also reflects aspirations toward direct mobilization of popular energies without intervention from state or political intermediaries. It is therefore important, in assessing LSM/LPSMs' potential contribution to political reform, to bear in mind their ambivalence as to the importance of such a project in the first place.

Core values of NGO/LSM/LPSMs center on "self-reliance" and "popular participation," linked to ideals of social justice and equity. They tend to see gaining social and economic benefits for the masses as more important than attainment of more "abstract" rights in the political sphere. Participation and self-reliance are seen both as instrumental to fulfilling equitable social and eco- nomic objectives at the grassroots level—and their absence as conversely dysfunctional—and as ends in themselves, essential to human dignity. Again, norms and goals of equity are primarily local in their conception and articulation, while it is central to LSM/LPSM philosophy that people can only be motivated around priorities they have determined for themselves and which affect their lives immediately. Developing understanding of and confronting forces bearing on their situation from outside is seen as a slow process by most who have worked for any extensive time among the urban or rural poor.

Intervention by the state is considered more likely to be coun- terproductive than beneficial, though Indonesian NGOs are not averse to support in the form of resources and facilitation of ac- cess by local authorities. Their interventions in various policy fields have been primarily aimed at achieving greater devolution of resources and decision making to community groups. Thus they encourage formation of primary health groups as key vehicles for providing health education and services at the village level; water users' associations to control distribution, maintenance, pric- ing, and revenue collection; associations of cultivators on official smallholder programs to manage distribution of seeds, credit, and other inputs;[5] savings and loan groups; informal cooperatives; and housing associations. Where they cannot avoid working through local units of government associated (GOLKAR) front groups, such as the Indonesian Farmers' Association (Himpunan Kerukunan Tani Indonesia—HKTI), Village Cooperative Unit (Koperasi Unit Desa—KUD), or Family Welfare Development Association (Pembinaan Kesejahteraan Keluarga—PKK),[6] they make every effort to orient them in a similar direction drawing, for example, on such traditional village institutions as *arisan*.[7]

LSM/LPSMs have low overall expectations of the state. One could even suggest that, like the "subsistence-minded" peasant of James Scott[8] and others, they would prefer that an exploitative state would leave them and the people they work with alone to develop their own survival strategies. However, accepting that this will not happen, they have pragmatically developed strategies for keeping the state at a distance while cooperating in numerous day-to-day contexts. NGOs' emphasis on "self-reliance," maximizing use of local resources and minimizing formal links with state and political processes could be seen as a modernized version of such subsistence mindedness.

Despite these caveats, there is evidence during the most recent period of shifts toward adopting a more explicit stance in favor of democratizing the political system in a direct sense. Such demands clearly go beyond long-standing efforts to influence policy in specific sectors, based on accumulated field experience. And they go beyond more recent efforts to establish freedom of association and legal certainty for popular organizations. In June 1993, fifty-two NGOs and related networks, supported by 109 individual activists, signed a Joint Declaration on Human Rights under the banner of Indonesian NGOs for Democracy.[9] This statement stressed the universality and indivisibility of political, civil, economic, social, and cultural rights, rejecting any notion of a trade-off among them.

Still more radical was the signatories' statement calling for "the guarantee of elections which are free, honest and just and which involve all section[s] of society and representative organizations in [the] electoral process."[10] This call for open political competition goes well beyond NGOs' normal social, developmental, and advocacy activities. While demands for freedom of political association represent a logical extension from longer-established demands for autonomous self-management of socioeconomic formations such as LSM/LPSMs, associations of workers, farmers, women, water users, and small enterprises. However, it also represents a conscious incursion into the political arena.

The catalyst for the joint statement was provided by the push by several Asian governments to amend the substance, or at least the interpretation and implementation of, the United Nations Charter on Human Rights, to make allowance for their history, culture, and development needs. Western countries, led by the USA under the newly elected Clinton administration resisted what they saw as an attack on the universal nature of the charter. The issues were thrashed out in United Nations-sponsored conferences on human rights held in Bangkok[11] and Vienna, where the final statement achieved a synthesis, at a rhetorical level at least.[12] Asian NGOs at a "counterconference" in Bangkok took a collective position in opposition to their governments, on which Indonesian NGOs later drew in the statement cited above.[13] Earlier, in opening a three-day UN workshop of Asian Pacific countries on human rights in Jakarta in January 1993, President Suharto had stressed the importance of culture and national sovereignty in determining how each country interprets and implements human rights. In response, the Foundation of Indonesian Legal Aid Institutes (Yayasan Lembaga Bantuan Hukum Indonesia—YLBHI) branded the Indonesian government as a major violator of human rights.[14]

The NGOs' June 1993 statement provides evidence of an emerging convergence between radical groups and important mainstream NGO networks clustered around the International NGO Group on Indonesia (INGI). INGI's strength is concentrated particularly in the fields of legal rights, labor, and the environment. Since around 1988 to 1990, entry points for the NGO community into debates among urban and intellectual elites about democratic reforms of the political structure have come via struggles around these issues. Nevertheless, at the time of writing, the breadth of support for the Indonesian NGOs for Democracy

Joint Declaration among mainstream NGOs cannot be gauged with any degree of certainty. Most major NGOs did not sign as individual organizations, although they could be seen as associated through NGO coalitions, such as INGI, YLBHI, WALHI (Wahana Lingkungan Hidup Indonesia—Indonesian Environment Network), or their regional forums. Some radical groups appear to have had some reservations, though on somewhat different grounds, as will be discussed below.

Indonesian NGOs and Competing Understandings of Democracy

It is possible to distinguish three broad understandings of democracy in the contemporary Indonesian context.

The first type is "representative" or "constitutional" democracy along Western lines. Although NGOs flourish in large numbers in India and the Philippines, where competitive electoral politics operates, they are subject to many strains and deviations from stated ideals. In principle, NGOs face two kinds of difficulties in relating to such a system. First, elected representatives are most effectively influenced through the formation of interest groups. NGOs' potential to trade votes for services is in part hampered by their underlying "nonpolitical" ideology and praxis. This can cause them to gain the worst of all worlds, since such scruples tend not to be understood by politicians, who may also see them as potential rivals. Second, politicians' expectations of reciprocal support in return for patronage and protection conflicts with NGOs' attempts to build capacity to organize and strength to demand services and legal entitlements as a right rather than a favor.

Evolution in a liberal-democratic direction holds growing appeal for significant sections of the Indonesian middle class, as lack of choice in political representation and lack of freedom of speech and association becomes increasingly irksome in business, professional, and intellectual quarters. By contrast, the mass of workers and peasants, for whom the costs and benefits of a more open and competitive representative process are uncertain, are more concerned with economic security and control over the means of subsistence. Consequently, in seeking to represent them, LSM/LPSMs tend to stress social and economic needs and are more ambivalent toward Western-style political reform. Radical groups who ally with workers and peasants face a similar dilemma, which they resolve by seeing liberal "freedoms" as a limited tool to achieve more sweeping "structural" transformation.

In practice, NGOs tend to emphasize group- and community-based decision making rather than that of individuals. They consequently tend to feel uncomfortable with the individualistic emphasis associated with liberal democratic ideology and look for understandings of democratic participation more in accord with their core values. In many ways, *pancasila* understandings of democracy can be seen as compatible with NGOs core values and practice, converging broadly with interpretations of *pancasila* drawn from earlier periods of Indonesian history emphasizing voluntarist modes of community cooperation (*gotong royong*) and "resilience."[15]

Processes of "deliberation and consensus," which have historically formed the core of *pancasila* concepts of decision making, fit well with NGOs' outlook and day-to-day practice. Equally, freedom of expression can be accommodated by *pancasila* to the extent that the ultimate goal is to achieve solutions for the whole group rather than a few individuals. Despite abuses by both present and former governments, ideals of *gotong royong* (working together) in pursuit of a common purpose retain considerable cultural and political resonance with the masses. NGOs have increasingly identified with criticism by students, intellectuals, and other activists of monopolization and centralization of power by the Suharto government. For the most part, however, rather than take up demands for sweeping structural change, they have concentrated their energies on working for more "open" and "participatory" interpretations of *pancasila* within their own sphere of operation.

Another tradition of democracy in Indonesia has been broadly expressed in terms of social revolutionary aspirations toward people's sovereignty (*kedaulatan rakyat*). Historically, the slogan *people's sovereignty* has been mainly associated with the left. However, it was interpreted in quite opposite ways by Mohammad Hatta and Tan Malaka during the period immediately after the proclamation of Indonesian national independence in 1945.[16] Whereas Hatta saw "popular sovereignty" in terms of government accountability through elected legislatures, Malaka and his supporters among radical youth, inspired by his ideas, stressed direct mass action. Parallel, albeit minority countertraditions to liberal and social democracy are to be found also in Western countries, expressed in demands for direct or participatory action and decision making.

Some elements of this third tradition have rubbed off on today's radical activist groups in Indonesia and even on elements among mainstream LSM/LPSMs. Values emphasizing mass action for social justice and an ethos of face-to-face decision making have obvious appeal in many local struggle contexts. They are also reflected in traditions of voluntary action which see diffusion of decision making beyond the formal processes of politics and administration as essential to any effective development of popular participation. In Indonesia, such ideals are not entirely utopian, insofar as they partly reflect people's experience of "direct democracy" at village level, although clearly the trend is toward greater bureaucratization.[17]

LSM/LPSMs draw on all three traditions of democratic participation in shaping both their critique of dominant power structures and their agenda for change. While they appear more comfortable and familiar with the second and third, all three are used eclectically in various struggles both by mainstream LSM/LPSMs and emerging radical groups, since each contains some potential countercultural challenge to dominant corporate statist ideology. Unfortunately, reiteration of vague slogans about participation, people's power, bottom-up decision making, and so forth serves to compress discussion of their meaning in ways which take no account of these three competing frameworks for understanding democratic participation. On the other hand, recent cooperation between different groups of activists on demands for the "right to organize" may provide a point of convergence. Although the right to organize is not readily associated with "*pancasila* democracy" as interpreted by the Suharto government, it nevertheless represents a common element within all three major traditions of democracy in Indonesia.

Achievement of any overall synthesis between competing understandings of democracy is likely to prove very difficult at both a conceptual and practical level. For example, without denying that ideals of decision making through deliberation (*musyawarah*) and consensus (*mufakat*) can sometimes be realized among small groups in face-to-face contexts, their extension from village and subvillage to regional and national arenas has never been satisfactorily achieved in Indonesia. At higher levels, "representative" or "functional" groups, in terms of the "integralist" or "family" theory within which Indonesian state and society officially operates, will inevitably become the creation of the government. This is because, as David Bourchier has put it, there is no other way of determining, in the absence of citizens' rights to organize freely, "which groups in society should be represented and in what proportion."[18]

Despite some notable exceptions, it is hard to see Indonesian NGOs posing any coherent, collective challenge to this dominant orthodoxy. They may even be reinforcing it with demands to be included in more regular and extensive ways in structures of national decision making. The GOI, for its part may well find ways to accommodate such demands as part of a more general process of promoting "openness." The overall effect could be to legitimize corporatist structures, though to some extent strengthening trends toward pluralism within established frameworks.[19]

Self-Reliance and Popular Participation

NGOs' ideas concerning democracy are derived from more fundamental values of self-reliance and people's participation indicated earlier. These are interpreted to mean, at least in an ideal sense, that those people most immediately concerned should determine their own organizational forms, decision making processes, priorities for action, and means for achieving them. The role of outside "animators" or "change agents" should be one of facilitation rather than direction, while indigenous human and material resources should be used to the greatest extent possible. While NGOs attempt to influence policy from time to time, either individually or jointly, their interventions should properly be seen as a scaling-up from field experience, which is overwhelmingly local in both context and orientation.

There are many barriers to realizing such ideals. For example, imbalances in organizational strength and access to external resources between NGOs and base-level groups which they support result in the latter's continuing dependence on the good offices of the former. This dependence occurs at two levels. First, foreign funding agencies (FFAs) are coming to rely on larger LPSMs to undertake evaluations of the growing number of LSMs for funding purposes. This issue has caused no little strain among so-called big and little NGOs. To some extent these misunderstandings are being overcome through joint workshops, training programs, and cooperative approaches in negotiating with FFAs. Second, larger NGOs undertake intermediary roles on behalf of base level groups, such as guaranteeing their creditworthiness in order to obtain bank loans, or negotiating secure stall locations for street traders.

Overcoming such dependence entails building up the self-management capacity of base-level groups, who can then form their own networks and federations for purposes of training, information sharing, and negotiation with outsiders. Such processes of "empowerment" entail building up the necessary confidence and skills. This is inevitably a slow process even if pursued with sustained will and systematic strategies. Realistically, to the extent that the cultural context of Indonesian villages and their relations with power holders retains strong elements of feudalism, NGOs and other activist outsiders cannot avoid some intervention in order to achieve these goals.

Notions of self-reliance (*swadaya*) in the Indonesian context were historically conceived in the context of the national struggle for independence, reinforced by local patterns of guerilla and territorial warfare evolved to suit the conditions of that struggle. Unilateral action by groups of youth (*pemuda*) and irregulars brought them into conflict with the fledgling Indonesian state, particularly the armed forces, during the revolutionary period following the proclamation of independence in 1945.[20] Ideas of self-reliance and popular sovereignty (*kedaulatan rakyat*) at that time found expression both independent from and even in conflict with Indonesian state structures.

Since that time, more quasi-Gandhian understandings of *swadaya* have emerged, emphasizing service to the community, encouragement of local initiative linked to an ethic of cooperation, and moderate lifestyles, with social action focusing on basic needs (*kebutuhan pokok*). However, analogy with Gandhian ideals falls short insofar as there has been no attempt even to conceive of an alternative polity, as in India, where Mahatma Gandhi's idea of a federation of village republics ran directly counter to the state-centered socialist ideals of India's first prime minister, Jawaharlal Nehru. The norm for NGOs working in the Indonesian rural context has been to cooperate with local authorities, either working through formal village structures or taking pains to legitimize new organizations through informal strategies capable of accommodating official ideology and structures.

Conflict Avoidance

The above stance reflects a more general orientation toward conflict avoidance. How far this derives from classical Geertzian, Javanese-style cultural values of harmony and consensus[21] and how far from considerations of political prudence is open to question. NGOs mostly concentrate on putting forward their own understandings, challenging those of the government only by implication and in relatively mild terms. Though NGOs do criticize government policy both individually and collectively in specific contexts,[22] their general style of conflict avoidance appears to result from deliberate strategic choice rather than lack of political resolve. They have developed considerable skill in exploiting areas of rhetorical convergence with official ideology, thus gaining access to decision-making processes and sometimes effecting reforms. Such norms and strategies are now being vigorously challenged by a cluster of more radical groups that has emerged since around 1988 to 1990.

An example of conflict avoidance is provided by the issue of finding a generic term to describe Indonesian NGOs. A tactical decision was taken in 1983 to abandon NGO (*Organisasi Non Pemerintah*—ORNOP) as a generic name. NGO/ORNOP was replaced by "self-reliant community institution" (*Lembaga Swa-daya Masyarakat*—LSM) and "institutions for developing community self-reliance" (*Lembaga Pengembangan Swadaya Masyarakat*—LPSM).[23] *Non-government*, it was argued, could easily be perceived as "anti-government."[24] *Swadaya* also conveys a clearer sense of popular self-determination, while carrying a more authentic ring in terms of national history and culture. Some observers have seen this last aspect as little more than post hoc rationalization. However, there is no reason why both explanations could not be valid. In practice, the term NGO is still widely used, both because of its wide international currency and its emphasis of an identity distinct from the government. In any case, defining their relations with the government continues to be a central question concerning LSM/LPSMs.

In order to avoid the impact of potentially threatening provisions of the 1985 Societies Law, many LSM/LPSMs have set up legal foundations (*yayasan*), which require only a very general statement of objectives. They can also be set up in the name of trustees and do not require any formal membership base. The *yayasan* arrangement allows for the establishment of institutions (*lembaga*) or executive bodies (*badan*) that can operate flexibly according to specific needs. Such flexibility is essential in negotiating with local authorities, which determine whether NGOs can operate effectively in an area or not. Such organizational forms have generally proved successful in evading potential takeover or co-optation by the government and associated front agencies. However, as a consequence, people have been held back from gaining experience of legal democratic processes, and structures of accountability have been prevented from emerging.

To a considerable extent, potential conflict is averted by informal negotiation. This applies both to intragroup relationships and LSM/LPSM relations with the authorities. Contrasts between formal and informal styles of decision making and debate in Indonesian public and social life are very striking to outside observers, though no doubt they are understood by insiders as forming a balanced whole. NGOs naturally emphasize informal modes of operating, where they enjoy advantages of flexibility and access at many levels and with which their people feel more comfortable. Such an ethos, in which the masses still look to influential persons (*tokoh*) to play mediating roles and provide protection and other tangible benefits, helps to explain the paradox of NGOs undertaking responsibility for fostering local self-reliance.

In practice, conflict cannot always be avoided, due to the government's insistence on formal registration of cooperatives and the monopoly granted to Village Cooperative Units (KUDs) in marketing of agricultural produce and supply of inputs. In practice, a very large number of informal cooperatives (*usaha bersama*) and credit unions now operate throughout Indonesia. Usually some kind of tacit understanding can be reached with local authorities that avoids the necessity for any direct rivalry or confrontation.

Contrasting approaches to mediating conflict between local people and the authorities can be observed in the Solo-Klaten Yogyakarta region of central Java, which has been regarded as politically "sensitive" since the upheavals in 1965 to 1966. In order to operate in this area, organizations such as the Prosperous Indonesia Foundation (Yayasan Indonesia Sejahtera—YIS), Bina Swadaya, the Social and Economic Research, Education and Information Institute (Lembaga Penelitian Pendidikan, Penerangan Ekonomi Dan Sosial—LP3ES), and the Yogyakarta Legal Aid Institute (Lembaga Bantuan Hukum Yogyakarta—LBHY) have been careful to avoid overt conflict with the authorities. In the legal rights field, LBHY for many years saw its main role as one of mediating individual cases rather than one of general advocacy. By contrast, the Legal Aid Study Group (Kelompok Studi Bantuan Hukum—KSBH), based in Yogyakarta and also affiliated to YLBHI, emphasized legal education and the "empowerment" of people to take up their own cases directly with the authorities. Training programs and handbooks in relation to issues such as land tenure and compensation for eviction are provided for this purpose. KSBH minimizes its own dealings with the authorities but has nevertheless felt itself to be under constant pressure. Since around 1988 to 1990, LBHY has moved closer to KSBH's position, in line with a general shift in policy within the YLBHI network.

Tensions between mainstream NGOs, particularly LBHY, and emerging, younger radical groups in this area came to a head over the conflict surrounding the Kedung Ombo dam struggle during the late 1980s. Radical student groups, particularly the Yogyakarta Students' Communication Forum (Forum Komunikasi Mahasiswa Yogyakarta—FKMY) supported by radical networks in Jakarta, notably the Indonesian Front for the Defence of Human Rights (INFIGHT) and the Indonesian Network for Forest Conservation (Sekretariat Kerjasama Pelestarian Hutan Indonesia—SKEPHI), undertook a program of direct mobilization and demonstrations both on site and in Jakarta. The YLBHI group concentrated on pursuing legal cases and, together with INGI and WALHI, in lobbying the World Bank and other Western governments. Through a combination of these efforts, some modest increase in compensation was obtained, although one village, Kedung Pring, with the assistance of a charismatic priest from Yogyakarta, Fr. Romo Mangunwijaya, adapted their lifestyle and dwellings, in defiance of the authorities, to survive the rising flood waters.

The intervention of radical students in Kedung Ombo and similar conflicts relating to land tenure and dispossession around the country has generated arguments about the sustainability of such strategies, particularly whether they can achieve empowerment and awareness building among local people over the longer term, whether local people are being used as tools in a political campaign, and whether some activists are "claiming credit" for the work of others.[25] It is hard, nevertheless, to know how much of this conflict is real and how far some tacit division of labor is emerging between radical and "mainstream" NGOs. Possibly the joint signature of the human rights statement cited earlier indicates some bridging of the gap between radical and mainstream NGOs on these issues.

Official Ideology vis-à-vis Self-Reliance and People's Participation

From the government's standpoint, *swadaya* implies an emphasis on the sovereignty and "national resilience" of the Indonesian state, unified "from Sabang to Merauke." No remotely complementary degree of self-rule has so far been envisaged by any government for Indonesia's villages and regions, although the importance of community self-reliance in local economic and social contexts is gradually becoming appreciated. Though keen for villages to mobilize their own resources, the government has so far been careful to maintain strong political and financial controls at the center. Thus BANGDES, the rural development arm of the Department of Home Affairs (Dalam Negeri) classifies *swadaya* as the highest of three stages of village development—the others being *swasembada* (self-sufficiency) and *swakarya* (self-development). As defined by BANGDES, *swadaya* seems to consist of having a long list of facilities in place, with little obvious regard to quality.

Popular participation (*berpartisipasi rakyat*) forms part of standard official rhetoric. This probably derives historically from the more radical slogan *kedaulatan rakyat* (people's sovereignty), which was prominent during the national independence struggle and its aftermath, although it is now little heard. Although some influential individuals display more than token commitment to popular participation, one suspects that the government as a whole sees it as consisting primarily of cooperation in implementing government programs, listening to speeches, and attendance at official functions. More recently, officially sponsored "dialogues" have been witnessed on TVRI (Televisi Republik Indonesia), featuring the president and other *tokoh* talking authoritatively to farmers about such matters as crops, credit, and cooperatives.

Commitment to "social justice" is enshrined as one of the five principles of Indonesia's official ideology of *pancasila*. Government pronouncements frequently refer to the aim of creating a "just and prosperous" (*adil dan makmur*) Indonesia. These aims are couched in terms sufficiently vague to deflect any too-specific demands for greater equity in resource distribution. Nevertheless, elements within the government who are concerned to see an improved flow of resources and effectiveness in programs for reaching the urban and rural poor are in part persuaded by the broad approach pursued by NGOs. For example, Yayasan Indonesia Sejahtera (YIS), based in Solo, has for many years run training programs relating to community development, health, and family planning that are attended by local government officials. YIS also undertakes many advisory and consultancy roles at higher levels. During the late 1970s and early 1980s their work came to the attention of Rustam Suparjo, then governor of Central Java and later Minister for Home Affairs. The supportive role he adopted toward NGOs was continued by his successor in this position, General Rudini, despite some stormy altercations in relation to the higher international profile on environmental and labor rights issues adopted by INGI since around 1989.

Patterns of NGO-Government Accommodation

In earlier writings I identified three broad approaches pursued by NGO/LSM/LPSMs in shaping their relations with the Indonesian government.[26] The first entails a twofold approach of (1) pursuing small-scale programs directly at the village level and ad hoc negotiation with local authorities; (2) cooperating in official development programs and seeking to enhance community participation. Although they are at pains to cultivate smooth working relations with relevant officials and agencies, NGOs in this group show no interest in changing or intervening in the political process as such but rather confine their efforts to influencing policy of those government agencies operating in fields with which their own work is directly concerned. They have always seen such an approach as the most effective means of preserving both their own autonomy and that of associated local groups. The main focus of their public advocacy is on promoting the importance of community participation and self-definition of the goals and strategies for achieving them. As they are both single-minded and versatile in conveying this relatively straightforward message, which is largely derived from direct field experience, they have probably proven more effective as advocates for bottom-up styles of development than those seeking to convey more complex prescriptions based on "structural analysis," "conscientization," and so forth.

Representatives of the first model include YIS, a primary health and community development organization based in Solo; Bina Swadaya, which specializes in promoting cooperative small enterprises and savings and loans clubs; and the Village Light Foundation (Yayasan Dian Desa) based in Yogyakarta, which has a special focus on appropriate technology. Although they have now become quite large organizations, all originated from quite small beginnings. In many ways, their growth has been unplanned, and they consequently tend to feel uncomfortable with many of their new roles.[27]

These LPSMs insist that their cooperation with the government is determined on a case-by-case basis according to whether benefits are likely to accrue to the people they serve, either directly or by influencing policy directions. In any case, cooperation with the government should not be facilely equated with cooption. The NGOs in question remain well aware of the need both to maintain effective grassroots links and to be clearly distinguished from "NGOs" initiated by the government,[28] such as the Family Welfare Development Association (Pembinaan Kesejahteraan Keluarga—PKK), which controls women's organizations at the village level,[29] and the Indonesian Labor Foundation (Yayasan Tenaga Kerja Indonesia—YTKI), established in 1969. The Minister of Manpower and representatives from GOLKAR-front organizations—such as the Indonesian Workers' Federation (SPSI), Indonesian Women's Corps (KOWANI), and Indonesian National Youth Committee (KNPI)—sit on YTKI's Board of Management.

The second approach is more explicitly critical of New Order development philosophy and practice. While promoting "consciousness raising" and capacity for self-management among specific target groups, it seeks legal status and protection for them against local officials and other influential persons, through contacts forged at higher levels of government. Conversely, their grassroots links and field experience serve to enhance their influence with and access to the authorities. Public advocacy and education programs are concerned not only with specific fields but are directed toward changing public opinion about developmental paradigms, particularly among middle-class professionals and intellectuals and among younger educated groups. LSM/LPSMs in this category initially expressed aversion to participating in official development programs but now cooperate extensively in fields such as urban development and ecology. Many NGOs in this second category are led by former student activists from the 1970s and have built up strong informal networks, to a considerable extent linked with broader Islamic networks.

Examples of NGOs in the second category include: (1) LP3ES, which combines research and publication (including the journal *Prisma*) with more conventional styles of community development activity in such fields as irrigation, appropriate technology, and small enterprises—LP3ES has been active in encouraging *pesantren*, traditional Islamic educational institutions, to take up community development work; (2) the Institute of Development Studies (Lembaga Studi Pembangunan—LSP), which has concentrated especially in the urban informal sector and housing programs and has indirectly supported various labor groups through economic programs; (3) major networks in the fields of legal aid and education (YLBHI) and the environment (WALHI), which, together with the Indonesian component of INGI,[30] operate as networks broadly within this second model. However, their individual affiliate organizations are representative of all three approaches.

The focus of action by groups in the third category is at the local rather than the national level, with emphasis on building awareness of rights rather than efforts to change policy. Rather than acting as intermediaries vis-à-vis the authorities, they seek to build confidence and skills among the people to conduct their own negotiations. Social and political change is seen as ultimately less dependent on "persuasion" and policy reform by the government than on the formation of strong, self-reliant groups, in the belief that eventually a strong, albeit informally structured popular movement will emerge. Emphasizing face-to-face dealings rather than formal organization, this group also tends to minimize involvement in large-scale networking arrangements. While they seek legal and bureaucratic niches within which to operate, they seek contact with government agencies only when necessary.

By its nature, such an approach is harder to pin down to particular groups, which are usually quite small and informally structured. Various study, popular theater, and church groups appear to fit into this category, as does the Yogyakarta-based Legal Aid Study Group (KSBH). Further examples include women's groups such as Yayasan Anisa Swasti (YAS) in Yogyakarta, which works among shop and factory workers; Kalyanamitra, a Jakarta-based research, documentation, study, and support group; and other informal networks supporting domestic servants.

The third model is in many respects the most difficult to sustain, though it also represents important ideals valued by most NGOs, particularly those relating to informality, empowerment, and autonomy of small groups. Many which start out in this direction move toward one of the other two larger categories as their operations grow in size and complexity. A more basic contradiction relates to the fusion between "awareness building" and minimizing contact with the government, which in the Indonesian context includes political parties. Such consciousness raising is likely to lead sooner or later to involvement in advocacy, resulting in a move toward either the second model or identification with more politically radical approaches. On the other hand, if the Indonesian political system does become more deregulated, this third model could provide an alternative strategy for building popular movements to more formal party structures favored by those who tend to see the state as the primary vehicle for effecting change.

These three models should be seen as ideal-types aimed at understanding patterns of action rather than rigid boxes for categorizing individual organizations. Most NGOs display mixed characteristics and tend to evolve through various stages. Also, despite very substantial differences in outlook and strategy, all three categories of NGO/LSM/LPSMs share several broad characteristics in common, which could be summarized as: (1) an orientation toward strengthening community groups as the basis for a healthy society and as a counterweight to government power; (2) a creative search for new strategies to confront changing social needs and emerging structures of disadvantage and powerlessness; (3) a strong commitment to ideals of popular participation in defining and implementing programs. Despite many tensions, bureaucratic and personal rivalries, and religious and ideological differences, it is legitimate to talk of an Indonesian NGO community which enjoys a good deal of exchange and mutual support.

Radical Upsurge since the Late 1980s

In recent years, this broad consensus has been explicitly challenged by the emergence of new groups and movements with aggressive and youthful leaders, who criticize established NGOs for what they see as their failure to mobilize workers and peasants or to develop any effective theoretical framework or strategies for change. In particular, they deplore the strategies for conflict avoidance outlined earlier.

Contemporary radical groups can certainly be credited with forging new patterns of alliance with workers, farmers, the landless, and squatters and have shown that it is possible to defy government restrictions on strikes and demonstrations to a greater extent than had previously been thought possible in New Order Indonesia. They take up issues of direct interest to various target groups, such as wages, land alienation, and environmental destruction that undermines poor people's bases of subsistence. However, they tend to link such struggles to wider political agendas. In time their macropolitical orientation is likely to come into conflict with the specifically local, survival-oriented focus of most peasants and workers. In that regard, traditional NGO approaches may well prove more durable.

Examples of such new radical groups are INFIGHT, SKEPHI, and FKMY, mentioned earlier; among women's groups are the Yogyakarta Women's Discussion Forum (Forum Diskusi Perempuan Yogyakarta—FDPY) and Women's Solidarity (Solidaritas Perempuan). The Institute for the Defense of Human Rights (Lembaga Pembelaan Hak-Hak Manusia—LPHAM), headed by veteran human rights activist Haji Princen, has provided a bridge between radical networks and mainstream NGOs active in the legal and human rights fields—notably YLBHI and INGI. Cooperation in this area has been strengthened by joint support for independent labor organizations. Groups involved in this area have recently joined in forming the Labor Solidarity Forum.

NGOs and Macropolitical Processes

Problems of how to scale up struggles to overcome poverty and exploitation beyond the local level and interact effectively with political and governmental structures are perennial issues among NGOs and social activists everywhere. These issues have been less explicitly recognized in Indonesia than in, say, India or the Philippines. To the extent that they have received recognition, many false hopes have been raised that NGO/LSM/LPSMs will somehow fill a gap left by political parties. However, even if fully representative political democracy were to be immediately restored in Indonesia, experience elsewhere indicates that there are powerful philosophical as well as practical reasons why the role of NGOs will remain distinct from that of political parties. Of those reasons, the most salient is that parties' prime focus is on capturing and holding power, for which purpose they need to effectively combine and aggregate interest groups across the social and political spectrum. By contrast, NGOs prefer to operate directly at a societal level and to keep governments and parties at arm's length as much as possible. Further, given their specific focus on poor and disadvantaged groups, NGOs are more likely to develop a long-term commitment to working alongside them.

The example of India is instructive here in that NGOs there generally view parties as an arm of the state. That perception also extends to more radical social activists, who have resigned even from left-wing parties in large numbers for such reasons. Politicians are seen by Indian NGOs and other social activists as seeking to coopt people's struggles and impose their own agendas. An inherent conflict is perceived between politicians, who commonly seek to build support by offering patronage plus protection from various forms of harassment in exchange for support, and voluntary activists, who seek to promote goals of popular empowerment and self-reliance in ways which politicians see as a threat to their power base. There is at least anecdotal evidence to suggest that on the rare occasions such activists stand for election (other than to village councils), they usually fail to receive popular support. This suggests that many villagers also draw clear distinctions between the two roles.

Conclusion

The emergence of new radical groups and recent calls by important elements among mainstream NGOs for a free and democratic political system obviously challenges the contention in this chapter that Indonesian NGOs are primarily local in orientation and relatively passive in relation to democratic reform in the political sphere. On the other hand, for all the reasons given, it is uncertain how deep-rooted or broad-based support for such a position will prove to be across the whole NGO spectrum. In that context, there have been reports of divisions among NGOs affiliated with INGI as to whether INGI's strategy is viable.[31] Particular concern centers on strategies of international lobbying aimed at exerting political leverage over the GOI. It may also be questioned as to whether the new radicals can properly be called NGOs or LSM/LPSMs. Indeed, the radicals themselves would probably reject those terms. This point is real rather than tautological, insofar as the radicals' prime focus is on changing state structures and the ultimate capture of political power by popular forces rather than on grassroots development, lobbying, advocacy, and autonomous group formation.

In summary, the dominant ideology and practice of most NGO/LSM/LPSMs is unlikely to place them in the forefront of struggles for democratic rights in the political sphere, although in a variety of indirect ways they are likely to continue to provide support. Even groups specializing in the building of legal awareness increasingly emphasize issues central to the daily survival of the common people, such as the environment, land alienation, and labor relations. In the longer term, some of today's young political activists may also come to structure their organizations according to LSM/LPSM models, though perhaps with an operating style more in line with India's social action groups.[32] However, this would not preclude individuals from "commuting" between party and nonparty organizations. In any case, it seems clear that although NGOs can be seen as playing important catalyst roles—together with other educators, reformers, and activists—in laying the groundwork for a more open political system in Indonesia, the responsibility for forming independent political parties and associated mass organizations will have to be taken up by others.

Finally, and perhaps more positively, NGOs, more than any other organization or grouping, continue to promote as their central objective the formation of self-managing organizations that are accountable to their members and possess some degree of autonomy from government agencies. Such a contribution is a vital precondition to the establishment of any stable democratic society and polity. However, it could be argued that such an assessment represents a Western rather than Indonesian formulation of the sociological and ideological cum power equation obtaining between NGOs and the state. It is also possible to see Indonesian NGOs' rejection of the nongovernment label in favor of *swadaya* not just as a strategy of conflict avoidance but as representing an alternative vision of *pancasila* democracy's "family principle," in which the Indonesian *negara dan bangsa* (state and nation) would be linked by strong networks of "self-reliant community institutions" existing side by side with formal administrative and political structures.

Inevitably, the state–civil society distinction is problematic in the Indonesian context, making it difficult in either a conceptual or practical sense to draw sharp lines between government (*pemerintah*) and state (*negara*). This is particularly true at the village level, where local government, societal, and family structures are closely intertwined. The distinctions between government and nongovernment spheres have correspondingly less significance to Indonesian than Western social activists. Nevertheless, this chapter has hopefully contributed toward establishing the broad "counterhegemonic" credentials of LSM/LPSMs in opposing the imposition of monolithic ideology and institutional structures from any direction.

Though space does not allow detailed argument of the case, it is worth adding that while they will obviously adapt their strategies to available social space and political opportunity, it would be quite misleading to see the future shape of Indonesian NGOs as a mere appendage to macro structures. So far, they have proved adept at taking initiative and creating space for themselves. During the period of increased social and political restrictions after 1978, they expanded both in numbers and range of activities.[33]

Finally, if ideological choices are posed in too stark terms between integralist-cum-corporatist versus liberal democratic strategies, many NGO/LSM/LPSMs could feel alienated from political involvement of any kind. At the other end of the spectrum, some radical agendas cause them equal unease. In such a climate, the whole issue of democratization could well cause serious splits between them. If, however, the middle ground in Indonesian politics is defined in terms of more societal and pluralist, less statist and corporatist understandings of *pancasila* than currently prevail, then nongovernment organizations, as part of a more broadly based coalition, seem well placed to contribute to the cause of reform in Indonesia. However, events may be moving too fast to achieve such a balance.

Notes

1. The original Indonesian of this highly debated article reads "Kemerdekaan berserikat dan berkumpul, megeluarkan pikiran dengan lisan dan tulisan dan sebagainya ditetapkan dengan Undang-undang" (literally, "Freedom to unite, gather together, and express one's thoughts orally, in writing, and by other means, is established according to law"). This formulation appears to fall short of a constitutional guarantee and is open to the interpretation that operation of such "freedom" is subject to laws passed by the government of the day.

2. Philip Eldridge, "NGOs in Indonesia: Popular Movement or Arm of Government?" (Monash University [Melbourne], Centre of Southeast Asian Studies, Working Paper no. 55, 1990), 6–8. For a more pessimistic view of the "ORMAS" legislation see Ben Witjes, "The Indonesian Law on Social Organisation" (internal study undertaken for NOVIB, Nijmegen, Netherlands, October-November 1986).

3. In principle, LSMs are primary or base-level groups, whereas LPSMs are larger, usually city-based groups which support or guide (*membina*) the development of smaller groups. This somewhat arbitrary distinction seems in practice to be determined by size. The terms NGO and LSM/LPSM are used more or less interchangeably in this chapter.

4. For more general discussion of the role of NGOs, see Philip Eldridge, "NGOs and the State in Indonesia,"in *The State and Civil Society in Indonesia,* ed. Arief Budiman (Monash Papers on Southeast Asia, no. 22), 502–38 and "The Political Role of Community Action Groups in India and Indonesia: In Search of a General Theory," *Alternatives* (Delhi and New York) 10, 3 (Winter 1984–85): 401–34; Anne Gordon Drabek, ed., *Development Alternatives: The Challenge for NGOs,* (Supplement to *World Development,* vol. 15, Autumn 1987).

5. For information on Bina Swadaya's role in relation to the Nuclear Smallholders Scheme (NSS) at Ophir, West Sumatra, see Eldridge, "NGOs and the State in Indonesia," 15–16.

6. The PKK is one of the two major official women's groups, with a virtual monopoly at village level. See, for example, Carol Warren, "The Bureaucratisation of Local Government in Indonesia" (Monash University, Centre of Southeast Asian Studies, Working Paper no. 66, 1990), 8.

7. *Arisan* are traditional social-cum-lottery clubs, which can be adapted to numerous social and developmental purposes such as cooperative small enterprises, purchase of animals, house building and repairs, family planning, and nutrition supplementation.

8. James C. Scott, *The Moral Economy of the Peasant: Rebellion and Subsistence in Southeast Asia* (New Haven: Yale University Press, 1977). (For a counterview, see Samuel L. Popkin, *The Rational Peasant* (Berkeley: University of California Press, 1979).

9. Indonesian NGOs for Democracy (IN-DEMO), "Joint Declaration on Human Rights," Jakarta, June 1993.

10. Ibid., 4.

11. "Final Declaration of the Regional Meeting for Asia of the World Conference on Human Rights," Bangkok, 29 March-2 April, 1993.

12. United Nations, "Vienna Declaration and Programme of Action, 25 June 1993" (obtainable from the United Nations, New York, and UN offices in other countries). On human rights issues, including the role of NGOs, see also *Far Eastern Economic Review,* 17 June, 1993, 5, 16–28.

13. For an account of both official and NGO statements, see United Nations, "Asian Preparatory Meeting for the World Conference on Human Rights Opens in Bangkok" (Sydney, United Nations Information Centre, Press Release no. G/10/93, 29 March, 1993).

14. Moses Manoharan, "Asia Supports National Human Rights Commissions," Jakarta, Reuters, 27 January 1993.

15. It has been argued that such traditions governed approaches to rural community development under Sukarno, compared with the current top-down ethos. N. Schulte-Nordholt, "From LSD to LKMD: Participation at the Village Level," University of Twente Technology and Development Group, Working Paper no. 25, 1985.

16. Benedict O'G. Anderson, *Java in a Time of Revolution: Occupation and Resistance 1944–46* (New York: Cornell University Press, 1972).

17. Warren, "Bureaucratization of Local Government in Indonesia.".

18. David Bourchier, "Contradictions in the Dominant Paradigm of State Organization in Indonesia" (Paper presented to the Conference on "Indonesia Paradigms for the Future," Murdoch University, Western Australia, Asia Research Centre on Social, Political and Economic Change, July 1993), 3–4.

19. Andrew MacIntyre, *Business and Politics in Indonesia* (Sydney: Asian Studies Association of Australia in association with Allen and Unwin, 1990), chap. 2 and pp. 258–62, states this argument in a more general context.

20. Cf. Anderson, *Java in a Time of Revolution.*

21. Clifford Geertz, *The Religion of Java* (Glencoe, Ill.: Free Press, 1960).

22. In a more recent and dramatic example related to the Kedung Ombo dam in central Java, the International NGO Group on Indonesia (INGI) issued a public statement coinciding with the World Bank Consortium meeting on aid to Indonesia in Brussels, May 1989. For this they were summoned by Home Affairs Minister Rudini for what turned out to be a relatively mild reprimand-cum-dialogue.

23. In principle, LSMs are primary groups of poor people or local groups which work directly with them, whereas LPSMs are larger, city-based support groups which support the development of smaller groups. This somewhat arbitrary distinction seems in practice to be determined by size.

24. Cf. *Prisma* (Jakarta) 12, 4 (April 1983—Issue on "Community Development Organizations"). See especially the article by Ismid Hadad

(3–25) and the "Dialogue" between Prof. Emil Salim, Minister for Population and Environment and Mrs. Erna Witular, at that time Executive Secretary of the Indonesian Environmental Association (WALHI) (65–69).

25. The issues here were succinctly captured in an exchange between George Adicondro and Arief Budiman in *Kritis* (Universitas Keristen Satya Wacana, Saltiga) 4, 3 (January 1990): 44–59.

26. Cf. Eldridge, "NGOs and the State in Indonesia" and "NGOs in Indonesia."

27. Cf., for example, Mary Johnson, "Non-Government Organizations at the Crossroads in Indonesia" in *Indonesian Economic Development: Approaches, Technology, Small-Scale Textiles, Urban Infrastructure and NGOs,* ed. Robert C. Rice, Monash University (AIA-CSEAS Winter Lecture Series 1988), 1990, 77–92. The late Mary Johnson, an Australian volunteer social worker, worked with YIS and its forerunner, the Christian Public Health Foundation (Yayasan untuk Kesehatan Umum— YAKKUM) for approximately twenty years.

28. Such NGOs could be better described as GONGOs—an acronym for "Government Organized Non-Government Organization," initiated in the Indian context, probably by Prof. Rajni Kothari (cf. "NGOs, the State and World Capitalism," *Economic and Political Weekly* [Bombay] 21, 50 (13 December 1986): 2177–82.

29. YIS sometimes works through local units of the PKK, claiming that they can provide a good deal of scope for informal participatory approaches.

30. INGI has separate networks of Indonesian NGOs and supporting NGOs overseas which meet periodically to formulate joint policies.

31. Mohtar Mas'oed, "INGI and the Politics of Development in Indonesia", (unpublished ms., Yogyakarta, Gadjah Mada University, ca. 1982).

32. W. Fernandes, ed., *Social Activists and People's Movements* (New Delhi: Indian Social Institute, 1985).

33. Cf. Artien Utrecht, ed., *Peranan LPSM di sektor non pertanian pedesaan Jawa Barat* (Bogor: IPB; Bandung: ITB; The Hague: ISS, May 1990), chap. 4.

Chapter Nine

Land Disputes, the Bureaucracy, and Local Resistance in Indonesia

Anton Lucas

Sangat sukar dipahami bagaimana seseorang bisa
tenteram menjadi pemimpin, sedang
dihadapannya beratus orang kehilangan
sawah nafkahnya demi satu lobi kecil
untuk bola mainan kanak-kanak yang bernama golf
Sangat tidak masuk akal bagaimana masih ada
kata-kata yang bisa muncul dengan mantap
dari mulut seorang pemimpin, tatkala
berjuta-juta orang membayarkan nasibnya
untuk kesejahteran sejumlah kecil
orang-orang sebangsanya sendiri
Sangat tidak bisa dipercaya bahwa mungkin ada
Menteri yang dipilih karena hatinya tuli, atau karena mata
    batinnya rabun
Namun juga sangat menakjubkan, bahwa ada rakyat
di suatu negeri, yang memiliki
pribadi sedemikian kuat, sehingga ketika
seluruh hidupnya dirampok, mereka tetap senyum dan ikhlas
Para malaikat menegur: "Betapa indahnya
keikhlasan namun bukan disitu tempatnya."

It is really difficult to understand
how a person can become a leader
with a clear conscience
while around him there are hundreds of farmers
who have lost their rice fields
on account of a small hole which is used
to play a child's game called golf.

> It really doesn't make sense that a leader
> can speak with conviction
> while millions of people loose their livelihood
> for a small group of their own countrymen.
>
> It is really unbelievable that maybe
> a minister was chosen because
> he cannot see what is going on
> or feel the atmosphere around him.
>
> It is really amazing that there is a country
> whose people have such strong wills
> yet when their livelihood is taken away,
> they can still smile willingly *[ikhlas]*
>
> The angels admonish us,
> "How glorious it is to be willing," they say,
> "but not regarding these things."
>
> —Emha Ainun Nadjib,
> "Syair heran" (A poem of amazement)

ONE OF THE ongoing encounters with bureaucratic culture in Indonesia is between the national, regional, and local administrations and landholders over compulsory land clearances. Since the late 1980s land disputes involving the bureaucracy and developers have become a major source of local and regional tension in Indonesia. Hardly a week goes by without another case of disaffected landholders in dispute with developers and the local bureaucracy concerning compensation which has been offered for their land, compensation that is well below market value. In a pattern that has now become common, local groups, often aided by NGOs and students, take their case either to provincial councils (DPRD), or more often to the national assembly (DPR) in Jakarta. While this action often briefly publicizes their case, and may provide some temporary advocacy, it seldom resolves the conflict between the local bureaucracy and the landholders themselves, concerning ownership of land or compensation for its expropriation.

This essay will explore the nature of the conflict between landholders and the bureaucracy in Indonesia, the bureaucratic processes involved in compulsory land clearances, and reactions of the people to loss of their land, often their only asset and major source of livelihood. The essay will also explore how local landholders have tried to come to terms with the bureaucratic culture in relation to disputes over compensation and ownership. To what extent do landholders use the legal system? Do they organize political protests? In what situations do both protesters and the state use violence to solve disputes?

As a case study, this essay will first discuss recent disputes and protests regarding the development of golf courses in Indonesia. The Plumpang (in north Jakarta) and Tubanan (in north Surabaya) disputes, as well as a land clearance in Jepara (on the north coast of Java), will then be discussed to illustrate the conflicts between landholders and the bureaucracy and how they are resolved.

I begin, however, with some general observations relating to compulsory land clearances in Indonesia, and how the bureaucracy acquires land for public projects, and facilitates the acquisition of land by private developers.

The enormous increase in land disputes in Indonesia over the past five years has been caused by the rapid expansion of foreign as well as domestic private investment. In order to facilitate private investment (as part of its industrialization program) the government has had to make it easier for investors to acquire land on which to build factories. It has also acquired land compulsorily for public projects, including housing (slum clearance), dams, roads, and urban renewal schemes.

The best-known land dispute in the 1980s arose from the compulsory clearance of 4,000 families from their traditional wet rice lands in order to build the Kedung Ombo dam in Central Java,[1] but others are nearly or already completed.[2] Other public projects involving land disputes arising from land clearances include urban redevelopment, which involves *kampung* improvement (including street widening), usually through a mixture of public and private financing. The biggest project is an urban redevelopment scheme in Surabaya.[3] Land is also compulsorily acquired for agricultural estates, reforestation, new plantations, and military use.[4] Land acquired with government assistance for private investment includes both industrial development as well as agribusiness, which involves large scale plantation development, including the highly lucrative forestry industry or HTI (Hutan Tanaman Industri).[5] The most lucrative source of private investment (and the area where many disputes occur) is the development of real estate complexes in Jakarta and Surabaya. Early in 1993 a new category of land disputes emerged, namely clearances for private golf courses in Indonesia.

Bureaucracy plays a pivotal role in the administration of land clearances and in the settling of land disputes. It is the bureaucracy of various ministries at the local (village), regional, and provincial levels which has the responsibility to implement government laws and regulations regarding land, from the Basic Agrarian Law of 1960 (which sets the legal framework for all land regulations) to the most recent government law, Keppres (Presidential Decree) no. 55 (June 1993), which covers the implementation of land clearances, definitions and interpretations of public interest (*kepentingan umum*), and the formation of committees that are now called Panitia Pengadaan Tanah. The committees consist of the provincial and local members of the bureaucracy to implement compulsory land acquisition for projects which are in the public interest, including negotiations with landholders regarding compensation. While in the past government Land Clearance Committees have also facilitated the clearance of land for large privately funded development projects (e.g., the proposed petrochemical factory in Cilacap, now canceled), it was not clear from the recently promulgated presidential decree how private developers would gain land for projects. This was clarified however in the "deregulation package" of 23 October 1992. Under these new regulations, local (*kabupaten*-level) government (*pemda*) has the responsibility for promulgating local zoning (*tata ruang*) regulations, and for providing land (up to ten hectares) for foreign and domestic investors. This responsibility gives local government a crucial role in deciding land use and in ensuring developers obtain the required land for development projects.

The Political Context

Disputes caused by compulsory land clearances take place in the context of both New Order Indonesia's economic development priorities and its political culture. I have already mentioned the implications of attracting private investment for industrialization. In their most recent report on human rights in Indonesia, the Indonesian Legal Aid Foundation (YLBHI) highlighted several characteristics of the political context that explain in part how land disputes arise and how the bureaucracy imposes solutions on landholders in New Order Indonesia.

First, land disputes take place in a system which has been de-politicized—a process that also entails the removal of competing ideologies (*deideologisasi*). *Pancasila* is the sole basis of the Indonesian state, to which all three parties contesting the election and all organizations must acknowledge allegiance. On another level, *pancasila* is used to underpin the ideology of development (*pembangunan*).

Second, in these two intertwined ideologies, loyalty is demanded by the government, and the people must be seen to be supporting both *pancasila* and *pembangunan*. This enables the culture of "compulsory suggestion" (*budaya petunjuk*) to work effectively. Those who do not follow the government's *petunjuk* (guidelines) are therefore considered disloyal, or worse, anti-development or anti-*pancasila*.

Characteristics of Disputes

Within this political culture, land clearance disputes over the past five years have shared certain features in common, according to the YLBHI. First, the importance of the involvement of civilian and military security apparatus, mainly Bakorstanas (Badan Koordinasi Keamanan dan Stabilitas Nasional, Body for the Coordination of National Security and Stability). This involvement has been obvious in disputes over land in East Java, particularly Surabaya, where manipulation by the bureaucracy in collusion with developers has been well documented and has reached dimensions hitherto unheard of.[6] Developers have their own privately funded security forces, called *satpam*, which are used to intimidate landholders who resist or who are known to organize protests. According to the human rights group Asia Watch, security forces involved in land clearances in Indonesia have not acted to uphold the law, rather "they have acted, often at the behest of local civilian officials, to bully the [resisting] farmers into acquiescence. Threats and harassment are clearly designed to stifle protest."[7]

Second, in the cases reported, the local bureaucracy always sides, or is perceived by landholders to side, with the developers. In public statements officials say the government is neutral in land disputes, or at least tries to ensure that landholders get a fair deal. On the other hand, according to the ideology of the government's development strategy, *pembangunan*, local government is expected to facilitate private investment in industrial development, natural resource development, industrial forestry, and estate agriculture, as well as tourism. Land is an essential resource for both foreign and domestic capital investment. Thus, in determining the level of compensation developers have to pay, the Land Clearance Committees (now called Land Procurement Committees or Panitya Pengadaan Tanah, rather than Panitya Pembebasan Tanah, a change that reflects opposition to the negative connotations of *pembebasan)*, always set compensation well below market rates, which is the chief cause of landholders' opposition to land clearances.

Third, the system of justice administered through the courts, as we shall see in the Plumpang dispute, does not provide landholders with an alternative to settling disputes over compensation. In other words the courts, very much under the indirect influence of *budaya petunjuk*, seldom if ever find in favor of landholders. Cumbersome bureaucratic legal procedures make it impossible to get speedy decisions, so most landholders are burdened with endless court appearances. If a judgment is given in favor of landholders, as in the Plumpang dispute, it is difficult to enforce. In short, the law gives victims of land clearances no legal protection in Indonesia.[8]

The recent Presidential Decree no.55 strengthens the power of the state against landholders, by reaffirming the right of the bureaucracy to revoke ownership rights if agreement cannot be reached on compensation, or if people refuse to move off their land when it is needed by the government for development projects.

The phenomenon of golf course development illustrates the nature of the bureaucracy and the responses of the landholders.

"Welcome to Indonesia: Islands of Endless Holes"

The recent controversy which erupted over land clearances for golf courses in Indonesia produced a spate of cartoon comment in the Indonesian print media. The heading above is the caption of a cartoon that appeared (in English) in the weekly news-magazine *Tempo* (suggesting that the recent golf mania is partly driven by demands of foreign business as well as tourism). The cartoon shows an attractive female Indonesian caddie waiting beside a male golfer (possibly a foreigner) who is about to play his shot. In the background we see that the entire archipelago has been turned into a golf course filled with hundreds of tiny flags denoting putting greens.[9] Other cartoon images depict the following themes: the overriding power of the developers (a developer is laying out a huge roll of instant turf which is about to engulf a farmer working in his wet rice fields);[10] the irrelevance of golf courses as sporting facilities for poor people;[11] and misplaced national pride in golf courses of international standard, which are "built on suffering."[12]

There is no consensus on how many operating golf clubs there are in Indonesia. *Tempo* says there are "roughly 93."[13] Minister of Politics and Security (Menpolkam) Soesilo Soedarman says 66 are operating, 27 are under construction, and 46 applications for new courses are being processed.[14] The majority are concentrated in West Java (reflecting the fact that golf is a sport of the national elite in Indonesia, as well as of expatriate businessmen, in particular Japanese), where 21 courses are operating, while another 30 are under construction, or seeking planning approval.[15]

Under the government's recent Deregulation Package, approval and permission to buy land for industrial, real estate, and recreational use is a matter for local (*tingkat II*) government authority, which is also responsible for promulgating local land use regulations. The central government retains planning authority for areas of special importance for resources or the environment, where special planning or zoning regulations apply. An example is the Puncak Region (*Kawasan Puncak*), a catchment and protected forest region, where state-owned companies operate large tea plantations. Because of its cooler climate and proximity to Jakarta, land in the Puncak region is keenly sought after for luxury developments, including country clubs with golf facilities. The regency of Tanggerang to the west of Jakarta, center of the government's industrial estate development, has also been targeted for new golf clubs by developers. The most exclusive and most expensive of these—Jaya Ancol (built in 1978), Bumi Serpong Damai (BSD), and Pantai Indah Kapuk—are owned by Ciputra, one of Indonesia's best-known Chinese business conglomerate tycoons. Transferable Membership Certificates (TMCs) of these exclusive clubs vary from $60,000 to $150,000. TMCs of less exclusive golf clubs start at $37,500.

The Bureaucracy's Perception of Golf Course Development

Most senior or upper-echelon members of Jakarta's bureaucratic elite *(pejabat teras)* are keen golfers, or aspire to be. This is not, as some have said publicly, because they are devoted to the game, but it is while playing golf that the deals are done. President Suharto and his generals play golf. Senior cabinet members play golf. Fifteen ministers of Development Cabinet V are reported to be honorary board members of BSD, while the board of advisers includes the managing directors of all state banks.[16]

Pressure on the government to clarify its policy on golf courses came after one of its ministers, Hayono Isman (Minister for Youth and Sport), said on Indonesian national television that "building golf courses is an indicator of the social welfare of the community."[17] As we shall see below, this led to a widely based protest campaign, which had similar features to other land disputes, except that this time the minister's controversial remarks seemed to legitimize the protests.

A characteristic of bureaucratic involvement in land clearance disputes is conflict between government departments. Solichin GP, a former governor of West Java, now responsible for overseeing development projects in the powerful State Secretariat, said publicly that newly appointed Minister of Home Affairs Yogie S. Memet's support for a country club in a state-owned tea plantation in the ecologically sensitive Puncak region was mistaken. According to the secretary, it contravened an earlier presidential decree imposing strict planning controls on Puncak Region. Other landholders in the area, namely the state company which owns adjacent tea plantations and Indonesian Safari Park, were concerned about the detrimental impact of the development on their projects, particularly the chemical herbicides used to destroy weeds in the golf course, which enter run off and pollute neighboring streams. This had all been foreshadowed in the presidential decree.

The rift between Solichin GP and Yogie S. Memet added fuel to the flames of the dispute started by the Minister of Youth and Sport the previous week. In Indonesia, senior officials seldom disagree in public. Students and human-rights groups seized the opportunity and organized action groups and demonstrations to oppose the minister's statement. The Union against Golf Course Development (Kaaplag), the Youth Front for the Protection of People's Rights (FPPHR), and United Action against Building Golf Courses (Kesatuan Aksi Anti Pembangunan Lapangan Golf) began to publicize the injustices in golf course development in other areas as well, and to question the overall development strategy which allowed so many golf courses to be planned or built in the first place.

These vocal protests, supported by strongly worded articles in the press (including the "Poem of Amazement" by Muslim activist and critic Emha Ainun Nadjib) as well as by more moderate voices from parliament, led to a "clarification" by Minister Hayono Isman, and a "correction" from Minister Yogie S. Memet, who reaffirmed the ban on planning approval for further development of golf courses in Puncak Region. Further attempts at damage control saw Coordinating Minister for Politics and Security (Menpolkam) Soesilo Soedarman announce seven Guidelines for Approval of Golf Courses.[18] The president subsequently announced a freeze on all new golf course development, saying that no more planning permits would be issued.

Land Disputes and Local Encounters with Bureaucratic Culture

A golf course development first needs a recommendation from the *bupati,* or head of local government. If the amount of land required by the developer is not more than ten hectares, the *bupati* issues a letter of planning approval, the level of compensation is agreed on, and an offer is made to landholders. A common complaint by villagers is that they are not given information about the reason for compulsory acquisitions. Until recently, landholders were not dealing with developers directly, although with the October 1993 Deregulation Package this will change. Quite often the local government acts on behalf of developers. Middlemen called *calo tanah* buy up the land before the developer gets planning approval; this has happened in many projects in the Surabaya region.

When the local bureaucracy can't get agreement from landholders, they use intimidation, physical violence, threats of arrest, and, in the last resort, terror squads. This happened in the case of the first major conflict over a golf course, in Cimacan in Cianjur regency, in the province of West Java, adjacent to the Cibodas National Park, in 1987. Farmers were invited to what was later described by SKEPHI, the NGO network for forestry conservation, as a "bogus meeting." Local officials told landholders that they would be paid compensation for vegetables in gardens bulldozed by the developer, PT Bandung Asri Mulya (BAM). They were also offered "discussions" about employment in the proposed tourist park. According to SKEPHI's English-language magazine, *Setiakawan*:

The farmers did not want jobs. They wanted their land. In great anger and feeling very much cheated, the farmers spontaneously staged [a] poster protest. They scribbled posters in the Sundanese language saying GOLF STICKS CANNOT REPLACE PLOUGHS; WE CANNOT PLAY GOLF FOR WE ARE FARMERS; WE CANNOT USE GOLF STICKS WE CAN ONLY HARVEST VEGETABLES. The protest was ended when 35 farmers were arrested as they marched out of the building where the bogus meeting was held. In addition personnel who claimed to be reporters of environmental bulletins, students and LBH [Legal Aid] staff were also arrested. They were all taken to Cianjur police station. Meanwhile villagers who had escaped the arrest wrote a letter of protest in solidarity to their friends. They warned the government that they would not cooperate with the government and the problem solving team if their friends [were] not released by Sunday 3 September [1989]. At 3 a.m. on Sunday 3 September, 20 farmers were released. They reported that the other 15 farmers were being beaten up and intimidated at the police station, while seven students, reporters and LBH staff were being intensively questioned. None of the arrested people were allowed lawyers from LBH. But finally on 3 September at five o'clock in the evening everyone was released without charges. However they can be called back by the police at any time for questioning.[19]

While this account deliberately portrays the Cimacan farmers' dispute as a victory for people's power, the victory was short-lived. The bulldozers later moved in to stay, farmers were powerless in the face of the unjust offer of thirty rupiahs per square meter of land they had cultivated since 1943, for which they claimed to have paid an annual rent to the village of 1.4 million rupiahs, or 2,000 rupiahs for one *patok* (one patok equals 400 square meters), although the village administration claimed to receive only 300,000 rupiahs. PT BAM offered the village 90 million rupiahs to lease the land for thirty years for a golf course. While senior bureaucrats, including Rudini, then Minister of the Interior, intervened with expressions of sympathy for the farmers, who visited the national parliament and the minister, these efforts have so far been to no avail.[20] When the recent golf course controversy erupted, journalists went to Cimacan to find out what the impact of the tourist park development had been on the livelihood of former landholders. In seven years has their welfare improved? Did they get the promised jobs in the Cibodas tourist park?

The journalists found that most of the approximately 200 farmers have remained unemployed since losing their land. The compensation they were paid (30 rupiahs per square meter) was not enough to obtain land elsewhere. The farmers themselves can no longer study, and they cannot educate their children past primary school. Some live only with financial assistance from their in-laws. Work was available with the golf course project at a wage of 2,500 rupiahs per day. However, because local people refused to work for the developer, people from other areas (Cianjur and Cipanas) were brought in. Refusing to work on the golf course was a kind of protest, a way for the farmers to keep their self-respect after being so badly treated. As the *santri* leader of the farmers resistance group (Kelompok Petani Bersama Cimacan) put it: "It is against our principles to work for BAM!" (*Haram hukumannya buat kami bekerja di BAM*).[21] "Who wants to become a slave working on land that once belonged to you?" asked another leader, Amir.[22] Instead they earn money selling food to tourists, working as unofficial parking attendants on weekends, or renting out umbrellas and woven mats to sit on. Only five of the two hundred or so stall vendors are former landholders, the rest are from outside the area. Some go into the forest and collect fruit to sell on weekends, others drive trucks when the regular drivers are not working.

Ijah, a forty-four-year-old woman, sums up the feelings of people who have lost their land through clearances for golf course development:

> Well, what other work can I do? I don't have any land now. I can't work on other people's land either. So I have to just pull out weeds like this. You don't earn much. I used to earn 200,000 rupiahs [each month],[23] now I get only 800 rupiahs a day. That's not including the cost of food that I have to bring from home. I'm tired, you know— I used to work six hours at the most before, now I have to work eight hours a day. I haven't got the energy, but what else can I do?[24]

According to former landholders, it is no coincidence that the building of the Cimacan golf course has taken seven years, is still not completed, and has been plagued by "misfortune." A number of key people have died—including a director of PT BAM, a bulldozer driver, the head of the local village LKMD (Lembaga Ketahanan Masyarakat Desa) that supported the project, the local military commander (Dansek) of Cimacan, and a village military security officer (*babinsa*)—all too much of a coincidence for the people of Cimacan, who regard the deaths as divine retribution for injustice.[25]

Parliament, the Bureaucracy and Land Clearances

> I wonder why you keep coming [to the parliament] although you realize the results [will] disappoint you. The DPR has no power to solve such problems because its job is to supervise the government, make laws, and prepare the state budget.
>
> —Armed Forces faction member and Commission II chairman Suparno, addressing a delegation of residents from Plumpang, North Jakarta.

Every year since 1989, landholders from throughout Indonesia, aided often by students and NGOs, have taken their grievances regarding arbitrary treatment by the bureaucracy and inadequate compensation to the national assembly in Jakarta. DPR fraction leaders offer comments (such as the quote above) and advice, and assure protestors that they will raise questions about disputes with local government administrations. Beyond this the DPR has so far been powerless to facilitate solutions to land disputes which are acceptable to all parties involved.

The disputed land of Plumpang or Tanah Merah in North Jakarta is an important case study of an encounter between land-holders and local bureaucratic culture. On 18 March 1992, 1,130 families living on 45 hectares covering three subdistricts, filed a law suit in the North Jakarta district court against the state oil company (Pertamina), the governor of Jakarta, and the mayor of North Jakarta. They demanded compensation for their land of 150,000 rupiahs ($75.00) per square meter, half the market price, for a total compensation bill of $33.75 million. The remaining 1,900 families, living on 15 hectares, accepted the compensation of 37,000 rupiahs ($18.50) per square meter offered by local government.[26] Pertamina claimed ownership of the land located behind its Plumpang storage depot, and announced plans to build further storage facilities there. The 1,132 occupants admitted that they were squatters, but argued that Pertamina had previously (in December 1991) agreed to pay compensation, and that it had never been paid. The group also sued the mayor of North Jakarta and the governor of Jakarta in the recently established state administrative court (PTUN) for demolition of the dwellings before the compensation dispute was settled by the court.

The mayor of North Jakarta made clear the government's position. The 1,132 residents were illegal squatters, living in dwellings that had been erected without approval, and the government is required by law to eradicate dwellings throughout Jakarta that are erected without building permits. The mayor thus ordered his security apparatus to pull the dwellings down. From May until 3 November 1992 the residents of Plumpang were continually harassed by two groups. One of these was the bureaucracy's security forces, known as *kamtib* (*keamanan dan penertiban*, security and order) under the direct control of the mayor, as head of the North Jakarta municipal administration.

Residents were also terrorized by a group calling itself the Three Dimension Brigade (Pasukan Tiga Dimensi). The only press report on this group described it as "a shadowy force" (*pasukan tak jelas*), meaning it was not clear to whom it was responsible, or on whose orders it acted. Members wore black, including a black beret with a skull badge. The Three Dimension Brigade terrorized the residents of Plumpang *kampung* each night:

> "They terrorized (*menteror*) the place and said they were ready to do away with (*membabat*) community leaders, especially those who lead protest actions," said Andi Cinge, aged 33, who said he had been assaulted by four members of the Three Dimension Brigade last October. "Luckily only my hand was hurt," he told JJ [*Jakarta Jakarta*], showing his injured hand.[27]

A journalist who visited Plumpang during this period reported seeing plywood doors and walls of temporary homes constructed by residents smashed in during raids by this group.

The Plumpang residents lost their legal battle in the Jakarta Administrative Court, but they appealed. By October the residents had visited the parliament fourteen times, asking the DPR to stop the administration from clearing their dwellings until the court had decided the issue of compensation.

On 3 November 1992 Judge Sarwono of the North Jakarta District Court announced his decision. Because the land was owned by the state (not by Pertamina) he ordered the government to pay 37,500 rupiahs per square meter for each dwelling. The ruling, apart from awarding compensation, also declared that the municipal administration's continuing dismantling of dwellings and eviction of people from their land was illegal. After the judge announced the decision the courtroom erupted in bedlam—people were crying, calling out hysterically, and embracing each other. Those outside the courtroom listening to the proceedings over loudspeakers went wild—"it was as if the people had won a victory after an extremely long and tiring war."[28] Judge Sarwono overnight became the hero of Tanah Merah residents.

The victory in court was short-lived. The mayor of North Jakarta said he would appeal. Meanwhile, the court said that the residents could stay on their land until there was a final ruling. Nevertheless, the administration continued to dismantle the dwellings, so residents resumed their visits to parliament. Their spokesman, Sugiyanto, said, "The North Jakarta Mayor just ignores the court order and shamelessly resorts to intimidation to evict us." Sugiyanto told parliament members that security forces "burned down makeshift shelters, ransacked household goods and filled wells with trash to force them to leave their land." The prolonged conflict had nearly drained the residents of their patience and economic resources, and many small-scale traders and peddlers had lost their livelihood. "We have nowhere to go and no one to help us. Every time we set up shelters, the brutal security forces immediately level them to the ground," said one of the peddlers.[29]

On 18 January 1993 Haji Muhidin HS, a prominent Muslim community leader from Plumpang, was sentenced to five months in prison for inciting the residents to resist the North Jakarta administrative security apparatus *(kamtib)* with bamboo spears. In April 1993 the North Jakarta mayor announced that the 2,664 illegal dwellings on the disputed land had been demolished.[30] In May residents sent a delegation of eighteen residents to the DPR to meet the PDI fraction representatives. They asked Pertamina to pay compensation of 37,500 rupiahs per square meter for dwellings destroyed and 5 million rupiahs per claimant as compensation for their land (which they claimed to have bought from Paguyuban Hardjontani Beloprodjo, an organization connected to the Kraton of Surakarta). "Where else can we turn to for protection?" asked the spokesperson of the group.[31] The parliament seemed powerless to act, and when it did the bureaucracy proved more powerful than the parliament. On 19 June, Pertamina security guards refused access to a DPR visiting team (including PDI leader Guruh Sukarnoputra) who wanted to observe the disputed *kampung* first hand. Pertamina bulldozers continued to flatten the temporary tents. Some were burned. H. M. Dault, a lawyer representing the 1,132 residents, protested to the North Jakarta District Court, asking for an order to stop the bulldozing of tents until the residents' appeal had been heard, but the court took no action.[32]

The encounters of the residents of Plumpang with the local bureaucratic culture have several features in common. First, the residents have resisted the eviction order of the mayor of North Jakarta, against the state's eviction force (called Team Penertiban Terpadu), who forcibly destroyed their dwellings and took away their building materials after the deadline (the end of December 1991) had passed for them to remove their dwellings themselves. However, they were unable to resist the actions of the vigilante squad's nightly visits.

Second, people have demonstrated against the decisions of the mayor, by placing the Indonesian flag at half mast over their dwellings. By December 1992, residents had made twenty-seven visits to the national parliament, without much concrete improvement in their situation. On one visit an Armed Forces faction spokesman told the residents that the DPR has no power to solve such problems.

Third, both the residents and the bureaucracy have resorted to legal action. Residents have filed a suit against the mayor of North Jakarta in the state administrative court for continuing evictions while the question of land ownership was not yet settled in the Central Jakarta district court. The case was lost and the residents appealed. The Central Jakarta district court awarded compensation to the families (5 million rupiahs per family) and the mayor of North Jakarta appealed. The North Jakarta administration took Haji Muhidin HS, one of the community leaders, to court for organizing "violent resistance" in the North Jakarta district court, and he was sentenced to five months in prison (the prosecution had asked for two years). So far the three different courts (PTUN and the Central Jakarta and North Jakarta district courts) have been unable to offer any solution or resolution for either the residents or the local administration. Meanwhile Pertamina, has resumed its "illegal" development of the site to extend its existing petroleum storage facilities.

Neither civil disobedience, violent protest, appeals to parliament, or legal action have resolved the dispute to the satisfaction of the people of Plumpang. In the view of the local bureaucracy, the residents are squatters whose illegal dwellings have to be removed by whatever means possible, including the use of a terror squad, as part of the government's program to develop Jakarta as a modern city.

One more avenue remained to Plumpang residents, and that was to vote against the government party at the last elections. We will now discuss this method of political action in relation to land disputes.

The Bureaucracy, National Elections, and Land Disputes

> Don't give up your land so it can be sold, even though people approach you with wonderful offers [*berbagai imbauan maupun iming-iming yang menggiurkan*]. Because land is our "soul."
>
> —Sukarno's daughter Megawati, in a campaign speech for the PDI in Pekalongan during the national election campaign in May 1992

Land issues were not widely discussed or aired during the national election campaign in May and early June 1992. Apart from PDI campaigner (now chairperson) Megawati's comments in the first week of the campaign (quoted above), there was no follow-up by leaders of the nongovernment parties. The government expected that land clearances would become a hot election issue. Three days after Megawati's speech in Pekalongan, Indonesia's top bureaucrat in charge of land affairs, National Land Board (Badan Pertanahan Nasional, BPN) chairman Sonny Harsono, said the government would welcome discussions about land issues during the campaign as long as they were "fair," constructive, used "objective data," and suggested solutions to the problems.[33] That was the end of the election campaign discussion about land clearances.

The reason for this lack of discussion lies in the local nature of these issues. Even a project as large and controversial as the Kedung Ombo dam, which affected over 5,000 families and flooded nearly 6,000 hectares of productive rice lands in central Java, affected voting in only two villages of Kemusu subdistrict, where a majority of farmers and their families refused to move from their land. In Mlangi village, P3 (the Development Unity Party) won, while in Kedungpring village, PDI won. While land issues tend to emerge at the village or hamlet level, separate results for individual polling booths below subdistrict level are not published, so it is not possible to pick up grassroots swings against the government party, Golkar, which would indicate an expression of opposition against local bureaucracy over land issues. The only way to pick up local swings (e.g., in areas of land disputes) is to observe the count at individual polling booths (TPS). In Jakarta, journalists went to observe results in polling booths in Plumpang, where P3 narrowly beat Golkar in all seven booths, with PDI placing third.[34] These results suggest that the Plumpang residents used the election to express their disapproval of the way the government had handled land clearance disputes.

One area with a twenty-year-old dispute between local land-holders and developers wanting land for luxury real estate is Tubanan *kampung* (actually an urban village, or *kelurahan*) in Surabaya. Living up to their reputation (among their fellow Javanese) for outspokenness, the people of Surabaya spoke out clearly after the election on why Golkar lost in Tubanan in the last two national elections in 1987 and 1992. According to the Surabayans, Golkar lost because the *kampung* administration had supported a developer in the attempts to obtain land, and because the dispute had gone on for so long and no solution had been found satisfactory to the parties concerned. According to one resident, "If the village bureaucracy (*para pamong*) here didn't take sides with the developer (PT Darmo Permai), maybe it wouldn't have happened like this" (i.e., PDI would not have won). PDI also won in the disputed Urip Sumoharjo *kampung* in Surabaya, where 25,000 residents have been threatened with eviction by a company controlled by Sudwikatmono, the president's brother-in-law. Said one resident, "We are disappointed with the attitude of the bureaucracy (*aparat pemerintah*) here. Because they don't consider our interests, in the end we were forced not to vote for Golkar."[35]

When disputes over land clearance become an important local political issue, people use elections to express disapproval, by voting for PDI instead of Golkar.

Tubanan Land Dispute: Violent Resistance in Response to Bureaucratic Corruption

Until the recent shooting of farmers by the army in Madura, the Indonesian armed forces have often been called in to play a role in land clearances, usually to support the local bureaucracy, which has been unsuccessful in getting landholders to move.

Thus the military, in the eyes of landholders, is seen to be backing private developers. But do landholders ever get support from the military when discussions with the bureaucracy break down? In the DPR (national assembly), the Armed Forces faction tried to support protesting landholders in the Plumpang dispute. Territorial units stationed at the provincial level who are responsible for enforcing security cannot support landholders since local administrations view resistance to land clearances as a threat to security and therefore potentially subversive.

When disputes and resentment due to bureaucratic corruption, intimidation, and inadequate levels of compensation are expressed, security forces move in and dismantle homes, as they did in Plumpang, where resistance was sporadic and disorganized. In Surabaya, landholders' resistance led to the military's backing down.

On the morning of Saturday 27 April 1991 security forces assembled at the edge of Tubanan *kampung* in north Surabaya. It is not clear exactly how these forces were constituted, but when municipal administrations send in teams to demolish *kampung* housing they are often combinations of civilian security and regular military forces. On this occasion they were met with "no less than one thousand" *kampung* inhabitants. The following eyewitness account appeared in the Muslim daily *Surya*:

Armed with wooden clubs, spears, and krises, the people angrily blocked and chased off every official who tried to enter the area. Seeing the residents' stubbornness [*kenekatan*], 150 civil and military personnel—including the local army commander [Dandim] of North Surabaya Lieut. Col. P. Gultom, the Muspika [officials] of Tandes [subdistrict], the police chief [Kapolres] of north Surabaya, police Lieut. Col. Fadilah Budiono, and officials from the Surabaya municipal government administration—withdrew and called off their planned demolition of houses in the area. . . . The distressing events began at 6:00 A.M., when residents, who were prepared, quickly scattered [*berhamburan*] as soon as they heard the sound of the wooden signal drum.[36] The drum signaled [to residents] that the security apparatus had arrived and were assembling near the Tubanan police station. As soon as they made their move toward the *kampung*, the people resisted. Facing the masses who were blocking their way, even attacking them, Lieut. Col. Gultom was forced to get up on the roof of a car, and started shouting to the people that they would not be harmed, and he wanted to help them. After shouting many times, the people sat down on the road. Lieut. Col. Gultom then asked the security forces to withdraw.[37]

This popular resistance humiliated the entire local bureaucracy, which had been assembled under the command of the military to dismantle "illegal" dwellings.

The problems in Tubanan had arisen over a long dispute which began in 1973. To begin with, residents were not involved in the original negotiations which determined the level of compensation (100 rupiahs per square meter). Furthermore, the area for which compensation was being paid (fifty hectares) was thirty hectares less than the total area of the Tubanan *kampung*. The residents had three demands: a resurvey of the area to determine the correct amount of compensation, adjustment of compensation levels (for those residents not yet paid) to new land values, and a resettlement scheme to provide replacement of land and housing, with water and electricity supplied. The dispute has dragged on and on. The East Java provincial military command tried to intervene, but then withdrew, the Governor's Directorate of Social and Political Affairs failed to find a solution, and finally the state secretariat's development watchdog which, as we have seen, intervened in the golf course disputes, requested the luxury real estate developer PT Darmo Permai, local government and residents to find an immediate solution. In September 1993 the municipal government held a meeting to discuss the developer's resettlement plan, which the government accepted. The plan involved resettling 477 families on 12.5 hectares of land, each family being offered 200 square meters as well as a certificate of permission to build (*hak guna bangunan*), with public facilities. No cash compensation payments would be offered. Because government municipal officials refused permission for lawyers with powers of attorney from Tubanan residents to attend the meeting with their clients, twenty residents left the meeting in protest.[38] The dispute dragged on for another three years, with the Indonesian National Human Rights Commission (Komnas HAM) instigating a full enquiry into the dispute in mid-1995, amid accusations that a leading national Golkar figure was a director of PT Darmo Permai. Finally in August 1996 after protests at more broken payment promises, the developer finally paid compensation to the remaining 50 families.

The Bureaucracy and Effective Land Clearances

Not all land clearances for development projects end in dispute like golf courses, luxury real estate development, or shopping malls built on urban *kampung*s or productive agricultural land. Many local development projects involving land clearances, although never publicized, are successfully implemented at the *kabupaten* level. The key to successful clearances is setting what landholders consider a fair level of compensation. Sometimes the bureaucracy has to twist the rules to do that.

Low-lying land in the *kabupaten*s of Kudus, Pati, Demak, and Jepara on Java's north coast was always exposed to flooding, and in 1982 and 1983 the government embarked on an ambitious flood control program known as the Jratunseluna River Basin Development Project, downstream from the Kedung Ombo dam.

In Jepara *kabupaten* flooding occurred in four subdistricts during the rainy season, and wet rice lands were also damaged by sea water in tidal flooding. Extensive flood control works, including the straightening of river beds, caused loss of irrigated rice land. According to a local official, only eleven out of more than one hundred families in one village refused the level of compensation offered. The money was handed over to the court (*dikonsinyasi*) to be paid out to those landholders when, as the government believed, they changed their minds. The project went ahead, the opposition died away (which was the purpose of depositing the money with the court in the first place), and remaining landholders claimed their compensation. The implementation of the Jratunseluna project in Jepara *kabupaten* was exceptional—there was no corruption of funds by the local bureaucracy (as in the Tubanan dispute), and no forced evictions (as in the Plumpang dispute).[39]

Another land clearance case which developed into a dispute in Jepara was unusual because it was the bureaucracy, the local land clearance committee, which wanted better compensation for local landholders, and tried to bend the rules on their behalf. Fifty-two hectares of state-owned land was needed for a university oceanography research center. According to a local government regulation, squatters on state land should be paid one-third of its market value as compensation for resettlement. Based on this regulation, the 100 families who had cultivated the land for more than twenty years were entitled to 333 rupiahs per square meter (one-third of the going market rate). The local land clearance committee (Panitya Pembebasan Tanah), agreed that that compensation was too low, so they inflated the reported area occupied by buildings on each property. This enabled the committee to pay 500 to 600 rupiahs per square meter in compensation, as well as to provide small replacement plots, each with an ownership certificate. The compensation package fell apart when the

State Auditing Board (BPKN) was told what had happened, accused the *bupati* of Jepara of "wasting government funds" (*memboroskan uang pemerintah*), and ordered that the money be repaid to the government. A member of the land clearance committee commented, "This is the difficulty of working at lower levels of government: if the committee hadn't carried out the clearance in the way it did, it wouldn't have succeeded" (i.e., the people would not have accepted 333 rupiahs per square meter for their land and buildings, and the university would not have secured land for its oceanography institute).[40]

Two factors are important in the success of the Jepara land clearances. First, both the bureaucracy and landholders could reach agreement on a fair level of compensation. Landholders believed the local land clearance committee was working in their interests, or at least trying to give them a just deal. Second, there was effective consultation between the local bureaucracy and landholders in regard to the level of compensation being offered, and the promise of providing new land with title was kept. Some landholders in Jepara also lost land to the widening of roads for the building of an electrical tower. Those landholders felt neither cheated nor deceived, as the head of the subdistrict explained the nature of the project and the reasons for it. Nor did he forget to enlist the support of the leading local *kyai* (Muslim leader).

Reflections on Land Disputes

A central aspect of disputes that arise from compulsory or forced clearances of land in contemporary Indonesia is the culture of state control. Key features of state control are control of the media (press and television), the bureaucracy, and, indirectly, the courts.

Control of the media is accomplished through a monopoly on

the supply of information, refusal of permission to film news footage in land clearance areas, and confiscation of sensitive film. But state control also includes self-censorship, as in the case of an analysis in the weekly *Jakarta Jakarta* of the participation of the Indonesian Armed Forces in land disputes, which journalists removed from the magazine before publication "to avoid being reprimanded" (*untuk menghindari adanya teguran*), an action usually carried out by a phone call from military intelligence. The article described the "mysterious" arrests of activists who tried to organize resistance, as well as the army's perception of its own role in land clearance disputes: namely, to enforce the law, to support local government, and to prevent physical clashes. Journalists felt the article, written before the national elections of May 1992, would "invite the anger of the armed forces."[41] Much of the sensitive information regarding the nature of community resistance to land clearances is expurgated in this way, which makes the *Surya* report of residents refusing to allow security forces into Tubanan *kampung* in Surabaya to demolish homes a unique report. The Muslim daily *Surya* is often outspoken on human-rights reporting; indeed, it has a general reputation for outspoken journalism. Violent resistance to evictions in urban land clearances is not reported in the national dailies.

The pivotal role of the Bakorstanas, particularly in East Java land clearance disputes, is another aspect of state control—that anything that hinders economic growth can also be seen as endangering national stability, which is the rationale for Bakorstanas involvement.

In some cases the government loses control of the agenda. The golf course protest movement, for example, linked students, parliament, and the media, and exposed a minister whose statement that golf improved poor people's welfare was an embarrassment to the government.

Student and NGO involvement in land disputes is another

common feature of landholders' resistance to the state bureaucracy. Student action groups formed around particular issues, such as the antigolf groups and the Plumpang student solidarity committee, and used different forms of protest, including lobbying, and (in the antigolf protest), an effective campaign in the national press. Critical news coverage of the issue was also provided by the privately owned television station RCTI.[42]

Student commitment to dispossessed landholders (whether farmers or urban dwellers) is usually short-lived. Once the issue has died down in the press, even if the basic question of compensation or alternative housing or livelihood remains, the students' involvement ends. According to one activist this is because student groups which support farmers and squatters are provisional, based as they are on "emotional ties," which are strongest at the beginning of a dispute, when it is a regional or national issue. Smaller NGOs, which are enthusiastic in their support of landholders initially, do not have funds or other resources to provide long-term programs to support landholders.

Terror squads (paramilitary vigilante groups), prolonged legal battles over an outcome which can't be enforced (even if adequate compensation is awarded by the courts, as in the Plumpang dispute), forced evictions, bureaucratic infighting, parliamentary powerlessness: these are some of the features of local encounters between landholders and the bureaucratic culture. There is no stronger symbol of parliamentary powerlessness and state control than the incident in which security guards refused to allow a fact-finding delegation from the DPR to visit the disputed area of Plumpang in north Jakarta.

The final question is whether the continuous reporting of land clearance disputes in the print media in Indonesia, in the context of increasing political openness, is changing the nature of local protest, or its effectiveness. While self-censorship is still in place (as well as the threat of formal censorship in the form of withdrawal of permission to publish) the press gives a lot of coverage to land disputes. Compensation disputes, and the numerous delegations to the national parliament and regional assemblies are all assiduously reported in the press. The past two years have seen the questioning (in letters to the editor) the integration of East Timor, the business interests of the president's family, the distribution of national lottery monies, and the sale of crude oil outside government quotas. Whether this questioning is a sign of greater political openness, or is an image which has been "created" by power holders remains to be seen. The view that the new press "freedom" is merely exploitation of friction within the elite is also held by many. In the golf course debate, greater press and political freedoms were apparent, although it was an issue that the government could not win, even if it had wanted to be repressive. While political openness may be a facade for some, for landholders locked in dispute with the government, under threat of eviction, the more open debate, whatever its political motivation, the better.

Notes

1. On the Kedung Ombo land dispute, see YLBHI (Yayasan Lembaga Bantuan Hukum Indonesia) and JARIM (Jaringan Informasi Masyarakat), *Laporan kasus* (Case reports) (Kedung Ombo: Kasus Arso, Cimacan), vol. 2 (June 1991), 1–59.

2. G. J. Adicondro, "Suatu kritik terhadap teori dan praktek Analisa Dampak Lingkungan (ADL) bendungan besar" (A citicism of the theory and practice of environmental impact analysis of large dams), *Kritis* (Journal Universitas Kristen Satya Wacana; special issue on Power and Democracy) 7, 4 (April-June 1993): 38–59.

3. See Anton Lucas, "Land Disputes in Indonesia: Some Current Perspectives," *Indonesia* 53 (April 1992): 87–89.

4. Nine of the largest land clearance disputes are summarized in Lucas, "Land disputes," table 1, p. 81.

5. Hardoyo, "Hutan Tanaman Industri (HTI) dalam mawas diri dan kilas balik pembangunan hutan di Indonesia" (Industrial forestry in the light of self-correction and a backward glance at forest development in Indonesia), mimeograph, Jakarta, October 1993.

6. The best-known case is that of the Surabaya Sports Centre (SSC), where developers deposited money in the private bank accounts of high-ranking officials, resulting in a number of court cases and removal or displacement of officials. See "Kasus Surabaya Sport Center (SSC) (Bagian 1): Proyek presisius yang memakan banyak "korban" pejabat," *Surya*, 6 January 1993.

7. *Injustice, Persecution, Eviction: A Human Rights Update on Indonesia and East Timor*, (New York: Asia Watch Committee, 1990), 71. The report notes that the United Nations Code of Conduct for Law Enforcement Officials states that the duty of such officials should be to protect all people from illegal acts; the report also notes that in Indonesia it is often the security forces who are responsible for such acts.

8. YLBHI, *Demokrasi di balik keranda: Catatan keadaan hak-hak asasi manusia di Indonesia 1992* (Jakarta: YLBHI, 1992), 170.

9. *Tempo*, 22 May 1993.

10. *Suara Pembaruan*, 17 May 1993.

11. In one cartoon, a poor farmer lines up his shot with his son, a caddie, the caption reads, "Memasyarakatkan golf dan menggolfkan mas. . . ." *Kompas*, 15 May 1993.

12. *Republika*, 16 May 1993.

13. "Protest dari Luar Lapangan," *Tempo*, 22 May 1993, 44.

14. "Masalah tanah tetap rawan," *Memorandum*, 28 May 1993.

15. G. J. Adicondro, "Dampak 'wabah' padang golf," *Suara pembaruan*, 2 April 1993.

16. "Boom golf di tengah protes," *DeTik*, 26 May-1 June 1993, 4.

17. As reported in "Protes dari luar lapangan," *Tempo*, 22 May 1993, 44, the minister's words were: "pembangunan lapangan golf bisa dapat menunjukkan tingkat kesejahteran masyarakat."

18. RCTI (Rajawali Citra Televisi Indonesia), "Golf dan kontroversi,"

on *Liputan berita* (a news program), 30 May 1993; see also *Memorandum*, 28 May 1993.

19. "A Call for International Solidarity on Indonesian Tropical Forest Issues," *Setiakawan*, no. 2 (September-October 1989): 23. This is a slightly edited version of the original English text.

20. The last reported visit was to the new Minister of Youth and Sport, whose favorable comments about golf courses as an index of community welfare have already been mentioned. See *Jawa Pos*, 19 May 1993. On the Cimacan golf course dispute, see also Lucas, "Land Disputes," 86.

21. "Dari Cimacan hingga rancamaya: Ribuan petani tergusur padan golf: Bagaimana nasib Mereka?" *DeTik*, 26 May-1 June 1993, 8.

22. "Belajar dari kasus Cimacan: Balada Mereka yang tergusur," *Republika*, 16 May 1993.

23. Farmers in the area were earning about 250,000 rupiahs per month from one *patok* (400 square meters) planted with vegetables such as broccoli, cabbage, onions, and lettuce, as well as orchids, roses, and even strawberries.

24. "Dari Cimacan hingga rancamaya," *DeTik*, 26 May-1 June 1993, 9.

25. *Republika,* 16 May 1993.

26. *Jakarta Pos*, 24 March 1992.

27. "Pesta kemenagan warga tanah merah," *Jakarta Jakarta*, 7-13 November 1992, 79.

28. "Isak tangis sambut putusan hakim," *Merdeka*, 3 November 1993.

29. "Plumpang land case still unsolved after 27th appeal to DPR," *Jakarta Pos*, 3 December 1992.

30. "Bangunan tanah merah plumpang sudah rata," *Kompas,* 3 April 1993.

31. "Warga tanah merah jakut kembali mengadu ke DPR," Merdeka, 19 May 1993.

32. "Hidup getir warga wanah merah," *Republika*, 20 July 1993.

33. "Kepala BPN [Badan Pertanahan Nasional] Soni Harsono: OPP [Organisasi Partai Politik] silahkan mengeritik soal tanah," *Kedaulatan rakyat*, 15 May 1992; "Isu Tanah harus ditampilkan Wajar," *Jawa Pos*, 15 May 1993.

34. "Sebuah kemenangan yang mengejutkan?" *Tempo*, 13 June 1993, 22.

35. "Warga Kecewa, Golkar Kalah di daerah Tubanan dan Urip," *Jawa Pos*, 13 June 1992. On the Urip Sumoharjo dispute, see Lucas, "Land Disputes," 87–89.

36. The wooden signal drum (*kentongan*) is traditionally used in villages to mark the passing of the night, to signal that a thief has been caught, or to warn that danger is threatening. The latter signal is a ceaseless fast beat, and was often used in the Revolution to summon people to act against corrupt officials.

37. "Ribuan warga tubanan unjuk rasa," *Surya*, 28 April 1991.

38. "Warga tubanan buat wawali [wakil walikota] terpana," *Surabaya Pos*, 15 September 1993.

39. In neighboring Pati and Demak, landholders complained about unilateral appropriation of their lands, and corruption of compensation as part of this project; G. J. Adicondro, "Several Cases of Resistance against the Adverse Impact of the Jratunseluna Project by Villagers Downstream from Gedung Ombo," unpublished paper, n.d.

40. The information on Jepara land clearances comes from interviews in July 1992 with a subdistrict official who wishes to remain anonymous.

41. I am grateful to a *Jakarta Jakarta* journalist, who wishes to remain anonymous, for this material.

42. RCTI, "Liputan khusus" (Special coverage report), 30 May 1993.

Chapter Ten

Samin in the New Order: The Politics of Encounter and Isolation

Amrih Widodo

SINCE THE 1930s, no major uprising by the Samin people has provoked significant government intervention. Some Samin people were imprisoned in 1965, when they were accused of being members of the Indonesian Communist Party (PKI) but in fact the local state functionaries were convinced from the beginning that the Samins were not communists. As the officials were in no doubt that they were "just Samin," the imprisonment was actually meant to force them to leave their Samin teachings and be "normal." Local authorities have always taken advantage of situations like this to put more pressure on the Samin people. Considering the intensity of government penetration into village life, especially through the development programs of the New Order regime, it is quite remarkable that Samin communities still exist. The Samin people have not been of major concern to local authorities, but they have the potential to be quite a nuisance. They can still show their "power," or intentionally demonstrate their potential for resistance, as illustrated by the following story.

In a village in Pati District, where a significant number of Samin families live, 7 August 1989 was a traumatic day. On that day, 117 Samin couples were to be married by the state. Before the wedding day, the state functionaries, guided by the village chief and two of his assistants, had made "approaches" to the Samin leaders. Four times the leaders were summoned by the village head to meet the district chief, the head of the district police, and the commander of the district military office. They were cajoled, warned, and threatened into having a "normal" official marriage. The ultimate threat was that they would be exiled abroad, just like their late founder, Samin Surontika. This threat was very effective, as it reminded them of the history of persecution of their fellow believers. They had no choice but to comply with the state's demands. The wedding ceremony was led by a Buddhist priest. The defeated Samins, given a choice of religions for their wedding celebration, chose Buddhism. The main reason for this choice, as they said,[1] was that *buda,* the Javanese word for Buddhism, also means *mlebune uda* (when entering you must be naked), which they consider to be the same as the basic principle of their own teachings—*sikep rabi* (having sexual intercourse).

The newly wed couples were upset, as were the elders and the leaders, because they felt that they were being made fools of in public (*digambar*).[2] The wedding ceremony was performed as a public event, to which regency and district officials, members of the regency legislature, leaders of women's organizations, and journalists were invited. It was arranged as a stage on which to demonstrate the success of the village chief in dominating the Samin community. In the following days, leading newspapers and magazines published reports on the wedding.[3] It signified the moment when "backward" communities, like that of the Samins, had come to an end, swept away by the "spirit" of the New Order development programs.

The village chief seemed to use this event to demonstrate to his superiors that he was a capable leader, deserving of a second term. However, although superiors do play a crucial role in the approval process of candidacy, a village head position is decided by election. This is where the Samin people regained their pride. They organized their people to choose another candidate to defeat the former village head. The former village head was said to have spent seventy million rupiah on this election; nonetheless, he lost. The Samins now have a new village head—a dedicated young farmer who knows that he owes his victory to them.[4] There may be other reasons for the defeat of the former village chief, but for the Samin people, it proved that they still had the "power" to defend their dignity and their identity.

This paper is a preliminary report and analysis of my research on Samin communities, particularly those in the *kabupaten* (regencies) of Blora, Pati, and Kudus. It will try to answer some questions concerning the state of the Samin communities at present, their teaching (*Agama Adam*), and its continuation in the context of the dynamics of the power relations between the Indonesian state and the Samin peasant communities. First, I will explain the nature of *Agama Adam* as conceived by the Samins, its relationship with the Samin "language", as well as its role in the proliferation of Samin communities. Second, I will describe and analyze the "discourse" on Saminism, that is, how its proliferation is also significantly influenced by the interests and interference of outside factors such as the state, the media, and observers-researchers. Finally, I will demonstrate the strategies, both economic-organizational and ideological-symbolic, employed by the Samins in the proliferation of themselves and of their teachings.[5] Finally, I will draw conclusions on how to explain theoretically the viability of such "millenarian" movements in the history of modern Indonesia.

Historical Background: Who Are the Samins?

The teachings known as Saminism were first preached by Samin Surontika, an ordinary Javanese peasant, in the Randublantung District in the southern part of Blora Regency in the mid 1890s.[6] Surontika was a *kulikencang* (peasants who controlled the land and were responsible for paying taxes and performing corvée labor for the king or *priyayi* [the Javanese aristocrats or officials] and thus to the colonial state), and he owned several acres of rice-field. Samin's teachings were called *Agama Adam* by his disciples, who called themselves *wong sikep,* meaning "those who are alert," "those who are liable to the state," or "those who embrace."[7] It has been outsiders—ranging from colonial officials, to nationalist leaders such as Tjipto Mangoenkoesoemo, and present day historians—who have called Samin's teachings Saminism, and one of its followers a Saminist. (In this paper, I use the terms *Saminism* and *Samin,* respectively.)

In the 1900s Saminism spread rapidly within and beyond the Regency of Blora to Bojonegoro, Grobogan, Ngawi, Pati, Rembang, and Madiun. In 1907 it was reported that its followers numbered 3,000. It was then that a *controleur* (lowest-level Dutch administrative official) caught wind of a rumor that the Samins were planning to revolt on March 1. Eight of Samin's disciples were arrested on the spot. Samin himself was not seized then, but a few days later he accepted the regent's invitation to Rembang, where he was arrested. The disciples were exiled to the Outer Islands; Samin died in exile in Padang, Sumatra, in 1914.[8] However, the activity of Samin's followers did not die down; on the contrary, they reached a peak in 1914. Samin refused to pay taxes or render corvée, dared to speak low-level (*ngoko*) Javanese and Samin "language" to Dutch officials and *priyayi,*[9] and ignored the authority of the religious functionaries who solemnized marriages and funerals and collected fees for their services. Again, in 1928, two groups of Samin people in the Juwana District were arrested for what the colonial government called *lijdlijk verzet* (veiled resistance) against the classification of their land. Their noncooperation included their persistent use of the Samin "language" when answering questions.

Before describing the state of Saminism at present, it is important to know why, historically, Samin people called themselves *wong sikep,* and the implications of this for the peasant-state relationship. At the end of the nineteenth century, a change occurred in the term used to refer to peasants: from *wong sikep* to *kuli ken-cang*. This change represented the social transformation brought about by the enforcement of the Cultivation System. Under the Cultivation System, the state commuted taxes into corvée, as it needed a ready labor supply. Thus, to have control over a share of land meant an obligation to render corvée. In an attempt to share the burden, the greater the demand for corvée, the more people were provided with shares of land. Trapped in this situation, the once-independent *wong sikep* were transformed into *kuli* (coolies), who were tied to the village communal land, and, hence, to corvée. The village community then became a pool of coolies.[10] It was at this time that the Samins revived the idea of *wong sikep*. They insisted that the term did not mean "those who are liable to the state"; instead, they introduced a new meaning with a sexual connotation: "those who embrace."[11] To understand what Saminism is, it is essential to understand this transformation, for this marks the beginning of the efforts of *kuli kencang*[12] to regenerate *wong sikep*, in an age when the state under which *wong sikep* had once lived was lost.

The end of the nineteenth century also marked a significant change in the nature of the relationship between the peasantry and the *priyayi*. With the hyperpenetration of government into the village sphere, whatever place the *priyayi* had managed to hold onto in the ideally interdependent-mutual relationship of *kawula-gusti* (servant-lord) was "taken" by the Dutch. In this time of crisis, Onghokham suggests, the royal authority gained through the possession of *wahyu* was not concentrated in a single selected individual, such as the king.[13] Instead, *wahyu* was distributed to individuals to whom royal authority would then be attributed. It was at this historical juncture that, I suggest, Samin "rediscovered" the ideology of his teachings.[14] It was the moment of being in need of independence, and of disillusionment with what the concept of *kawula-gusti* had become. This disillusionment and need for independence prompted the desire for a "perfect" internalization of the group (*gusti*) with the individual (*kawula*), which was the stage of "pureness" that Samin taught his disciples.

The history of the Samins' sense of property can be traced back to the management of teak forests. In theory, the king owned all the land and forest, but such ownership was defined in a way that it was different from the Dutch sense of property.[15] The "new sense of property" introduced by the Dutch through the state's control over forest access, which was the villagers means of survival, brought about the emergence of what the state called *maling kayu* (teakwood theft). Nancy Peluso reports that the number of teakwood thefts began to mushroom at the end of the nineteenth century, after the colonial state ratified the forestry laws and set up an efficient network for the enforcement of laws, and that, in a number of villages, most of the members were involved in teakwood theft. In this forest environment there also appeared "rebellions" by others on the social periphery: *tegal* (robbers), *blandhong* (woodcutters), and *blantik* (livestock dealers). Saminism was born within the context of these "rebels." *Tempo* reports that in the past Saminists sought *kasekten* (possession of magic power [often] attained by means of ascetic practice), *ngelmu*, (esoteric knowledge), and *kadigdayan* (the art of magic combat).[16] All these skills were important requirements for being a *maling aguna*. This is not altogether in keeping with the nonviolent image with which the Samin movement has been identified.

The Discourse on Saminism

In *The Moral Economy of the Peasant*, James C. Scott introduces the subsistence ethic as the key to making a causal analysis of peasant resistance.[17] This ethic, he argues, is rooted in the economic practices and social exchanges of peasant society. It is within the context of this ethic that the causes of peasant resistance should be understood. In *The Weapon of the Weak,* Scott continues his analysis of the forms of peasant resistance, based on this subsistence ethic. His studies do not really reveal why the resistance of a certain group of peasants, in a given location at a given time, takes its particular form. Nor does he discuss the ideology or beliefs upon which a particular form of resistance is based. Thus, he never explains why the Saya San rebellion in Burma intended to restore the Old Kingdom, or why the Samin revolt took the form of what he calls folk anarchism.

There were two studies on the Samin movement during the colonial period. The first inquiry was conducted in 1917 by Jasper, the assistant resident of Tuban, under the auspices of the Dutch governor general, who felt that the Samins' uncooperativeness had finally exceeded the limits of the colonial government's tolerance. Jasper's report concluded that *Agama Adam* was a form of Javanese mental deviance (*mentaal afwijking*), which had resulted from the enormous social changes generated by the Ethical Policy. Thus, he contended, it was not worth looking at in any detail. *Het Saminisme* (1918), the second study, was carried out by Tjipto Mangoenkoesoemo, one of the most outspoken critics of Dutch colonial rule and exploitation. Tjipto's perspective was, however, similar to Jasper's. He saw Saminism as little more than an amalgam of Hinduism and archaic agrarian anarchism, important only as an expression of the profound contradictions brought about by Dutch colonial domination and capitalist exploitation.

Historians writing about the Indonesian nationalist movement and peasant rebellions have tended to describe only briefly the Samin movement.[18] Benda and Castles, The Siauw Giap, and Onghokham sketch the history of the Samin movement and its sociological background. The brief article by Benda and Castles addresses the question of what Saminism is, but the limited secondary materials they used for their analysis prevent them from answering this question satisfactorily. King's and Korver's studies are so preoccupied with "theoretical" concerns that they disregard the question of what Saminism is. However, King's anthropological observations, and Peluso's study on forest management, do give some background on the local forest economy. The Gadjah Mada Report is the only survey that compiles linguistic data about Saminism, but this report is superficial and nonanalytical.

Indonesian observers such as Njoman Dekker and Sudomo, Suripan Hutomo, and Budiman give more attention to the linguistic aspects of Saminism. Their analyses have not yet reached a satisfactory explanation of the relationship between Samin language and *Agama Adam*. They and other observers such as Anwar, Mulder, Prasongko, Prawoto, Sastroatmodjo, and Soesanto highlight, in the main, the role of the Samin people in fighting against the colonial state, their "strange," language and their good qualities. The writings usually convey humanistic and cultural missions, portraying Samin people as the "pure" Javanese, and arguing that their *adat* should be preserved. A significant number of articles have been written in newspapers and magazines, usually describing Saminism in the exotic tone of a eulogy.

Nowadays, the Samins usually wish to avoid being called Samin because of the established connotations of that term.[19] When non-Samin Javanese hear the term *wong Samin* (Samin people), what usually comes to mind are people whose behavior or speech are ludicrous (*kocak*) and foolish (*konyol*); irrational and ungrammatical; stupid and backward; or simply crazy and uncontrolled.[20] On the other hand, outsiders also believe that the Samin people are trustworthy, honest, and hardworking.

Outsiders and the state have been facing the dilemma of how to appropriate and place the Samins into their own sociocultural map. The discourse on Saminism has always implied that Samins were heroes who have been effective in their use of foolishness and hilarity, as a means of resistance to the colonial government.[21] Ironically, the Indonesian state since independence has been annoyed by the same "foolish" and "hilarious" behavior that used to be directed at the state functionaries during the colonial era.

Attempts to subdue and domesticate the Samin "issue" have been made by both the Sukarno and Suharto governments of postindependence Indonesia. In 1952 a directive from the Ministry of Information claimed that "the much-discussed Saminist community has now, in the era of independence, started to behave normally, just like other folk" (Benda and Castles, 1969, 207). In a similar vein, in 1987 New Order functionaries claimed that Samins were currently participating fully in the government's development programs, and were even engaged in monetary exchange and the market economy (*Tempo,* 23 May 1987). Although articles about the Samin people never fail to claim that they are already as "normal" as other Javanese, nonetheless, the image of the Samins' ludicrous and foolish behavior is still perpetuated,[22] and is used to refer to such behavior even when it does not belong to the Samins.

The word *nyamin,* which means "to act like a Samin," has been coined by the state to refer to such behavior. The New Order officials in many regencies no longer acknowledge the existence of the Samin people. Anybody behaving like a Samin is accused of being *nyamin*—that is, pretending to act a Samin to gain certain benefits or to avoid or resist state policies. This treatment means that the present Samin people have been severed from their historical heroic heritage. They are subject to sanctions and other consequences whenever they do not comply with state regulations and laws. Their actions are no longer considered heroic, but simply crazy and resistant.

The particular characteristics of Samin communities seem to have the potential to attract outsiders' interest in them, with the purpose of encouraging the Samins' interest in some activity—political, religious, economic, or cultural—in order to include them in their groups or ideologies. The Sarekat Islam in the 1930s, the Indonesian Communist Party in the 1960s, and the New Order Golkar are examples of those who have penetrated Samin communities using Samin terms, and have gained some success, but never full support. The Samins always slip from their grasp.

Since what distinguishes Samins from non-Samins is their behavior, particularly their linguistic behavior, language is the most important access to their world. Although Samins understand and may be able to speak high-level *krama* to state officials and strangers, they dare to speak *ngoko* in those situations, or deliberately and systematically use vocabulary assigned with second meanings. My data show that there have always been some outsiders who have learned the Samin language, in order to act as translators between the two worlds. These people include some government officials who learn and use the "language" of the Samins: they aim to gain Samin cooperation through the coopting of their language. Political appeals, tax collections, corvée, and other government programs need to be "translated" when they are delivered to the Samin community, otherwise they will be met with some resistance.

On the other hand, intensive penetration by the New Order development programs has brought about significant structural changes in rural areas. In response to this situation, and realizing how powerful the state is, the Samin people have been trying to minimize negative images of them by paying their dues to the state (e.g., paying taxes on time, volunteering to do communal work, and so on). Their strategy seems to be to accommodate the state's demands, so that they can be left alone to do what they want. This "leave me alone" ideology can be seen in their religious, linguistic, and economic behavior. This means that an analysis of the relationship between the state and the Samin communities should not be based on the concept of state in a strict political sense. Instead, political meaning should be looked for elsewhere.[23]

Agama Adam *and the Samin Language*

Whenever devout Samins are asked about their belief in the existence of hell and heaven, they tend to shake their heads, smile, and answer softly: "When you say there is a heaven . . . yes, it's true, there is a heaven. In your tongue. If you say no, then there is not."[24] For the Samins, life ends with death. They believe that human beings' obligation to do good things is just for their benefit when they are alive, not for any forms of afterlife. Hardjo Kardi, a Samin, describes death as freedom.[25] One of their conceptions of religion is that "religion is a weapon."[26] How should we make sense of such contentions? Is religious truth for the Samins embedded in speech? From what constraints and obligations will they be free after death? What is religion for them, that they see it as a weapon?

The above statements suggest that the Samin conceptualization of religion is quite different from that which is usually used in anthropology. Yet, in the history of anthropological studies of religion, the various conceptualizations of religion develop in response to, and in the context of, the development of anthropological studies and social science in general. The Indonesian and Javanese term that is comparable to the conceptualizations of religion, as the term is used in anthropology, is *agama*. One of the main Javanese conceptualizations of religion is expressed in the saying *Agama ageming ratu,* which means "Religion is the king's outfit." The notion of outfit of the king suggests some kind of ideology that underlies the process and politics of symbolization. The Samins' contention that religion is a weapon (*agama iku gaman*), indicates the perspective from which the Samins view and live life, as well as the "ideology" they adhere to in response to the surrounding hegemonic Javanese worldview and ethos. Indeed, although the Samin are Javanese, they are considered as of the "other" by "mainstream" Javanese. The Samins' conceptualization of religion is consistent with their conception of language—it is viewed as something secret and sacred. The Samin language also serves as a weapon to fight against or avoid the king's or state's interference in their life. "Rituals" for the Samin seem to be the linguistic encounters with the "other" (the mainstream Javanese and Indonesians) within which the secretness and sacredness of their language and religion are revitalized. Thus, for the Samins, religion and language are embedded in each other, and both involve the politics of symbolization—the politics in which Samins have to be engaged before they are "free" with the coming of death.

Takashi Shiraishi suggests that central to the teaching of Samin was an idea of purity.[27] Ordinary language concepts such as the state, the *priyayi,* taxes, corvée, and *wong sikep,* were all transformed according to that central idea. The transformation involved the assignment of second meanings to these ordinary language concepts. The ideology or belief that constitutes the logic of these second meanings, perhaps embodied in *Agama Adam,* is still a mystery. The Gadjah Mada team reports that *Agama Adam* includes many sets of formulae in the Samin "language," the second meanings of which usually refer to agricultural and sexual activity. It has been the operation of these two sets of meanings that have vexed and enraged state functionaries in their encounters with the Samin, both in situations where they do and do not understand the Samin "language."

To see how this mechanism of transformation works to subvert the ordinary language that the state speaks through its officials, we can turn to the often quoted courtroom dialogue between a Samin who refused to pay taxes, and his *priyayi* judge.[28] The state functionary became vexed and enraged, and hastily decided the sentence, whereas the Samin defendant remained calm. He remained calm because it was he who entertained linguistic control over the situation. The Samins could always win at this linguistic power play, for they understood what the officials said, and yet they deliberately and systematically employed an exclusive language of their own that challenged the "hegemony" of the pre-established meanings appropriated by the Javanese linguistic and social hierarchy. This calmness, I would suggest, assumes some kind of "faith" that serves as the ideological-religious basis for its expression, the Samin language.

The Samin people believe that they are the purest Javanese (*Jawa Asli* or *Lugu*). They divide existence in the world into two categories: *wong* (human being) and *sandhang pangan* (the necessities of life; e.g., food and clothing). Every human being, regardless of his or her social and economic status, race, nationality, or religion, is conceptually the same for the Samin: *wong*. They refer to everyone with the egalitarian term *sedulur*, meaning something like "sibling."[29] *Wong* is the origin and the center of everything, and all existence must be able to be translated into, and interpreted on the basis of, this idea of *wong*.[30] As I explained above, the Samins like to call themselves *wong sikep* to show that their ultimate duty and goal in life is *sikep rabi*, to embrace or make love. They believe that every human being makes love, and this is what makes everybody the same. The difference, according to the Samin, is that they are the only ones who acknowledge, even profess (*ngakoni*), it openly and religiously. They believe that other people (non-Samin) *nglakoni*, do it, but do not profess it. Therefore, non-Samins can never be pure. For Samins, to be pure means to be *lugu*—simple, plain, innocent, literal. Consequently, to profess their faith, Samins have to behave and speak in a *lugu* way. It is this *lugu*-ness in their behavior—especially their linguistic behavior, in which sexual matters are spoken about blatantly —that has been considered hilarious and foolish by outsiders. Mainstream Javanese like to make sexual jokes, usually in a subtle ways, and sex for them has ideologically been connected to power.[31] In contrast, the Samin people talk about sexual matters in a plain, nonglorifying, religious way.

To illustrate this point, let us look at the Samin profession of faith (*sadat*, from Arabic *syahadat*), which is said as a marriage oath on a couple's wedding day, after the couple have consummated the marriage (*rukun*, lit. "harmonious"):[32]

Kula wong	I am a human being
Jeneng lanang	of a male kind
Pengaran X	called X
Damel kula sikep rabi	my duty is to marry / have sexual intercourse
Demen janji	(I am) determined to make an oath
Tata-tata wedok	to work with a female kind
Buk nikah pun kula lakoni	sleeping together, I have done it.

This spoken oath is then answered by one of the elders, who says that since the man makes his oath voluntarily, he should remember and watch his own words (*niteni omonge dhewe*). The attending members of the community will also watch and remember (*niteni*) his words.

This is the minimum requirement to be a Samin today. The complete *sadat* is only spoken once, on the "wedding day," since Samin people believe in one marriage for life (*sepisan kanggo selawase*). However, part of the *sadat* is repeated over and over, when the couple introduces themselves to new people. When Samins introduce themselves, each is supposed to say, "*Tepangke, kula jeneng lanang/wedok, pengaran X*" (Let me introduce myself,

I am of the male/female kind, called X). This means that whenever they encounter new people their *sadat* is renewed and their identity is confirmed. In a group situation, every person present will go individually to a guest, hold the guest's hand firmly, and not let it go until they have finished the introduction. Each person continues to hold the guest's hand until they hear the guest's name clearly. To outsiders visiting a Samin community for the first time, the impact of this encounter is overwhelming. With the understanding that Samin people have their own "language," after a few introductions, one cannot help but imitate the way the Samins introduce themselves, and when conversation occurs the outsider becomes tongue-tied.

In such gatherings, one of the unavoidable topics of discussion is *Agama Adam*. The Samins seem to be very familiar with the guest's assumptions about *Agama Adam,* which is interpreted as the religion of the first man, Adam. Indeed, this meaning is tacitly accepted by the Samins, for it also called *Agama Kawitan* (the first religion), or *Adam Kawitan* (Adam, the first), implying the authority Saminism assumes in being the first of all religions, even of all existences. However, Samins will give a second explanation of the meaning of *Agama Adam,* and during the explanation, the guest is taken aback by the double meanings given, mostly implicitly, to each explanation.

Agama iku gaman	*Agama* means "weapon"; it indicates a political weapon to resist or avoid outside intervention, especially state interference.
gaman lanang	Sexual meaning is introduced by explaining that *agama* is the weapon of the male kind.
Adam pangucape	*Adam* is the term used to say it, because *Adam* is *pangucape* (speech). Before sexual intercourse, one has to *jawab* (speak), especially during the ceremony of marriage, as explained above. All relations between *wong* and *sandhang pangan* need *Adam*. *Adam* is, then, language for the Samin. Thus the weapon is language.

Dam, damel rabi   *Adam* (the penis and the language) is to be used for the relationship between *wong,* especially between the male and female.

From the explanation above, it can be concluded that *Adam* is given a meaning that contains both sexual and linguistic means of relations, where both are embedded in the teachings of *Agama Adam.* Furthermore, the explanation indicates that existence, for Samin people, is always in speech (i.e., the voice).[33] Things and human beings exist only when they are being spoken (about) by *wong.* Thus, *wong* and *sandhang pangan,* the two forms of being, exist simultaneously within speech.[34] To be a Samin, *wong* has to speak the truth, which is meant to be tangible or concrete. Lying, which denotes an incongruity between speech and reference, is the most serious "sin" for a Samin. They believe that only Samins can be "true Javanese," *Jawa Jawah,* meaning the Javanese who speak the truth. The introduction of new words usually brings about problems of signification and appropriation for Samins. All words with abstract or conceptual meanings can enter and be accepted into their signification system after they are "converted" into their language, the logic of which centers on their "religion," *Agama Adam,* the means of which is *keratabasa.*[35] Consequently, those words are given second meanings, with reproductive (sexual or agricultural or both) connotations. Since the Samins control the assignment of second meanings, they put themselves in a controlling position, with the condition that they dare to persist in using their "language."

The assignment of second meanings, instead of being formulaic and static, is very generative,[36] which means that the more stable and hierarchical symbolic order of the dominant Javanese and Indonesian languages are put in a continuously threatened position. The case of the mass wedding ceremony is an example of this. Although some Samin teachings are thought to be very similar to Buddhism by observers,[37] and by some Samins themselves, when the Buddhist ceremony was accepted, *buda* was understood to be *mlebune uda* (when entering you must be naked). The assignment of this new meaning serves two functions. First, it denies the forced meaning of the term, and this denial implies the refusal of the sociocultural transformation of their status and identity. Second, it serves as a confirmation of the Samins' own identity, as well as a confirmation that they are still in control of themselves, although it may only be at the symbolic level.

When asked about their life goals, the Samins say that they are *seneng* and *rukun*.[38] The location for *seneng* could be food, clothing, shelter, cattle, or other forms of *sandhang pangan,* but the ultimate form of *seneng* is *sikep rabi.* Therefore, *rukunan* (spouse) is the very location of the ultimate form of *seneng.* There are a set of rules that a Samin is not allowed to violate: *noh drengki, srei, dahwen, panasten* and *moh pethil, jumput, bedhog, colong, nemok wae, moh.*[39] All those rules basically mean "not desiring others' possessions." Unlike the common meaning of *kepengin* (wanting), or *seneng* (liking), which the gap in meaning implies an object of desire outside the self, Samin teaching conceptually locates the object of desire within the self. They say that what they want is what they have, and that the ultimate want is their own spouse.

This is a case where interest is not placed within a power relationship between the self and others: instead it is confined within the self or within the things already belonging to, and thus part of, the self.[40] I have explained above that the characteristics of the Samin language are its egalitarian tone in the use of *ngoko,* and the assignment of second meanings. During the New Order era, the process of "*krama*-ization" has intensively penetrated rural life, and has brought about some change in the nature of the Samin language. With everything becoming increasingly "*krama*-ized," I get the impression that nowadays the efficacy of the Samin language does not so much lie in the equalization of the interlocutors through the use of *ngoko,* but more in the carefully designed language use which does not imply any commitment of interests. The Samin people seem to realize that control and domination can operate only within the realm of power relations, and that power relations mean interest relations. Once they invest their interests within the hierarchical social relations and the imbalance of power relations, they will be trapped and coopted by hegemonic state control. They also seem to realize that encounters with state officials and other outsiders are unavoidable, and they are always in a politically and economically disadvantaged position. By combining the strategy of confining interests within the self, and assigning second meanings to a set of vocabulary, the Samins can defend their world, a world in which they still have some control over the politics of signification.

Last Words

The so-called Samin language, belonging to the nonleader Samin, consists of a set of answers for a set of questions. The Samins memorize the mantralike phrases in great detail, with an understanding that Samin Surontika will come again to check his offspring.[41] He is believed to be able to recognize his offspring from the way they answer his questions—that is, from their language. To my question on the coming of Samin Surontika, the Samins in Pati and Kudus gave two different explanations.

The first answer is millenarian and mystical in essence: Samin Surontika actually did not die in exile because he could live for hundreds of years. Sometimes he is believed to visit his offspring to see how they are, but only certain people can see him. At other times, I was told that Samin Surontika is only *salin sandhangan* (to be in different outfits) and that he will come one day to take care of his offspring. The second answer is based on the Samin teaching in which existence is in speech: Samin Surontika will be present when his name is being uttered, or when he is being talked about. In my opinion, this phenomenon is peculiarly Samin, and it has played an important role in the process of the proliferation of Saminism. The unstable position of the Samin people in the political discourse of modern Indonesian will invite debates and revive interest in discussion about them. Journalists, students, and government officials will still use issues of Saminism for their own purposes.[42] The realization of their interests will allow the Samins to have encounters with outsiders. Both the Samin people and the mainstream Javanese-Indonesians see each other as "the other," and each party negotiates its own identity during the encounters.

The proliferation of Saminism seems to depend very much on their encounters with outsiders, especially the language encounters. In the eyes of Samin people, each encounter then serves as a rite to test his or her faith. When the encounters take place in their house, many people will gather to participate in the rite, where their leaders demonstrate the efficacy of the Samin language, and thus the truth of *Agama Adam*. In this rite, each member of the Samin community is given the opportunity to confirm his or her identity, and to practice using Samin "language" by confirming the leaders' statements, commenting on the topics of the discussion, laughing at the guests' "illogical" words, and trying to explain some of the Samin teachings they have mastered. Each encounter, then, becomes an arena where the efficacy of Samin "language" is exercised, and thus the "truth" of *Agama Adam* is reevaluated, reconfirmed, and revived.

Appendix

When the Samins' property was seized to cover their tax arrears, they refused to accept the surplus money back from the state.[43] The Samins' state of mind is reflected in the following description of a courtroom scene, written by a Javanese journalist who visited Rembang in December 1914. The interrogation proceeds between the *patih,* a court official, and an accused Samin.

> "You still owe the state ninety cents."
> "I have not borrowed anything from the state."
> "You have to pay taxes, though."
> "*Wong Sikep* [i.e., the Saminist] knows no taxes."

This answer the *patih* found too bold, and he told the policeman sitting next to the Saminist to slap him in the face. But the Samin-disciple remained calm, and when he had received the blow, said:

> "Naturally the *priyayi* is offended, and finds me vexing. The state orders him to collect taxes, and I don't want to pay them. Naturally, he becomes annoyed."
> "Are you crazy, or are you pretending to be crazy?"
> "I am not crazy nor do I pretend to be."
> "You used to pay taxes; why not now?"
> "Formerly is formerly, now is now. Why doesn't the state stop asking for money?"
> "The state spends money, too, for the native population. If the state did not have enough money, it would be impossible to maintain the roads properly."
> "If we find the state of the roads troubling us, we'll fix them ourselves."
> "So you won't pay the tax?"
> "*Wong Sikep* knows no tax."

Such people are naturally difficult to persuade to another opinion. So the District Court rendered the following decision: "The District Court orders you to pay your debt to the state. If you have not paid within eight days, your goods will be seized. Go!"

And the Saminist left calmly, saying, "As far as I know, I have not borrowed anything from the state."

When eight days had passed and the Saminists had maintained their refusal to pay, their goods were seized. . . . None of [them] . . . resisted the seizures. . . . On the 8th or 9th of January the goods were sold. From the proceeds the taxes were paid; the rest of the money was to be returned to the owners, but they would not accept it. Each of them said: "As far as I know, I haven't sold anything."

Notes

1. The other important reasons that were unspoken were financial and ideological-religious. The government decided to subsidize half of this wedding ceremony, for which each couple had to pay 20,500 rupiahs (about $11). The Samins have inherited attitudes toward Islam from their elders, who had had unpleasant experiences with obligatory state-Muslim weddings. This particular community has also been influenced by teachings derived from "Serat Darma Gandhul," which contains critical views of Islam, but looks favorably on Buddhism.

2. *Digambar* literally means "being painted." In this case the Samin people felt that the state functionaries, especially the village chief, had publicly shamed them by forcing them to show their deference and admit their defeat.

3. See, for instance, *Kompas*, 11 and 14 August 1989; *Suara Karya*, 14 August 1989; *Jawa Pos*, 18 August 1989; *Surabaya Post*, 1 June 1989; *Sarinah*, 25 September 1989.

4. The election was held in January 1990, five months after the mass wedding ceremony. Out of five candidates, four passed the written test and the interview test. Out of 3,124 total votes, 990 went to the new village chief, 917 to the former village chief, 870 to the new chief's uncle, and the remaining 347 to the other candidates. The new village chief told me that the population of his village was about 6,600 from 664 families, so on average one family consists of 10 people. But, he said, the

big families are usually the Samin families. This supports the argument that the organization of Samin families to vote for the new village chief helped ensure his victory.

5. I will discuss the economic aspects of the proliferation of Saminism in another paper. It is sufficient here to say that it is also due to the relative autonomy of the Samin farmers, in that agriculture has given them a better position to create borders—economic, political, and ideological—with outsiders.

6. The actual number of Samin people and *Agama Adam* followers is not known. Any statements or articles indicating the existence of Samin people in a *kabupaten* will invite negative responses from the *bupati*—it is considered to be a sign of failure to include Samin people in the development programs, since Saminism is perceived as backwardness. All *bupati* have claimed that there are no more Samin people in their areas; Samins are considered to be ex-Saminists, the offspring of Samin families, or those who act like Samins (Javanese: *nyamin*). My data suggests, however, that there are still many villages in Blora, Grobogan, Rembang, Kudus, and Ngawi where Samins live and still adhere to their teachings, albeit with differing degrees of commitment.

7. For an example of the transformation of those terms and their meanings over time, see Onghokham, "Penelitian sumber-sumber gerakan mesianis," *Prisma* 1 (January 1977): 64–70.

8. See H. Benda and L. Castles, "The Samin Movement," *Bijdragen tot de taal-, land- en volkenkunde* 125 (1969): 211–12; Suripan Sadi Hutomo, "Bahasa Orang Samin," *Majalah Konggres Bahasa Jawa* (1991).

9. As far as we know, the Samin "language" consists of a set of *ngoko* vocabulary to which are assigned second meanings that resist or ignore the established meanings. Peasants usually speak high-level *krama* Javanese to *priyayi*, complying with the linguistic hierarchy and convention of meanings. Thus, speaking *ngoko* or Samin "language" is a blatant challenge to the *priyayi*.

10. Onghokham, "Penelitian sumber-sumber gerakan mesianis," 64–70. Under the Dutch rule in the nineteenth century, taxes rested on the land, not on the individual, and taxes were collected from the village instead of the individual.

11. *Sikep* can mean "alert" or "ready," perhaps referring to the physical and mental state that forest dwellers should possess. The term implies that the Samins are people who adhere rigorously to their principles.

12. Most of the Saminists were *kuli kencang*.

13. Onghokham, "The Residency of Madiun: *Priyayi* and Peasant in the Nineteenth Century." (Ph.D. dissertation, Yale University, 1975), 234–41. *Wahyu* means a divine token of greatness and honor, the owner of which is entitled to be a leader or even a king. See Soemarsaid Moertono, *State and Statecraft in Old Java* (Ithaca: Cornell Modern Indonesia Project Monograph Series 43, 1968), 56–58; and for the connection of *wahyu* and power, see Benedict Anderson, "The Idea of Power in Javanese Culture," in *Culture and Politics in Indonesia*, ed. Claire Holt (Ithaca: Cornell University Press, 1981), 1–28.

14. I suggest that Samin *rediscovered* the idea that *wahyu* was anybody's right, because the idea was not absolutely new: instead it was rejection of what had become the colonial dynastic "tradition."

15. See T. Pigeaud, *Java in the Fourteenth Century*, vol 1 (The Hague: M. Nijhoff, 1962), 472; Onghokham, "The Inscrutable and the Paranoid," in *Southeast Asian Transitions*, ed. R. Mcvey (New Haven: Yale University Press, 1976), 115; and Soemarsaid Moertono, *State and Statecraft in Old Java*, 111–18.

16. *Tempo*, 23 May 1987.

17. I have collected more than one hundred writings on Saminism: scholarly articles, articles from newspapers and magazines, theses, reports, and so on; most of them have been based on very short visits to one of the communities, and a reading of the previously written material. See the explanation below.

18. See G. Kahin, *Nationalism and Revolution in Indonesia* (Ithaca: Cornell University Press, 1952), 43–44; Sartono Kartodirdjo, "Agrarian Radicalism in Java: Its Setting and Development" in *Culture and Politics in Indonesia*, ed. Claire Holt (Ithaca: Cornell University Press, 1972), 119–22; and Sartono Kartodirdjo, *Protest Movements in Rural Java* (Singapore: Oxford University Press 1973).

19. Basically, all Samin people, following the basic principle of their

teachings, call themselves *sikep*, which means *sikep rabi* (having sexual intercourse). *Samin* has, then, been given the meaning of *sami-sami*, with the egalitarian sense that everyone is *sami*, the same. Samin people in Klapadhuwur call themselves *peniten*, meaning "those who recognize and remember."

20. See Njoman Dekker and Sudomo, *Masyarakat Samin*; Paulus Widiyanto, "Samin Surontika dan Konteksnya" *Prisma* 8 (1983): 59–67. See also works by Suripan Hutomo: "Masyarakat Samin ing Daerah Ngraho," *Penyebar Semangat* 11 (17 March 1972); "Kronologis Sejarah Gerakan Samin" *Penyebar Semangat* (2 October 1972); *Masyarakat Samin di Jawa Timur (Sebuah feasibility study)* (Jakarta: Dept. Pendidikan dan Kebudayaan, 1980); "Bahasa dan Sastra Lisan Orang Samin" *Basis* 32 (January 1983); "Samin Surontika dan Ajaran-Ajarannya" *Basis* 34 (January 1985); "Bahasa Orang Samin," *Majalah Konggres Bahasa Jawa* (1991); and *Tempo*, 23 May 1987. The verb *nyamin* was coined, and is very widely used, to mean "to act or to speak like a *wong Samin*"—that is, in a foolish (*konyol*) or half-witted (*kocak*) way.

21. From my interviews with Saminists, state functionaries, and observers of the Samin movement, it is increasingly evident that the Samins did not have direct encounters with the Dutch. Instead, they always had to deal with indigenous state functionaries who, in carrying out their duties for the colonial government, used their authority for their own benefit. Nevertheless, the discourse on Saminism never fails to portray Samin people as heroes who fought without violence against the Dutch.

22. The word *samin* does not now refer to the Samin people only, but is used to signify any behavior considered similar to that of the Samin people.

23. Benedict Anderson has suggested such an approach for examining the political aspects of millenarian movements. See "Millenarianism and the Saminist Movement," in *Religion and Social Ethos in Indonesia*, ed. J. Mackie (Clayton, Victoria, Australia: Monash University Press, 1975), 48–61.

24. I am interested in the Samin "language" as Samins and others define it—that is, as a social construct. Therefore, I am not approaching the concept of language from a linguistic or sociolinguistic perspective.

25. *Tempo*, 23 May 1987, 46.

26. *Agama iku gaman*. See Suripan, "Bahasa dan Sastra Lisan Orang Samin."

27. Takashi Shiraishi, "Dangir's Testimony: Saminism Reconsidered," *Indonesia* 50 (April 1990), 95–120.

28. See the appendix at the end of the chapter for a rendition of a courtroom dialogue in which a court official (*patih*) is questioning a Samin who was accused of being in arrears over tax payment.

29. Unlike in the past, when *ngoko* was the language level suggested for addressing outsiders, nowadays Samin people, especially the younger generation, speak *krama* to outsiders. They do not acknowledge that the reason for using *krama* is the hierarchy in society, since they conceptually reject hierarchies. They say *krama* is used voluntarily because someone will be *rugi* (ashamed of himself or herself; lit., losing out or suffering financial loss) if they do not use it.

30. Mbah Tarno, the leader of the Samin community in the above story, is very fond of being challenged to give the second meaning to any words given to him, that is, the meanings given on the basis of the central idea of *wong*. The second meaning always reflects the basic teachings of Saminism as described above: the idea of reproduction (sexual and agricultural), and the unison of spoken words with their "concrete" or "tangible" meanings. Some examples follow:

gunung (mountain)	=	*guneme sing dumunung* (speeches have to match reality)
sembahyang (prayer)	=	*mesem tambah nggrayang* (after smiling, then you touch)
bumi (earth, land)	=	*mlebume diemi-emi* (the penetration should be done carefully)
lemah (land to be tilled)	=	*lumah* (lying on one's back i.e., a woman ready for sexual intercourse)
wali (friend of God, saint)	=	*sing disuwali* (the thing you cover with cloth; i.e., the penis)

(In traditional Javanese texts, the term is used for the group of [usually nine] lords to whom the Islamization of Java is attributed.)

negara (state)	=	*neg-nege wong loro* (the intention of two people)

swarga (heaven) = *sakwaregan* (once you are full)
pancasila = *pathokan tata cara sikep rabi sing kudu*
(the state philosophy) *dilakoni* (the principles of the Samin lifestyle)

31. On this matter, see, for instance, Benedict Anderson, *Language and Power: Exploring Political Cultures in Indonesia* (Ithaca: Cornell University Press, 1990). A number of Javanese texts, epitomized by "Serat Centini," demonstrate the glorification, and thus domestication, of sex and power.

32. In the Samin marriage system, a bachelor is supposed to stay with the family of the woman he wants to marry (*nyuwita*) until they have consummated the marriage. They immediately report to the woman's parents once they have had intercourse. The parents will then gather some people to witness the man professing his marriage oath (*seksenan*), after which the marriage is considered legal.

33. Whenever the Samin are faced with new abstract conceptual words, particularly those that they do not like for political and religious reasons, they usually acknowledge their existence only in speech (when they are being uttered). The existence of written words is denied because they are not *muri*, which means "voiced" or "spoken," but which can also mean "meaningful." It is the speaking mouth that makes the words meaningful, not the written letters. Thus, for the Samin people, the domain of meanings is always in speech.

34. In his book *Solo in the New Order* (Princeton: Princeton University Press, 1986) James Siegel argues convincingly that translation and hierarchy are intimately intertwined in Java. He demonstrates that language can either constitute or work against hierarchy through translation. The Samin "language," like *ngoko,* is what Siegel terms the "authentic" in language, the domain of which is voice. The "authentic" cannot be appropriated to hierarchy without being "translated" into the "unauthentic"—*krama* or Indonesian. This model, to some degree, fits the way the Samin people view language.

35. *Keratabasa* is a kind of Javanese etymology to search for underlying or original phrases from which words are derived. In Javanese grammar, *keratabasa* does not occupy a significant place as a productive means for giving meanings or creating new words, but in reality this

does occur. In the case of Samin people in Pati, Kudus, and parts of Blora (Klapadhuwur), *keratabasa* seems to have become the basis for logic and etymology. See Suripan Hutomo, "Bahasa Orang Samin."

36. There are certainly words that do have stable second meanings. They are for the most part words such as *Agama Adam, sikep rabi, rukun,* and *seksenan* that are used for the Samins' teachings.

37. See Niels Mulder, "Saminism and Buddhism: A Note on a Field Visit to a Samin Community," *Asian Quarterly* 3 (1983): 62–67.

38. For the Samins, *seneng* means: (1) to desire, (2) fulfillment of desire, (3) the state of being free or unburdened, (4) something like fun. *Rukun* means: (1) to make love, (2) to live together harmoniously.

39. *Drengki, srei, dahwen,* and *panasten* indicate a restless state of mind and emotion relating to wanting things belonging to others; *pethil, jumput, bedhog,* and *colong* all mean "to steal" in different ways.

40. *Self* here could be an individual or collective self.

41. In some places it is not Samin Surontika, but the twin princes, who come again to free the people from suffering. See Mailrapport no. 238x1929.

42. In his article "Dangir's Testimony: Saminism Reconsidered," Shiraishi indicates how biased the report on the Samin movement by a Javanese state official is. It could be read that this type of interest, or other kinds of interests of outsiders, have been playing an important role in the proliferation of Saminism.

43. Rendered from Benda and Castles, "Samin Movement," 225; Anderson, "Millenarianism and the Saminist Movement," 55; and Shiraishi, "Saminism Reconsidered."

Chapter Eleven

What's in a Name? Appropriating Idioms in the South Sulawesi Rice Intensification Program

Greg Acciaioli

> Situru' bicarapi pabbanuaé siengkalinga paupi pamarentana pabbanuaé, naweddi madécéng busesaé, mabbija wolo-woloé, nasawé taunna.
>
> If the inhabitants of a realm are of one mind, if the government and the village inhabitants listen to each other's words, then the contents [of the land—i.e., crops] can be good, the livestock can multiply, and the people can come to maturity as well.
>
> —customary words of a Bugis *pallontara'* upon opening a discussion of farming matters

Introduction: National Culture and Development

UNDER INDONESIA'S New Order the endeavor of nation building has been crucially linked to the promulgation of an ideology of development (*pembangunan* [I]).[1] Government exhortations have emphasized the need to concentrate national energy and spirit on the task of development in order to facilitate an economic take-off (*lepas landas* [I]), as well as justifying the stifling of dissent by positing the need for political stability to foster economic progress (Reeve 1990, 161). The ongoing realization of national economic integration has been invoked to justify such policies as the involvement of the armed forces in local development efforts, as dictated by the notion of *dwi fungsi* (I), their dual social and military functions. The orientation to economic development has become one of the major sources of legitimation for the New Order, as indicated by President Suharto's great pride in his title Father of Development (*Bapak Pembangunan* [I]). Foreign economists have lauded Indonesia's attainment of greater economic integration and the accompanying "dramatic improvement in Indonesia's economic fortunes since 1965," noting the role of a strong central government in this achievement (Hill and Weidemann 1989, 3, 53).

Development in Indonesia cannot be seen solely as an economic phenomenon, however. As required by Article 32 of its constitution, the Indonesian state has assumed the task of developing a "national culture" as a crucial aspect of its project of nation building (Foulcher 1990, 301; Davis 1972). Part of this national culture[2] under the New Order has been precisely the construction of an ideology of economic development. This national culture has been continually invoked in order to mobilize the populace to attain economic goals set by the state. Linguistic strategies have been crucial not only for the formulation, but also for the implementation, of economic development efforts. Language policy has been crucial to the construction and imposition of a development ethos:

> The state is attempting to manage the evolution of the Indonesian language in such a way that it will play a key role in realizing the particular understanding of development which the state wishes to see advanced. As such, language becomes an all-pervasive agent of cultural hegemony, strengthening the position and nature of the state in so far as it gives social existence to the realities it transmits. [Foulcher 1990, 305]

The fabrication of new terms to designate national aims, often from Sanskrit-derived roots in high Javanese, has been a common linguistic strategy in formulating and labeling national culture.[3] The term for the core civic philosophy, *Pancasila* (I) (i.e., the five principles), is perhaps the best exemplification of this tendency, although even the less pretentious guidelines to help farmers to grow their crops, the *Panca Usaha Tani* (I), or the Five Endeavors for Farmers, evidence this tendency. Acronyms have been coined to designate development efforts in the New Order with as much ideological relish as they were invented in the Old Order to label political aspirations. To take but one example, the Five-Year Development Plans (*Rencana Pembangunan Lima Tahun* [I]) are referred to with the acronym *Repelita,* thus harnessing the metaphor of serving as a lamp (*pelita* [I]) or beacon for guidance of the masses.

Perhaps the central instrument in the linguistic construction of development policy—its institutionally sited discourse or "policy speak," as Raymond Apthorpe (1985) aptly terms it with chilling echoes of George Orwell—is the invocation of certain key terms in *Bahasa Indonesia* (I) which are presented as designating proper Indonesian ways of doing things. Just as terms like *musyawarah* (I) (mutual consultation) and *mufakat* (I) (consensus) conjure visions of a distinctively Indonesian mode of political deliberation, while terms like r*ukun* (I) (harmonious) and *tertib dan damai* (I) (ordered and peaceful) evoke the proper sociopolitical ambience desired by the government, so too a term like *gotong royong* (I) (mutual cooperation) is invoked to depict the Indonesian ideal of cooperative economic activity. John R. Bowen (1986) has convincingly portrayed how this term was invented by nationalist politicians to model coordinated resistance against colonial domination (in Hatta's view) and to formulate a vision of conjoining political opposites in a unified nationalist enterprise (in Sukarno's view). With its orientation to development, the Indonesian state has appropriated this term to model collaborative efforts by villagers in carrying out specific development projects. Although intended to lend the aura of participation from below, this label has largely been used to mask the coercive quality of top-down implementation that has characterized New Order development programs (Bowen 1986, 552–53).[4] For example, the early rice intensification program that forced farmers to plant high-yielding varieties and use chemical inputs, for which they were automatically charged with debts, was labeled *BIMAS Gotong Royong* (I) (Mass Guidance [*BImbangan MASsal* (I)] in accordance with mutual cooperation) in an effort to make the program appear as a cooperative endeavor of farmers with the government.

The use of such national symbols as "Sanskrit words and pseudo-traditional terms" (Bowen 1986, 554) by the Indonesian state can be seen as part of a homogenizing (and some would say Javanizing) strategy central to the Indonesian nation-building effort. In fact, through the development of its national language, the extension of verbal and visual media throughout the archipelago, and various other disseminations (and restrictions), the Indonesian state has been quite successful in what Christine Drake (1989) has identified as the sociocultural dimension of integration. One of the indications of this success is the degree to which the content of local idioms and symbolic forms is increasingly penetrated by national symbols. Even in such relatively isolated regions as the highlands of Central Sulawesi, the *pantun* (I) that formerly expressed in local metaphors the aspirations of courtship now extol the virtues of *pancasila* (I) (Acciaioli 1985). However, given the dialogic construction of national tradition (Bowen 1986, 546; Warren 1989, 1990), the imposition of national symbols must sometimes be complemented by the appropriation of local idioms. While embodying national ideology, development programs must also be implemented in local contexts in a manner that resonates with regional understandings. The way in which local and national labels have been used in rice intensification programs in South Sulawesi not only demonstrates the state's intentional misrecognition and appropriation of local idioms of leadership and consultation, but it also reveals how local participants may usurp national idioms to further their own interests.

Appropriation from Above: Searching for an Appropriate Name

A curious document issued by the Department of Agriculture of the province of South Sulawesi in Indonesia chronicles the search for a fitting public name for the program intended to accelerate rice intensification efforts in the regencies of Bone, Bulukumba, and Sinjai. The program's official name, Operasi Khusus Peningkatan Produksi Pangan di Sulawesi (Special Operation for Increasing Food Production in Sulawesi), with its emphasis on the term *operation*, announces the military cast of this effort. Indeed, the organizational structure of the operation is described as a network of "posts," the channels of communication between levels of implementation as "commando lines," its leaders as "attackers," and its measures as "shots." The introduction to this document describes the program as a "campaign" aiming at a "breakthrough" that will lead other regency governments to adopt the lightning (with intentional echoes of *Blitzkrieg?*) measures leading to "shortcut increases of production" (Dinas Pertanian Tanaman Pangan 1982). As the head of the provincial agriculture department states in the introduction to the document, "There is no success without struggle, and there is no struggle without sacrifice." [5] The military idioms used to describe and implement this program are nothing new in Indonesian development rhetoric. Economic development in the New Order, and within that rubric the rice intensification program, is seen as a continuation of the nationalist revolutionary struggle for independence, calling for the same fervent commitment and martial tenacity.

Motivating participation in government programs through nationalist idioms has been, however, only part of development rhetoric in the rice intensification campaigns in the province of South Sulawesi. Appropriate implementation has depended also on another rhetorical development: the harnessing of local idioms to the task of transformation. Efficacy depends not only on effective organizational structure and timely intervention, but also on the appropriate labeling of the effort. As the document alluded to above declares:

> "WHAT'S IN A NAME?" says SHAKESPEARE, but for the Eastern people who happen to live in the East part of Indonesia, it [a name] has a very important meaning in life. Because of this the governor of the province of South Sulawesi has proposed that this special operation to be implemented in South Sulawesi be given a name that has an important meaning in its relation to the social and cultural organization of South Sulawesi. [Dinas Pertanian Tanaman Pangan 1982, 1][6]

Thus, in naming this specific campaign, the provincial Office of Agriculture rejected general terms that had been used to label similar development efforts in other provinces. The simple term Prosperous (*Makmur* [I]) had been the name chosen for the rice intensification program in the provinces of Nusa Tenggara Barat and Nusa Tenggara Timur. Building on this example, the compound title First-Class Prosperous (*Unggul Makmur* [I]) had been proposed for the South Sulawesi program in order to emphasize the centrality of using prime, or first-class, seed varieties resistant to the most devastating pests (VUTW—*varietas unggul tahan wereng* (I).[7] But what was settled on was the name Operasi Lappo Asé (B).

The phrase *lappo asé* (B) can be translated from the Bugis language as "piles of paddy" or, less poetically rendered, "heaps of rice."[8] Not only does the name Operation Piles of Paddy have the advantage of graphically depicting the desired outcome of the campaign, but this result is also represented by the acronym OLA[9] formed from the plan name, for *ola* (B) is the Bugis term for a unit of volume. Although this unit was originally equal more or less to the capacity of a coconut shell (Matthes 1874, 882), in recent times it has been given the approximate modern gloss "liter." Hence the acronym seeks to depict the program's aim of helping farmers to produce ever more liters of rice. The document mentioned above, whose title *Kesan dan Peristiwa Operasi Lappoase di Kabupaten Bone, Sinjai dan Bulukumba Propinsi Sulawesi Selatan* can thus perhaps best be translated as *Impressions and Incidents of Operation "Piles of Paddy" in the Regencies Bone, Sinjai, and Bulukumba in the Province of South Sulawesi,* vividly justifies the naming of the development program as follows:

For a long time South Sulawesi has borne the title of Food Granary of East Indonesia, so that for the people of South Sulawesi the meaning of *paddy* has been welded to their life and their livelihood. Seen from another perspective, this special operation about to be implemented has the purpose of adding to the vitality of South Sulawesi in the matter of increasing rice production. Due to these two factors, the name of this special operation was formulated as a regional version, which would be popular later under the name Operasi Lappo Ase (OLA). It was hoped that the bestowal of this name would serve a double purpose—that is, besides serving as a sociocultural igniting, it would be able to facilitate the remembering[10] [of the program] by all levels of South Sulawesi society, so that finally the people of South Sulawesi would be fervent for Lappo Ase. This hope, as it turns out, was achieved. Lappo Ase has succeeded in creating a terrific resonance not only in the three regencies that are its first executors, but also for all the regencies of South Sulawesi, and perhaps even for other provinces in Indonesia. [Dinas Pertanian Tanaman Pangan 1982: 1][0]

By creating a program title using a local idiom of traditional expectations rather than the technocratic jargon of projected results, the government planners sought to elicit the cooperation of local farmers to achieve the aims of this stage of the rice intensification effort in South Sulawesi.

While the use of indigenous terms in the name of a specific development campaign may facilitate the integration of novel techniques and imposed schedules into the quotidian rhythms of a local culture, the manner in which that program is carried out—the strategy of its implementation—must also resonate with the local patterns of organizing and adjudicating members' activities. The particular means used by the government to require the use of prime seed varieties and enforce the adherence to imposed planting schedules in the heartland of South Sulawesi's rice bowl—the regencies of Pinrang and Sidenreng-Rappang (Sidrap)—illustrate the government's recognition of the importance of appropriating not only names, but also indigenous structures of control.

Indonesia's Rice Intensification Program: Aims, Institutions, and Implementation

In order to fulfill such national objectives as increasing incomes, agricultural output, and labor opportunities, goals articulated in the succession of five-year plans (*Repelita*) laying out the general strategy of development (National Development Information Office 1990–91, 24–27), Indonesia's rice intensification program has included measures to increase both the extent and intensity of rice production. A major aspect of the rice intensification program has been a heavy reliance on a technocratic strategy involving the following aspects: construction (and reconstruction) of infrastructure such as technical irrigation systems; introduction of mechanized labor, especially minitractors; the use of modern rice varieties—the "miracle" seeds of the Green Revolution, whose short growing periods have allowed double-cropping and in some areas even triple-cropping; and all the chemical inputs needed for these miracle seeds to attain maximum yields. Implementation has also required the fostering of a distribution system not only for prime seeds, but also for the chemical inputs —fertilizers, pesticides, and (in labor-deficient areas like parts of South Sulawesi) herbicides. The government has also organized an extension (*penyuluhan* [I]) system to instruct farmers in the most fruitful use of these inputs, as well as the operation of tractors and other machinery, and created several credit programs with low-interest loans made even more alluring by subsidies that keep down the prices of inputs. In addition, the government has overseen the erection of a marketing system intended to facilitate not only farmers' obtaining a profitable price for their product, but also the provisioning of a national stockpile in warehouses spread through the countryside that buy rice of a suitable quality at a guaranteed price.

Such development efforts have involved organizing farmers in various associations to ensure their participation in this program: farmers' groups (Kelompok Tani [I]) through which extension is provided; water users' associations (P3A, Persatuan Petani Pemakai Air [I]) to regulate the use and cleaning of irrigation facilities; and village cooperatives (KUD, Koperasi Unit Desa [I]). These latter groups have been delegated the tasks of overseeing the distribution of inputs through a network of kiosks, arranging for credit through local branches of the People's Bank of Indonesia (BRI, Bank Rakyat Indonesia [I]), providing such postharvest facilities as cement rice-drying floors and motorized rice mills for hulling rice. They have also been accorded the role of purchasing the lion's share of the crop from the farmers and serving as the primary channel to the national stockpile[12] (See below.) This latter function has been linked to the maintenance of a floor price for the crop deemed adequate to recompense farmers for their labors and spur them to seek higher incomes through increasing productivity and production by making use of the total package of goods and services offered through the rice intensification program.

One of the most difficult obstacles faced by the program has been the design of procedures to protect the more abundant and frequent crops from the depredation of pests. This difficulty springs in part from the very marked success of the program in increasing production by bringing more land into rice cultivation for a greater portion of the year, for the practice of double- and triple-cropping provides a continuously favorable environment in which pests can breed. Protection can be only partially accomplished through the use of pesticides, and that only at great cost, both for farmers to guard their crops and for research organizations and companies to develop new chemical agents. Environmental costs have hardly been negligible, as many farmers have lost a major protein source in the fish that used to inhabit their flooded paddy fields, and have been locked into a spiral of ever-greater dependence on ever less effective pesticides, since many of the natural predators of these pests were also decimated by pesticides.

In recent years Indonesia has drastically reduced its reliance on pesticides, even banning many varieties earlier provided at subsidized cost to farmers. Instead, it has implemented an Integrated Pest Management Program (National Development Information Office 1990–91, 84–85), that depends on such measures as improved-resistance varieties[13] and pest-specific, synthetic hormones rather than broad-spectrum pesticides. Implementation of the Integrated Pest Management Program has once again allowed a partial reliance on the natural predators of such pests as the brown planthopper and green leafhopper, since those predators are un-affected by the application of pest-specific hormones.

However, even earlier South Sulawesi had experimented with its own unique program to combat the incursions of pests prey-ing on rice, especially the attacks of the tungro virus as transmit-ted by the green leafhopper (*Nephotettix virescens*). By the mid-1980s, plant scientists of the Food Research Institute in Maros, just north of the provincial capital, Ujung Pandang, had stan-dardized a classification of the most popular miracle rice varieties used locally in terms of their different levels of resistance to tun-gro and other pests. Based on this classification, regency govern-ments annually stipulated to farmers which varieties they were allowed to plant in the wet and dry seasons. In general, after a wet-season planting of permissible varieties of a given level of re-sistance, only designated varieties of a higher level of resistance could be planted in the following dry season.[14] By varying the levels of resistance in successive planting seasons each year, the re-gency government hoped to forestall, or at least postpone, the loss of resistance to tungro and other depredations that had be-fallen previous miracle rice varieties when continuously planted across wide areas. However, although the model underlying this government policy was basically technocratic, originating in the experiments of research scientists trained outside the local con-text, it has been implemented by the appropriation of a local tra-dition of adjudication and stipulation within Bugis villages.

Appropriation from Above: Institutionalizing Tudang Sipulung

Before the transformation of rice cultivation practices in South Sulawesi—a process initiated under the Dutch colonial authori-ties and intensified by national government intervention under the auspices of the rice intensification program—decisions as to when to begin the planting season, what local varieties to use, and how water would be allocated depended on meetings of farmers from a single hamlet (*kampong* [B]). The meetings were termed *tudang sipulung* (B), which may be glossed literally as "to sit gathered together with each other." Such meetings convened to decide these issues were led by *pallontara'* (B), indigenous savants who had learned to read and interpret the palm leaf manuscripts (*lontara'* [B]) written in the Bugis script. Although the term *lontara'* (B) encompasses all genres recorded in this form, ranging from chronicles and diaries to spells and prayers, the palm leaf manuscripts of specific interest with regard to the planting season are almanacs detailing how such factors as the relative brightness and location of the stars, the colors of the clouds, and other meteorological phenomena in the lead-up to the planting season can be interpreted to predict such future conditions as the duration and intensity of rains, the extent of pest depredation, and the success of planting different varieties of rice. Based on the reading of these signs, the *pallontara'* (B) stipulated the schedule of seedbed preparation and of transplantation (including the auspicious days for organizing rituals to propitiate the guardian spirits of the rice fields), the seed varieties most likely to produce abundant harvests, the projected harvest time, the pattern of water allocation for that season, and a determination of the fines to be imposed for failing to observe these terms. (Sumhudi 1979, 24ff.) The implementation of this program was largely in the hands of the *mado* (B), a local village warden who had inherited this position by virtue of his aristocratic descent. Although the village headman, and possibly even the district head appointed as part of the colonial regime, might attend such meetings, they were present primarily as ratifiers, not as leaders. Throughout the colonial and early independence periods, the specific rice varieties to be planted and the manner of their cultivation were thus determined at the local level, rather than being imposed by government authorities from above.

The role of such traditional institutions as the hamlet *tudang sipulung* (B) meetings was subject to a process of erosion with the introduction of government-sponsored rice intensification programs. The first of those programs was known by the acronym DEMAS (Demonstrasi Massal [I], Mass Demonstration), and was introduced to South Sulawesi in 1964 by government planners working with students from the Faculty of Agriculture of Hasanuddin University in the provincial capital. The government intensified operations with the Komando Operasi Pangan Sangiang-Seri (I), begun in selected Bugis regions in the 1966–67 season and extended to the Makasar areas further south in 1969. The program underwent several name changes through the late 1960s and the beginning of the 1970s, but continued under the auspices of BIMAS (Bimbingan Massal [I], Mass Guidance) schemes emphasizing an imposed package of credit for inputs which farmers were required to obtain (Abdullah et al. n.d.; Leibo 1983, 24ff.). Problems experienced with credit repayment by the farmers who had been forced to participate in the program led to a reorientation in government policies as early as 1971 with the introduction of INMAS (Intensifikasi Massal [I], Mass Intensification) and later INSUS (Intensification Khusus [I], Special Intensification).[15] These programs moved away from the BIMAS strategy of distributing credit to whole groups of farmers, whose group leaders were then responsible for loan repayment. INMAS and subsequent programs emphasized instead the initiative and responsibility of farmers as individuals in obtaining credit for modern inputs. Managing the transition from BIMAS to INMAS was not the only problem facing government officials charged with implementing the rice intensification program. The disastrous drought of 1971 not only brought insoluble quandaries of water allocation,[16] but farmers were concomitantly faced with the declining resistance of not only local varieties, but also the prime varieties (*varietas unggul* [I]) provided by the government to the increasing depredations of tungro in the 1972–73 and 1973 planting seasons. Faced not only with those cumulating setbacks but also with the general reluctance of farmers to adhere to all the stipulations of DEMAS and subsequent intensification plans, government officials at the regency (*kabupaten* [I]) level charged with the implementation of agricultural policy sought to find a way of motivating farmers to participate in further phases of the rice intensification program.[17] In order to ensure the coordination of all the stages of production and distribution necessary to provide real increases, and to improve profitability for farmers, these officials needed a strategy to institutionalize adherence to the integrated program combining all these aspects of the rice intensification effort.

Like the planners of Operasi Lappo Ase in the regencies of Bone, Bulukumba, and Sinjai to the south, the regency government of Sidenreng-Rappang (Sidrap) chose to harness a local idiom to the yoke of technocratic innovation. The local institution of *tudang sipulung* (B) was raised to the status of a regency-wide conference to which were invited government officials responsible for the implementation of rice intensification, technical advisors from the Food Research Institute at Maros and elsewhere, representatives of all the villages in the regency, and the most esteemed *pallontara'* (B) of the regency. Thus began in 1974 the institution of Tudang Sipulung congresses held annually in February under the chairmanship of the governmental head of the regency, the *bupati* (I).

The indigenous *tudang sipulung* (B) was thus transformed from a local gathering into an official government-sponsored occasion at which is now announced the following series of stipulations:[18] the prime rice varieties allowed to be planted each season; the schedule of their planting in each district (*kecamatan* [I]) for both the wet and dry seasons for each type of rice field—rain-fed, irrigated by semitechnical irrigation, or irrigated by full technical irrigation; the schedule of water availability through both semitechnical and technical irrigation channels, specifying the dates on which sluice gates in each district will be opened and closed; the schedule of the three-week harvest period allowed for each district. The schedules for planting such crops as soybeans, peanuts, cassava, and corn (collectively labeled *palawija* (I) by the Department of Agriculture) between the rice-planting seasons are also announced. Farmers are exhorted to follow the Five Endeavours for Farmers (Panca Usaha Tani [I])—use of prime seed varieties, measures to fight pests, use and improvement of irrigation, intensified fertilizer use, and regular planting rows—and the penalties for noncompliance are alluded to, though not specified.

The government deems essential the presence of *pallontara'* (B) at these regency *tudang sipulung* (B) meetings to legitimize the acceptance of state stipulations. But their continuing presence at *tudang sipulung* (B) conceals a basic transformation in the grounds of their participation: their former constitutive role in designing these stipulations has been reduced to a contemporary commentarial one. Although hailed by government officials as experts at weather prediction and ancestral custom (*adat* [I]), including traditions for tilling the soil, the *pallontara'* (B) are allowed only to comment on the plans already independently drawn up by the Agriculture Department, Public Works Department, People's Bank of Indonesia, Cooperatives Office, the Regency Government, and experts invited from the provincial Agricultural Research Institute and the Faculty of Agriculture of Hasanuddin University. Government reports and coverage in the popular press have hailed this "meeting of technology and tradition" (Myala 1980) as a forum where farmers can face the government and declare their opinions, but other observers (and even officials who have participated) have noted the absence of any impact from the words of those below. One researcher described the situation as follows: . . . although farmers are given the opportunity to give voice to their problems, this opportunity is always limited by the time available or receives insufficient attention for their solution, as their input is only inventoried rather than a way out [of their difficulties] being sought. But in fact those who talk the most and all the stipulations come from the government elements, while the others sit and listen to round out the proceedings [literally, "as finishers"]. Thus, each decision is regarded as the result of mutual deliberation. [Daud 1985, 27][19]

Although the *bupati* (I) of Sidrap may once have replied in an interview that "We always accept reports from below," (Myala 1980, 12), the reports accepted have tended to be only affirmations of the declared government program. As one retired Ministry of Information official put it, the *pallontara'* (B) and farmers are allowed the opportunity to declare their allegiance to the governmental scheme.

Further *tudang sipulung* (B) meetings are subsequently held at the district (*kecamatan* [I]) and village (*desa* [I]) levels after the issuing of the results of the regency level meeting. However, only certain *pallontara'* (B) are allowed to participate: those that have been recognized and accorded the title of district *pallontara'* (B) by the regency government. The district head (*camat* [I]) and village headman (*lurah* [I] or *kepala desa* [I]) preside at these meetings. One informant described the role of the *pallontara'* (B) at these meetings: they tell the ancient tales that stress the wisdom of the regency government's plan and "the necessity of the people obeying the decisions of their superiors" (Sumhudi 1979, 78). Effective power for the enforcement of these stipulations rests with the hierarchy of government officials. The *tudang sipulung* (B) has thus been transformed as an institution. Although during the colonial period the village and district government officials were mere onlookers present at a set of deliberations whose decisions were formulated and enforced by local officiants, now the *pallontara'* (I) have been disenfranchised from the policymaking process, reduced to the status of public relations specialists advertising the virtues of the one-and-only course of action that the farmers are allowed to follow (Sumhudi 1979, 90).

As in the instance of the care taken in choosing the name Operasi Lappo Asé and its acronym OLA for the rice intensification campaign in Bone, Sinjai, and Bulukumba, the Sidrap government's creation of regency-level *tudang sipulung* (B) to transmit each year's rice-growing regimen to the local populace represents a harnessing of local Bugis idioms to impose a technocratically devised plan conceived from above. Whereas a general appeal to the national spirit of *gotong royong* (I), a suspiciously Javanese-sounding solicitation, may have limited effect in the context of motivating Bugis farmers to adhere to government prescriptions in agriculture, the appropriation of *tudang sipulung* (B) allows officials to claim that they are merely continuing the local practices of farming regulation, while actually legitimating such novel technocratic practices as the rotation of miracle rice varieties.

But the picture is not quite so neat. For if the government can redefine tradition to fit its policies, so too individual Bugis entrepreneurs can use imposed institutions to continue their own organizational forms. While maintaining the appearance of adherence to institutions established by the government to foster development for the populace as a whole, local entrepreneurs can subvert the development process to attain their own ends. Appropriation can be accomplished from below as well as from above.

Appropriation from Below: "Acting in the Name of" KUD

This process of appropriation from below can be exemplified in the disparity between formulation and actualization in the rice-marketing system found in Sidenreng-Rappang. As part of the integrated plan of rice intensification designed by the government, village cooperatives, or KUD (Koperasi Unit Desa [I]), have been charged with a major role in organizing the distribution of inputs, channeling credit, providing postharvest facilities for rice processing, and buying rice directly from the farmers and selling it directly to government warehouses for the national stockpile. Although the KUD are designed to be the major intermediaries between farmers as producers and the government as purchaser, the actual passage of rice from sellers to buyers is a maze of options. Figure 1 is a flowchart representation of rice-marketing channels in the regency.[20] Amid this diversity of flows, only one is stipulated by the government as the primary channel for surplus rice in the intensification plan: that given by the bottommost (dashed-and-dotted) line proceeding from farmers to the cooperatives and then to the national stockpile. Yet, that is precisely the most rarely used channel.[21] One researcher in the regency encountered only 18.6 percent of his sample of farmers *ever* having sold rice to the KUD of his study village (Sumhudi 1979, 63)—a figure in keeping with the more recent observations of my colleagues and myself in two other villages in the regency.[22] Throughout the regency, despite government premiums paid for rice passing through the KUD, almost all rice is handled by a network of private rice merchants operating at various scales depending on their position in the network.

The particular channels chosen by growers and buyers are quite diverse, depending on the immediate needs of producers, sellers, and laborers. Harvest laborers tend to sell their harvest shares (in most cases, 10 percent of what they are able to pick) immediately to roadside buyers.[23] These low-volume purchasers, termed *papétépété* (B) after a variety of very small fish,[24] are mostly young men who set up temporary tripod weighing stations on the roads next to fields in the process of being harvested. There they purchase small amounts of rice by paying on the spot a cash price of 110 rupiahs per kilogram for unhulled rice received

FIGURE 1

MARKETING CHANNELS FOR UNHULLED RICE (*GABAH*) AND HULLED RICE (*BERAS*)

A Flowchart representation for Sidenrong-Rappang (Sidrap), 1985

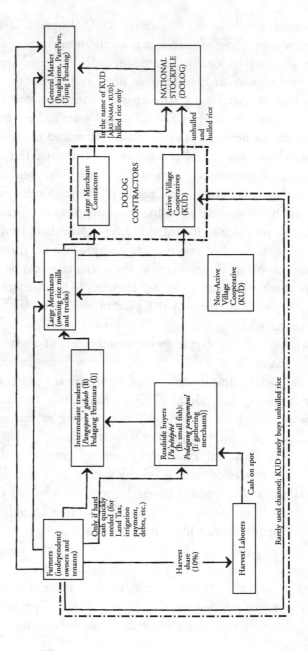

Rarely used channel; KUD rarely buys unhulled rice

directly from the field (*gabah kering sawah* [I]) with the capital they have borrowed from intermediate traders (*pangoporo' gabah* [B]).[25] Farmers, both owner-operators and tenants, most often bypass this option unless sorely pressed for immediate cash, selling instead directly to intermediate traders, who pay from 120 to 125 rupiahs/kg., depending on the volume purchased and the allocation of responsibility for transport costs. If already in a stable customer (*langganan* [I]) relationship with a large merchant (*padangkang loppo* [B]), a dealer who owns his own rice mill, drying floor, warehouse, and one or more trucks, the farmer will sell to that merchant at 130 to 135 rupiahs/kg. for unprocessed rice directly from the field. Whereas these high-volume buyers will pay cash to intermediate merchants to maintain the latter's supply of capital, they will only pay farmers in installments once they have processed the rice and sold it on the market or on more favorable terms to the warehouses of the regional stockpile DOLOG (Depot LOGistik), whose floor price at the time of harvest is usually higher than on the open market.

However, DOLOG's pricing is not homogeneous. DOLOG will buy only from those who have been able to negotiate a contract to supply the warehouse. According to government policy, the major recipients of these contracts should be the village cooperatives (i.e., KUD) of the region served by the warehouse. However, a limited number of private merchants may be designated as contractors supplying DOLOG. These latter designees should receive only 279 rupiahs per kilogram of hulled rice (*beras* [I]), while the village cooperatives receive a price of 285 rupiahs/kg., thus obtaining a six-rupiah premium. In fact, what has happened is that private contractors have been receiving the same price.

The actual granting of premium prices to large private rice merchants has arisen as a result of the circumstance that only eighteen of twenty-four village cooperatives established in the regency of Sidenreng-Rappang were still active as DOLOG contractors in 1986. Of these, only twelve were still capable of obtaining credit from the People's Bank of Indonesia (BRI—Bank Rakyat Indonesia [I]) to cover rice processing and marketing. The other KUD had forfeited the right to obtain credit from BRI due to their outstanding debts. Along with other informants, recently appointed KUD managers[26] attributed this inability on the part of the KUD to pay their bank debts to the tendency of these village cooperatives to lend money to private rice merchants. Such a policy was, in fact, counter to one of the primary purposes for which KUD had been established, namely providing for farmers an alternative buyer to the private rice merchants. Specifically, KUD were established in part to help farmers avoid the losses of the *ijon* (I) system, whereby a crop was purchased in its entirety by a merchant a considerable time before the actual harvest at a price well below what could be obtained if the harvest were indeed successful. All too often farmers have resorted to such a sale when pressing needs for cash have arisen before the harvest. By allowing farmers' credit to cover their expenses for the high inputs needed for proper cultivation of the miracle rice varieties (i.e., the prime seed with resistance to *wereng* [I]), the KUD sought to minimize farmer indebtedness to private third parties. Yet, it is precisely those people to whom they were indebted before the establishment of village cooperatives who have been able to obtain the funds that were allocated to the KUD in order to establish an alternative marketing network.

This seeming anomaly becomes intelligible when we see which people have managed to become the local officials in charge of the KUD. In two villages subjected to scrutiny, the very rice merchants whom the cooperatives were established to circumvent have become the custodians of the KUD. In those villages private rice merchants managed to gain enough farmers' votes to win elections within the KUD to management positions by gaining the endorsement of the regency-level cooperatives office.[27] State sponsorship of these rice merchants has, ironically enough, proven to be the major factor determining their continued domination of marketing channels, despite the state's avowed purpose in setting up the cooperatives as an alternative to allow farmers to compete with them. Precisely they, and the associates to whom they grant the privilege, have been able to use KUD funds to finance their private operations providing DOLOG with rice.

Ironically, the private rice merchants were able to effect this continued control of the rice market by adopting a tactic recalling the very facet that the provincial government had considered crucial to the success of the rice intensification program. It is once again a matter of names. Private rice merchants have been able to provide rice to the national stockpile warehouses by acting "in the name of" (*atas nama dari* [I]) the cooperatives. Indeed, this role has spawned a new verb—*mengatasnamakan* (I), "to act in the name of"—in the national language, Bahasa Indonesia. With certificates issued by the KUD, these rice merchants have been able to bring their rice to DOLOG, where it was accepted (if it met standards for water content, chaff, broken grains, etc.) under the quota of rice to be provided by the village cooperatives. Receiving the price officially accorded to the KUD, the private merchants have been obliged to present the difference of six rupiahs per kilogram to the KUD treasury. However, as (ruling) members of the cooperatives, they have also been eligible to determine the uses of these KUD treasury funds and to obtain credit under KUD auspices to expand their operations further. In one village, the head of the KUD had been able to finance a new rice mill and warehouse for his private operations, while next door the KUD warehouse served only to contain the disassembled broken huller belonging to the cooperative. The cement rice-drying floor in front of the KUD warehouse was in a state of such disrepair that cattle were grazing on the tufts of grass that had burst through the cracks in the floor. Even those six cooperatives of the eighteen who had permission to remain rice suppliers to DOLOG, but were ineligible for credit from Bank Rakyat

Indonesia, used what was termed the relationship system (*sistem relasi* [I]), delegating to large merchants (*padangkang loppo* [B]) the quota they had agreed to supply to DOLOG. By these means the KUD not only received the six-rupiah premium, but managed to remain on the active list of suppliers. But the actual transactors have continued to be the private merchants who have thus continued to reap their profits by acting "in the name of KUD" and in some cases serving as the official heads of the cooperatives in whose name they acted.

Conclusion: The Dialectic of Mutual Appropriation in Development

The appropriation of names in the implementation of the rice intensification program in South Sulawesi is thus not a unilateral operation. On the one hand, the regency government in Sidenreng-Rappang has harnessed a traditional deliberative form—*tudang sipulung* (B)—to impose the technocratically conceived system of varietal choice and scheduling. On the other, the rice merchants of Sidenreng-Rappang, an area long famous for providing intermediate traders throughout the island and indeed the archipelago, have managed to use the name of KUD to continue their domination of the rice market, despite the institutional purpose of the KUD being precisely to reduce their control over farmers' disposal of production. In fact, such practices as *ijon* (I) have continued unabated, but under a somewhat different guise. Those KUD ineligible for credit due to defaulting in loan repayments have been unable to purchase the inputs necessary to stock their kiosks. Private rice merchants have thus assumed this role of providing inputs to local farmers, but in return have required that crops grown with inputs obtained with credit from them be reserved exclusively for their purchase.

As revealed by the case of Sidrap regency, rice intensification efforts in South Sulawesi have followed the typical Indonesian pattern of top-down implementation. What such measures as the appropriation of *tudang sipulung* (B) have sought to facilitate is the illusion of participation on the part of the farmers in the villages. Michael R. Dove (1988, 33) has pointed out how the very term for the interface between officials and peasants—*penyuluhan* (I), "extension"—depicts "a situation in which the officials talk and the peasants listen (or pretend to listen, as is more often the case)."[46] Indeed, the root *suluh* (I), from which this term is formed means "torch"; it thus reinforces the image of light being bestowed on an ignorant (*bodoh* [I]) populace formerly all in the dark, an image that is part of the resonance of the term for the orienting framework of Five-Year Plans (*Repelita*). Yet, although Indonesian officials may see themselves as the agents who must impose change (Dove 1988, 22), the populace that is the object of such changes often finds ways of asserting its own right to affect, if not control, the direction of local development. Warren (1989, 1990a) has demonstrated how Balinese villagers invoke ideals of equity and dialogue implicated by such terms as *musyawarah* (I) and *mufakat* (I) and by the civic philosophy of *Pancasila* (I) itself in order to call officials to account and hence promote their own participation in the development process.

However, as the South Sulawesi case illustrates, the local participants who effectively resist the transformation envisaged by development programs may not be the peasant farmers. Entrepreneurs in Sidrap have been able to continue in their profitable positions by appropriating the cooperative idioms as the guise for continuing their private operations. Such an example not only compromises the nature of participation and confutes the aims enunciated by development planners, but it also confounds the nature of the development process. On the one hand, a modern development scheme has resorted to the authority of traditional local forms; on the other, indigenous entrepreneurs have used the modern idiom of cooperatives to increase their control of the market. Distinguishing just what is tradition and modernity in this setting becomes problematic. Theorists of political development (e.g., Rudolph and Rudolph 1967) and more recently social historians and anthropologists analyzing the continual reconstitution and invention of local tradition and custom (Keesing and Tonkinson 1982; Hobsbawm and Ranger 1983; Lindstrom and White 1993) have questioned the dichotomy of modernity and tradition. In the case of South Sulawesi the characterization of the agricultural sector certainly does not lend itself to neat categorization in these terms. Even figuring out who represents what or what represents whom can be puzzling. The "authoritative discourse" of the state (Asad 1979) is couched in traditional indigenous idioms, while the countering voice of the region's prosperous elite invokes the modern organizations whose names they assume in order to continue the very activities that the state had sought to undermine. Determining whose interests are being advanced under traditional and modern idioms becomes problematic, just as assessing the degree and amount of "participation" in development seems an ever more chimerical task. In the analysis of such deliberate development efforts as rice intensification, a theory of replacement and breakthrough into modernity is as oversimplified as a model of conflicting discourses. Just as the nation-state may exalt its harnessing of tradition as the key to modernization, so interested local elites may usurp the idioms of modernity to continue their regional control.

Notes

Acknowledgments

In its long gestation period, this paper has been nursed through successive phases with the solicitous assistance of numerous organizations and individuals. Many of the data were obtained while I was working on a project investigating the rice intensification program in South Sulawesi under the auspices of the Center for Policy and Implementation Studies (CPIS) and the Harvard Institute for International Development. My coworkers in that project, Ilyas Saad and M. Nawir Messi, were invaluable partners in the quest to penetrate just how rice intensification was being carried out in this region far from the center. Our work included two field trips to South Sulawesi, the first from August to October 1985 and the second from May to June 1986. Further details about the effects of the intensification program on rice production and marketing in South Sulawesi are available in Acciaioli, with the assistance of Messi and Saad, "Greening the Periphery." Special thanks are due to the Pusat Latihan Penelitian Ilmu-Ilmu Sosial, Universitas Hasanuddin, in Ujung Pandang for the access provided to their library and especially for permission to photocopy the PLPIIS reports that had been written on rice intensification. Other colleagues in CPIS were valuable advisors in helping orient me to the problems of development, especially in Outer Indonesia. John Bowen deserves special thanks in this regard. James J. Fox saved me from some overexuberant misinterpretations and has in general curbed my errant enthusiasms, though not as much as he would have liked. I have also benefited from the comments of Carol Warren, Jim Taylor, and Jennifer Nourse on an earlier draft of this paper. Barbara Martin-Schiller's meticulous comments on a near-final draft once again prevented me from some very embarrassing overstatements and errors. Some sections of the paper were first presented at the conference "Rethinking Development in Southeast Asia," sponsored by the Center for South and Southeast Asia Studies of the University of California at Berkeley on 14–15 March 1987. A more integrated version of this paper was delivered at the panel "Far from the Centre" at the conference "Indonesian Culture: Asking the Right Questions," sponsored by the Asian Studies Discipline at Flinders University of South Australia. An abbreviation of that version was then delivered at the panel "State Rhetoric and Indigenous Response: The Dynamic of Resistance and Cooptation in Insular Southeast Asia," held at the American Anthropological Association Meetings, 1–6 December 1992. I wish both to thank all these organizations and individuals for their encouragement and assistance and to absolve them of any responsibility for errors or idiosyncracies in this exploration of the dynamic of development in South Sulawesi.

1. The letter (I) after an italicized term, phrase, or sentence indicates the term is from the Indonesian language (*Bahasa Indonesia* [I]), while (B) marks those from the Bugis language.

2. Drake defines national culture as "shared national values, customs, organisations, and institutions that transcend local and ethnic boundaries, extend nationwide, and promote national consciousness and interregional contact." *National Integration in Indonesia: Patterns and Policies* (Honolulu: University of Hawaii Press, 1989), 60.

3. Foulcher (1990, 305–6) argues that the use of a Sanskritized vocabulary of high Javanese has lent to modern bureaucratic notions the aura of authority and associated requirement of deference that attached to the court culture of the Javanese nobility. Such an interpretation would seem to give the lie to Davis's argument that in the process of modernization Indonesia is simply becoming Westernized, more and more "like us," with "no core, however sacred, which cannot be sacrificed if the price is right." (1972, 316).

4. As Bowen points out in his case studies, peasants in various regions continue to identify *gotong royong* (I) with labor obligations imposed from above, such as the Friday morning "village clean-up" (*bersih desa* [I]) in the Gayo highlands of northern Sumatra (1986, 556). Whereas the government may conspicuously misrecognize local cultural realities, lumping together in regional compilations of local customs quite divergent local traditions of labor cooperation as mere examples of a pan-Indonesian *gotong royong* (I) tradition, local farmers recognize this labor form as the successor to the government demands heaped upon them in colonial times (i.e., the Dutch *herendiensten*).

5. "*Tidak ada sukses tanpa perjuangan dan tidak ada perjuangan tanpa pengorbanan*" (I). In the case of this particular program the invocation of a medical idiom of justification is also particularly salient, as evident in the words of the director of Bank Rakyat Indonesia at the beginning of the implementation effort on 10 January 1981:

The vitality of South Sulawesi will be heightened to a greater extent in the [process of] increasing rice production. The therapy to be used in increasing this vitality is not the technique of using colored capsules or injected solutions, but by means of the "surgeon's knife." This means "life or death," as the consequence of the carrying out of an operation.

Vitalitas Sulawesi Selatan dalam peningkatan produksi padi akan lebih ditingkatkan. Therapy yang digunakan dalam meningkatkan vitalitas yang dimaksud bukan melalui penggunaan kapsul berwarna atau dengan cairan injeksi akan tetapi melalui "pisau bedah" . . . (Operasi). Ini berarti "hidup atau mati", sebagai konsekwensi dari pelaksanaan suatu operasi. [Dinas Pertanian Tanaman Pangan 1982, 3]

6. The original Indonesian text reads:

"WHAT'S IN A NAME", kata SHAKESPEARE, tapi bagi orang Timur yang kebetulan hidup di Indonesia bagian Timur, mempunyai arti yang sangat penting dalam kehidupan, sehingga oleh karenanya Bapak Gubernur Propinsi Sulawesi Selatan menganjurkan agar supaya Operasi Khusus yang akan dilaksanakan di Sulawesi Selatan diberikan nama yang mempunyai arti penting dalam hubungannya dengan sosio-cultural masyarakat Sulawesi Selatan. [Dinas Pertanian Tanaman Pangan 1982, 1]

7. *Wereng* (I) is a term encompassing both the brown planthopper (*wereng coklat* [I]) whose depredations had a devastating impact in the eighties, after pesticides destroyed its natural predators, and the green leafhopper (*wereng hijau* [I]), which has also been quite destructive in its role as the carrier of tungro virus.

8. The Bugis, formerly known as the *Boegineezen* in Dutch and the Buginese in English (and actually labeling themselves as *To Ugi'* [B]) are the predominant ethnic group in the province of South Sulawesi. Concentrated in the northern and central lowland regencies of the province, although scattered throughout the southern regencies and in the northern mountain regencies and indeed throughout the Indonesian archipelago, the Bugis totaled 1,605,000 members in the 1930 census conducted by the Netherlands East Indies government, the last census to include a breakdown by ethnic groups. This number also included

153,000 Bugis in regions of Indonesia outside their home province of South Sulawesi. In 1965 the number of ethnic Bugis was estimated at 2,930,000 by the Institute of Ethnography, USSR Academy of Sciences (Sirk 1979, 12) and in a slightly later estimate at more than 3 million (Chabot 1967, 190). Their numbers probably now hover around 4 million, though the lack of an ethnic breakdown in census figures renders this number merely an educated guess. For a recent thumbnail ethnological sketch of this ethnic group, see Greg Acciaioli (1993).

9. The Indonesian government, perhaps following Dutch colonial usages, has attempted to label major government departments, projects, and even events with acronyms. The evocative power of these acronyms should never be underestimated, as witnessed by such singularly arousing examples as GESTAPU for Gerakan S Tigapuluh (I) (the Movement of September 30th) to mark the events surrounding the abortive coup led by a Communist colonel that led to the downfall of Sukarno and to the assumption of power by the generals who forged the New Order.

10. Although at this point the Indonesian term *ingat* (I) is used, the force of this term for the Bugis audience can only be realized when the significance of the cultural concept of remembering (*inge'* in the Bugis language) as a mode of apprehending the world is taken into account. In fact, the Bugis term *inge'* is often used to translate the term *sadar* (I) "to be or become aware." It is no accident that *sadar* (I) is the word chosen by Indonesian government officials and others to describe the attitude of those who have come to realize the basic rightness of government programs as opposed to "backward" village methods. See Errington (1983, 1989) and Acciaioli (n.d.) for further discussion of the centrality of *inge'* (B) in the culture of courtly Luwu', and the conceptions of Bugis pioneer migrants to the frontiers of Central Sulawesi respectively.

11. In the original Indonesian:

Sejak dahulu Sulawesi Selatan mendapat gelar sebagai "Lumbung Pangan Indonesia Timur," sehingga dengan demikian bagi masyarakat Sulawesi Selatan arti "padi" sudah terpateri dalam hidup dan kehidupannya. Dilain pihak Operasi Khusus yang akan dilaksanakan mempunyai makna untuk menambah vitalitas Sulawesi Selatan dalam hal peningkatan produksi padi/beras. Dari kedua hal ini, dirumuskan nama Operasi khusus ini adalah versi daerah, yang kemudian populer dengan nama 'Operasi Lappo Ase' (OLA). Pemberian nama ini, diharapkan dapat memberikan tujuan ganda, yaitu disamping sebagai pencetusan sosio-cultural, juga dapat memudahkan semua lapisan masyarakat Sulawesi Selatan untuk mengingatnya, sehingga pada akhirnya masyarakat Sulawesi Selatan akan 'demam Lappoase'. Harapan ini ternyata dapat dicapai. Lappoase telah berhasil membuat resonansi yang hebat, tidak hanya pada tiga Kabupaten sebagai pelaksana Lappoase yang pertama, tapi juga pada semua Kabupaten di Sulawesi Selatan, mungkin juga pada Propinsi lain di Indonesia. [Dinas Pertanian Tanaman Pangan 1982, 1–2]

12. According to Kristanto, Parenta, and Sturgess (1989, 392), 40 to 50 percent of South Sulawesi's annual rice surplus of 500,000 to 600,000 tons is absorbed by the national stockpile network. However, as is argued later, little of this rice actually is processed and transported to the regional warehouses by the KUD.

13. Fox (1991) provides genealogies of the lines of hybridization for all the miracle seed varieties that have been used in Indonesia's rice intensification program up to the beginning of the 1990s.

14. The monograph prepared by Acciaioli with the assistance of Messi and Saad (n.d.) presents in greater detail the classification of varieties in terms of their resistance to tungro, the brown planthopper, and other pests. It also displays the departure of government stipulations from the theoretical model of varying levels of resistance, levels of pest depredation before and after implementation of this varietal rotation scheme, as well as the extent to which farmers have adhered to government stipulations of permissible rice varietal sequences.

15. Since the fieldwork providing the data for this paper was undertaken, a new intensification program known as Super INSUS has been implemented in South Sulawesi. I have not yet obtained sufficient information regarding how Super INSUS is being implemented, so the latest phases of the processes described here may have introduced new considerations that would have to be taken into account in a fully contemporary treatment.

16. Although Jacqueline Lineton's analysis of the effects of this drought was intended to account for why so many Bugis left their homes in the regency of Wajo' in the early 1970s, her description also reveals why local government officials continue to be so concerned to insure farmers' adherence to *all* the stipulations in the integrated rice intensification program:

> In 1971, the rains failed and the area of *sawah* [I] planted shrank by two-thirds; half of the rice-fields actually sown were eaten out by mice because of the irregular planting pattern—swampy areas had been sown a month or more before the dryer fields. Consequently, a crop was received from only 327 out of 2497 hectares of *sawah* [I] in the whole *wanuwa* [B]. The total rice crop amounted to only about 350,000 kilograms of rice—less than 46 kilograms of rice per head or far below the national average of 80–119 kilograms per head. In a survey of ten per cent of village households, it was found that a majority had harvested no rice at all from their *sawah* [I] in 1971. [188]

17. Despite the introduction of the rice intensification program in South Sulawesi as early as 1964, not until 1976 did the use of government-inspected prime seeds with resistance to tungro become general in such ricebowl areas as Pinrang Regency. One of the major problems with such early programs as DEMAS in South Sulawesi was precisely the lack of an institutional mechanism to motivate farmers to adhere punctiliously to the government guidelines.

18. The list compiled here follows closely the contents listed for each edition of the *Resultant Formulations of the Tudang Sipulung Deliberations* (*Hasil Rumusan Musyawarah "Tudang Sipulung"* [I]), issued annually by the Office of the Bupati in Sidrap Regency (Kabupaten Daerah Tingkat II Sidenreng-Rappang 1983–86).

19. The original Indonesian text reads as follows:

> . . . walaupun diberikan kesempatan pada pihak petani untuk mengungkap permasalahan selalu dibatasi dengan waktu atau kurang mendapat tanggapan untuk pemecahannya, hanya saja diinfentarisir input yang masuk dan bukan mencari bagaimana jalan

keluar. Tetapi kenyataannya yang banyak bicara dan segala keten-
tuan dari unsur pemerintah sedangkan lain sebagai pelengkap
duduk mendengar, maka setiap keputusan dianggap hasil
musyawarah.

Daud reiterates further on in his report (41) that participants in the
tudang sipulung simply follow along in supporting (*turut mendukung*
[I]) what the government enunciates.

20. This figure is adapted from Saad (1985).

21. Given its emphasis on the idioms rather than the accomplish-
ments of the rice intensification program in South Sulawesi, this essay
does not provide detailed documentation of the relative amounts of rice
entering the national stockpile via the KUD as opposed to those being
brought by private entrepreneurs both to the national stockpile and to
public markets within the regency and beyond. Such documentation is
provided in Acciaioli, with the assistance of Messi and Saad (n.d.).

22. Farmers give various reasons for their reluctance to sell rice to the
village cooperative. Among them are the following: (1) the inability of
farmers to process their crop to the level of dryness demanded by the
national stockpile; (2) their inability to pay the cost of transporting their
rice to the location of the cooperative; (3) the cooperative's refusal to
buy farmers' rice due to limited storage facilities and lack of capital; (4)
compared with the readiness of some private buyers to pay cash on the
spot (though usually at a price below what the KUD is obligated to
pay), the failure of the KUD to pay cash for rice delivered. When the
KUD does purchase rice on credit, the time interval before payment is
received by the farmers is substantially longer than when private rice
merchants purchase their rice on credit.

23. Besides neighbors and relatives from the field operator's village,
these harvest laborers include traveling teams of workers from such depressed areas as Jeneponto in the Makassarese region to the south, as
well as Javanese from transmigrant communities to the north in the
Polewali-Mamasa region.

24. The term *papétépété* (B) is also used for the small motorcycle-en-
gine-driven vehicles carrying up to eight people in a covered passenger
area behind the driver's cab, a major means of public transport in the

provincial capital Ujung Pandang. Elsewhere, as in Java, such transportation is known as *bemo* (I).

25. All prices quoted here refer to the 1985 harvest season in the regency.

26. These new managers, many of them recent graduates of agriculture programs, had been hired just prior to our 1986 fieldwork by the regional cooperatives office to help with straightening out local finances for those KUD that had lost the right to obtain credit from the government bank.

27. The South Sulawesi case parallels the situation in Java reported by Frans Husken and Benjamin White, where not large landowners, but large marketers "dominate village-level power structures and have access to state patronage both in and outside agriculture." "Java: Social Differentiation, Food Production, and Agrarian Control," in *Agrarian Transformations: Local Processes and the State in Southeast Asia*, ed. Gillian Hart, Andrew Turton, and Benjamin White, with Brian Fegan and Lim Teck Ghee, 235–65 (Berkeley: University of California Press, (1989, 258).

Glossary

abangan	a nominal Muslim
adat	custom or tradition
arisan	a rotating credit association
azas kekeluargaan	the family principle; the idea that the society is one family and that the state is the head of that family
Bakorstanas	Badan Koordinasi Stabilitas Nasional, the National Stability Coordinating Board, which replaced Kopkamtib in 1988
Bappenas	Badan Perencanaan Pembangunan Nasional, the National Planning Agency
Bimas	Bimbingan Massalan, an early New Order agriculture extension program
budaya petunjuk	a culture in which people are expected to follow the "directions" of those in authority
Bulog	the government's food (rice) procurement and storage agency
bupati	a regent or head of district government—the level below provincial government
camat	a subdistrict officer
Dharma Wanita	an official organization of wives of civil servants
Dolog	the regional offices of Bulog
DPR	Dewan Perwakilan Rakyat, the People's Representative Council, the national parliament
DPRD	Dewan Perwakilan Rakyat Daerah, the Regional People's Representative Council (at the provincial or kabupaten level)
dwifungsi	literally, "dual function"; the notion that the military is entitled and required to play the dual role of protecting the nation and managing the state

Golkar	Golongan Karya, the political organization through which the government contests elections and controls national and local legislatures
gotong royong	mutual cooperation
ICMI	Ikatan Cendiakawan Muslim Indonesia, the Indonesian Muslim Intellectuals Association
ijon	the practice of selling rice or other crops before the harvest
INGI	the International Non-Governmental Group on Indonesia, a consultative body made up of Indonesian and other NGOs with an interest in Indonesian development
Inmas	Instruksi Masyarakat, a rice agriculture extension and credit program
kabupaten	a regency or district that has its own partly elected council; an administrative unit below the province
kampung	an urban community or neighborhood; village
kecamatan	a subdistrict, an administrative unit below the kabupaten
kelurahan	village-level local government (in either rural or urban areas); headed by an appointed civil servant
keroncong	popular Indonesian music using violins and guitars
keterbukaan	political openness
kethoprak	"traditional" Javanese popular theater
Korpri	Korps Pegawai Republik Indonesia, the official organization for all Indonesian civil servants
krama	high (respectful) Javanese speech
KUD	Koperasi Unit Desa, village coop
kyai, kiai	a respected Islamic teacher
lebaran	the day ending the Islamic fasting month
Lekra	the Institute of People's Culture—a communist-linked cultural organization
LKMD	Lembaga Ketahanan Masyarakat Desa, a consultative organization for village-level government

LSM	Lembaga Swadaya Masyarakat, community self-reliance organizations, NGOs
ludruk	a form of East Javanese popular theater
lurah	a village head
Malari	the 15th of January (1974) Affair
Masjumi	a pre-'New Order' Islamic political party whose main support lies outside Java
mufakat	consensus
musyawarah	consensual decision making involving deliberation and discussion
NU	Nahdatul Ulama, an Islamic organization with strong support in East and Central Java
ngoko	informal, low-level Javanese
Ormas	Organisasi Masyarakat, a social organization (in the 1970s and before) affiliated with a political party
palawija	secondary food crops
Pancasila	the five principles that make up the official national philosophy of Indonesia
PDI	the Indonesian Democratic Party, a government engineered coalition of nationalist and other non-Muslim parties
pembangunan	development
Pemda	local government
pemuda	youth organization
Pertamina	the Indonesian state oil company
pesantren	an Islamic residential school
PKK	Pembinaan Kesejahteraan Keluarga, the Family Welfare Development Association, a government-sponsored community development organization
PPP	Partai Persatuan Pembangunan, the Development Unity Party, a government-engineered coalition of Muslim parties
pribumi	an indigenous Indonesian

priyayi	a Javanese aristocrat and state official
Repelita	Rencana Pembangunan Lima Tahun, Five-Year Development Plan
rukun	harmony
santri	a devout Muslim or student at a pesantren
Setiakawan	*Solidarity*, an environmentalist magazine
Taman Siswa	a nationalist, educational organization
SKEPHI	Sekretariat Kerjasama Pelestarian Hutan Indonesia, an Indonesian environmentalist organization
syaria	Islamic law
tayub, tayuban	Javanese popular dancing in which males in the audience may dance with the dancer; frequently performed with a gamelan orchestra at social functions
ulama	the body of (Islamic) religious scholar-leaders
umat, ummat	the faithful, the Islamic community
WALHI	Wahana Liugkungan Hidup Indonesia, a federation of Indonesian environmental organizations
wereng	the brown plant-hopper, a rice pest
YLBHI	Yayasan Lembaga Bantuan Hukum Indonesia, an association of legal-aid organizations
zakat	a religious tax or tithe

Bibliography

Abdul Hakim G. Nusantara. *Politik hukum Indonesia* (The politics of law in Indonesia). Jakarta: YLBHI, 1988.

Abdulkadir Besar. "Academic Appraisal tentang tata tertib MPR" (Academic appraisal of procedural aspects of the MPR). In *Laporan pimpinan MPRS tahun 1966–1972.* Jakarta: Penerbitan MPRS, 1972.

————. "'Negara Persatuan': Citanegara integralistik anutan UUD 1945" ("The unitary state": The integralist state-philosophy as the basis of the 1945 Constitution). In Guru Pinandita, *Sumbangsih untuk Prof Djokosoetono SH.* Jakarta: Lembaga Penerbit Fakultas Ekonomi Universitas Indonesia, 1984.

Abdullah, Syukur, et al. "Rice Intensification Program in Sulawesi Selatan." Report prepared for the Center for Policy and Implementation Studies, Jakarta., n.d.

Acciaioli, Greg. "Bugis." In *Encyclopedia of World Cultures,* David Levinson, editor-in-chief. Vol. 5, *East and Southeast Asia,* ed. P. Hockings, 48–52. New Haven: Human Relations Area Files Press, 1993.

————. "Culture as Art: From Practice to Spectacle in Indonesia." *Canberra Anthropology* 8, 1–2 (special volume: Minorities and the State, 1985): 148–72.

————. "Searching for Good Fortune: Knowledge, Fate and Hierarchy among the Bugis of Lake Lindu, Central Sulawesi (Indonesia)." Manuscript., n.d.

Acciaioli, Greg, with the assistance of M. Nawir Messi and Ilyas Saad. "Greening the Periphery: Aspects of the Rice Intensification Program in Sidrap, South Sulawesi." Research Papers Series issued by the Centre of Asian Studies, University of Western Australia., forthcoming.

Achdiat K. Mihardja, ed. *Polemik kebudayaan 1948* (The 1948 cultural polemic). Reprint, Jakarta: Dunia Pustaka Jaya, 1986.

Adicondro, G. J. "Dampak sistemik dan kritik kultural yang terlupakan: Suatu refleksi terhadap kampanye Kedung Ombo yang lalu" (The impact of a forgotten cultural critique: A reflection on the past Kedung Ombo campaign). *Kritis* 4, 3 (January 1990): 44–54.

———. "Dampak 'wabah' padang golf" (The impact of the golf course epidemic). *Suara Pembaruan*, 2 April 1993.

———. "Several Cases of Resistance against the Adverse Impact of the Jratunseluna Project by Villagers Downstream from Gedung Ombo." Unpublished manuscript.

———. "Suatu kritik terhadap teori dan praktek analisa dampak lingkungan (ADL) Bendungan Besar" (A critique of the theory and practice of the environmental impact analysis of large dams). *Kritis* (a journal of Universitas Kristen Satya Wacana, special issue on Power and Democracy) 7, 4 (April-June 1993): 38–59.

Ahmad Subardjo Djoyoadisuryo. *Kesadaran nasional: Otobiografi* (National consciousness: An autobiography). Jakarta: Gunung Agung, 1978.

Ali Boediardjo. "Volksconcert P.P.R.K. jang pertama" (The first P.P.R.K. folk concert). *Poedjangga Baroe* 8, 10 (April 1941): 252–55.

Alisjahbana Takdir. *Layar terkembang* (With sails unfurled). Batavia: Balai Pustaka, 1936.

———.Review in *Poedjangga Baroe* 8, 7 (1941): 176–77.

Almond, Gabriel, and Sidney Verba. *The Civic Culture: Political Attitudes and Democracy in Five Nations*. Princeton: Princeton University Press, 1963.

Andaya, Barbara Watson. "The Changing Religious Role of Women in Pre-Modern Southeast Asia." Paper presented at the Fourth Women in Asia Conference, University of Melbourne, October 1993.

Anderson, Benedict R. O'G. "The Idea of Power in Javanese Culture." In *Culture and Politics in Indonesia*, ed. Claire Holt, 1–28. Ithaca: Cornell University Press, 1981.

———. *Java in a Time of Revolution: Occupation and Resistance 1944–46*. Ithaca, N.Y.: Cornell University Press, 1972.

———. *Language and Power: Exploring Political Cultures in Indonesia.* Ithaca: Cornell University Press, 1990.

———. "Millenarianism and the Saminist Movement." In *Religion and Social Ethos in Indonesia*, ed. J. Mackie, 48–61. Clayton, Victoria: Monash University Press, 1975.

———. *Mythology and the Tolerance of the Javanese.* Ithaca: Cornell Modern Indonesia Project, 1965.

———. "Old State, New Society: Indonesia's New Order in Comparative Historical Perspective." *Journal of Asian Studies* 42 (May 1983): 477–96.

Apthorpe, Raymond, "Pleading and Reading Agricultural Development Policy: Small Farm, Big State, and the 'Case' of Taiwan." In *Social Anthropology and Development Policy*, ed. Ralph Grillo and Alan Rew, 88–101. A.S.A. Monographs, no. 23, London: Tavistock Publications, 1985.

Armijn Pané. "Belenggu." *Poedjangga Baroe* 7(10- 12) (April-June 1940).

———. "Boekoe, pers, radio dan film" (Books, the press, radio, and film). *Poedjangga Baroe,* Nomor Peringatan (Anniversary issue) (1938): 3–16.

———. "Dardanella", *Poedjangga Baroe* 1, 12 (1934): 38 1–83.

———. *Gamelan djiwa* (Gamelan of the spirit). Jakarta: Bagian Bahasa, DPPK, 1960.

———. "Gamelan tegenover krontjong, droom tegenover werkelijkheid" (Gamelan as opposed to *krontjong,* dream as opposed to reality). *Poedjangga Baroe* 9, 1 (July 1941): 9–30.

———. "Kerontjong disamping gamelan" (*Kerontjong,* not just gamelan). *Poedjangga Baroe* 8, 10 (April 1941): 256–60.

———. "Kesoesastraan baroe" (New literature). Part 1. *Poedjangga Baroe* 1, 1 (1933): 9–15.

———. "Lagoe Indonesia Raja" (The anthem "Indonesia Raya"). *Poedjangga Baroe* 2 (1934– 1945): 27–30.

———. "Produksi film tjerita di Indonesia, perkembangannja sebagai alat masjarakat" (Film production in Indonesia, its development as a tool of society). *Indonesia, Madjallah Kebudajaan* 4, 1–2 (January–February 1953): 5–112.

———. "Radio dan keboedajaan" (Radio and culture). *Poedjangga Baroe* 5, 9 (1937–1938): 197–98.

———. *Shackles*. Translated by John H. McGlynn. Athens: Ohio University Monographs in International Studies, 1985.

———. *Shackles*. Rev. ed. Translated by John H. McGlynn. Jakarta: Lontar Foundation, 1988.

Asad, Talal. "Anthropology and the Analysis of Ideology." *Man* 14, 4 (1979): 607–27.

Asia Watch Committee. *Injustice, Persecution, Eviction: A Human Rights Update on Indonesia and East Timor*. New York: Asia Watch Committee, 1990.

Aswab Mahasin. "NGOs and Political Alternatives: Awaiting Surprises." Background paper untuk seminar: Pembangunan masyarakat desa yang berorientasi kerakyatan antara mitos dan realita (Background paper for a seminar: Development of village society that is democratically oriented between myth and reality). Yogyakarta: Fakultas Ilmu Sosial dan Politik, Universitas Gadjah Mada, 1989.

Attamimi, Abdul Hakim. "Peranan keputusan presiden Republik Indonesia dalam penyelenggaraan pemerintahan negara" (The role of presidential decisions in the governance of the Indonesian Republic). Dissertation for the degree of Doctor of Laws, University of Indonesia, Jakarta, 1990.

Austin-Broos, Diane. "Clifford Geertz: Culture, Sociology and Historicism." In *Creating Culture*, ed. D. Austin-Broos, 141–62. Sydney: Allen and Unwin, 1987.

"Bahasa dan Sastra Lisan Orang Samin" (The language and oral literature of the Samin). *Basis* 32 (January 1983).

"Bahasa Orang Samin" (The language of the Samin). *Majalah Konggres Bahasa Jawa*. 1991.

Bailey, F. G. *Humbuggery and Manipulation: The Art of Leadership*. Ithaca: Cornell University Press, 1988.

Bakdi Soemanto. *Pergeseran makna sakral dalam pertunjukan wayang kulit* (The shift of sacred meaning in shadow play performance). Yogyakarta, Pusat Penelitian Kebudayaan Lit-UGM, Universitas Gadjah Mada, 1988.

Bambang S. Sulasmono. "Kristalisasi pemikiran kenegaraan" (A crystalization of constitutional thinking). *Kompas*, 14 May 1991.

Bellah, Robert. *Beyond Belief.* Berkeley: University of California Press, 1970.

Bellah, Robert N., et al. *Habits of the Heart: Individualism and Commitment in American Life.* Berkeley: University of California Press, 1985.

Benda, H. and L. Castles. "The Samin Movement." *Bijdragen tot de taal-, land-, en volkenkunde* 125 (1969): 211–12.

Bloch, Maurice. *Ritual, History and Power: Selected Papers in Anthropology.* London: Athlone Press, 1989.

Bourchier, David. "Contradictions in the Dominant Paradigm of State Organization in Indonesia," Paper presented to the Conference on 'Indonesia Paradigms for the Future.' Murdoch University, Western Australia, Asia Research Centre on Social, Political and Economic Change, July 1993.

———. "Reflections on the Integralist Tradition of Political Thought in Indonesia." Paper presented to the Asian Studies Association of Australia 9th Biennial Conference, Armidale, New South Wales, 5–9 July 1992.

Bowen, John R. "On the Political Construction of Tradition: Gotong Royong in Indonesia." *Journal of Asian Studies* 45, 3 (1986): 545–61.

Brenkman, John. *Culture and Domination.* Ithaca: Cornell University Press, 1987.

Brown, R. E. "The Performing Arts: Modernity and Tradition." In *What Is Modern Indonesian Culture?* ed. G. Davis, 48–52. Papers in International Studies, Southeast Asia Series, no. 52, Athens: Ohio University Press, 1972.

Budi Darma. "The Origin and Development of the Novel in Indonesia." *Tenggara* 25 (1990): 9–35.

Budiman, Arif. "Gerakan mahasiswa dan LSM ke arah sebuah reunifikasi" (The student movement and nongovernmental organizations in the movement toward reunification). *Kritis* 4, 3 (January 1990): 53–59.

Chabot, Hendrik T. "Bontoramba: A Village of Goa, South Sulawesi." In *Villages in Indonesia*, ed. Koentjaraningrat, 189–209. Ithaca: Cornell University Press, 1967.

Choy, Peggy. "Texts through Time: The Golek Dance of Java." In *Aesthetic Tradition and Cultural Transition in Java and Bali*, ed. Stephanie Morgan and Laurie Jo Sears. Madison: University of Wisconsin Press, 1984.

Chudori, Leila. *Malam Terakhir* (The last right). Jakarta: Grafitipers, 1989.

Clancy, Anna. *The Cultural Constructions of Javanese Women in Modern Indonesian Literature*. Honors thesis, University of Sydney, 1988.

Colson, Elizabeth. "Power at Large: Meditation on 'The Symposium on Power.'" In *The Anthropology of Power*, ed. Raymond D. Fogelson and Richard N. Adams, eds, 375–86. New York: Academic Press, 1977.

Cribb, Robert. "Heirs to the Late Colonial State? The Indonesian Republic, the Netherlands Indies, and the Revolution, 1945–1949." Manuscript, 1989.

Darji Darmodiharjo. *Pancasila dalam beberapa perspektif* (Several perspectives on *pancasila*). Jakarta: Aries Lima, 1982.

Darnton, Robert. *The great cat massacre and other episodes in French cultural history*. New York: Vintage Books, 1985.

Daud, Darmuni. *Air melimpah sawah tak tergarap: Studi kasus tentang sebab timbulnya pemberoan sawah di desa Mattongang-Tongang, kecamatan Mattiro Sompe, kabupaten Pinrang—Sulawesi Selatan* (Water exists in abundance, but the wet-rice fields are not cultivated: A case study concerning the causes of wet-rice land being kept fallow in the village Mattongang-Tongang, Mattiro Sompe district, Pinrang regency—South Sulawesi). Laporan Penelitian PLPIIS, Ujung Pandang: Pusat Latihan Penelitian Ilmu-Ilmu Sosial, Universitas Hasanuddin, 1985.

Davis, Gloria. "What is Modern Indonesian Culture? An Epilogue and Example." In *What is Modern Indonesian Culture?*, Papers in International Studies, Southeast Asia Series, no. 52, Athens: Ohio University Press, 1972.

Davis, Gloria, ed. *What Is Modern Indonesian Culture?* Papers in International Studies, Southeast Asia Series, no. 52, Athens: Ohio University Press, 1972.

Dhakidae, Daniel. "Pahlawan." *Tempo*, 25 May 1991, p. 107.

Dinas Pertanian Tanaman Pangan. *Kesan dan peristiwa Operasi Lappoase di kabupaten Bone, Sinjae dan Bulukumba propinsi Sulawesi Selatan* (Impressions and incidents of Operation Lappoase in the regencies of Bone, Sinjae, and Bulukumba in the province of South Sulawesi). Ujung Pandang: Dinas Pertanian Tanaman Pangan, Propinsi Daerah Tingkat I, Sulawesi Selatan, 1982.

Dini, N. H. *Jalan bandungan* (Bandungan Street). Jakarta: Penerbit Jambatan, 1989.

Djoko Quartanto. "Jatidiri" (Identity). *Kompas*, 16 September 1990.

Dove, Michael R. "Introduction: Traditional Culture and Development in Contemporary Indonesia." In *The Real and Imagined Role of Culture in Development: Case Studies from Indonesia*, ed. Michael R. Dove, 1–37. Honolulu: University of Hawaii Press, 1988.

Drabek, Anne Gordon, ed. "Development Alternatives: The Challenge for NGOs." Supplement to *World Development* 15 (Autumn 1987).

Drake, Christine. *National Integration in Indonesia: Patterns and Policies.* Honolulu: University of Hawaii Press, 1989.

Drakeley, Stephen. "Torture, Terror and Titillation: The Mysogynous Myth of Lubang Buaya and the Mass Killings in Indonesia." Paper presented at the Fourth Women in Asia Conference, University of Melbourne, October 1993.

Eldridge, Philip. "NGOs and the State in Indonesia." In *The State and Civil Society in Indonesia*, ed. Arief Budiman, 502–38. Monash Papers on Southeast Asia, no. 22.

———. "NGOs in Indonesia: Popular Movement or Arm of Government?" Monash University, Centre of Southeast Asian Studies, Working Paper no. 55, 1990.

———. "The Political Role of Community Action Groups in India and Indonesia: In Search of a General Theory." *Alternatives* (Delhi and New York) 10, 3 (Winter 1984-85): 401–34.

Ellen, Roy F. "Ritual, Identity and Management of Interethnic Relations on Seram." In *Time Past, Time Present, Time Future*, ed. David Moyerd and H.J.M. Claessen, 117–35. Doordrecht: Foris Publications, 1988.

Emha Ainun Nadjib. "Mereka menyangka saya Kiai" (They suppose that I am a Kiai). *Matra*, February 1992.

———. "Syair heran" (A poem of amazement). *Opini plesetan* column in *DeTik*, 26 May– 1 June 1993, p. 3.

Enloe, Cynthia. *Does Khaki Become You? The Militarization of Women's Lives*. London: Pluto, 1983.

Eros Djarot. "Membangun sinema Indonesia" (Developing Indonesian cinema). *Kompas*, 1 July 1990.

Errington, Shelly. "Embodied Sumange in Luwu." *Journal of Asian Studies*, 42, 3 (1983): 545–70.

———. *Meaning and Power in a Southeast Asian Realm*. Princeton: Princeton University Press, 1989.

Evans, Peter B., Dietrich Rueschemeyer, and Theda Skocpol. *Bringing the State Back In*. Cambridge: Cambridge University Press, 1985.

Faruk, H. T., and Ryadi Goenawan. "Dimensi-dimensi *Pudjangga Baru*" (Dimensions of *Pudjangga Baru*). *Basis* 32, 7 (July 1983): 257–64.

Feith, Herbert and Lance Castles, eds., *Indonesian Political Thinking, 1945–1965*, (Ithaca: Cornell University Press, 1970).

Fernandes, W., ed. *Social Activists and People's Movements*. New Delhi: Indian Social Institute, 1985.

"Final Declaration of the Regional Meeting for Asia of the World Conference on Human Rights." Bangkok, 29 March–2 April 1993.

Foucault, Michel. *Power/Knowledge: Selected Interviews and Other Writings, 1972–1977*. New York: Pantheon Books, 1980.

Foulcher, Keith. "The Construction of an Indonesian National Culture: Patterns of Hegemony and Resistance." In *State and Civil Society in Indonesia*, ed. Arief Budiman, 301–20. Monash Papers on Southeast Asia, no. 22. Clayton, Victoria: Centre of Southeast Asian Studies, 1990.

————. "Post-Modernism or the Question of History: Some Trends in Indonesian Fiction since 1965." In *Culture and Society in New Order Indonesia*, ed. V. Matheson-Hooker. Kuala Lumpur: Oxford University Press, 1993.

————. *Pudjangga Baru: Literature and Nationalism in Indonesia, 1933–1942*. Bedford Park: Flinders University, 1980.

Fox, James J. "Managing the Ecology of Rice Production in Indonesia", In *Indonesia: Resources, Ecology, and Environment*, ed. Joan Hardjono, 61–84. Singapore: Oxford University Press, 1991.

Frederick, William. "Rhoma Irama and the *Dangdut* Style: Aspects of Contemporary Indonesian Popular Culture." *Indonesia* 34 (October 1982): 103–31.

Freire, Paulo. *Pendidikan sebagai praktek pembebasan* (Education as liberation). Jakarta: Gramedia, 1984.

Gans, Herbert. *Popular Culture and High Culture*. New York: Basic Books, 1974.

Geertz, C. Afterword ("The Politics of Meaning") to *Culture and Politics in Indonesia*, ed. C. Holt, 319–36. Ithaca: Cornell University Press, 1972.

————. *The Interpretation of Cultures*. New York: Basic Books, 1973.

————. "Javanese Village." In *Local, Ethnic and National Loyalties in Village Indonesia: A Symposium*, ed. W. Skinner. Cultural Report Series, Southeast Asian Studies, Yale University, 1959.

————. *The Religion of Java*. Glencoe, Ill.: Free Press, 1960.

Gerth, H. H., and C. Wright Mills, eds. *From Max Weber*. New York: Oxford University Press, 1946.

Glassburner, Bruce. "Economic Openness and Economic Nationalism in Indonesia under the Soeharto Government." Paper presented at a conference on Comparative Analysis of the Development Process in East and Southeast Asia, Honolulu: East-West Center, May 1990.

Goenawan Mohamad. "Aku." *Tempo* 22, 29 (19 September 1992).

———. *Catatan Pinggir* (Marginal notes). Jakarta: Grafiti, 1982 (vol. 1), 1989 (vol. 2), 1991 (vol. 3).

———. *Potret seorang penjair muda sebagai si Malin Kundang* (Portrait of a young poet as *Malin Kundang*). Jakarta: Pustaka Jaya, 1972.

———. *Seks, sastra, kita* (Sex, literature, us). Jakarta: Sinar Harapan, 1980.

Guru Pinandita. *Sumbangsih untuk Prof Djokosoetono SH* (Dedication for Professor Djokosoetono). Jakarta: Lembaga Penerbit Fakultas Ekonomi Universitas Indonesia, 1984.

Hardjono, Ratih. "Wanita tersiksa dalam novel sentimental" (Tortured women in sentimental novels). *Prisma* 16, 5 (1987).

Hardoyo. "Hutan Tanaman Industri (HTI) dalam mawas diri dan kilas balik pembangunan hutan di Indonesia" (Industrial Forestry in the light of self-correction and a backward glance at forest development in Indonesia). Mimeograph, Jakarta, October 1993.

Hatley, Barbara. Introduction to *Time Bomb and Cockroach Opera*, ed. John McGlynn and Barbara Hatley. Jakarta: Lontar Press, 1992.

———. "The New Indonesian Pujanggas." Paper presented at a conference on multilingualism in Indonesia, Pacet, West Java, 1981.

Hefner, Robert. *The Political Economy of Mountain Java: An Interpretive History*. Berkeley: University of California Press, 1990.

Heins, Ernst. "*Kroncong* and *Tanjidor:* Two Cases of Urban Folk Music in Jakarta. *Asian Music* 7, 1 (1975): 20–32.

Hellwig, Tinneke. *Kodrat Wanita: Vrouwbeelden in Indonesische Romans*

(Women's nature: Women's image in Indonesian novels). (Leiden: C. M. S. Hellwig 1990), 83–84.

Heryanto, Ariel. *Perdebatan sastra kontekstual* (The debate over contextual literature). Jakarta: Rajawali, 1985.

Hill, David T. "Interpreting the Indonesian National Character: Mochtar Lubis and *Manusia Indonesia*." In *Text/Politics in Island Southeast Asia*, ed. D. M. Roskies, 288–321. Athens: Ohio University Center for International Studies, Monographs in International Studies, Southeast Asia Series, No. 91, 1993.

———. "Mochtar Lubis: The Artist as Cultural Broker in New Order Indonesia." *Review of Indonesian and Malaysian Affairs* 21, 1 (1987): 54–87.

Hill, Hal, and Anna Weidemann. "Regional Development in Indonesia: Patterns and Issues." In *Unity and Diversity: Regional Economic Development in Indonesia since 1970*, ed. Hal Hill, 3–54. Singapore: Oxford University Press, 1989.

Hirschman, Albert. *Essays in Trespassing: Economics to Politics and Beyond*. Cambridge: Cambridge University Press, 1981.

Hobsbawm, Eric, and Terence Ranger, eds. *The Invention of Tradition*. Cambridge: Cambridge University Press, 1983.

Hocking, B., and M. Smith. *World Politics*. London: Harvester, 1990.

Husken, Frans, and Benjamin White. "Java: Social Differentiation, Food Production, and Agrarian Control." In *Agrarian Transformations: Local Processes and the State in Southeast Asia*, ed. Gillian Hart, Andrew Turton, and Benjamin White, with Brian Fegan and Lim Teck Ghee, 235–65. Berkeley: University of California Press, 1989.

Indonesian NGOs for Democracy [IN-DEMO]. "Joint Declaration on Human Rights." Jakarta, June 1993.

Jassin, H. B. *Pudjangga Baru: Prosa dan puisi* (*Pudjangga Baru:* Prose and poetry). Jakarta: Gunung Agung, 1963.

Jayadiningrat, R. M. A. *Serat man jenthu inggih mas nganten* (The tale of Mas Jenthu, also known as Mas Nganten). Vol. 1. Surakarta: Albert Rusche, 1907.

Jayawardena, K. *Feminism and Nationalism in the Third World*. London: Zed Press, 1986.

Jenkins, David. *Suharto and His Generals: Indonesian Military Politics, 1975–1983*. Ithaca: Modern Indonesia Project, Cornell University, 1984.

Johns, Anthony H. Introduction to *Road with No End*, by Mochtar Lubis. Translated by A. H. Johns. London: Hutchison, 1968.

———. "The Novel as a Guide to Indonesian Social History." *Bijdragen tot de taal-, land-, en volkenkunde* 115, part 3 (1959): 232–48.

Johnson, Mary. "Non-Government Organizations at the Crossroads in Indonesia." In *Indonesian Economic Development: Approaches, Technology, Small-Scale Textiles, Urban Infrastructure and NGOs*, ed. Robert C. Rice, 77–92. Monash University (AIA-CSEAS Winter Lecture Series 1988), 1990.

Kabupaten Daerah Tingkat II Sidenreng-Rappang, Hasil Rumusan Musyawarah. "Tudang Sipulung." Pangkajene (a government publication of kabupaten Pangkajene), 1983–86.

Kahin, G. *Nationalism and Revolution in Indonesia*. Ithaca: Cornell University Press, 1952.

Karim Halim. Untitled review of *Belenggu* by Armijn Pané. *Poedjangga Baroe* 8, 6 (1940): 132.

Katalogus: Seni Rupa Baru Proyek Satu "Pasaraya Dunia Fantasi" (Catalogue: The new Visual Arts Project One, "A fantasy-world department store"). Jakarta: Galeri Baru, Taman Ismail Marzuki, 15–30 June 1987.

Keesing, Roger, and Robert Tonkinson, eds. "Reinventing Traditional Culture: The Politics of Kastom in Island Melanesia." *Mankind* 13, 4 (special issue, 1982).

Koentjaraningrat. *Kebudayaan Jawa* (Javanese culture). Jakarta: Balai Pustaka, 1984.

Kornhauser, Bronia. "In Defense of *Kroncong*." In *Studies in Indonesian Music*, ed. Margaret J. Kartomi, 104–83. Clayton, Victoria: Monash University Centre of Southeast Asian Studies, 1978.

Kristanto, Kustiah, Tajuddin Parenta, and Neil Sturgess. "South Sulawesi: New Directions in Agriculture?" In *Unity and Diversity: Regional Economic Development in Indonesia since 1970*, ed. Hal Hill, 387–408. Singapore: Oxford University Press, 1989.

Lane, Max. *Openness, Political Discontent and Succession in Indonesia: Political Developments in Indonesia, 1989–91.* Nathan, Queensland: Centre for the Study of Australia-Asia Relations, Griffith University, Australia-Asia paper, No. 56, 1991.

Leibo, Jefta. "Kehidupan petani kecil di bawah terpaan revolusi hijau: Studi kasus tentang implikasi penggunaan input pertanian moderen terhadap kehidupan sosial ekonomi petani kecil di desa Minasa Baji, kabupaten Maros, Sulawesi Selatan" (The life of small farmers under the assault of the green revolution: A case study concerning the implications of the use of modern agricultural inputs on the socioeconomic life of small farmers in the village Minasa Baji, Maros regency, South Sulawesi). Laporan Penelitian PLPIIS, Ujung Pandang: Pusat Latihan Penelitian Ilmu-Ilmu Sosial, Universitas Hasanuddin, 1983.

Lerner, Daniel. *The Passing of Traditional Society*. Glencoe, Ill.: Free Press, 1958.

Lewis, Bernard. *The Political Language of Islam*. Chicago: University of Chicago Press, 1988.

Liddle, R. William, "Indonesia's Threefold Crisis." *Journal of Democracy* 3, 4 (October 1992).

———. "Political Entertainment." Manuscript, Ohio State University, 1990.

———. "The Relative Autonomy of the Third World Politician: Soeharto and Indonesian Economic Development in Comparative Perspective." *International Studies Quarterly* 3, 4 (December 1991): 403–27.

———. "Rumah seorang penulis" (The address of a writer). In *Catatan Pinggir* (Marginal Notes), by Goenawan Mohamad. Vol. 3, pp. x–xi. Jakarta: P. T. Grafiti, 1991.

Lindstrom, Lamont, and Geoffrey White, eds. "Custom Today." *Anthropological Forum* 6, 4 (special issue, 1993).

Lineton, Jacqueline. "Pasompe' Ugi': Bugis Migrants and Wanderers." *Archipel* 10 (1975): 173–201.

Logemann, J. H. A. *Keterangan-keterangan baru tentang terjadinya UUD 1945* (New accounts of the origins of the 1945 Constitution; a translation of the 1962 essay "Nieuwe gegevens over het ontstaan van de Indonesische Grondwet van 1945," translated by Darji Darmodihardjo). Jakarta: Aries Lima, 1982.

Lohanda, Mona. "Majoor Jantje and the Indische Element of Batawi Folkmusic." Paper presented to the Third Dutch-Indonesian Historical Congress, Leiden, 23–27 June 1980.

Lubis, Mochtar. *The Indonesian Dilemma*. Translated by Florence Lamoureux. Singapore: Graham Brash, 1983.

———. *Maut dan cinta* (Death and love). Jakarta: Pustaka Jaya, 1977.

———. *Situasi manusia Indonesia kini* (The situation of the Indonesian people today). Jakarta: Yayasan Idayu, 1977.

Lubis, T. Mulya. "In Search of Human Rights: Legal Political Dilemmas of Indonesia's New Order, 1966–1990." Doctor of Laws dissertation, University of California, Berkeley, 1990.

Lucas, Anton. "Land Disputes in Indonesia: Some Current Perspectives." *Indonesia*, 53 (April 1992).

MacIntyre, Andrew. *Business and Politics in Indonesia*. Sydney: Allen and Unwin, 1990.

Madjid, Nurcholish. "Ibn Taimiya on Kalam and Falsafah: The Problem of Reason and Revelation in Islam." Ph.D. dissertation, University of Chicago, 1984.

———. *Islam: Doktrin dan Peradaban* (Islam: Doctrine and civilization). Jakarta: Yayasan Wakaf Paramadina, 1992.

———, ed. *Khazanah intelektual Islam* (The intellectual treasure of Islam). Jakarta: Bulan Bintang, 1984.

Madjid, Nurcholish, Abdul Qadir Djaelani, Ismail Hasan Metarieum S.H., and H. E. Saefuddin Anshari. *Pembaharuan Pemikiran Islam* (The renewal of Islamic thought). Jakarta: Islamic Research Centre, 1970.

Mangunwijaya, Y. B. "Budaya yang menculik kita" (A culture that carries us away). *Tempo* 3 (January 1987).

———. *Burung-burung manyar* (The weaver birds). Jakarta: Penerbit Jambatan, 1981.

———. *Durga-Umayi*. Jakarta: Grafitipers, 1991.

———. "Renungan Agustus 1990" (Remembering August 1990). *Kompas*, 15 August 1990.

———. *Roro Mendut*. Jakarta: Gramedia, 1983.

Manoharan, Moses. "Asia Supports National Human Rights Commissions." Reuters, 27 January 1993.

Marah Rusli. *Siti Nurbaya*. Batavia: Balai Pustaka, 1922.

Marsillam Simanjuntak, "Konstitutionalisme dan Demokrasi di Indonesia" (Constitutionalism and Democracy in Indonesia) *DeTik*, No. 565, 30 November 1992.

———. "Unsur Hegelian dalam pandangan negara integralistik" (Hegelian elements in the integralist view of the state). Master of Laws thesis, Faculty of Law, University of Indonesia, Depok, 1989.

Masyarakat Samin di Jawa Timur (The Samin society of East Java: A feasibility study). Jakarta: Dept. Pendidikan dan Kebudayaan, 1980.

Matthes, B. F. *Boegineesch-Hollandsch woordenboek* (Bugis-Dutch dictionary). The Hague: M. Nijhoff, 1874.

de Mendelssohn, Peter. *Japan's Political Warfare*. London: George Allen and Unwin, 1944.

Menuju masyarakat Baru Indonesia: Antisipasi terhadap tantangan abad XXI (Toward a New Indonesian society: Anticipating the challenges of the twenty-first century). Jakarta: Kompas and Gramedia, 1990.

Misbach Jusa Biran. "Film Indonesia memerlukan kaum terpelajar" (Indonesian films require an educated class). *Prisma* 19, 5 (1990): 40–44.

Mochtar Pabottingi. "Bahasa mobil kelas menengah" (Automobile language of the middle class). *Tempo*, 23 March 1991, p. 104.

Mohammad Yamin. *Naskah persiapan undang-undang dasar 1945* (Documents relating to the preparation of the 1945 Constitution). Vol. 1. Jakarta: Jajasan Prapantja, 1959.

Mohtar Mas'oed. "INGI and the Politics of Development in Indonesia." Unpublished manuscript, Yogyakarta, Gadjah Mada University, circa 1982.

Morris, Ivan, ed. *Japan 1931–1945: Militarism, Fascism, Japanism?* Boston: Heath, 1963.

Mulder, Niels. "Saminism and Buddhism: A Note on a Field Visit to a Samin Community." *Asian Quarterly* 3 (1983): 62–67.

Myala, Fahmy. "'Tudang Sipulung': Pertemuan teknologi dan tradisi di Sidrap" ('Tudang Sipulung': A meeting of technology and tradition in Sidrap). *Kompas*, 8 February 1980, pp. 1, 12.

Nagazumi, Akira. *The Dawn of Indonesian Nationalism: The Early Years of the Budi Utomo, 1908–1918.* Tokyo: Institute of Developing Economies, 1972.

Nasution, Adnan Buyung. "Adakah hak asasi manusia di Dalam UUD 1945?" (Does the 1945 Constitution Contain Human Rights?) *Forum Keadilan*, nos. 20, 21 (January 1993).

———. "The Aspiration for Constitutional Government in Indonesia: A Socio-legal Study of the Indonesian Konstituante, 1956–1959." Ph.D. dissertation, Rijksuniversiteit, Utrecht, 1992.

National Development Information Office. *Indonesia: Source Book 1990–91.* Jakarta: National Development Information Office, 1991.

Natsir, M. *M. Natsir versus Sukarno.* Padang: Yayasan Pendidikan Islam, 1968.

Nichterlein, Sue. "An Essay on Transcultural Intellectual Biography: Sutan Takdir Alisjahbana." In *Spectrum*, ed. S. Udin, 61-91. Jakarta: Dian Rakyat, 1978.

Njoman Dekker and Sudomo. *Masyarakat Samin: Suatu tunjauan singkat sosiokulturil* (The Samin people: A brief sociocultural observation). Malang: Lembaga Institut Keguruan Ilmu Pendidikan, 1970.

Nugroho Notosusanto. *Proses perumusan pancasila dasar negara* (The process of formulating the *pancasila* state philosophy). Jakarta: Balai Pustaka, 1981.

Onghokham. "The Inscrutable and the Paranoid." In *Southeast Asian Transitions*, ed. R. Mcvey. New Haven: Yale University Press, 1976.

————. "Penelitian sumber-sumber gerakan mesianis" (Research on the sources of messianic movements). *Prisma* 1 (January 1977): 64–70.

————. "The Residency of Madiun: *Priyayi* and Peasant in the Nineteenth Century." Ph.D. dissertation, Yale University, 1975.

Padmasusastra. *Serat Subasita* (A tale of etiquette). Surakarta: Budi Utama, 1914.

Padmo Wahyono. "Integralistik Indonesia" (Indonesian integralism). *Majalah Persahi*, no.3 (January 1990).

Palmier, Leslie. *Social Status and Power in Java*. London: Athlone Press, University of London, 1969.

Pangeran Aria Sasraningrat, *Wedamadya* (Middle way). Comp. Padmasusastra. Surakarta: 1898.

Pigeaud, T. *Java in the Fourteenth Century*. Vol 1. The Hague: M. Nijhoff, 1962.

van der Plas, Ch. O. "Nota van der Plas van 7 December 1927" (The van der Plas note of 7 December 1927). In *Onderwijsbeleid in Nederlandsch-Indië 1900–1940*, ed. S. L. van der Wal, 437–44. Groningen: J. B. Wolters, 1963.

Popkin, Samuel L. *The Rational Peasant*. Berkeley: University of California Press, 1979.

Pramudya Ananta Tur, *Anak semua bangsa* (Child of all nations). Jakarta: Hasta Mitra, 1982.

————. *Bumi Manusia* (This earth of mankind). Jakarta: Hasta Mitra, 1980.

————. *Cerita dari Blora* (Stories of Blora). Jakarta: Balai Pustaka, 1950.

————. *Jejak langkah* (Footsteps). Kuala Lumpur: Wira Karya, 1986.

————. *Rumah kaca* (House of glass). Jakarta: Hasta Mitra, 1988.

Propinsi Daerah Tingkat I, Sulawesi Selatan. *Operasi Lappo Ase (OLA)* (Operation Lappo Ase). Seri Tanaman Pangan 05/IV/AR/81. Ujung Pandang: Balai Informasi Pertanian, 1981.

Pye, Lucian, and Sidney Verba. *Political Culture and Political Development*. Princeton: Princeton University Press, 1965.

Rae, L. "Liberating and Conciliating: The Work of Y. B. Mangunwijaya." In *Indonesian Political Biography*, ed. Angus McIntyre. Melbourne: Monash University, Centre of Southeast Asian Studies, 1993.

Rajni Kothari. "NGOs, the State and World Capitalism." *Economic and Political Weekly* (Bombay) 21, 50 (13 December 1986): 2177–82.

Ramadhani Aksyah. "Paham integralistik dan oposisi" (Integralism and opposition). *Kompas*, 28 October 1989.

Ramage, Douglas. "Pancasila Discourse in Soeharto's Late New Order." Paper prepared for the conference on Indonesian Democracy: 1950s and 1990s. Monash University, 17–20 December 1992.

Rasjidi, H. M. *Koreksi terhadap Drs. Nurcholish Madjid tentang sekularisasi* (Correction of Drs. Nurcholish Madjid concerning secularization). Jakarta: Bulan Bintang, 1977.

RCTI [Rajawali Citra Televisi Indonesia]. "Golf dan kontroversi." On *Liputan berita* (a news program), 30 May 1993.

———. "Liputan khusus" (Special coverage report), 30 May 1993.

Reeve, David. "The Corporatist State: The Case of Golkar." In *State and Civil Society in Indonesia*, ed. Arief Budiman, 151–76. Monash Papers on Southeast Asia, no. 22. Clayton, Victoria: Centre of Southeast Asian Studies, 1990.

Remy Sylado. "Benarkah mengangkat lagu menjadi populer?" (Can you make a record popular?). *Kompas*, 29 July 1990.

Resink, G. J. "Indonesische toekomstmuziek" (The future music of Indonesia). *Kritiek en opbouw* 4, 5 (April 1941): 74–77.

Ricklefs, M. C. "Unity and Disunity in Javanese Political and Religious Thought of the Eighteenth Century." *Modern Asian Studies* 26, 4 (October 1992): 663–78.

———. "Yogyakarta under Mangkubumi, 1749–1792: A History of the Division of Java." Ph.D. dissertation, Cornell University, 1973.

Rodgers, Susan. "Imagining Tradition, Imagining Modernity: A Southern Batak Novel from the 1920s." *Bijdragen tot de taal-, land-, en volkenkunde* 147, 2–3 (1991): 27 1–97.

Rudolph, Lloyd I., and Susanne Hoeber Rudolph. *The Modernity of Tradition: Political Development in India*. Chicago: University of Chicago Press, 1967.

Rukiah. "An Affair of the Heart." In *Reflections on Rebellion: Stories of the Indonesian Upheavals of 1948 and 1965*, ed. William Frederick and John McGlynn. Athens: Ohio University Press, 1983.

Saad, Ilyas. "Pola pemasaran gabah dan beras di kab. Sidrap" (The pattern of unhulled and hulled rice marketing in Sidrap regency). Report prepared for the Centre for Policy and Implementation Studies, Jakarta, 1985.

Salim Said. *Genesis of Power: General Sudirman and the Indonesian Military in Politics 1945-1949*. Singapore: Institute of Southeast Asian Studies, 1991.

———. *Profil dunia film Indonesia* (A profile of the Indonesian film world). Jakarta: Grafitipers, 1982.

———. *Shadows on the Silver Screen: A Social History of Indonesian Film*. Jakarta: Lontar Foundation, 1991.

Sama, Shagir, and S. Anwar H. Rizvi. "Evaluasi penerapan pergiliran varietas padi dalam pengendalian tungro" (An evaluation of the practice of rotating paddy varieties in the control of tungro virus). *Kumpulan Makalah TEMU TUGAS I*, a collection of papers from Workshop 1, 29–30 July 1985. Maros: Badan Penelitian dan Pengembangan Pertanian, Balai Penelitian Tanaman Pangan Maros, 1985, pp. 1–11.

Santa-Maria, Luigi. "L'Essor officiel: 1900- 1942." In *Sastra, Introduction à la littérature Indonésienne contemporaine*, ed. H. Chambert-Loir, 29–55. Paris: Cahiers d'Archipel, 1980.

Sartono Kartodirdjo, "Agrarian Radicalism in Java: Its Setting and Development." In *Culture and Politics in Indonesia*, ed. C. Holt. Ithaca: Cornell University Press, 1972.

———. "Kesadaran sejarah dan kepribadian nasion" (Historical consciousness and national identity). *Kompas,* 4 (October 1990) (pt. 1), 5 (October 1990) (pt. 2).

————. *Protest Movements in Rural Java.* Singapore: Oxford University Press 1973.

————. "Rakyat jangan dianggap bodoh" (Don't treat the people as if they are stupid). *Prisma* 6 (1989).

Sartono Kartodirdjo et al. *Perkembangan peradaban priyayi* (The development of the *priyayi* ethos). Yogyakarta: Gadjah Mada University Press, 1987.

Sayidi Surjohadiprojo. "Jatidiri dan kebudayaan bangsa" (Identity and national culture). *Kompas,* 9 August 1990.

————. "Kemampuan menyadari perubahan" (The capacity to understand change). *Kompas,* 8 October 1990.

Scherer, Savitri. "Introducing Yudhistira Ardi Noegraha." *Indonesia* 31 (April 1981): 31–52.

————. *Keselarasan dan kejanggalan: Pemikiran-pemikiran priyayi nasionalis jawa awal abad XX* (Harmony and disharmony: Javanese nationalist *priyayi* thought at the beginning of the twentieth century). Jakarta: Sinar Harapan, 1985.

Schulte-Nordholt, N. "From LSD to LKMD: Participation at the Village Level." University of Twente, Technology and Development Group Working Paper no. 25, 1985.

Schwarz, Adam. "All Is Relative." *Far Eastern Economic Review* 155 (30 April 1992): 54–58.

Scott, James C. *The Moral Economy of the Peasant: Rebellion and Subsistence in Southeast Asia.* New Haven: Yale University Press, 1977.

Sears, Laurie J. *Fantasizing the Feminine in Indonesia.* Durham: Duke University Press, 1996.

Siegel, James. *Solo in the New Order.* Princeton: Princeton University Press, 1986.

Sen, Krishna. "The Image of Women in Indonesian Films: Some Observations." *Prisma: The Indonesian Indicator* 24 (March 1982): 17–29.

Serat Pamoring Jaler Estri (Propriety for husband and wife). Surakarta: Vogel van der Heijde for Waradarma Association, 1905.

Shils, Edward. "Intellectuals in the New States." *World Politics* 12, 3 (April 1960): 329–68.

Shiraishi, Takashi. "Dangir's Testimony: Saminism Reconsidered." *Indonesia* 50 (April 1990).

Sirk, U. H. *La langue Bugis* (The Bugis language). Translated from Russian by Nicle Pacory. Cahiers D'Archipel, vol. 10. Paris: Association Archipel, 1979.

Sjahrir. *Ekonomi politik kebutuhan pokok: Sebuah tinjauan prospektif* (The political economy of basic needs: A prospective view). Jakarta: LP3ES, 1986.

————. *Kebijaksanaan negara: Konsistensi dan implementasi* (State policy: consistency and implementation). Jakarta: LP3ES, 1987.

Soemarsaid Moertono. *Negara and usaha Bina-Negara di Jawa masa lampau: Studi tentang masa mataram II abad XVI sampai XIX* (State and statecraft in Old Java: A study of the second Mataram period, from the sixteenth to the nineteenth centuries). Jakarta: Yayasan Obor Indonesia, 1985.

————. *State and Statecraft in Old Java: A Study of the Later Mataram Period, Sixteenth to Nineteenth Century.* Ithaca: Cornell University Modern Indonesia Project, 1968.

Soewarsih Djojopoespito. *Manusia bebas* (Free people). Jakarta: Pustaka Jaya, 1975.

Sri Pudyastuti R. "Gencar semarak Pasaraya" (Boom in Pasaraya). *Tempo*, 30 March 1991, p. 108.

Subagio Sastrowardoyo. "Upacara bendera" (Flag ceremony). *Tempo*, 13 April 1991, p. 101.

Sudharmono. "Wawasan masa depan kita dan peranan ilmu-ilmu sosial" (Our conception of the future and the role of the social sciences). *Pelita* 16 December 1986.

Sudomo. *Kebijaksanaan Kopkamtib dalam penanggulangan ekstremitas kiri,* (Kopkamtib's policy to tackle the extreme left); *terbatas* (restricted). Jakarta: Sekretariat Komando Operasi Pemulihan Keamanan dan Ketertiban, 1982.

Suhunan Situmorang et al. "Revivalisasi negara integralistik: Polemik yang belum selesai" (The revival of the integralist state: An unfinished polemic). *Forum Keadilan*, no. 22 (1990).

Sukarno. "The Birth of Pantja Sila." In *Man, State and Society in Contemporary Southeast Asia*, ed. Robert O. Tilman, 270–76. New York: Praeger Publishers, 1969. [Excerpted from a speech delivered 1 June 1945, whose text was originally published in Sukarno, *Toward Freedom and the Dignity of Man* (Jakarta: Republic of Indonesia Department of Foreign Affairs, 1961), 1–21].

Suluardi, Raden Bagus. *Serat Riyanta* (The story of Riyanta). Weltevreden, Papyrus, 1920.

Sumardjo, Jakob. "A Peaceful Home: Women in Indonesian Literature." *Prisma: The Indonesian Indicator* 24 (March 1982): 41–52.

———. "Sastra Pudjangga Baru" (The new *pudjangga* literature). *Basis* 32, 7 (July 1983): 242–55.

Sumarkoco Sudiro. "Kualitas manusia Indonesia" (The quality of the Indonesian people). *Kompas*, 11 October 1990.

Sumhudi, Aslam. *Konsekuensi sosial dari pembangunan pertanian di Sidrap: Studi kasus di desa Lancirang, kecamatan Dua Pitue, kabupaten Sidrap* (The social consequences of agricultural development in Sidrap: A case study of the village Lancirang, Dua Pitue district, Sidrap regency). Laporan Penelitian PLPIIS, Ujung Pandang: Hasanuddin University Press, 1979.

Suripan Sadi Hutomo. "Bahasa Orang Samin" (The language of the Samin). *Majalah Konggres Bahasa Jawa*, 1991.

Suryakusuma, Julia I. "Siti Nurbaya pada dekade 1990." *Tempo*, 4 May 1991, pp. 47–61.

Sutherland, Heather. *The Making of a Bureaucratic Elite: The Colonial Transformation of the Javanese* Priyayi. Singapore: Heinemann, 1979.

———. "Pudjangga Baru: Aspects of Indonesian Intellectual Life in the 1930s." *Indonesia* 6 (1968): 106–27.

Sutton, R. Anderson. "Who Is the Pesindhen? Notes on the Female Singing Tradition on Java." *Indonesia* 37 (April 1984): 119–34.

Svensson, Thommy. "The Making of the Local Colonial State in Historical Perspective." Paper presented at the conference on The Socio-Economic Foundations of the Late Colonial State in Indonesia, 1880–1930, Leiden, 1989.

Swara. *Bab alaki rabi: Wayuh kaliyan boten* (About marriage: Whether to have a second wife or not). Semarang: H. A. Benyamins, 1913.

Tanter, Richard. "Intelligence Agencies and Third World Militarisation: A Case Study of Indonesia, 1966–1989." Ph.D. thesis, Dept. of Politics, Monash University, 1991.

Tanter, Richard, and Kenneth Young, eds. *The Politics of Middle Class Indonesia*. Clayton, Victoria: Monash University Centre of Southeast Asian Studies, 1990.

Taufik Abdullah. "Pola Kepemimpinan Islam di Indonesia" (The pattern of Islamic leadership in Indonesia). In *Islam dan Masyarakat: Pantulan Sejarah Indonesia* (Islam and society: An Indonesian historical reflection), ed. Taufik Abdullah, 54–87. Jakarta: LP3ES, 1987.

———. "Siti Nurbaya: Roman, wanita, dan sejarah." *Tempo*, 4 May 1991, pp. 47–6 1.

Taylor, Charles. "Interpretation and the Sciences of Man." *Review of Metaphysics* 25 (Fall 197 1): 49.

Teeuw, A. *Modern Indonesian Literature*. 2d ed., 2 vols. The Hague: M. Nijhoff, 1979.

Tiwon, Sylvia. "Models and Maniacs: Articulating the Female in Indonesia." In *Representing and Resisting the Feminine in Indonesia*, ed. Laurie J. Sears. Durham: Duke University Press, 1996.

Umar Kayam. *Para Priyayi* (The *priyayi*). Jakarta: Grafitipers, 1992.

———. *Sri Sumarah dan Bawuk* (Sri Sumarah and Bawuk). Jakarta: Pustaka Jaya, 1975.

United Nations. "Asian Preparatory Meeting for the World Conference on Human Rights Opens in Bangkok." Press Release no. G/10/93. Sydney, United Nations Information Centre, 29 March 1993.

————. "Vienna Declaration and Programme of Action 25 June 1993." Obtainable from United Nations, New York, and UN offices in other countries.

Utrecht, Artien, ed. *Peranan LPSM di sektor non pertanian pedesaan Jawa Barat* (The role of NGOs in the West Java nonagricultural rural sector). The Hague: Institute of Social Studies, May 1990.

Vatikiotis, Michael. *Indonesian Politics under Suharto: Order, Development and Pressure for Change.* London: Routledge 1993.

Verba, Sidney. "On Revisiting the Civic Culture: A Personal Postscript." In *The Civic Culture Revisited,* ed. Gabriel Almond and Sidney Verba, 394–410. Boston: Little, Brown, 1980.

Walsh, James. "Asia's Different Drum." *China News Digest Book and Journal Review,* 14 June 1993.

Warren, Carol. "Balinese Political Culture and the Rhetoric of National Development." In *Creating Indonesian Cultures,* ed. Paul Alexander and Jennifer Alexander, 39–54. Oceania Ethnographies, no. 3. Sydney: Oceania Publications, 1989.

————. "The Bureaucratization of Local Government in Indonesia." Monash University (Melbourne), Centre of Southeast Asian Studies, Working Paper no. 66, 1990.

————. "Rhetoric and Resistance: Popular Political Culture in Bali." *Anthropological Forum* 6, 2 (1990): 191–206.

Weinstein, Frank. *Indonesian Foreign Policy and the Dilemma of Dependence.* Ithaca: Cornell University Press, 1976.

Widiada Gunakaya and Surayin. *Penuntun pelajaran tata negara* (Constitutional studies manual; based on the 1984 curriculum and revised in accordance with the 1987 teaching guidelines). Bandung: Ganeca Exact, 1987.

Widiyanto, Paulus. "Samin Surontika dan Konteksnya" (Samin Surontika and its context) *Prisma* 8 (1983): 59–67.

Williams, M. T. "Integralism and the Brazilian Catholic Church." *Hispanic American Historical Review* 53, 4 (August 1974): 431–52.

Witjes, Ben. 'The Indonesian Law on Social Organization." Internal study undertaken for NOVIB, Nijmegen, Netherlands, October-November, 1986.

YLBHI [Yayasan Lembaga Bantuan Hukum Indonesia]. *Demokrasi di balik keranda: Catatan keadaan hak-hak asasi manusia di Indonesia 1992* (Democracy behind the screen: Notes on the human rights situation in Indonesia in 1992). Jakarta: YLBHI, 1992.

————. "Hukum, politik dan pembangunan" (Law, politics, and development; a submission to the DPR concerning the Social Organisations Bill). Jakarta: YLBHI, 1985.

YLBHI and JARIM [Jaringan Informasi Masyarakat]. *Laporan kasus* (Case studies) Kedung Ombo, Kasus Arso, Cimacan, vol. 2 (June 1991): 1–59.

Yudhistira Ardi Noegraha. *Arjuna mencari cinta* (Arjuna drop-out). Jakarta: Cypress, 1977.

————. *Arjuna mencari cinta II*. Jakarta: Cypress, 1980.

————. *Arjuna Wiwahahaha . . .* ! (Arjuna versus Arjuna) Jakarta: Garuda Metropolitan Press, 1984.

Yusuf, Mas'ud. *Bandak dan irri di Mattombong: Pola pemakaian beras asli dalam sebuah desa Bugis yang DiBIMASkan.* (Indigenous rice varieties and mirace rice in Mattombong: the pattern of using indigenous rice in a Bugis village that has undergone the BIMAS program). Ujung Pandang: Pusat Latihan Penelitian Ilmu-Ilmu Sosial, Hasanuddin University. (Laporan Penelitian PLPIIS), 1977.

Zurbuchen, Mary. "The Cockroach Opera: Image of Culture and National Development in Indonesia." *Tenggara* 23 (1989): 124–50.

List of Contributors

Greg Acciaioli is senior lecturer in the Department of Anthropology at the University of Western Australia in Perth.

Amrih Widodo is a graduate student in the Department of Anthropology at Cornell University.

David Bourchier is lecturer in the Department of Asian Studies at Murdoch University in Perth.

Philip Eldridge is associate professor in the Department of Politics at the University of Tasmania in Hobart.

Fachry Ali is a Jakarta based social commentator.

William Frederick is associate professor in the Department of History at Ohio University in Athens, Ohio.

Barbara Hatley is senior lecturer in the Department of Asian Languages and Studies at Monash University in Melbourne.

Kuntowijoyo is senior lecturer in the Department of Anthropology at Gadjah Mada University in Yogyakarta.

R. William Liddle is professor in the Department of Political Science at The Ohio State University in Columbus, Ohio.

Anton Lucas is senior lecturer in the Department of Asian Studies and Languages at Flinders University of South Australia in Adelaide.

The late **Barbara Martin-Schiller** was a lecturer in the Department of Asian Studies and Languages at Flinders University of South Australia in Adelaide.

Moelyono is an artist and social activist in Java.

Jim Schiller is lecturer in the Department of Asian Studies and Languages at Flinders University of South Australia in Adelaide.

Paul Tickell is a lecturer in the Centre for Asian Studies at the University of Western Australia in Perth.

Monographs in International Studies

Titles Available from Ohio University Press, 1996

Southeast Asia Series

* Southeast Asia Translation Project Group

No. 75 Lockard, Craig A. From Kampung to City: A Social History of Kuching, Malaysia, 1820–1970. 1987. 325 pp. Paper 0-89680-136-5 $20.00.

No. 76 McGinn, Richard, ed. Studies in Austronesian Linguistics. 1986. 516 pp. Paper 0-89680-137-3 $20.00.

No. 77 Muego, Benjamin N. Spectator Society: The Philippines Under Martial Rule. 1986. 232 pp. Paper 0-89680-138-1 $17.00.

No 79 Walton, Susan Pratt. Mode in Javanese Music. 1987. 278 pp. Paper 0-89680-144-6 $15.00.

No. 80 Nguyen Anh Tuan. South Vietnam: Trial and Experience. 1987. 477 pp., tables. Paper 0-89680-141-1 $18.00.

No. 82 Spores, John C. Running Amok: An Historical Inquiry. 1988. 190 pp. paper 0-89680-140-3 $13.00.

No. 83 Malaka, Tan. From Jail to Jail. Tr. by Helen Jarvis. 1911. 1209 pp., three volumes. (SEAT V. 8) Paper 0-89680-150-0 $55.00.

No. 84 Devas, Nick, with Brian Binder, Anne Booth, Kenneth Davey, and Roy Kelly. Financing Local Government in Indonesia. 1989. 360 pp. Paper 0-89680-153-5 $20.00.

No. 85 Suryadinata, Leo. Military Ascendancy and Political Culture: A Study of Indonesia's Golkar. 1989. 235 pp., illus., glossary, append., index, bibliog. Paper 0-89680-154-3 $18.00.

No. 86 Williams, Michael. Communism, Religion, and Revolt in Banten in the Early Twentieth Century. 1990. 390 pp. Paper 0-89680-155-1 $14.00.

No. 87 Hudak, Thomas. The Indigenization of Pali Meters in Thai Poetry. 1990. 247 pp. Paper 0-89680-159-4 $15.00.

No. 88 Lay, Ma Ma. Not Out of Hate: A Novel of Burma. Tr. by Margaret Aung-Thwin. Ed. by William Frederick. 1991. 260 pp. (SEAT V. 9) Paper 0-89680-167-5 $20.00.

No. 89 Anwar, Chairil. The Voice of the Night: Complete Poetry and Prose of Chairil Anwar. 1992. Revised Edition. Tr. by Burton Raffel. 196 pp. Paper 0-89680-170-5 $20.00.

No. 90 Hudak, Thomas John, tr., The Tale of Prince Samuttakote: A Buddhist Epic from Thailand. 1993. 230 pp. Paper 0-89680-174-8 $20.00.

No. 91 Roskies, D. M., ed. Text/Politics in Island Southeast Asia: Essays in Interpretation. 1993. 330 pp. Paper 0-89680-175-6 $25.00.

No. 92 Schenkhuizen, Marguérite, translated by Lizelot Stout van Balgooy. Memoirs of an Indo Woman: Twentieth-Century Life in the East Indies and Abroad. 1993. 312 pp. Paper 0-89680-178-0 $25.00.

No. 93   Salleh, Muhammad Haji. Beyond the Archipelago: Selected Poems. 1995. 247 pp. Paper 0-89680-181-0 $20.00.

No. 94   Federspiel, Howard M. A Dictionary of Indonesian Islam. 1995. 327 pp. Bibliog. Paper 0-89680-182-9 $25.00.

No. 95   Leary, John. Violence and the Dream People: The Orang Asli in the Malayan Emergency 1948–1960. 1995. 275 pp. Maps, illus., tables, appendices, bibliog., index. Paper 0-89680-186-1 $22.00.

No. 96   Lewis, Dianne. *Jan Compagnie* in the Straits of Malacca 1641–1795. 1995. 176 pp. Map, appendices, bibliog., index. Paper 0-89680-187-x. $18.00.

No. 97   Schiller, Jim and Martin-Schiller, Barbara. Imagining Indonesia: Cultural Politics and Political Culture. 1996. 384 pp., notes, glossary, bibliog. Paper 0-89680-190-x. $30.00.

No. 98   Bonga, Dieuwke Wendelaar. Eight Prison Camps: A Dutch Family in Japanese Java. 1996. 233 pp., illus., map, glossary. Paper 0-89680-191-8. $18.00.

No. 99   Gunn, Geoffrey C. Language, Ideology, and Power in Brunei Darussalam. 1996. 328 pp., glossary, notes, bibliog., index. Paper 0-89680-192-6. $24.00.

No. 100   Martin, Peter W., Conrad Ozog, and Gloria R. Poedjosoedarmo, eds. Language Use and Language Change in Brunei Darussalam. 1996. 390 pp., maps, notes, bibliog. Paper 0-89680-193-x. $26.00.

Africa Series

No. 43   Harik, Elsa M. and Donald G. Schilling. The Politics of Education in Colonial Algeria and Kenya. 1984. 102 pp. Paper 0-89680-117-9 $12.50.

No. 45   Keto, C. Tsehloane. American-South African Relations 1784–1980: Review and Select Bibliography. 1985. 169 pp. Paper 0-89680-128-4 $11.00.

No. 46   Burness, Don, ed. Wanasema: Conversations with African Writers. 1985. 103 pp. paper 0-89680-129-2 $11.00.

No. 47   Switzer, Les. Media and Dependency in South Africa: A Case Study of the Press and the Ciskei "Homeland." 1985. 97 pp. Paper 0-89680-130-6 $10.00.

No. 51   Clayton, Anthony and David Killingray. Khaki and Blue: Military and Police in British Colonial Africa. 1989. 347 pp. Paper 0-89680-147-0 $20.00.

Latin America Series

No. 13 Henderson, James D. Conservative Thought in Latin America: The Ideas of Laureano Gomez. 1988. 229 pp. Paper 0-89680-148-9 $16.00.

No. 17 Mijeski, Kenneth J., ed. The Nicaraguan Constitution of 1987: English Translation and Commentary. 1991. 355 pp. Paper 0-89680-165-9 $25.00.

No. 18 Finnegan, Pamela. The Tension of Paradox: José Donoso's *The Obscene Bird of Night* as Spiritual Exercises. 1992. 204 pp. Paper 0-89680-169-1 $15.00.

No. 19 Kim, Sung Ho and Thomas W. Walker, eds. Perspectives on War and Peace in Central America. 1992. 155 pp., notes, bibliog. Paper 0-89680-172-1 $17.00.

No. 20 Becker, Marc. Mariátegui and Latin American Marxist Theory. 1993. 239 pp. Paper 0-89680-177-2 $20.00.

No. 21 Boschetto-Sandoval, Sandra M. and Marcia Phillips McGowan, eds. Claribel Alegría and Central American Literature. 1994. 233 pp., illus. Paper 0-89680-179-9 $20.00.

No. 22 Zimmerman, Marc. Literature and Resistance in Guatemala: Textual Modes and Cultural Politics from El Señor Presidente to Rigoberta Menchú. 1995. 2 volume set 320 + 370 pp., notes, bibliog. Paper 0-89680-183-7 $50.00.

No. 23 Hey, Jeanne A. K. Theories of Dependent Foreign Policy: The Case of Ecuador in the 1980s. 1995. 280 pp., map, tables, notes, bibliog., index. paper 0-89680-184-5 $22.00.

No. 24 Wright, Bruce E. Theory in the Practice of the Nicaraguan Revolution. 1995. 320 pp., notes, illus., bibliog., index. Paper 0-89680-185-3. $23.00.

No. 25 Mann, Carlos Guevara. Panamanian Militarism: A Historical Interpretation. 1996. 243 pp., illus., map, notes, bibliog., index. Paper 0-89680-189-6. $23.00.

No. 26 Armony, Ariel. Argentina, the United States, and the Anti-Communist Crusade in Central America, 1977–1984. 1997. 312 pp., illus., maps, notes, bibliog., index. Paper 0-89680-196-9. $26.00.

Ordering Information

Individuals are encouraged to patronize local bookstores wherever possible. Orders for titles in the Monographs in International Studies may be placed directly through the Ohio University Press, Scott Quadrangle, Athens, Ohio 45701-2979. Individuals should remit payment by check, VISA, or Master-Card.* Those ordering from the United Kingdom, Continental Europe, the Middle East,. and Africa should order through Academic and University Publishers Group, 1 Gower Street, London WC1E, England. Orders from the Pacific Region, Asia, Australia, and New Zealand should be sent to East-West Export Books, c/o the University of Hawaii Press, 2840 Kolowalu Street, Honolulu, Hawaii 96822, USA.

Individuals ordering from outside of the U.S. should remit in U.S. funds to Ohio University Press either by International Money Order or by a check drawn on a U.S. bank.** Most out-of-print titles may be ordered from University Microfilms, Inc., 300 North Zeeb Road, Ann Arbor, Michigan 48106, USA.

Prices are subject to change.

* Please add $3.50 for the first book and $.75 for each additional book for shipping and handling.

** Outside the U.S. please add $4.50 for the first book and $.75 for each additional book.

Ohio University
Monographs in International Studies

The Ohio University Center for International Studies was established to help create within the university and local communities a greater awareness of the world beyond the United States. Comprising programs in African, Latin American, Southeast Asian, Development and Administrative studies, the Center supports scholarly research, sponsors lectures and colloquia, encourages course development within the university curriculum, and publishes the Monographs in International Studies series with the Ohio University Press. The Center and its programs also offer an interdisciplinary Master of Arts degree in which students may focus on one of the regional or topical concentrations, and may also combine academics with training in career fields such as journalism, business, and language teaching. For undergraduates, major and certificate programs are also available.

For more information, contact the Vice Provost for International Studies, Burson House, Ohio University, Athens, Ohio 45701.